D1540503

Infants and Children with Prenatal Alcohol and Drug Exposure: A Guide to Identification and Intervention

Keeta DeStefano Lewis, R.N., P.H.N., M.S.N.

SUNRISE
River Press

The publisher and authors have made a conscientious effort to ensure any recommendations or procedures outlined in this book are proper, accurate, and in accordance with accepted professional practices at the time of publication. As in the case with health care, education, and/or human service work in general, each specific issue and each individual question combine to form a unique situation, not easily addressed at a distance or from the pages of a book designed to provide generic information on a wide range of subjects. While this work provides recognized structures, processes, and procedures, it is mandatory for the reader to realize that recommendations found within this book are not a substitute for professional on-site assessments and recommendations. The publisher and authors make no representations or warranties of any kind regarding the materials in this work nor shall they be liable for any damages resulting, in whole or in part, from the use of or reliance upon this material.

Library of Congress Cataloging-in-Publication Data

Lewis, Keeta DeStefano
    Infants and children with prenatal alcohol and drug exposure : a guide to identification and intervention / Keeta DeStefano Lewis.
        p.   cm.
    Includes bibliographical references and index.
    ISBN 0-9624814-2-4
    1. Children of prenatal substance abuse.   I. Title.
RJ520.P74L49   1995
618.92'86--dc20   94-47669
                                                                          CIP

Copyright © 1995 Keeta DeStefano Lewis

Printed & bound in the U.S.A.

All rights reserved. No part of this book may be reproduced or transmitted in any form by any means without the written permission of the copyright holder, except where permitted by law.

For additional copies of this work, contact:
Sunrise River Press, 11481 Kost Dam Rd.
North Branch, MN 55056, 612-583-3239

Dedication

To Stretch

a maverick—

one who believed in the power of self determination

never afraid to challenge the system

a man of principle

a humorist

with quick wit

and who cared

about me, my work, our family

and was the impetus for this book.

I'll always love you.

Contributors

Keeta DeStefano Lewis, R.N., P.H.N., M.S.N.

Doctoral Candidate, University of California San Francisco.
Early Intervention School Nurse, Napa Infant Program, Napa, California

Sue Bakley, B.F.A., M.A.

Special Education Teacher, Early Childhood Special Education Program
San Diego Unified School District
San Diego, California

Bonnie M. Bear, R.N., B.S.N., P.H.N.

School Nurse Health Specialist, San Diego Unified School District Infant Development Program, San Diego, California

Barbara Bennett, M.D.

Chief, Developmental Behavioral Pediatrician, Child Development Center, California Pacific Medical Center, San Francisco. Associate Clinical Professor of Pediatrics, University of California San Francisco. Consultant, Haight Ashbury MAMA Program, San Francisco, California

Dale Berry, R.N., B.S.N., P.H.N.

Director, Children's Medical Service, Napa County Health and Human Services Napa, California

Beverly J. Bradley, R.N., M.S., Ph.D.

School Health Consultant, San Diego Unified School District, San Diego, California

Lynette S. Chandler, B.S., P.T., B.A., M.Ed., Ph.D.

Professor and Director of Physical Therapy, University of Puget Sound Tacoma, Washington

Gay M. Chisum, B.A., R.N., C.D.

Executive Director, Perinatal Addiction Education Consultants, Chicago, Illinois

Dan R. Griffith, Ph.D.

Clinical Associate, Department of Psychiatry and Behavioral Sciences, Northwestern University Medical School, Chicago, Illinois. Consultant/Faculty, Center for Substance Abuse Prevention, National Resource Center for the Prevention of Perinatal Abuse of Alcohol and Other Drugs, Fairfax, Virginia

Marci J. Hanson, Ph.D.

Professor, Early Childhood Special Education, San Francisco State University, San Francisco, California

Eleanor W. Lynch, Ph.D.

Professor, Department of Special Education, San Diego State University, San Diego, California

Laura Mahlmeister, R.N., Ph.D.

Consultant, Legal Nursing Issues, and Staff Nurse, San Francisco General Hospital, San Francisco, California

Lora-Ellen McKinney, Ph.D.

Director, Clearinghouse for Drug Exposed Children, University of California Medical Center, San Francisco, California

Marion D. Meyerson, CCC-SP/A, Ph.D.

Lecturer, Communication Disorders and Sciences, San Jose State University, San Jose, California

Marie Kanne Poulsen, Ph.D.

Psychologist, Center for Child Development, Children's Hospital, Los Angeles, California

Mary Anne Theiss, R.N., M.S., J.D.

Practicing Attorney, Manlius, New York, and Federal Court, Northern District of New York. Adjunct Professor, New School of Social Research, New York

Helen Bosson Thomson, R.N., B.S.N., P.H.N.

School Nurse, Napa County Office of Education, Napa, California

Mark F. Whitney, Ph.D.

Assistant Professor, College for Human Development, Department of Child and Family Studies, Syracuse University Syracuse, New York

Reviewers

Virginia Armstrong, R.N., M.S.
NICU Nurse Educator
Children's Hospital NICU
Oakland, California

Gordon R. Bear, LCSW, BCD
Psychotherapist, Family Life Educator
    and Consultant
San Diego, California

Jean Brunelli, R.N., M.A.
School Nurse/Team Leader
Tracy Infant Program/ABC Unified
    School District
Cerritos, California

Margaret Ellickson, R.N., SNP
School Nurse
Tacoma, Washington

Janet Gonzalez-Mena, M.A.
Faculty, Child/Family Studies
Napa Valley College
Napa, California

Joan Larson Havard, M.Ed., CCC/A
Teacher of the Deaf, Audiologist
Fremont, California

Cathy A. Janis, M.A., CCC/SLP
Speech/Language Pathologist
Napa Infant Program
Napa, California

Art Javar, B.A.
Staff Development Trainer
Sonoma Development Center
Sonoma, California

Lisa K. Lewis Javar, R.N.
Sonoma Development Center
Sonoma, California

Etta Jones, B.A.
Community Relations Specialist
San Francisco Unified School District
San Francisco, California

Jeanette Koshar, R.N., M.S.N.
Nurse Practitioner
Women's Reproductive Health
Napa, California

Donna P. Le Claire, R.N.
University of California Medical Center,
    NICU
San Diego, California

Marie Leech, M.A.
Director, Case Management
Options for Recovery
University of California
San Diego, California

Constance Mukherjee, MAT, CCC/SLP
Speech/Language Pathologist
Turnstone Center for Physically Disabled
    Children and Adults
Fort Wayne, Indiana

Lois Pearson, R.N., B.S.N.
School Nurse
Napa, California

Barbara Quackenbush, R.N., M.S.N.
School Nurse
Coordinator, Hope Infant Program
San Diego, California

Jan Sampson, R.N., M.S.N.
Faculty, ADN Program
Santa Rosa Junior College
Santa Rosa, California

Nadya Hellinger Schmeder, R.P.T.,
    O.T.R., M.A.
Educational Specialist
Napa Infant Program
Napa, California

Karla Snorf, P.T.
Physical Therapist
Napa Infant Program
Napa, California

Contents

Introduction

Chapter 1. Historical Perspective on Women, Drug Use, and Their Children. ... 1
Beverly J. Bradley

Chapter 2. Drugs and the Effects on Health and Development of the Fetus,
Neonate, Infant, and Child 21
Bonnie M. Bear

Women, Infants, and Drugs

Chapter 3. Pregnancy and Chemical Dependency 57
Gay M. Chisum, Keeta DeStefano Lewis

Chapter 4. Nursing Care of the Newborn with Prenatal Alcohol and
Drug Exposure: The Immediate Postnatal Period 79
Laura Mahlmeister

Chapter 5. Alcohol-Related Effects on the Infant, Child, and Adult 111
Helen Bosson Thomson, Keeta DeStefano Lewis

Infants, Children, and Health

Chapter 6. Physical Health Concerns of the Infant and Child with
Prenatal Alcohol and Drug Exposure. 129
Barbara Bennett, Keeta DeStefano Lewis, Helen Bosson Thomson

Chapter 7. Nursing Interventions and the At-Risk Infant and Child
with Prenatal Alcohol and Drug Exposure. 147
Keeta DeStefano Lewis, Bonnie M. Bear

Developmental Concepts

Chapter 8. Cognitive Development of Children Prenatally Exposed
to Alcohol, Tobacco, and Other Drugs 167
Dan R. Griffith

Chapter 9. Vulnerability and Resiliency Factors of the At-Risk Infant
and Young Child with Prenatal Alcohol and Drug Exposure. 187
Marie Kanne Poulsen

Chapter 10. Motor Development of Neonates, Infants, Toddlers, and
Children with Prenatal Alcohol and Drug Exposure. 203
Lynette S. Chandler

Chapter 11. Communication Development and Disorders of Children
with Prenatal Alcohol and Drug Exposure and Pediatric AIDS..... 229
Marion D. Meyerson

Service Delivery

Chapter 12. Establishing and Maintaining Connections: Strategies for
Working with Children Prenatally Exposed to Alcohol and Drugs. 253
Sue Bakley, Mark F. Whitney

Assessment Approach

Chapter 13. Developmental Assessment of Infants and Children
Who Are At-Risk Due to Prenatal Alcohol and Drug Exposure. ... 275
Eleanor W. Lynch

Environmental and Legal Influences

Chapter 14. The Impact of Family Diversity on Addiction, Treatment,
and Recovery 297
Marci J. Hanson, Marie Kanne Poulsen, Lora-Ellen McKinney

Chapter 15. Legal Issues and the Rights of Infants and Children 325
Mary Anne Theiss

Resources

Chapter 16. 345
Dale Berry, Keeta DeStefano Lewis

Index   353

Acknowledgments

My utmost appreciation is extended to the numerous people who gave their time, talent, encouragement, and support during the writing of this book: Beverly Bradley, my dear friend, who carefully read many drafts, attending to details, making important comments and humorous anecdotes which helped redirect my cluttered thoughts and keep me on track. Bonnie Bear, another dear friend, was always there when I needed her, day or night, and also read numerous drafts of the manuscript and provided support, keeping me at peace. Gordon Bear, a friend and a man of intellectual and spiritual wisdom, enthusiastically supported me. With expertise he answered many questions about children and families whenever I was in need of clarification. He did this unconditionally as did my other friends. To his tribute his proverb "out of home not out of family" is found in the introduction. Paige Grove, a wonderful woman, friend, and spiritual supporter, typed much of this book, never growing tired—or at least, she didn't show it. Laura Mahlmeister, whose encouragement and contagious enthusiasm was invaluable and always there for me even through my most difficult times. A special thank you to Dave Arnold, the publisher, and his wife Martha, a school nurse in Minnesota, for being understanding and patient, attending to the details for delay that were caused due to the sudden death of my husband Robert Stretch Lewis after the inception of the book. I am thankful for and gratefully indebted to all of these special people who are my mentors, teachers, and trusted colleagues, but most of all my friends.

A special thanks also to all of the authors of various chapters and to those people who took time out of their busy everyday lives to review these chapters. Their many comments and suggestions were helpful in the making of this book.

Last, but by no means least, I especially thank my family for their love and support. My daughter Lisa, son-in-law Art, and grandchildren Da-Naii and Dante, and my son John. Even in the midst of losing their beloved father and grandfather they encouraged me, gave up much of their time with me, and cheered me on. Of course their comment when I questioned them about certain statements was always "Dad made me say that." And to my mother who is proud of me and believes I can do anything I choose. All of these people provided the light at the end of the tunnel.

I hope that this book will raise questions about how we value our children who are the now and the future. Furthermore, I hope that in the near future we become a responsible society and books on this topic will not be necessary.

Introduction

In the United States 375,000 infants are reported to have been born annually with prenatal drug exposure (PDE). These infants represent a population whose short- and long-term developmental and educational needs have not been identified. Research studies are just beginning to focus on the effects that combinations of drugs have on the infant and child; why some infants and children are affected and others escape any noticeable symptoms; why some have behavioral and social disabilities; and what are the best practices for prevention and treatment when working with the affected neonate, infant, child, or parent.

As with other children, children with prenatal drug exposure should be afforded the same health and physical rights as adults. Children are vulnerable due to their physical, mental, and social immaturity, and therefore need a certain amount of special protection from society to facilitate normal growth and development.

The United Nations General Assembly in 1989 adopted a legal document which articulates universally acceptable standards called the *Convention on the Rights of the Child.* The United Nations *Convention on the Rights of the Child* states that:

> Children have the right to **survival**: through the provision of adequate food, shelter, clean water, and primary health care; the right to **protection**: from abuse, neglect, and exploitation, including the right to special protection in times of war; and the right to **develop**: in a safe environment through the provision of formal education, constructive play, advanced health care, and the opportunity to participate in the social, economic, religious, and political life of the culture—free from discrimination.

The editor, and a major contributor to this book, believes in the basic rights of the child as described by the United Nations General Assembly. This book was designed to provide the reader with knowledge and understanding about the issues and needs of neonates, infants, and children with prenatal drug exposure. With this information the reader is urged to advocate providing basic survival needs, protecting the children from abuse and neglect, and developing an environment conducive to normal growth and development. Such advocacy comes out of a sound knowledge base and a belief that all infants, children, and their families are important!

This book is written primarily to provide health care, school and social service professionals with information and up-to-date research and knowledge obtained from clinical experience. This information will be valuable to the global community of caregivers of infants and children prenatally drug exposed, especially teachers, parents, foster parents, physicians, social workers, counselors, psychologists, speech and language therapists, physical and occupational therapists, day care providers, attorneys, and judges. This community of individuals has an impact on the child's life and plays a key role in the potential development of children that can result in a happy and successful life. Many individuals are part of intervention teams for at-risk children and their families. All participants in the child's life need to recognize, not label, the at-risk child who is prenatally drug exposed, establish therapeutic partnerships with their families, be able to identify any special needs, and provide linkage to identified resources for successful outcomes to take place.

There is an almost universal premature assumption that prenatal drug exposure equates to disabilities in health, motor, language, learning, social, or behavioral domains. It is unclear exactly how many infants and children with prenatal drug exposure exhibit or will exhibit limitations in these areas. Factors that influence disabilities in these domains are varied and numerous and many are discussed in this text. Awareness of the vulnerability of infants and children with prenatal drug exposure to disabilities warrants the need for further professional knowledge and understanding of the issues. However, predicting negative outcomes needs to be tempered with realistic optimism for individuals and groups of children with prenatal drug exposure.

The contributing authors in this book are professionals from a variety of disciplines with varying educational and ethnic backgrounds. They are multidisciplinary, multicultural professionals who have special clinical experience and knowledge about neonates, infants, and children with prenatal drug exposure and their families. They also have a personal interest in sharing their knowledge and expertise with those individuals working with pregnant women using drugs; caregivers of neonates, infants and children; and other individuals who make decisions which affect women's and children's lives.

The book has a research and clinical orientation. Research can establish correct information upon which infants, children, and their families can be understood. Research provides evidence to challenge or dispute individual health, educational, or social needs and the much-needed bridge from research to practice. Only through an awareness of the logic, methods, and shortcomings of research can individuals judge for themselves the merits of various scholars' research findings and conclusions. It is with this in mind that relevant research is threaded throughout the chapters of this book.

The main purpose of this book is to provide a better understanding and general knowledge about the pregnant substance abuser and the effects such abuse has on the growth and development of their infants and children. To facilitate this objective this book includes eight sections: Introduction; Women, Infants, and Drugs; Infants, Children, and Health; Developmental Concepts; Service Delivery; Assessment Approach; Environmental and Legal Influences; and Resources.

Chapter 1 includes a historical overview of women and drug use. Past findings of researchers and observations of clinicians about children with prenatal drug exposure are compared to contemporary findings. Prevalent public perceptions of the specific substances—such as tobacco, alcohol, and opiates—often determined whether or not the substances were the subject of scientific study. Social acceptance of drugs often delayed their classification as addictive, illegal, or hazardous to the developing fetus. Even when scientific evidence indicated that a particular drug had potential for causing addiction, malformation of the fetus, miscarriage, low birth weight, increased neonate/infant mortality, and neonatal withdrawal symptoms, social acceptance of the drug adversely affected medical practice, nursing practice, and public health education efforts. Review of the literature from the late 1800s reveals a consistent pattern of inequitable access to care as well as a lower standard of care for females who used drugs as compared to their male counterparts.

Chapter 2 has a research and clinical prospectus on the effects of maternal substance abuse on the neonate, infant,

and child. A review of the literature reveals that serious scientific study of the newborn with prenatal drug exposure began about twenty-five years ago and supports potential adverse outcomes for the newborn. The cause of the adverse effects remains in question. The chapter presents current research data and clinical observation on common drugs of abuse including cocaine, marijuana, opiates, phencyclidine (PCP), and tobacco. Origin and pharmacology of the drugs; maternal, fetal, and neonatal effects; neurobehavioral and developmental effects; and long-term outcomes are explored.

Chapter 3 provides nurses and other health care professionals with a foundation for understanding maternal chemical dependency. A model of chemical dependency, attitudes of health care providers, and contributory factors in maternal drug dependency are explored. Discussions focus on nursing and interdisciplinary interventions which are implemented in the antepartum, intrapartum, and postpartum setting with the pregnant woman who is chemically dependent.

Chapter 4 discusses nursing care of the newborn with prenatal drug exposure and the immediate postnatal period. Nurses who care for delivering mothers and their newborns face an unprecedented crisis in health care. With short turnaround hospital stays, it is difficult to appropriately evaluate the pregnant woman who presents for delivery and may be a user of drugs or the newborn after birth prior to discharge. The chapter discusses identifying the pregnant woman who is chemically dependent in relation to safe care; identifying major neonatal risks and complications; and planning and providing immediate post-birth care to the mother and newborn, including assessment, intervention, and evaluation .

Chapter 5 provides the reader with an overview of alcohol-related effects on the neonate, infant, and child. The nurse's role in the identification of pre-natal alcohol abuse and the nursing skills necessary to provide services to the child and family affected by the abuse are also discussed. Research shows fetal alcohol syndrome includes lifelong physical, mental, and behavioral disabilities. Early identification of harmful maternal drinking patterns and a humanistic approach to intervention are critical in the effort to prevent alcohol-related effects.

Chapter 6 presents the current physical health care challenges of neonates, infants, and children born prenatally drug exposed. The conditions and concerns discussed in this chapter may occur prenatally, perinatally, or postnatally and may leave the infant or young child with significant neurologic, developmental, or sensory deficits. These deficits may require special treatment or early intervention services.

Chapter 7 focuses on school health services. School nurses are serving increasing numbers of children who have risk factors associated with prenatal drug exposure that may interfere with their school performance and success. Included in this chapter are the physical influences (vision, hearing, growth and clinical measurements, immunizations, and nutrition), the environmental influences (child abuse and neglect), and the cultural influences on child develop-ment. Home visiting and staff safety issues are discussed, and individualized developmental plans are also included.

Chapter 8 addresses the cognitive development of children prenatally exposed to alcohol, tobacco, and other drugs. Interventions to promote optimal cognitive development with this group of children, including emotional and behavioral development, are included. Sparse research evidence to date indicates that a small percentage of children prenatally drug exposed may suffer damage to their central nervous systems, which results in identifiable cognitive deficits ranging from subtle learning problems to severe mental retardation. Another avenue under investigation which produces damage to cognitive achievement and performance appears to be related to the effects the drug-using maternal/family lifestyle has on other areas of child development. Children with insecure attachments and/or behavioral problems can be emotionally and cognitively unable to engage in learning or demonstrate what they already know.

Chapter 9 discusses the vulnerability and resiliency factors of the at-risk infant and young child with prenatal drug exposure. A wide range of psychosocial and biological factors influence the social, emotional, and behavioral development of this group of children. Case management, assessment, and intervention issues are identified and discussed. The early identification of infant/child and family risk indicators, child and family needs, and available resources can lead to provision of the preventive intervention services that are critical for augmenting resilience in developmentally vulnerable children and their families.

Chapter 10 reviews the motor development of children with prenatal drug exposure to legal and illegal drugs. The effects of prenatal drug exposure as described in controlled clinical trials are reviewed for neonates from birth to one month, infants and toddlers one month to two years, and children three to nine years. There is sufficient evidence of prenatal drug exposure effects on motor development and related areas of development to cause concern. There is also considerable variation in the degree of response, which is not yet understood. Treatment models, goals, and intervention strategies are suggested for various documented drug effects.

Chapter 11 provides information on communication development and disorders of children with prenatal drug exposure and pediatric AIDS. Children prenatally drug exposed to licit and illicit drugs and those with human immunodeficiency virus are reported to have speech, language, and hearing problems. A continuum of effects from normal to severely compromised is reported in the research and clinical literature. Recommendations for remediation of communicative disorders are suggested which can occur within the context of the family and cultural communities. Thorough, individualized assessments followed by appropriate therapeutic approaches are needed.

Chapter 12 addresses the preschool child with prenatal drug exposure and examines the child's behaviors in order to define the problems those behaviors create in both school and home settings. Information as to why the at-risk preschool child is best served by using sound principles of child development and effective practice rather than in special programs in segregated settings is provided. Interven-

tion strategies are included for managing difficult behaviors and learning problems, modifying the preschool environment, and collaborating with other community agencies. Strategies for helping children cope with potential effects of life stresses, such as foster home placements, family separations, and chaotic home environments, are discussed.

Chapter 13 provides information about developmental assessment of infants and young children who are at risk. A comprehensive assessment of a child's development, health status, and behavior is needed to determine eligibility for special programs or services. The assessment can provide families and professionals with a more complete understanding of the child's strengths and needs. This chapter also discusses supporting and working with families during the assessment process, parent-professional partnerships, partnerships when families are at risk, and other special considerations.

Chapter 14 describes the diversity among families in the United States and the influence of this diversity on the delivery of family services, including health, educational, and social service approaches as they relate to chemical dependency. The impact of chemical dependency on family functioning and parenting is also described, as well as the impact of cultural diversity on addiction, treatment, and recovery. The characteristics, roles, and importance of extended family/kinship networks and foster family care in providing care for children of chemically dependent women are included. Finally, recommendations are suggested for the provision of services to families, particularly the children, from a wide range of backgrounds and belief systems.

Chapter 15 summarizes the legal issues surrounding the fetus, infant, or child with prenatal drug exposure and the pregnant substance abuser. The mother's rights may conflict with what is in the best interest of the child. The rights of the child, maternal-fetal conflict, refusal of treatment, maternal rights versus the state's interest in protecting life, compelled hospitalization and treatment during pregnancy, rights of the father, and criminalization of maternal conduct are discussed with case examples and case law. Nursing intervention and recognition of the chemically dependent mother are discussed within a legal framework, as are hints for the health care provider in documentation and the role as a court witness.

This book allows the reader to observe some of the emerging *trends* that may be helpful to this population of children and their families. Many infants and children with prenatal drug exposure are moved out of the home into foster homes for a variety of reasons; however, whenever possible these children need to be placed within the homes of extended family members. If they need to be removed from their natural parent, attempts should be made first to keep them in kinship homes whenever it is feasible. A phrase by Gordon Bear, psychotherapist and family life educator in San Diego, summarizes this option— "out of home but not out of family." Support systems whereby these families can receive financial aid need to be in place.

Methods to identify family types and risk, and a clearer definition of family,

need to be articulated. This will allow identification of high-risk families in need of intervention. It might be that parents attend their child's early intervention program, day care, or classroom, learning how to teach and care for their children as their children learn and develop.

Family-centered care includes specialized day care to meet the needs of infants and children living in culturally and ethnically diverse environments and families, as well as those infants and children with special needs related to health and care.

Credential requirements for special certification in early childhood for individuals working with these infants and children and their families are being developed and implemented across the United States. Home visits will be a part of early intervention programs as required by PL 99-457. Professionals working in the school system are now required to implement options for children and families, including home visits and small group class services in a variety of natural environments, such as in churches, community centers, or parks.

Diagnosis and outpatient care for children may be part of the service provided by a school system. Schools can provide pediatric outpatient service to help parents help kids. Post-traumatic stress syndrome is often a part of children's lives. Observations of divorce, drug use, homicides, suicides, gang warfare, riots, and drive-by shootings are not an uncommon occurrence in many children's everyday lives. The abduction of children from their homes and community makes children fearful of the possibility. Recently a television interviewer asked a group of children what their greatest fear was. A common response was *Will I be killed* or *will I be taken from my home*? Schools can provide a safe place where children and their families can receive a comprehensive, inclusive education accompanied by needed social and health care services.

This book is not meant to address or answer every issue or question concerning this population of infants and children, but to provide available, up-to-date information and resources for professionals, parents, and agencies. There will continue to be new considerations for both child and family not addressed in this book. Professionals working with children and families are encouraged to review new research findings, emerging knowledge derived from clinical practice, and changes in laws about tobacco, alcohol, and drug use, child abuse, and testing of pregnant women and neonates.

1

Historical Perspective on Women, Drug Use, and Their Children

Beverly J. Bradley, R.N., M.S., Ph.D.

Past findings of researchers and observations of clinicians about children prenatally exposed to drugs are compared with contemporary information. When significant numbers of women of childbearing age in the United States began to use alcohol, tobacco, marijuana, cocaine, hallucinogens, heroin, or other opiates, clinical observations and research about the effects on their infants and young children followed. However, prevalent public perceptions of the specific substances, such as tobacco and alcohol, often determined whether or not the substances were the subjects of scientific study. Social acceptance of drugs often delayed their classification as addictive or illegal, or hazardous to the developing fetus. Even when there was scientific evidence that a drug had potential for causing addiction, malformation of the fetus, neonatal withdrawal symptoms, miscarriage, low birth weight, and increased infant mortality, social acceptance of the drug adversely affected medical practice, nursing practice, and public health education efforts. A review of the literature from the late 1800s reveals a persistent pattern of inequitable access to care and lower standards of care for females who use drugs as compared with their male counterparts.

"He was normal in size but thin. His movements were jerky and he was very nervous, crying for sixty hours without sleeping. After this his symptoms abated and he recovered." *Fere—1883 (Terry & Pellens 1928)*

". . . particularly sensitive to motion, was pale and pinched and prostrate." *Earle—1884 (Terry & Pellens 1928)*

". . . excessive nervousness, rapid breathing and convulsive movements. She had nursed with difficulty." *Bureau—1895 (Terry & Pellens 1928)*

". . . are restless and cannot be stilled in their crying." *Lambert—1907 (Terry & Pellens 1928)*

"The restlessness increased; it began to yawn and sneeze. Its face became pinched and its color poor. It drew up its legs as if in cramps, and cried out as if in pain. Its pupils became widely dilated. The chin was in a constant tremor reminding the observer of the chattering of an adult in a chill. Finally diarrhoea began, and the infant showed signs of collapse, with general convulsions." *Laase—1919 (Terry & Pellens 1928)*

"The pulse became weak and almost imperceptible; the skin was pale and bathed in cold perspiration; mucous membranes and extremities cyanotic; respiration rapid and shallow; vomiting and diarrhoea marked, the child presented a clinical picture of distinct surgical shock." *Van Kleek—1920 (Terry & Pellens 1928)*

Signs of neonatal abstinence include:

Irregular sleep patterns
Yawning
Fever
Ineffective sucking and swallowing
Increased oral drive
Regurgitation and loose stools
Hyperirritability
Increased muscle tone
Increased and exaggerated reflexes
Tremors
Restlessness
High-pitched cry
Mottling of the skin
Excessive nasal secretions
Sneezing
Sweating
Rapid and irregular respirations
Intermittent cyanosis
(Finnegan 1988)

"But if this holds for one drug, opium, must it not hold for all drugs, alcohol, chloral, cocaine, etc., the activities of which depend on soluble substances?" *Sainsbury—1909 (Terry & Pellens 1928)*

"Psychoactive drugs, such as opiates, cocaine, marijuana, and alcohol, are generally fat soluble and of small molecular size, so that they also easily cross the blood-brain barrier." (Zuckerman 1991)

"Abstinence symptoms in the neonate exposed to non-narcotic drugs in utero have been described for phenobarbital, diazepam, marijuana, cocaine and alcohol." (Chasnoff 1988)

Before the turn of the century, medical literature contained descriptions of symptoms displayed by infants born to women who used drugs, primarily opium, which are remarkably similar to current descriptions of neonatal abstinence. In the late 1800s and early 1900s, opiates were common ingredients in patent medicines that were marketed creatively, and cocaine was an ingredient in the popular soft drink, Coca Cola, until replaced with caffeine in 1903.

Prior to the Harrison Narcotic Act in 1914, which made narcotics illegal, women were addicted to narcotics more often than men. Narcotics were prescribed frequently by physicians to relieve either physical or emotional distress of female patients and could be obtained easily and legally without a prescription. A 1910 case study of a woman who had taken McMunn's elixir of opium for thirty-one years illustrates the extent to which opium was available. The woman had delivered a total of eighteen children. The only survivors were the two born before she was prescribed the elixir to prevent a miscarriage during her third pregnancy and the last who was treated with paregoric until withdrawal symptoms subsided (Terry & Pellens 1928). Since the ratio of women to men addicted to narcotics in the United States at the turn of the century was estimated to be two to one, the prevalence of prenatal drug exposure in that time period was undoubtedly substantial (Nyswander 1956).

The substances most frequently used by women of childbearing age in the United States are reflected in the literature about maternal health, conditions of the neonate, and congenital anomalies. The effects of morphine, heroin, methadone, alcohol, thalidomide, LSD, cocaine, dilantin, phenobarbital, diazepam (Valium), marijuana, and tobacco upon the mother and child parallel the time in history when the substances were used frequently by women of childbearing age.

A review of the literature about children prenatally exposed to drugs and their mothers reveals trends in the perceptions of health care providers and the public about the nature of addiction. Those views range from a disease model to a spiritual deficit model (McBride 1910; Hare 1913; Jellinek 1950; Nyswander 1956). Males and females who are dependent upon substances are viewed differently by health care providers, legislators, and jurists,

with an unchanged pattern of more sympathy, more research about effective treatment models, and more accessibility to treatment for males than for females (Wood 1944; Nyswander 1956; Bresnahan, Brooks & Zuckerman 1991; Murray 1991; Kelley, Walsh & Thompson 1991).

Even when a drug had a potential for causing addiction, malformation of the fetus, neonatal withdrawal symptoms, miscarriage, low birth weight, and increased infant mortality, social acceptance of the drug influenced medical practice, nursing practice, and public health education efforts. For example, the term addiction was not commonly used in relation to alcohol until long after clear evidence of addiction of the user, abstinence symptoms in the neonate, and fetal alcohol syndrome. In like manner, habit was the term associated with tobacco use until recently, despite scientific evidence of physical changes in the user upon withdrawal from tobacco and the negative effects of smoking on fetal development. Prior to the availability of a cheaper form of cocaine—crack—that drug was described as causing habituation and psychological dependence in health education materials and professional publications despite widespread use in the middle and upper classes since the 1970s (Willgoose 1972; Sleet & Estrada 1974; Ensor & Means 1975; Anderson & Creswell 1980). After increased use among lower socioeconomic classes, cocaine began to be described as a drug that caused physical dependence or addiction (Adams & Kozel 1985; Udell 1989).

While technical knowledge about the

effects of drugs on the health of mothers and their children has changed dramatically in the last century, some attitudes toward both the women and their children remain similar. Historically, women who use drugs have been faced with more public censor for their behavior, more punitive responses, and less access to care when desiring to cease using drugs than men (McBride 1910; Hare 1913; Terry & Pellens 1928; Wood 1944; Nyswander 1956). This pattern is remarkably unchanged (Paltrow 1991; Johnson & Cole 1992; Child Welfare League of America 1992; March of Dimes 1990). Labeling and categorizing offspring of drug-using mothers as idiots, monsters, and degenerate beings was described by McBride in 1910 only to be followed eighty years later by the media's use of terms such as "drug babies," "children of the damned," and "crack babies" (Matthiessen 1992). Another similarity is initial pessimism about the prognosis for infants prenatally exposed to specific substances, followed by realization that some infants prenatally exposed to drugs are not affected at all, and that the negative effects may not be permanent (McBride 1910; Jones et al 1973; Smith 1976, 1982; Streissguth et al 1991; Chasnoff 1992).

Early in the 1960s, the congenital anomalies associated with the prescription antinausea drug thalidomide spurred research into teratogens as well as embryology and dysmorphology (Neuberger 1963; Zuckerman 1991). Since then, threats to the developing fetus by a wide variety of nongenetic, extraneous substances (teratogens) that have been studied include prescription drugs such as dilantin and thalidomide; chemicals such as lead and mercury; infectious agents such as the rubella and herpes viruses; and maternal use of alcohol and other nonprescription drugs (Crain 1984; Chasnoff 1988).

Views of Addiction and Substances

Historically, the problem of being addicted to substances like alcohol, morphine, heroin, barbiturates, and prescription drugs has been viewed as a disease, a psychological disorder, a social deviation, or a spiritual deficit. In general, the trend has been away from psychological, social, and spiritual disorders and toward emphasis on genetic and physical factors that predispose individuals to become addicted to substances. However, this trend did not eliminate the social stigma associated with being addicted to substances, especially those substances that are illegal or widely used by the poor.

As early as 1910, Dr. C. A. McBride wrote, "I do not think the question of heredity as a cause of inebriety is denied by any authority of the present age." While one would think this view of the cause of addiction to alcohol would lead to a nonjudgmental view of the patients who were alcoholics, this same health care provider went on to say his data may be invalid because those who gather family histories and statistics "know how stupid such patients can be regarding their family history and statistics gathered from an institution containing only this class of patient would naturally vary greatly from those compiled in one where only a better class was received" (McBride 1910).

Even though the concept of alcoholism as disease was popular among health care providers in the United States early in the twentieth century, few studies were done to test the disease model because of the political and emotional issues associated with Prohibition and the criminalization of alcohol (Jellinek 1950). After the repeal of Prohibition in 1933, the idea of alcoholism as disease returned to the United States from Europe where research about the etiology of alcoholism had not been stifled by the political climate. The disease concept became prominent in the field of psychiatry for both clinical treatment and research hypotheses. In 1950, Jellinek concluded that the medical profession had officially accepted alcoholism as an illness even if a minority of the medical profession "is disinclined to accept the idea." Between 1939 and 1955, six thousand Alcoholics Anonymous (AA) groups were formed and began meeting in the United States and Canada. By 1955, the organization claimed 150,000 recovering alcoholics (Alcoholics Anonymous 1955). Alcoholics Anonymous meetings in communities throughout the United States and Canada were central in making the illness concept part of public opinion, in addition to the most common theoretical base for research and treatment models.

Despite the predominance of the disease model of addiction to alcohol and some other substances in professional publications, there is no consensus among health care providers about the etiology of addiction. The disease model continues to be competitive with several other models; the social model, which emphasizes social factors such as poverty as causative; the learning theory, which

suggests that individuals learn to use substances in response to certain cues; post-traumatic stress disorder hypothesis, which theorizes that experiences like physical and sexual abuse trigger addictions; and the psychological model, which highlights the role of underlying psychological deficits (Bresnahan, Brooks & Zuckerman 1991). During the last decade, etiology research, primarily about illicit drug users, has resulted in identification of risk factors or predictors of drug abuse. These risk factors emphasize social and environmental influences, not biological predisposition or psychopathology, and serve as the basis for many of the current school-based and public health prevention programs (Hawkins, Lishner & Catalano 1987).

Whether or not an individual using nicotine, morphine, heroin, cocaine, or other substances could become addicted has been influenced more by the social acceptance or rejection of the drugs than by the scientific information available. Smoking tobacco and using cocaine were called "habits" that could lead to "psychological dependence" and "normal hedonistic response" in publications for health care providers and health educators until very recently. On the other hand, use of heroin, barbiturates, and morphine has more consistently been described as "dangerous" and "addictive," and leading to "physical dependence" (School Health Education Study 1967; Wilgoose 1972; Sleet & Estrada 1974; Ensor & Means 1975; Anderson & Creswell 1980; Neuberger 1963; Adams & Kozel 1985; Bresnahan, Brooks & Zuckerman 1991).

Views of Male and Female Substance Users

After describing a strong-willed man with a splendid physique who leapt from a window after turning into a "cocaine fiend" as a result of his cocaine "habit," Dr. McBride wrote that he trembled "to think of the likely result upon delicate women and even children" (1910). Dr. Francis Hare (1913), who treated women "alcoholists" in his sanitorium, noted that women seemed to do as well as the men. However, he concluded that the prognosis for women was actually worse than for men because the women only appeared to respond to treatment as well as men because they were influenced by "propriety" to seek treatment earlier and were more carefully guarded when they went home. Forty years later, an equally negative view of females being treated for addiction was written by a female psychiatrist. She stated that "female addicts seem to sink to a much lower level of degradation than male addicts. It may be that males can better withstand the degrading effects or perhaps they do not represent as socially deteriorated a type as the females who succumb to drugs" (Nyswander 1956). Thirty-five years later, Bresnahan, Brooks and Zuckerman (1991) reported that female addicts are viewed as revolting, disgusting, and bad. Sexual terms which are commonly used to describe women addicts that seriously erode self-esteem and lead to depression include "lush," "coke whore," and "slut" (Bresnahan, Brooks & Zuckerman 1991).

In 1944, Dr. Wood asserted that smoking has a degenerating influence on women and is "prejudicial in every way to their highest efficiency as sweethearts, wives and mothers" whereas the men who were smokers were encouraged to quit in order to set a good example for their mates. A young man who married a smoker was warned that he may not experience "normal mating" (Wood 1944). Fifty years later, Bresnanhan, Brooks, and Zuckerman (1991) theorize that the inability to stop using drugs during pregnancy results in guilt and self-hate for women. Recently, mandated testing and reporting, criminalization, and child abuse reporting are examples of punitive actions taken against women who use drugs during pregnancy (March of Dimes 1990; Larson 1991; Child Welfare League 1992).

In relation to causing neonatal problems, fathers have historically shared the blame but not with the same intensity as the mothers. In 1910, McBride wrote that a drunken women will produce a drunken offspring. In 1928, Terry and Pellens asserted that a father will pass on the morphia influence present at conception and contribute to "the circulating poison." While public reaction to women who use drugs that may damage their unborn children arouses moral outrage, a contemporary bioethicist suggests that the anger is focused primarily on poor and powerless women (Murray 1987) and contends that the father is equally or more at fault if he does not assure that the mother has adequate prenatal care (Murray 1991).

Women's Access to Treatment Programs

As early as 1913, female addicts were perceived to be less successful in treatment programs than their male counterparts. Even when female patients in his sanitorium recovered, Dr. Hare gave credit to the men who brought the females in for early treatment and watched them carefully after they returned home (Hare 1913). A female psychiatrist who treated male and female addicts in a Lexington federal prison reported less crime among women than men, but described the women she treated for drug addiction as socially deteriorated and made up primarily of those arrested for prostitution, for robbing drunks, and for petty thievery. She described her female patients as far more unstable and unruly than her male patients (Nyswander 1956).

There has been—and remains—a lack of appropriate treatment facilities for all who need help for drug addiction. In addition, research about drug treatment is based primarily on studies involving men. Women, particularly pregnant women, have even fewer choices about treatment than men. Of the few treatment programs available for women, many exclude pregnant women and very few of them permit children to remain with their mothers (Kumpfer 1991; Paltrow 1991; Bresnahan, Brooks & Zuckerman 1991; Child Welfare League 1992). In a survey of drug treatment programs in New York City, 87% of the programs did not provide services for pregnant addicts on Medicaid. Of those surveyed, only two had facilities for children (Kuehne & Warguska 1992). Clearly a change in public policy is needed, since women have lacked access to effective treatment for drug abuse throughout the century and patterns of drug use have changed.

Patterns of Substance Use Among Young Women

Substance use among women of childbearing age is not a new phenom-enon in the United States. In 1914, the Harrison Narcotic Act made use of narcotics a criminal act. Prior to that, the ratio of female addicts to male was estimated to be 2 to 1. Narcotics, primarily opium, were available in many nonprescription remedies and elixirs as well as in prescriptions used liberally by physicians to treat both the physical and mental distress of women (Nyswander 1956). Medicines with opium often were prescribed to treat the discomforts of dysmenorrhea and pregnancy and to prevent miscarriage (Hare 1913; Terry & Pellens 1928). When use of narcotics was criminalized in 1914, the ratio of female to male addicts was reversed. By 1956, Nyswander estimated the ratio to be one female to three or four males as compared to two females to one male fifty years earlier. During the 1980s, the ratio of female to male addicts approached one to one.

Women were active in the social movements against alcohol use, the most famous being the Women's Christian Temperance Union led by Carrie Nation before the turn of the century. Men preached about the "evils of liquor" and "demon rum" from the pulpits of major religious denominations and voted to make alcohol use and drunkenness a sin in church doctrines and rules of membership (Howell 1928).

In 1920, possession and use of alcohol was criminalized in the United States by the Volstead Act; the legislation was repealed thirteen years later, ending what is commonly called the Prohibition Era (Allsop 1961). After Prohibition, purchasing alcohol before the age of majority and being drunk in public remained illegal for both men and women of any age. During the last 100 years, the religious, political, and legal environments have had more influence on information about the physiological effects of alcohol use than on information gained from science-based studies. For example, in literature for health educators, alcohol was separated from "dangerous drugs" and was not classified as a "drug" with potential for addiction until the last two decades (School Health Education Study 1967; Sleet & Estrada 1974; Ensor & Means 1975).

Beginning in 1980, many state and national organizations began programs to educate pregnant women about the negative effects of alcohol on their unborn children. By 1991, eight states had enacted laws that required posting warning signs for pregnant women where alcoholic beverages were served or sold (Serdula et al 1991).

In 1975, a twelve-year study of drug use patterns among high school seniors, college students, and young adults was begun by Johnston, O'Malley, and Bachman (1989), and it included alcohol and tobacco use (Figure 1). A decline in the use of all drugs except for cocaine began in 1982. In 1987, use of crack cocaine leveled at low prevalence rates, and in 1988 crack use among high school seniors dropped. However, the level of use of illicit drugs by high school students and young adults in the United States remains higher than in any other industrialized nation (Johnston, O'Malley & Bachman 1989).

During the twelve years studied by Johnston, O'Malley, and Bachman (1989) drug use by males and females approached parity. While the disparity between the sexes is converged toward zero, survey results revealed differences in drugs chosen and frequency of use.

Young males were more likely to use illicit drugs and alcohol, marijuana, and cocaine more frequently than their female counterparts. Young females were more likely than males to smoke cigarettes, especially female college students (1989). Figures 1 and 2 illustrate these survey results (Johnston, O'Malley & Bachman 1989).

Since the differences between the drugs chosen by females and males are minimal and the male-female differences have been basically parallel since 1975, with some narrowing of those differences, it is possible to make some generalizations about drug use by females in the childbearing years from data for the age-group (see Figure 2).

Alcohol

In the last twenty years, alcohol has been increasingly categorized as a drug. Organizations and governmental agencies that originated to combat and treat alcohol abuse and regulate the sale of alcohol still exist. The recognition of alcohol's status as a drug has led to the AA model for recovery being adapted to address other addictions as well. Meetings of Narcotics Anonymous and Cocaine Anonymous are now offered. The National Council on Alcoholism is now the National Council on Alcoholism and **Other Drug Addictions**.

Interest in the effects of alcohol on the unborn child and the neonate appeared in medical literature beginning in the 1800s. Malformations of children born of alcohol-using women were first described by French physicians (Lemoine, Harrousseau & Borteyru) in 1968 and confirmed in 1973 by Seattle physicians Jones, Smith, Ulleland, and Streissguth. These teratogenic effects of alcohol are now known as fetal alcohol syndrome. In 1976, Smith added fetal alcohol syndrome to the second edition of his classic publication *Recognizable Patterns of Human Malformation,* which includes photographs and descriptions of hundreds of malformations of newborns. In the third edition published in 1982, Smith noted that alcohol was the most common major teratogen to which a fetus is likely to be exposed.

Twenty years after the first reports of alcohol-related malformation of neonates, over two thousand scientific reports have been published that confirm the teratogenicity of alcohol (Streissguth et al 1991). The public health objectives for the year 2000 call fetal alcohol syndrome the leading preventable cause of birth defects and contains an estimate of 3 infants per 1,000 live births affected by their mother's alcohol use (*Healthy People 2000* 1990).

In 1967, Nichols described symptoms in a newborn that he attributed to alcohol withdrawal. He noted that while there were a few such reports, medical authorities disagreed about an abstinence syndrome in newborns whose mothers used alcohol excessively. Alcohol withdrawal for newborns is now well documented, described as less severe than withdrawal from narcotics and characterized by tremors, irritability, hypertonicity, and restlessness (Chasnoff 1988; Kuehne & Warguska 1992).

Alcohol is a substance with teratogenic potential to the fetus and addiction potential for both mother and fetus. In 1990, *Youth Risk Behavior Surveillance System* (1991), a survey administered to high school students, showed that 92.4% had drunk alcohol at least once and 30.4% of the female seniors reported heavy drinking on one or more recent occasions. Similarly, Johnston, O'Malley, and Bachman (1989) reported 92% of seniors in high school had used alcohol at least once, with 27% of the female high school seniors having five or more drinks in a row within the previous two weeks.

Education about fetal damage from alcohol may be changing the behavior of pregnant women. A four-year study of alcohol use among pregnant and nonpregnant women from the ages of 18 to 45 indicated a 38% decline in alcohol use among the pregnant women (Serdula et al 1991). In 1985, 32% of the pregnant women reported alcohol use within the previous month but in 1988 only 20% made that claim. Use of alcohol by nonpregnant women in the study declined as well, from 57% in 1985 to 53% in 1988. Alcohol use among pregnant women was highest for those who also smoked and were unmarried.

Tobacco

Fifty years ago, members of an obstetrical association for physicians responded to a survey about the effects of cigarettes on pregnant women. When asked if inhaling twenty-five cigarettes daily had an unfavorable effect on maternal health, 84% said yes; only 2.66% said no and 5% answered that they did not know (Wood 1944). Wood also reported more miscarriages and premature births among women who smoked and advocated for no smoking at all during pregnancy. In a widely used text for nurses published in 1952, the authors acknowledged that most obstetricians disapproved of excessive smoking during pregnancy, but concluded there was no reason to believe that a woman who

(text continues on page 14)

Figure 1. Trends in Illicit Drug Use by High School Seniors

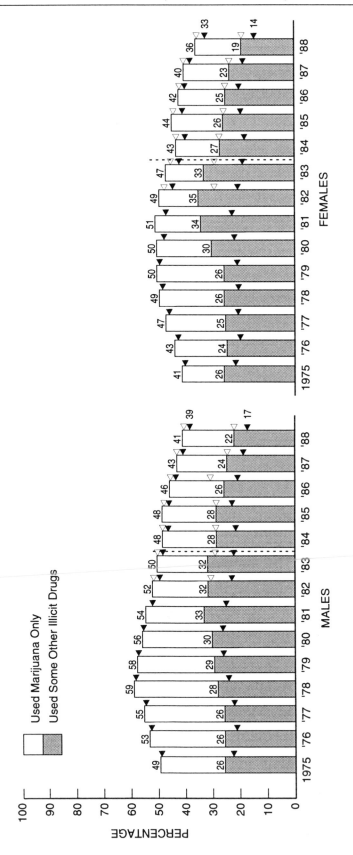

Taken from Johnston LD, O'Malley PM, Bachman JG. Drug Use, Drinking, and Smoking: National Survey Results from High School, College and Young Adult Populations: 1975-1988. Washington, D.C.: U.S. Government Printing Office, 1989 (DHHS publication No. ADM 89-1638).

Figure 2. Use of Fourteen Types of Drugs

Prevalence of Use of Fourteen Types of Drugs, by Sex, 1988
Among Respondents of Modal Age 19-30

	Males	Females	Total
Approx. Wtd. N =	(3600)	(4300)	(7900)
Marijuana			
Annual	34.6	27.7	30.8
Thirty-Day	21.4	14.2	17.5
Daily	4.5	2.2	3.3
Inhalants[b]			
Annual	2.1	1.2	1.6
Thirty-Day	0.7	0.4	0.5
Inhalants, Adjusted[b,e]			
Annual	3.4	1.4	2.4
Thirty-Day	1.5	0.5	0.8
Nitrites			
Annual	1.7	0.5	1.1
Thirty-Day	0.7	0.2	0.4
Hallucinogens			
Annual	5.2	2.4	3.6
Thirty-Day	1.4	0.6	1.0
Hallucinogens, Adjusted[g]			
Annual	5.2	2.4	3.6
Thirty-Day	1.5	0.6	1.0
LSD			
Annual	4.0	1.7	2.7
Thirty-Day	1.1	0.5	0.7
PCP[f]			
Annual	0.5	0.3	0.4
Thirty-Day	0.4	0.1	0.2
Cocaine			
Annual	16.9	11.2	13.8
Thirty-Day	7.0	4.6	5.7
Crack[c]			
Annual	4.0	2.3	3.1
Thirty-Day	1.6	1.0	1.3
Other Cocaine[f]			
Annual	14.7	9.9	12.0
Thirty-Day	5.1	4.5	4.8
Heroin			
Annual	0.2	0.2	0.2
Thirty-Day	0.1	0.1	0.1

Taken from Johnston LD, O'Malley PM, Bachman JG (1989).

Figure 2. Use of Fourteen Types of Drugs (continued)

Prevalence of Use of Fourteen Types of Drugs, by Sex, 1988
Among Respondents of Modal Age 19-30

	Males	Females	Total
Approx. Wtd. N =	(3600)	(4300)	(7900)
Other Opiates[a]			
Annual	2.8	2.3	2.6
Thirty-Day.	0.7	0.5	0.6
Stimulants, Adjusted[a,d]			
Annual	7.4	6.7	7.0
Thirty-Day	2.6	2.7	2.7
Sedatives[a]			
Annual	2.3	1.9	2.1
Thirty-Day	0.7	0.8	0.7
Barbiturates[a]			
Annual	2.0	1.7	1.9
Thirty-Day	0.6	0.7	0.7
Methaqualone[a]			
Annual	0.7	0.4	0.5
Thirty-Day	0.1	0.1	0.1
Tranquilizers[a]			
Annual	4.0	4.5	4.3
Thirty-Day	1.3	1.5	1.4
Alcohol			
Annual	89.8	87.1	88.4
Thirty-Day	79.8	68.7	73.7
Daily	9.4	3.7	6.3
5+ drinks in a row in last 2 weeks	45.4	24.3	33.9
Cigarettes			
Annual	36.3	38.0	37.3
Thirty-Day	28.0	29.6	28.9
Daily (Any)	22.2	23.7	23.1
Half-pack or more per day	18.3	18.3	18.4

[a] Only drug use which was not under a doctor's order is included here.
[b] This drug was asked about in four of the five questionnaire forms. N is four-fifths of N indicated.
[c] This drug was asked about in two of the five questionnaire forms. N is two-fifths of N indicated.
[d] Based on the data from the revised question, which attempts to exclude the inappropriate reporting of non-prescription stimulants.
[e] Adjusted for underreporting of amyl and butyl nitrites. See text.
[f] This drug was asked about in one of the five questionnaire forms. N is one-fifth of N indicated.
[g] Adjusted for underreporting of PCP. See text.

smoked moderately (ten or fewer cigarettes a day) needed to change her custom (Zabrinski & Eastman 1952). Currently, the results of exposure of unborn babies to tobacco are accepted by health care providers to include increased rates of miscarriage, prematurity, low birth weight, increased perinatal mortality, and respiratory problems (Chasnoff 1992; Kuehne & Warguska 1992). Ironically, Dr. Wood had suggested the first two tobacco-related complications fifty years earlier.

Estimates indicate that 18 million women of childbearing age in the United States smoke cigarettes (Chasnoff 1992), with 38% of all children being prenatally exposed to tobacco (Gomby & Shiono 1991). The US public health goal for the year 2000 is to increase abstinence from tobacco during pregnancy from 75% to 90%; the 1987 baseline used in setting the goal revealed that 27% of all women smoked and 25% of pregnant women smoked (*Healthy People 2000* 1990). Similarly, a 1988 survey of 19- to 30-year-old females indicated that 23.7% use cigarettes daily, with 18.35% using a half-pack or more each day (Johnston, O'Malley & Bachman 1989). More recently, Gomby and Shiono (1991) estimated that 37.65% of pregnant 12 to 34 year olds smoked.

Marijuana

After the end of World War II, there was public concern about increased use of narcotics and the role of organized crime in drug trafficking. The Boggs Act, which was passed by Congress in 1951, increased the severity of penalties for drug-related offenses and included marijuana as one of the drugs for which the penalties were to be applied. A dominant theory in the early 1950s contended that marijuana was a stepping-stone to heroin use. According to Abel, during the late fifties and early sixties, the main users of marijuana were African-Americans and Mexican Americans. But later in the sixties, large numbers of middle-class, white college students began using the drug. It was then that the harsh penalties began to be questioned and the dialogue about decriminalizing and legalizing the drug began. In 1972, the National Commission on Marijuana estimated that twenty-four million Americans had tried it, eight million still used it occasionally, and a half million used it daily. Marijuana use rapidly grew more commonplace during the seventies. Abel (1980) reported that fifty million Americans had tried it and twelve million used it regularly by the mid-1970s.

While marijuana remains a drug used frequently by young adults, its use by high school seniors began to decline in 1979 (Johnston, O'Malley & Bachman 1989). Use by high school seniors during the thirty days before the survey was taken in 1979 reached a peak of 27.7% and was reported to be 13.9% in 1990 (Johnston, O'Malley & Bachman 1989; *1990 Youth Risk Behavior* 1991). Gomby and Shiono (1991) estimated that 17.4% of 12- to 34-year-old women use marijuana during pregnancy.

Beginning in the sixties, an explosion of studies and publications reported on behavior changes with marijuana use and its social issues and physiologic effects. Abel (1980) reported finding more than 8,000 articles about marijuana published between 1965 and 1979. Many of the studies were about the drug being a stepping-stone, inciting criminal behavior, and having addiction potential. Many early findings were refuted by later studies with improved methodology. Tennes (1984) reported that most studies she reviewed about marijuana's effects on pregnancy, the neonate, and teratogenicity were flawed because of the polydrug use of the subjects and small sample sizes. She concluded that marijuana made no significant contribution to variance in birth weight and no consistent signs and symptoms were present at birth which could be attributed to prenatal exposure to marijuana when use of tobacco, alcohol, and other drugs was factored out. However, Zuckerman (1991) and Chasnoff (1988) reported that children born of mothers who smoke marijuana are more likely to have low birth weights similar to mothers who smoke tobacco. In 1988, Chasnoff reported withdrawal symptoms of the neonate, including irritability, tremulousness, and some visual functioning deficits, which differs from the conclusion of Tennes' metanalysis of numerous studies and her observation that there were few reports from clinicians despite frequent marijuana use among pregnant women (1984).

Researchers and clinicians have observed a variety of physical, neurobehavioral, and developmental manifestations among infants prenatally exposed to marijuana. However, studies of teratogenicity of marijuana have not yielded consistent results suggesting adverse effects on the fetal brain, fetal growth, or child development (Tennes 1984; Zuckerman 1991; Kronstadt 1991).

Cocaine

Cocaine use among young females increased markedly with the availability of "crack," the cheaper form of the drug, in the mid 1980s. Prior to the development of this easily used and inexpensive form of cocaine, a complicated way of making crack was called freebasing (Udell 1989). Use of cocaine increased rapidly beginning in the mid-1970s and ending in 1988 with a sharp decline among high school seniors and a leveling off of use by young adults (Johnston, O'Malley & Bachman 1989; Adams & Kozel 1985). Gomby and Shiono (1991) estimated that 4.5% of pregnant women use cocaine. One percent of female high school students surveyed in 1990 reported cocaine use in the prior thirty days (*1990 Youth Risk Behavior* 1991), which is consistent with the baseline used to develop the public health goals for the year 2000—1.1% for 12 to 17 year olds and 4.5% for 18 to 25 year olds (*Healthy People 2000* 1990).

While there are many anecdotal reports of the condition of neonates exposed to cocaine during pregnancy, the association between prenatal cocaine use and smaller head size and intrauterine growth retardation has been well established (Chasnoff 1988; Zuckerman 1991; Lewis, Schmeder & Bennett 1992). The neurobehavioral symptoms of irritability and tremulousness may be attributed either to withdrawal or to a direct effect of cocaine on the central nervous system of the infant (Chasnoff 1988.)

Recent studies of children prenatally exposed to cocaine indicate significant progress by the age of three and four that places them into a normal range of social, emotional, and intellectual development. Of the nearly 400 children studied, 30% to 40% continue to have varying degrees of attention deficits and delays in language development but all tested within the normal range cognitively (Chasnoff 1992).

Hallucinogens

Use of hallucinogens has declined sharply since 1975. Less than 1% of American youth and 0.5% of females reported using LSD within the last thirty days in a study by Johnston, O'Malley, and Bachman in 1988. During the sixties LSD was the hallucinogenic drug that attracted public attention because of its use by the "love" or "flower" genera-tion. Questions about the drug's terato-genicity and ability to cause chromo-somal damage were raised. In 1970, Aase, Laestadius, and Smith published a study that produced evidence of neither teratogenic effect nor chromosomal damage.

Use of another hallucinogen, PCP, dropped sharply at the beginning of the 1980s and was reported by less than one half of one percent of all youth surveyed in 1988. Female use of PCP within thirty days of the survey was 0.1% (Johnston, O'Malley & Bachman 1989).

Heroin and Other Opiates

Use of opiates among women of childbearing age was prevalent at the turn of the century and prior to the Harrison Narcotic Act in 1914 that criminalized narcotic use (McBride 1910; Terry & Pellens 1928; Nyswander 1956). After that, men were more likely than women to use illegal narcotics such as morphine and heroin. In 1988, survey results reported that heroin use within the last thirty days among 18 to 30 year olds was 0.1% (the same rate for males and females); use of other opiates was 0.6% (Johnston, O'Malley & Bachman 1989). However, in some health care fa-

cilities and specific urban areas the rate of use is reported to be much higher (Gomby & Shiono 1991).

Problems associated with neonatal withdrawal have been described with accuracy in the literature since the turn of the century. It is interesting that the drug of choice used to treat neonatal withdrawal was and is still paregoric, or tincture of opium (Terry & Pellens 1928; Zuckerman 1991). Recently, the interrelationship between use of illegal opiates and other behaviors such as prostitution and sharing of needles to in-ject drugs makes it clear that the fetus is also at increased risk of being infected with human immunodeficiency virus (HIV) and a myriad of sexually trans-mitted diseases, including hepatitis B. Recent studies (Zuckerman 1991; Kuehne & Warguska 1992) also indicate that neonates exposed to opiates may be at increased risk for sudden infant death syndrome (SIDS).

The possibility of opiates as terato-gens was the subject of research in the 1970s when heroin use was perceived to be a serious drug threat facing the na-tion. Naeye and others (1973) reported that offspring of mothers who were ad-dicted to heroin were subnormal in size and were frequently delivered preterm (1973). Those researchers were unable to determine if the poor fetal growth was a result of inadequate nutrition or drug use. Subsequent research about offspring of women who use heroin, morphine, and methadone has led to speculation that postnatal experiences may be as im-portant as prenatal drug exposure in de-termining development of the child (Kronstadt 1991).

Polydrug Use

Studies of the effects of prenatal exposure to drugs have been complicated because few pregnant women who use drugs use a single substance. Use of secondary drugs, especially tobacco, alcohol, and marijuana, as well as inadequate dietary intake make evaluation of the infant prenatally exposed to narcotics or cocaine very complex (Chasnoff 1988; Lewis, Bennett & Schmeder 1989; Gomby & Shiono 1991; Zuckerman 1991). Abma and Mott (1991) reported data from the National Longitudinal Survey of Youth about the alcohol, cigarette, and marijuana use of women aged 15 to 30 during their first pregnancies. In this study, 45% of the women used at least one substance; the least educated and youngest were most likely to use both marijuana and tobacco; older mothers were most likely to use alcohol. When cocaine use became popular in the 1980s, it was most often used in combination with marijuana, alcohol, methamphetamines, PCP, and/or sedatives. This made research about the effects of cocaine on the fetus and neonate far too complicated to be used accurately in headlines. Unfortunately, the media began using terms like "crack babies," which oversimplified the cause of neonates' problems and contributed to catastrophic outcomes for the children.

Summary

The reproductive casualty for children prenatally exposed to drugs ranges from fetal death and spontaneous abortion to premature birth, intrauterine growth retardation, mental retardation, learning problems, and normalcy (Howard 1992). Undoubtedly, this continuum has existed throughout history for children born of mothers who used the substances available at that time. However, a pattern emerges when reviewing medical literature about children prenatally exposed to drugs. Throughout the twentieth century, health care providers observed and reported malformations, growth retardations, and excessive fetal and perinatal deaths that were perceived to be related to the mother's use of a drug. Initial research studies involved only a small sample of the population, such as heroin-, morphine-, cocaine-, or alcohol-abusing mothers or women using one urban medical facility. Initial research findings may have overestimated the number of children that were negatively affected by their mothers' prenatal drug use. Studies indicate that there are a variety of effects on the developing fetus and young child and that there is conflicting evidence on the long-term effects of some of the drugs on the fetus and young child. Despite the fluctuations and patterns of drug abuse, the observations of health professionals beginning at the turn of the century remain relevant.

REFERENCES

Aase JM, Laestadius N, Smith DW. Children of mothers who took L.S.D. in pregnancy. *Lancet* 1970; II(2): 7663.

Abel EL. *Marihuana: The First Twelve Thousand Years*. New York: Plenum Press, 1980.

Abma JC, Mott FL. Substance use and prenatal care during pregnancy among young women. *Family Planning Perspectives* 1991; 23(3): 117-128.

Adams EH, Kozel NJ. Cocaine use in America: Introduction and overview. In Kozel NJ, Adams EH, eds. *Cocaine Use in America: Epidemiologic and Clinical*

Perspectives. Washington, DC: U.S. Government Printing Office (National Institute on Drug Research Monograph 61; DHHS publication no. ADM87-1414).

Alcoholics Anonymous. New York: Alcoholics Anonymous Publications, 1955.

Allsop K. *The Bootleggers and Their Era.* Garden City, NY: Doubleday, 1961.

Anderson CL, Creswell WH. *School Health Practice.* St. Louis: CV Mosby, 1980.

Bresnahan K, Brooks C, Zuckerman B. Prenatal cocaine use: Impact on infants and mothers. *Pediatric Nursing* 1991; 17(2): 123-9.

Chasnoff IJ. Newborn infants with drug withdrawal symptoms. *Pediatrics In Review* 1988; 9(9): 273-7.

Chasnoff IJ. Hope for a 'lost generation.' *School Safety* 1992; (Winter):4-6 (published by National School Safety Center. Westlake Village, California).

Child Welfare League of America. Pregnant drug abusers: Rights vs. responsibilities. *School Safety* 1992; (Winter): 26-8.

Crain LS. Prenatal causes of atypical development. In Hanson M.J. *Atypical Infant Development.* Austin, TX: PRO-ED,1984.

Ensor P, Means RK. *Instructor's Resource and Methods Handbook for Health Education.* Boston: Allyn and Bacon, 1975.

Finnegan LP. Drug addiction and pregnancy. In Chasnoff IJ, ed. *Drugs, Alcohol, Pregnancy and Parenting.* Boston: Kluwer Academic Publishers, 1988.

Gomby DS, Shiono PH. Estimating the number of substance-exposed infants. *Future of Children* 1991; 1(1): 17-25 (published by the Center for the Future of Children, the David and Lucile Packard Foundation, Los Altos, California.

Hare F. *On Alcoholism: Its Clinical Aspects and Treatment.* Philadelphia: P. Blakiston, 1913.

Hawkins JD, Lishner DM, Catalano RF. Childhoold predictors and the prevention of adolescent substance abuse. In Jones DL, Battjes RJ, eds. *Etiology of Drug Abuse: Implications for Prevention.* Washington, D.C.: U.S. Government Printing Office (National Institute on Drug Abuse Research Monograph 56; DHHS publication No. ADM87-1335).

Healthy People 2000. Washington, D.C.: U.S. Government Printing Office (DHHS publication No. PHS 91-50213), 1990.

Howell GC. *The Case of Whiskey.* Altadena, CA: No publisher, 1928.

Howard J. Developing strategies for educational success. *School Safety* 1992; (Winter): 14-7.

Jellinek EM. *The Disease Concept of Alcoholism.* New Haven, CT: Hillhouse Press, 1950.

Johnson DJ, Cole CK. Extraordinary care for extraordinary children. *School Safety* 1992; (Winter):7-13.

Johnston LD, O'Malley PM, Bachman JG. *Drug Use, Drinking, and Smoking: National Survey Results from High School, College, and Young Adult Populations: 1975-1988.* Washington, D.C.:U.S. Government Printing Office, 1989 (DHHS publication No. ADM89-1638).

Jones KL, Smith DW, Ulleland CN, Streissguth AP. Pattern of malformation in offspring of chronic alcoholic mothers. *Lancet* 1973; I(7814):1267-71.

Kelley SJ, Walsh JH, Thompson K. Birth outcomes, health problems, and neglect with prenatal exposure to cocaine. *Pediatric Nursing* 1991; 17(2):130-6.

Krogh D. Nicotine: The most addictive drug? In *Nicoteen.* New York: Scholastic, 1992, pp 26-7.

Kronstadt D. Complex developmental issues of prenatal drug exposure. *Future of Children* 1991; 1(1): 36-49.

Kuehne EA, Warguska M. Prenatal cocaine exposure. In Jackson PL, Vessey JA, eds. *Primary Care of the Child with a Chronic Condition.* St. Louis: Mosby Yearbook, 1992.

Kumpfer KL. Treatment programs for drug-abusing women. *Future of Children* 1991; 1(1): 50-60.

Larson CS. Overview of state legislative and judicial responses. *Future of Children* 1991; 1(1): 72-84.

Lemoine P, Harrousseau H, Borteyru JP, Menuet JC. Les enfants de parents alcooliques: Anomalies oberees: A propos de 127 cas. *Ouest Med* 1968; 8: 476-82.

Lewis KD, Bennett B, Schmeder NH. The care of infants menaced by cocaine abuse. *MCN (Maternal Child Nursing)* 1989; 14(5): 324-9.

Lewis KD, Schmeder NH, Bennett B. Maternal drug abuse and its effects on young children. *MCN (Maternal Child Nursing)* 1992; 17(4): 198-203.

March of Dimes. *March of Dimes Statement on Maternal Substance Abuse.* San Jose, CA: March of Dimes, 1990 Fall.

Matthiessen C. A fighting chance. *Image* 1992; (May 3): 9-16.

McBride CA. *The Modern Treatment of Alcoholism and Drug Narcotism.* New York: Rebman Company, 1910.

Murray TH. Moral obligations to the not-yet born: The fetus as patient. *Clinics in Perinatology* 1987; 14: 329-42.

Murray TH. Prenatal drug exposure: Ethical issues. *Future of Children* 1991; 1(1): 105-12.

Naeye RL, Blanc W, Leblanc W, Khatamee MA. Fetal complication of maternal heroin addiction: Abnormal growth, infections, and episodes of stress. *Journal of Pediatrics* 1973; 83(6): 1055-61.

Neuberger MB. *Smoke Screen: Tobacco and the Public Welfare.* Englewood Cliffs, NJ: Prentice Hall, 1963.

Nichols MM. Acute alcohol withdrawal syndrome in a newborn. *American Journal of Diseases of Children* 1967; 133: 714-5.

1990 Youth Risk Behavior Surveillance System. Atlanta, GA: Centers for Disease Control, National Center for Chronic Disease Prevention and Health Promotion, 1991.

Nyswander M. *The Drug Addict as a Patient.* New York: Grune & Stratton, 1956.

Paltrow LM. Perspective of a reproductive rights attorney. *Future of Children* 1991; 1(1): 85-92.

School Health Education Study. St. Paul, MN: 3M Education Press, 1967.

Serdula M, Williamson DF, Kendrick JS, Andra RF, Byers T. Trends in alcohol consumption by pregnant women. *Journal of the American Medical Association* 1991; 265(7): 876-9.

Sleet D, Estrada J. *Essentials of Life and Health: Instructor's Manual.* 2nd ed. New York: CRM/Random House, 1974.

Smith DW. *Recognizable Patterns of Human Malformation.* 2nd ed. Philadelphia: WB Saunders, 1976.

Smith DW. *Recognizable Patterns of Human Malformation.* 3rd ed. Philadelphia: WB Saunders, 1982.

Streissguth AP, Aase JM, Clarren SK, Randels RP, LaDue RA, Smith DF. Fetal alcohol syndrome in adolescents and adults. *Jour-*

nal of the American Medical Association 1991; 265(15): 1961-7.

Tennes K. Effect of marijuana on pregnancy and fetal development in the human. In Braude MC, Ludgord JP, eds. *Marijuana: Effects on the Endocrine and Reproductive Systems.* Washington, D.C.: U.S. Government Printing Office (National Institute on Drug Abuse Research Monograph 44; DHHS publication No. ADM84-1278).

Terry CE, Pellens M. *The Opium Problem.* New York: Committee on Drug Addictions, in collaboration with the Bureau of Social Hygiene, 1928.

Udell B . Crack cocaine. *Special Currents: Cocaine Babies.* Columbus, OH: Ross Laboratories, 1989.

Willgoose CE. *Health Teaching in Secondary Schools.* Philadelphia: WB Saunders, 1972.

Wood FL. *What You Should Know About Tobacco.* Grand Rapids, MI: Zondervan Publishing House, 1944.

Zabrinski L, Eastman NJ. *Nurses Handbook of Obstetrics.* 9th ed. Philadelphia: JB Lippincott, 1952.

Zuckerman B. Drug-exposed infants: Understanding the medical risk. *Future of Children* 1991; 1(1): 26-35.

ANNOTATED BIBLIOGRAPHY

Terry CE, Pellens M. *The Opium Problem.* New York: Committee on Drug Addictions, in collaboration with the Bureau of Social Hygiene, 1928.
This book, written in 1928, is a delightful, candid, and easy-to-read volume with colorful descriptions of observations of physicians about opium addiction beginning in the late 1800s. The book gives the reader new respect for keen professional observation as the descriptions of neonatal withdrawal were no less detailed than those currently available.

Future of Children: Drug-Exposed Infants.
Volume 1, Number 1, Winter 1991.
Published by:
> **David and Lucille Packard**
> **Foundation**
> **Center for the Future of Children**
> **300 Second Street, Suite 102**
> **Los Altos, CA 94022**

This publication provides an up-to-date overview from multiple perspectives of the problems of infants prenatally drug exposed. The perspectives include: epidemiologic, medical, nursing, legal, ethical, economic, and social and public policy. Each section has current resources that are useful to the researcher and clinician who work in the health, educational, or social service arenas.

Drug-Exposed Babies—The Newest Cry for
Help in the War on Drugs. *School*
Safety, **Winter 1992.**
> **Published by: School Safety News**
> **Service**
> **National School Safety Center**
> **4165 Thousand Oaks Boulevard,**
> **Suite 290**
> **Westlake Village, CA 91362**

This is a special edition of a news journal which contains information particularly useful to educators who are challenged to provide instruction and support for children prenatally exposed to drugs. The seven articles include a hope-filled update from Dr. Ira Chasnoff; educational strategies from Dr. Judy Howard; practical experiences from classroom teachers; discussion of legal issues from the Child Welfare League of America; and policy suggestions for school board members.

Drug Use, Drinking, and Smoking: National
Survey Results from High School, Col-
lege, and Young Adult Populations,
1975-1988. **1989. A publication of the**
U.S. Department of Health and Human
Services, Public Health Service, Alco-
hol, Drug Abuse, and Mental Health
Administration, publication no. (ADM)
89-1638, and for sale by the:
> **Superintendent of Documents**
> **U.S. Government Printing Office**
> **Washington, DC 20402**

This publication summarizes the findings of a twelve- year study of use of alcohol, tobacco, and other substances among American youth. The text, tables, graphs, and charts describe substances used by high school seniors, college students, and non-college youth and allow the reader to visualize patterns of use of substances since 1975.

2

Drugs and the Effects on Health and Development of the Fetus, Neonate, Infant, and Child

Bonnie M. Bear, R.N., B.S.N., P.H.N.

This chapter reviews the last three decades of research into the adverse effects of prenatal substance exposure on the fetus, infant, and child. A host of methodological issues can affect the research, such as the nature of prenatal care, unreliable self-reporting of the mother, limitations of urine screening, the biological variability of the fetus, the amount or strength of the substances used, the validity of the research tools, and polydrug use. These confounding research issues thus lead to a body of literature with inconclusive results about the major variables, including the pharmacology of specific drugs, the drug-using lifestyle of the mother, and the postnatal environment. Whereas there are definite adverse effects of drugs, both temporary and long term, it is difficult to truly isolate the specific cause of the adverse effects on the fetus. Further research is needed into the cumulative and interactive effects of the multiple risk factors which impact children prenatally exposed to drugs. This review includes the substances of cocaine, marijuana, narcotics, phencyclidine, and tobacco. Recent research has focused on cocaine, and it is given more consideration in this review.

A review of the research literature regarding newborns subjected to maternal substance abuse indicates that serious scientific study began approximately twenty-five years ago. Research in the 1960s began to show a correlation between pregnant women using cigarettes, heroin, and/or alcohol and early childhood developmental problems. In the 1980s, medical researchers published studies suggesting adverse effects of marijuana, cocaine, and methamphetamines on the fetus and neonate. The accumulated body of research available in the 1990s, in general, supports potential adverse outcomes for newborns prenatally exposed to substances. However, the cause of the adverse effects remains in question. Some studies suggest that the postnatal environment plays a vital role, perhaps even more than drugs, in the long-term outcome of this population (Coles et al 1992; Lifschitz et al 1983; Wilson 1992).

Many studies report conflicting findings regarding the effects of particular drugs on the fetus, newborn, infant, and young child. A look at the confounding factors involved in studying these effects provides some understanding of the challenges faced in this area of research. Therefore, this chapter deals first with the methodological research issues and then reviews the literature pertaining to the effect of specific substances on the mother and her offspring. Substances covered in this chapter include cocaine, marijuana, narcotics, phencyclidine, and tobacco. Alcohol-related birth defects are well established and will be covered in a separate chapter. However, alcohol abuse is a prominent factor in many, if not most, drug users' lives. It must be remembered that the prevalence of polysubstance use makes ascribing a specific perinatal effect to the use of one specific substance during pregnancy very difficult.

Methodological Research Issues

Yonekura (1989) found that pregnant women who are drug dependent may have little or no prenatal care, have infections or other medical complications, and generally have poor nutrition. These factors alone put these women at risk for poor pregnancy outcome. In addition, drug-dependent women seldom use or abuse only one substance. For example, a woman using cocaine often uses alcohol and/or opiates to deal with depression that may follow the euphoria of cocaine. Also, drugs are seldom pure, and the strength varies over time and geographic area. Some of these factors may be dealt with in research studies by the use of various statistical methods for sorting out the effects of interrelated risk factors; this is usually very expensive and requires a large sample.

Another compounding factor for research is the reliability of self-reporting by substance abusers, especially since denial is a known part of addictive behavior. Understandably, women also may be reluctant to report the use of substances for which they may face legal sanctions or social disapproval. This can lead to erroneous conclusions by not correctly identifying the at-risk population, as was demonstrated by Zuckerman and associates (1989). The use of urine or blood samples throughout pregnancy can reduce the possibility of error. However, serial testing is hampered by the irregularity or absence of prenatal care by untreated drug-dependent women. Even if serial urine screening is possible it may not always give an accurate picture, due to the rapid clearance of some drugs. For example, cocaine metabolites are present in the urine of a nonpregnant woman less than a week and amphetamines are present only one to two days (Dixon 1989). During pregnancy, renal function is enhanced, thus limiting the window of time for testing even further. The possible margin of error, if relying on urine toxicologies alone, was illustrated by Christmas, Penz, and Dinsmoor (1991) who found that only 40% of their patients who admitted to using drugs actually had positive urine toxicology test results. Some researchers support the use of hair or meconium samples, which would be easier to collect and in which substance abuse can be detected over a three-to-four-month period (Callahan et al 1992). Recently, the procedure for analysis of meconium for drugs has been modified, making this test feasible for large-scale clinical and research use (Ostrea, Romero & Yee 1993).

Many biological variables must also be considered when researching the impact of substance abuse on a newborn. Some infants are more vulnerable than others to the insult of prenatal substance exposure. This was dramatically demonstrated by Christoffel and Salafsky (1975) in the report of a fraternal twin pregnancy in which fetal alcohol syndrome (FAS) developed in one twin and the other twin was only minimally affected. The reasons for this variance in fetal effects are unknown. Genetic differences also influence the effect of substance abuse on the fetus. For example, liver and plasma enzymes metabolize cocaine into the inactive water-soluble metabolites. Enzyme activity is gener-

ally decreased in a pregnant woman and her fetus, thus the fetus is more sensitive to small doses of cocaine due to this prolonged exposure. However, in some pregnant women the enzyme level stays the same or may actually increase during pregnancy therefore decreasing the risk to the fetus (Christmas 1992).

Yet another variable is the amount of substance used, for example, binge usage versus repeated low doses of drugs. The timing of the exposure is also critical. During the first trimester, spontaneous abortions are a risk and congenital malformations may occur because this is the time of organogenesis. All organs are susceptible the first three months but the brain continues to be vulnerable throughout pregnancy due to its longer period of development. During the last trimester, premature labor or abruptio placentae may occur and growth may be affected, resulting in intrauterine growth retardation (IUGR).

Several studies link substance-abusing males to an increased incidence of negatively affected offspring (Little & Sing 1987; Tanaka, Suzuki & Armina 1982; Yazigi, Odem & Polakoski 1991). The mechanism for this adverse effect has not been identified. However, a recent study by Yazigi, Odem, and Polakoski (1991) demonstrated that cocaine can bind to human spermatozoa. They hypothesized that the sperm could then transport the cocaine into the egg and cause abnormal development of the fetus, adding another variable to consider in substance abuse research.

Finally, there are problems with the research tools used to assess infant/child development. For example, some measurements are not sensitive enough to adequately evaluate the quality of motor skills of an infant prenatally drug exposed (Schneider & Chasnoff 1992). With an older child, the assessment tool may be highly structured thus allowing for a great deal of examiner intervention. This external structure may mask some of the self-regulatory difficulties experienced by children prenatally drug exposed.

With all of these confounding issues, the findings of research in this area should be read carefully. Table 1 outlines factors that affect research.

Questions to ask when reviewing research literature include:

1. What were the selection criteria for the drug-exposed population and the control group?

2. How large was the sample?

3. What methods were used to determine which substances were taken, amount taken, route of administration, and period of exposure?

4. Were the examiners "blind" to infant exposure?

5. What methods were used to control for confounding variables?

6. What tests were used to assess the infant/child?

7. Are the purported effects consistent with the pharmacologic action of the substance?

8. Have other studies supported similar findings?

9. What is the clinical importance of the outcome?

The following material in this chapter reviews research into the adverse effects of prenatal substance exposure on the fetus, the infant, and the growing child. The substances of cocaine, marijuana,

narcotics, phencyclidine, and tobacco are covered, with a particular empahsis on cocaine because of a recent focus on cocaine research. Table 2 helps elaborate on the effects of each drug, and Table 3 covers the effects of drug use on breast-feeding.

Cocaine

Cocaine is a natural alkaloid derived from the *Erythroxylon coca* plant grown in the mountains of South America.

Origin and Pharmacology

More than 5,000 years ago, the natives of the Andes were chewing coca leaves to decrease hunger and fatigue (Dixon 1989). Cocaine was first isolated in Germany in 1857, and its local anesthetic properties were applied in ophthalmology in the early 1880s (Gawin & Ellinwood 1988). By the 1890s, Coca-Cola and patent medicines containing cocaine were marketed in the United States. Coca-Cola contained cocaine until 1903 when it was replaced with caffeine. Subsequently, due to the extensive abuse of cocaine in the United States, cocaine was restricted to controlled medical use by an act of Congress in 1914.

In the late 1960s and early 1970s, the illegal use of cocaine reemerged as a public issue, but widespread use in the United States didn't occur until the early 1980s. Cocaine has now become the largest source of illicit drug income in this country, and its use has spread across all demographic lines and socio-economic classes (Kleber 1988). Estimates of the number of pregnant women using cocaine have ranged from 3% to 17% (Slutsker 1992).

Cocaine is a central nervous system

Table 1. Confounding Factors Affecting Research

1. Unreliable self-reporting.

2. Limitations of urine screening.

3. Variance in amount of substance and time of exposure.

4. Implications of sperm being altered by paternal substance abuse.

5. Problems in maintaining a cohort of infants and children for follow-up studies.

6. Strength of drug varies over time and geographical area.

7. Contamination of drugs.

8. Varied vulnerability of fetus.

9. Lack of sensitive, effective assessment tools.

10. Multiple variables associated with maternal substance abuse, such as:

    a. Inconsistent or no prenatal care.

    b. Inadequate maternal nutrition.

    c. Poor maternal health.

    d. Polydrug use.

    e. Socioeconomic factors, both prenatally and postnatally, such as poverty, fractured families, multiple caretakers, homelessness, abuse, and neglect.

(CNS) stimulant, an appetite suppressant, and a local anesthetic. The physiologic effects of cocaine occur through a variety of mechanisms. These mechanisms include blocking peripheral nerve impulses, which contributes to its local anesthetic effect; direct stimulation of the CNS and blocking the reuptake of neurotransmitters (Young, Vosper & Phillips 1992). The neurotransmitters (norepinephrine, epinephrine, and dopamine) carry impulses from one nerve to the next and when they are blocked, the signals are exaggerated. For example, dopamine is thought to produce feelings of contentment and happiness. When excess levels of dopamine are present, the cocaine user becomes euphoric or feels "high." Norepinephrine and epinephrine produce vasoconstriction and tachycardia with a concomitant rise in blood pressure as well as overall increased body temperature (Young, Vosper & Phillips 1992). With excess norepinephrine, there is a powerful vasoconstrictive action that is believed to be the most important deleterious effect of cocaine (Dixon 1989). Virtually every organ system is vulnerable and this vasoconstriction could explain many of the reported adverse perinatal effects associated with prenatal cocaine exposure (Dixon 1989).

Acker and associates (1983) published the first report of adverse effects of maternal cocaine use in which they described two cases of abruptio placentae. Subsequent studies have cited a variety of potential deleterious effects; however, the inconsistent findings make it difficult to conclusively establish independent effects of cocaine exposure in utero. Rather, the negative neonatal outcomes may be the result of an overall potentially detrimental milieu in which cocaine exposure is an important factor (Coles et al 1992; Richardson & Day 1991). Although we may not know the exact cause of an individual child's delays, children prenatally exposed to cocaine will most likely receive more positive intervention if approached as "at risk" rather than assuming deficits. As we look for answers to the problem of prenatal drug exposure, we tend to focus on the negative influences in a child's life; but we must not forget to factor in some of the positive forces that may counterbalance some of the risks. For example, some children are raised by supportive grandparents or by adoptive or foster parents who provide a stable, consistent environment. Other children are involved in early intervention programs while their parent(s) is involved in recovery. Thus, the impact of prenatal drug exposure may be mitigated by these positive influences. Prenatal drug exposure is a potential, but not inevitable, insult.

Maternal Effects

Women who use cocaine during pregnancy are at increased risk for nutritional and vitamin deficiency due to cocaine's appetite suppressant property and/or their general lack of interest in caring for themselves, for example, eating and sleeping properly. They may also lack motivation to seek prenatal care, or may avoid medical care for fear of discovery. Furthermore, their lifestyle may put them in danger of injury through violence as well as increasing the probability of infectious diseases which may be passed on to the fetus, in-

cluding HIV infection, syphilis, hepatitis B, herpes virus type II and other sexually transmitted diseases. These factors alone, aside from the effects of cocaine, put both mother and baby at increased risk for perinatal complications.

Pregnant women using cocaine are subject to the same general medical risks as nonpregnant cocaine-using individuals. These risks include cerebrovascular accidents, hypertension, seizures, aortic rupture, subarachnoid hemorrhage, malignant hyperthermia, ruptured aneurysms, bowel problems, acute myocardial infarction, and sudden death (Cregler & Mark 1986). In addition, cocaine use during pregnancy has been associated with a range of adverse maternal effects such as abruptio placentae, premature rupture of membranes (PROM), preterm labor and delivery, and precipitous delivery or abnormally rapid cervical dilatation (Chasnoff, Burns & Burns 1986).

Abruptio placentae, or premature separation of the placenta, has been linked with maternal cocaine use in several studies (Bingol et al 1987; Chasnoff et al 1989; MacGregor et al 1989; Dixon 1989) and is associated with poor perinatal outcome including maternal hemorrhage and fetal hypoxia (Young, Vosper & Phillips 1992). The exact mechanisms of cocaine-induced placental abruptio are still unknown, but the pharmacologic effects of cocaine offer a plausible explanation. A high incidence of stillbirths related to abruptio placentae has been cited in several studies (Acker et al 1983; Bingol et al 1987; Hadeed & Siegel 1989). However, in another study comparing thirty-four women who reported using cocaine during pregnancy with six hundred who re-

(text continued on page 30)

Table 2. Effects of Prenatal Drug Exposure during Pregnancy, on the Newborn, and on the Growing Child.*

Effects of Cocaine

During Pregnancy	On the Newborn	On the Growing Child
Poor weight gain	Premature birth	Disorganized form of attachment
Sexually transmitted diseases	Intrauterine growth retardation	Easily frustrated
Fetal hypoxia	Meconium staining	Mood dysfunction
Intrauterine strokes	Smaller head circumference	Seizures
Spontaneous abortion	Tremulousness	Autism
Preterm labor	Increased startles	Learning disability
Premature rupture of membranes	Shrill cry	Language processing problems
Precipitous delivery	Abnormal muscle tone/reflexes	Difficulties with articulation
Stillbirths	Restlessness, irritability	Attention deficit
Abruptio placentae	Rapid state changes	Hyperactivity
	Irregular sleep pattern	Abnormal oculomotor functioning
	Difficult to console, decreased cuddliness	
	Poor feeding, vomiting, diarrhea	
	Impaired habituation	
	Gaze aversion	
	Facial defects	
	Neural tube defects	
	Visual defects	
	Limb defects	
	Genitourinary defects	
	Congenital heart defects	
	Intestinal impairments	
	Central nervous system lesions	
	Intraventricular hemorrhage	
	Seizures	

Effects of Marijuana

During Pregnancy	On the Newborn	On the Growing Child
Difficulty conceiving	Intrauterine growth retardation	Leukemia
Spontaneous abortion	Meconium staining	Myopia
Precipitous labor	Increased tremors	Strabismus
Tachycardia	Features compatible with fetal alcohol syndrome	
Hypertension	Poor habituation to visual stimuli	
	Abnormal oculomotor functioning	
	Abnormal sleep and arousal patterns	

Effects of Narcotics

During Pregnancy	On the Newborn	On the Growing Child
Difficulty conceiving	Premature birth	Strabismus
Sexually transmitted diseases	Meconium staining	Attention deficit
Hepatitis A, B, C	Intrauterine growth retardation	Developmental delay

* Most effects listed are purported, not conclusive. There are no identified prenatal drug exposure syndromes other than fetal alcohol syndrome and neonatal abstinence syndrome (opiates).

Table 2. Effects of Prenatal Drug Exposure during Pregnancy, on the Newborn, and on the Growing Child.* (continued)

Effects of Narcotics (continued)

During Pregnancy	On the Newborn	On the Growing Child
HIV	Smaller head circumference	Learning disability
Bacterial endocarditis	Neonatal abstinence syndrome	Hyperactivity
Septicemia	SIDS	Slowed psychomotor level
Cellulitis	Apnea	Temper tantrums
Toxemia		Delayed speech
Eclampsia		Impaired visual motor functioning
Placental insufficiency		
Abruptio placentae		
Preterm labor		
Premature rupture of membranes		
Breech presentation		
Stillbirths		
Spontaneous abortion		

Effects of PCP

During Pregnancy	On the Newborn	On the Growing Child
Tachycardia	Intrauterine growth retardation	Attention deficit
Hypertension	Tremulousness	Diminished social interaction
Hyperthermia	Irritability	Dull with flat affect
Seizures	Hypertoxicity	Poor fine motor coordination
	Meconium staining	Oppositional behavior
	Diarrhea	Delayed speech/language
	Vomiting	
	Temperature instability	
	Poor visual tracking	
	Difficulty consoling	
	Rapid state changes	
	Nystagmus	

Effects of Tobacco

During Pregnancy	On the Newborn	On the Growing Child
Difficulty conceiving	Premature birth	Increased respiratory illnesses
Ectopic and tubal pregnancies	Intrauterine growth retardation	Diminished lung function
Poor weight gain	Smaller head circumference	Chronic otitis media
Chronic fetal hypoxia	Tremulousness	Childhood cancer
Vaginal bleeding	Hypertoxicity	Attention deficit
Spontaneous abortion	Poor habituation to sound	Hyperactivity
Preterm labor	SIDS	Diminished reading, verbal, and math skills
Premature rupture of membrane	Cleft palate/lip	Lower IQ
Placenta previa	Hernias	Poorer social skills
Abruptio placentae	Eye and ear malformations	
	Congenital heart defects	
	Central nervous system abnormalities	

Table 3. Effects of Drug Use on Breast-feeding

Cocaine	Transmitted in breast milk. Infant may demonstrate increased startle response, marked tremulousness or seizures.
Marijuana	Transmitted in breast milk and remains there a long time. Effects on infant are unknown but breast-feeding is not recommended.
Narcotics	Transmitted in breast milk. Withdrawal symptoms in the infant can be alleviated by breast-feeding from a mother using heroin. There is danger the infant may become excessively drowsy or may become addicted. Prescription narcotics may cause drowsiness and failure to thrive in nursing infants. Methadone, specifically: Breast-feeding may be considered up to 4 to 6 months of age if mother is: 1. In well supervised methadone treatment program. 2. Not using other substances. 3. Eating an adequate diet. 4. Not infected with HIV, tuberculosis, or Hepatitis B, which may be transmitted via breast milk.
Phencyclidine	Transmitted via breast milk. Animal research demonstrates significant activity changes in nursing offspring of female animals given PCP.
Tobacco	Transmitted in breast milk. Inhibits milk production. Reduces level of vitamin C in milk. May cause nausea and vomiting with abdominal cramping and diarrhea.

ported no cocaine use, the cocaine users did not differ from the controls in terms of abruptio placentae or other obstetrical complications. There was also no difference in gravidity (number of pregnancies) between the two groups. There was, however, a significant difference in parity (live births), indicating that the women using cocaine had more previous fetal losses (Richardson & Day 1992).

Premature rupture of membranes, which may put the fetus at increased risk of infection, was reported in 33% of pregnant cocaine users in a study by Cherukuri and associates (1988). However, when Oro and Dixon (1987)

matched cocaine users with controls by prenatal care status, no increased risk of PROM was noted in cocaine users compared with controls.

There are also inconsistent findings regarding maternal cocaine use and preterm labor and delivery. Several studies have reported an increase in preterm births (< 37 weeks gestation) in pregnancies complicated by cocaine use as compared to control groups (Chasnoff, Griffith et al 1989; Cherukuri et al 1988; Christmas, Penz & Dinsmoor 1991; Dixon 1989; Oro & Dixon 1987), but it is not a consistent finding (Hadeed & Siegel 1989; Richardson & Day 1992;

Zuckerman et al 1989). Less commonly cited complications associated with maternal cocaine use include meconium-stained amniotic fluid, a sign of fetal distress (Christmas 1992) and precipitous delivery (Chasnoff, Burns & Burns 1986).

Fetal/Neonatal Effects

Despite the increasing body of research on the reproductive risks associated with maternal cocaine use, few independent effects of cocaine on the fetus have been confirmed (Slutsker 1992). There are, however, a number of purported adverse effects, including impaired fetal growth, congenital anomalies, and sensory effects.

Fetal Growth

Several studies indicate that in utero cocaine exposure adversely affects fetal growth parameters such as birth weight, length, and head circumference (Bingol et al 1987; Chasnoff, Lewis et al 1989; Cherukuri et al 1988; Hadeed & Siegel 1989; Neerhoff et al 1989; Oro & Dixon 1987). These studies revealed that 15% to 35% of the babies prenatally exposed to cocaine were small for gestational age (SGA) compared to a high of 7% in babies not prenatally exposed to drugs. Small for gestational age is usually defined as below the tenth percentile for a given gestational age. This intrauterine growth retardation (IUGR) is of concern because low birth weight (LBW) is a major factor in infant mortality in the United States (Zuckerman 1991). Low birth weight is defined as an infant weighing less than 2,500 grams (5 pounds) at birth. The two major contributors to LBW are preterm birth and IUGR; IUGR ranks second to prematu-

rity as a cause of perinatal loss (Wolfe & Gross 1989).

Although there are multiple risk factors for IUGR, making it difficult to evaluate the impact of maternal cocaine use on fetal growth, some studies have documented an independent effect of cocaine (Bingol et al 1987; MacGregor et al 1989; Oro & Dixon 1987). Chasnoff, Griffith, and others (1989) noted that maternal cocaine users who discontinued use after the first trimester had infants with significantly higher mean birth weights than those who continued use throughout pregnancy. Prenatal care also reduces the risk of IUGR as found by MacGregor and associates (1987). In this study, maternal cocaine users who received adequate prenatal care had infants with higher birth weights than those who did not have prenatal care. However, infants of both groups had significantly lower mean birth weights than did infants who were not prenatally exposed to cocaine. As demonstrated in this study, prenatal care can improve the outcome of a pregnancy complicated by maternal cocaine use, but the effects on growth are not completely ameliorated.

Reduced placental blood flow, associated with cocaine use, is a reasonable explanation for reduced birth weight and length and may also contribute to a smaller head circumference (microcephaly). Reduced head circumference secondary to in utero cocaine exposure has been reported (Chasnoff, Griffith et al 1989; Cherukuri et al 1988; Hadeed & Siegel 1989; Little & Snell 1991; Zuckerman et al 1989). This decreased head circumference is of concern because it may reflect a smaller brain, and infants with IUGR and microcephaly are more likely to demonstrate developmental and learning problems compared to infants with normal head size (Chasnoff et al 1992). Furthermore, it is of interest that Eckerman, Lynne, and Gross (1985) found that head growth after birth may be a more powerful predictor of developmental outcome than head circumference at birth. Thus, postnatal nutrition and other environmental factors affecting brain growth may be critical in the long-term outcome of infants exposed to cocaine in utero. Further studies are needed to evaluate the relative impact of cocaine on head circumference when other risk factors, such as poor maternal nutrition, lack of prenatal care, and poor maternal health, are present.

Congenital anomalies

Cocaine use during pregnancy has been associated with numerous congenital anomalies but a specific syndrome has not been identified (Table 2). Data from both human and animal studies indicate that fetal vascular disruption caused by vasoconstriction or hemorrhage secondary to maternal cocaine use may be the cause of congenital anomalies (Hoyme et al 1990; Oro & Dixon 1987). Vascular disruption may occur at any time in gestation, thus the fetus is at risk for potential damage throughout the pregnancy if cocaine exposure continues.

Fetal anomalies have been reported affecting the genitourinary tract (Chasnoff, Griffith et al 1989; MacGregor et al 1987), the brain (Bader & Lewis 1990; Bingol et al 1987; Kobori, Ferriero & Golabi 1989), skeletal system (Kobori, Ferriero & Golabi 1989), bowel (Chasnoff, Griffith et al 1989; Hoyme et al 1990), and cardiovas-

cular system (Lipshultz, Frassica & Orav 1991; Neerhoff et al 1989). Some of the purported congenital anomalies are "remediated" with surgery, for example, hypospadias or ventricular septal defect. Conversely, no congenital anomalies were reported in three studies of infants exposed to cocaine in utero (Cherukuri et al 1988; Richardson & Day 1992; Zuckerman et al 1989). The inconsistencies in these reports may be related to the differences in timing, dosage, route of cocaine administration, and other variables. Furthermore, some of the studies were conducted on a very small number of cases. Larger, well controlled studies are needed to determine the individual risk of anomalies associated with cocaine use during pregnancy.

There are reports of intrauterine or perinatal cerebrovascular accidents that may have long-term implications for future learning or behavior difficulties (Chasnoff, Lewis et al 1989; Dixon 1989; Kobori, Ferriero & Golabi 1989). Dixon (1989) found that 35% of stimulant (cocaine, methamphetamine)-exposed, asymptomatic, full-term infants exhibited cranial abnormalities as documented by cranial ultrasound at three days of age. The abnormalities observed included small hemorrhages or cysts (resolution of a hemorrhage) located in the basal ganglia, frontal lobes, and posterior fossa. The distribution of these lesions could explain some of the motor abnormalities documented by Schneider and Chasnoff (1992). However, these lesions may be "silent" until higher level cognitive functions are required (Dixon 1989). It must be noted that the clinical significance of these cranial abnormalities is not known at this time.

A more recent study by Dusick and

colleagues (1993) failed to establish any association between prenatal cocaine exposure and increased incidence of intraventricular hemorrhage (IVH) or ischemic events. In this prospective study of 323 consecutively born very low birth weight infants (about 1,499 grams) there were 86 infants exposed to cocaine and 146 infants not exposed who did not differ significantly in incidence of IVH (35% vs 36%) and periventricular leukomalacia (2% vs 4%). However, there was an increased risk of abruptio placentae (18% exposed vs 8% nonexposed), surgical ligation of patent ductus arteriosus (7% exposed vs 1% nonexposed), and seizures (17% exposed vs 5% nonexposed).

Sensory effects

Some studies have reported abnormalities of the visual system associated with in utero exposure to cocaine, such as optic nerve hypoplasia, strabismus, nystagmus (Dominguez et al 1991), delayed visual maturation, prolonged eyelid edema (Good et al 1992), and abnormal dilatation of iris blood vessels (Isenberg, Spiero & Inkelis 1987). Delayed visual maturation is manifested by visual inattention in infancy, with a normal eye examination. Vision eventually develops normally, but visual inattention has continued to age 4 months in some studies and may have a negative impact on mother-infant bonding unless the caregiver can make the necessary adaptations. The reported cases of eyelid edema and abnormal dilatation were resolved without any long-term effects.

The studies cited involved small samples and polydrug use was usually a compounding issue. Thus cocaine may be a contributing, but not independent,

factor for these ophthalmologic anomalies. The anomalies would be consistent, however, with the pharmacologic action of cocaine. In fact, Good and colleagues (1992) ask the question, "Why do so many infants escape cocaine's potentially devastating effects?"—suggesting that there could be a greater incidence of anomalies than is reported.

There are conflicting studies regarding the effects of prenatal cocaine exposure on the auditory system of the developing fetus. Shih, Cone-Wesson, and Reddix (1988) report auditory brainstem responses (ABRs) in neonates prenatally exposed to cocaine that indicate dysfunction in the auditory system and neurologic impairment. Similar findings were reported by Salamy and associates (1990). In both studies the ABRs were normal by three to six months after birth. Conversely, another study comparing fifty infants with prenatal cocaine exposure to fifty controls found no increased incidence of hearing deficits as determined by ABRs (Carzoli et al 1991).

Neurobehavioral and Developmental Effects

Cocaine affects the neurobehavioral outcome of the developing fetus directly via action of the drug or its metabolites on the brain, or indirectly through cerebral vascular compromise, cerebral hypoxia, or fetal malnutrition (Neuspiel & Hamel 1991; Singer, Arendt & Minnes 1993). Some newborns exposed to cocaine in utero exhibit neurobehavioral deficits in state regulation, interactive ability, and habituation as measured by the Brazelton Neonatal Behavior Assessment Scale (NBAS) (Chasnoff, Griffith et al 1989; Chasnoff, Lewis et al

1989; Fulroth, Phillips & Durand 1989). Habituation is considered a primitive form of learning because it involves gradual adaptation to aversive or repetitive stimuli, in order that the infant is protected from the abundance of new stimuli faced every day. Impaired habituation places the infant at risk for overstimulation and disorganization or they may go into a deep, unresponsive sleep state to avoid overstimulation. These deficits are of concern because they may be indicators of possible long-term effects of cocaine on neuro-psychologic functioning (Dixon 1989). On the other hand, the deficits may be only temporary, interfering with mother-infant attachment, thus indirectly affecting long-term outcome.

Nurses in neonatal units observe in infants prenatally exposed to cocaine a spectrum of behaviors from lethargy and deep sleep to panicked awake states and irritability. When infants prenatally exposed to cocaine are scored on the neonatal abstinence scale (developed for newborns exposed to heroin), they have not shown significant dysfunction (Hadeed & Siegel 1989; Ryan, Ehrlich & Finnegan 1987), perhaps because the scale does not encompass the neurobehavioral abnormalities and physiologic effects observed in some of these infants. More comprehensive assessment tools such as the Lewis Protocol (1990) are being developed and may provide a more sensitive measure of neurobehavioral functioning. At present, Brazelton's NBAS offers a means of describing the alterations in behavior noted in infants and can be used to train caregivers to understand and respond appropriately to the infant's cues.

The dysfunctional behaviors observed

in the infant prenatally exposed to cocaine may represent withdrawal or may be reflective of CNS damage occurring early in the pregnancy. Results of one study demonstrate that neurobehavioral deficiencies are just as severe whether the mothers quit during the first trimester or continued use until delivery (Chasnoff, Griffith et al 1989). This study, which was done on a small sample, supports the theory that there is damage to the CNS rather than a withdrawal syndrome. Furthermore, the clinical signs of prenatal cocaine exposure—including hyperirritability, difficult feeding patterns, increased tremors, and irregular sleep patterns—may persist for weeks or months, long after withdrawal would be completed (Lewis 1990; Schneider, Griffith & Chasnoff 1989). However, withdrawal from cocaine in adults, especially in habitual users, may last from one to ten weeks, so it is difficult to predict what pattern of withdrawal might occur in neonates exposed to cocaine in utero (Coles et al 1992).

In contrast to the studies noted above, other researchers have not found neurobehavioral deficits in infants prenatally exposed to cocaine. Coles and colleagues (1992) found that cocaine exposure had considerable impact on birth weight and head circumference. However, they found cocaine exposure had minimal effects on the behavioral outcome in infants. The study was designed to control for prematurity, various medical problems, polydrug exposure, examiner effects, and duration and time of exposure. However, Coles and associates discuss other limitations of the study that make it difficult to compare it with previous studies.

Richardson and Day (1992) evaluated

the outcomes of infants whose mothers were light to moderate users of cocaine and had decreased cocaine use during pregnancy. They compared thirty-four infants who were exposed to cocaine in utero with six hundred controls and found the exposed infants did not differ from the controls in growth, physical anomalies, or neurobehavioral outcome. Considering the discrepancy in these studies on prenatal cocaine exposure, the effects of cocaine have not yet been independently linked to a specific pattern of neurobehavioral deficits (Neuspiel & Hamel 1991).

In the area of motor development, Schneider and Chasnoff (1992) used movement assessment of infants (Chandler, Andrews & Swanson 1980) to demonstrate increased muscle tone and persistence of primitive reflexes in a group of 4-month-old infants. Although the authors recognized the impact of parenting skills on motor development, tone and reflexes are more reflective of neurophysiologic functioning. It is unlikely that environmental factors would be the causative agent in increased muscle tone or increased tremors in the extremities.

Development beyond the neonatal period is dependent on an expanding number of interactive factors, making it increasingly difficult to isolate the effects of cocaine exposure in utero. Despite the biologic vulnerability associated with prenatal cocaine exposure, responsive caretaking and/or early intervention can modify or remediate the insult (Zuckerman 1991). The effect of the social environment was demonstrated in a study involving two groups of premature infants. One group in which the infants were neurologically immature received responsive caretaking and by 7 years of age had IQ levels similar to those of the group of infants who were neurologically mature (Beckwith & Parmalee 1986). These findings agree with the study of children with similarly high levels of perinatal stress (Werner 1989). Children from families with a high level of stability had much better outcomes than those who faced both high perinatal stress and poor family stability.

Long-term Effects

Early studies suggested a link between prenatal cocaine exposure and sudden infant death syndrome (SIDS) (Chasnoff, Lewis et al 1989; Chavez et al 1979). Subsequently, a larger study failed to demonstrate the same association (Bauchner et al 1988). It is of note that SIDS cannot be readily attributed to the pharmacologic action of cocaine. Even the highest alleged risk between maternal cocaine use and SIDS does not qualify an infant for home apnea monitoring on the basis of cocaine exposure alone, according to the risk standards of the National Institutes of Health Consensus Group (Bresnahan, Brooks & Zuckerman, 1991).

Postnatal drug exposure has been linked to SIDS and this clouds the relationship of prenatal drug exposure, including cocaine, for SIDS even further. Kandall and Gaines (1991) discuss three mechanisms whereby postnatal drug exposure increases the risk for SIDS:

1. Exposure to drugs via breast milk.

2. Accidental environmental exposure, including passive tobacco smoke.

3. Administration of drugs by the caretaker to calm a fussy baby, to cause direct harm to the baby or out of ig-

norance of the drug's potential side effects.

Thus, many factors must be considered when investigating the issue of SIDS if drugs are involved either prenatally or postnatally. Further studies are needed to clarify the relationship between prenatal exposure to cocaine and SIDS, but at this time it appears the increased risk is minimal.

Very few studies have been published regarding the long-term effects of prenatal cocaine exposure on child development. In a two-year study comparing three groups of children (cocaine-exposed, marijuana- and/or alcohol- exposed without cocaine, and nondrug- exposed) there were relatively few significant differences among the groups on the Bayley Scale of Infant Development (Chasnoff et al 1992). The authors caution that the Bayley scales may not be reflective of the self-regulatory problems noted in children prenatally drug exposed, because the scale is highly structured and allows for a great deal of examiner intervention. If external regulation of problems is not provided, the lack of self-regulation often negatively affects the child's performance. Further research is being done to examine the extent of external regulation required by drug-exposed children in varying test situations (Chasnoff et al 1992)

The majority of the cocaine-exposed children followed to ages 3 and 4 at Chicago Center for Perinatal Addiction are functioning at age-appropriate levels in social, emotional, and intellectual development (Griffith 1991). It is important to note that these children have received intensive assessment and intervention from pediatricians, psychologists, physi-

cal therapists, speech therapists, and developmental programs. However, even with this extensive intervention, 30% to 40% of the children still have problems with language development and/or attention of widely varying severity. These included difficulties with articulation and severe language processing problems. The attentional problems ranged from mild distractibility to attention deficit disorders. This study demonstrates the need for early educational intervention, family therapy focusing on the development of healthy, nurturing relationships, and psychotherapy for the children to work through emotional problems resulting from their chaotic environment. Several studies support the belief that the home environment is a more important factor than the biologic vulnerability created by cocaine/ polydrug exposure (Chasnoff 1988; Chasnoff, Burns & Burns 1986; Chasnoff, Hatcher & Burns 1982; Lifschitz et al 1985; Wilson 1992).

Davis and colleagues (1992) in a retrospective study found autism, as defined by *Diagnostic and Statistical Manual of Mental Disorders (DSM-III-R)* criteria, in children with prenatal cocaine exposure. Hyperactivity was also noted in these children. In a study of seventy children, ages 1 month to 5 years, a high frequency of autism (11.47%) and language delay (94%) was reported. The study suggests caution in the interpretation and thereby generalization as complete information was not always available. This was a retrospective study in which it was impossible to ascertain all of the variables, for example cigarette smoking, duration of exposure, and polydrug use. However, this high rate of autism is not known to occur in children exposed to opiates or alcohol alone.

Further studies need to be conducted on this new disturbing finding using methodological designs discussed earlier in this chapter. Autism is reported to occur in 2 to 21 per 1,000 live births (Ritvo et al 1989) but has not been previously reported in association with in utero drug exposure.

Marijuana

Origin and Pharmacology

Marijuana is a drug made from the dried leaves and flowering tops of the plant *Cannabis sativa*. More than 400 chemicals are found in the plant, but delta -9 tetrahydrocannabinol (THC) is the main mind-altering ingredient in marijuana (Turner 1980). The amount of THC in the marijuana determines its potency. Today the strength of marijuana is ten times greater than the marijuana produced in the 1970s, resulting in an increased risk of health problems for the user (Zuckerman 1988). Marijuana is a very complex drug that is metabolized in stages by the liver. It accumulates in fatty tissue and a single dose may take up to thirty days to be excreted. The metabolites can be measured in the urine up to seven days after use (Nahas 1976).

Although marijuana has been referred to as a "soft drug" and no more damaging than tobacco or coffee, recent studies report prolonged deleterious effects on the heart and lungs, and transitory effects on the immune system and reproductive functions (Nahas & Latour 1992). Marijuana can increase the heart rate by 50 percent and it disrupts pulmonary function, thereby reducing the oxygen level in the blood (Zuckerman et al

1989). The lungs are also susceptible to damage because marijuana contains up to 50 percent more tar and cancer-causing chemicals than found in cigarettes. These tars and chemicals are especially harmful because marijuana users often inhale unfiltered smoke deeply and hold it in the lungs as long as possible. Studies are now documenting a link between marijuana and cancer of the upper aerodigestive tract (Endicott & Skipper 1991; Nahas & Latour 1991; Taylor 1988). Damage to the immune system is usually only temporary, but it puts the user at risk for multiple infections. By inhibiting the secretion of reproductive hormones, marijuana may cause dysmenorrhea, lower sperm production, and diminished sexual growth and development (Zuckerman 1988). Studies indicate that with repeated exposure, most of these hormonal changes return to normal in adults because the body develops a tolerance to the inhibitory effects (Zuckerman 1988).

Animal Studies

Much of the research on the effects of marijuana has been done in animals because it is difficult to isolate marijuana use in humans. Abel (1983) reviewed the research in animal studies and found that intrauterine growth retardation (IUGR), preterm delivery, and developmental problems were observed in animals. The IUGR could be attributed to poor nutrition associated with marijuana use (Abel 1975). Even the developmental problems noted in animals may respond to a better diet. This was demonstrated in a study by Charlebois and Fried (1980) where marijuana-induced developmental problems in rats were prevented by providing a high protein diet. Is it possible, then, that some of the deleterious effects of marijuana exposure during human pregnancy could be prevented by a well-balanced diet?

Maternal Effects

Marijuana is certainly not a new substance in the drug market, and the number of infants exposed to marijuana in utero in the late 1980s was estimated to be 611,000, or 17% of newborns (Gomby & Shiono 1991). Even so, there are limited human studies of marijuana use during pregnancy and these studies have not produced conclusive results regarding the effects of marijuana on the fetus (Zuckerman 1991). A small study by Greenland, Statish, Brown, and Gross (1982) found a significant increase of precipitous labor and meconium staining associated with maternal use of marijuana. The mothers using marijuana also exhibited poor weight gain, higher levels of anemia, and prolonged labor, although not to a significant degree. Other larger studies have not found adverse maternal effects (Zuckerman 1988).

Fetal/Neonatal Effects

It is known that marijuana crosses the placental barrier (Indanpaan-Heikkila 1969). Due to the lengthy and complex metabolism of marijuana, the fetus is subject to prolonged exposure from even a single episode of marijuana use. However, as discussed earlier in this chapter, methodological problems have often contributed to inconsistent reports regarding the effects of marijuana on the fetus. For example, some studies show no correlation between maternal marijuana use and IUGR when relying on self-reporting to determine substance abuse (Fried, Watkinson & Willan 1984;

Linn et al 1984). To the contrary, when Zuckerman and colleagues (1989) conducted a study using urine assay to test for marijuana by-products, they found that marijuana use was indeed associated with IUGR. Another study by Hingson and associates (1986) designed to evaluate the validity of self-reporting, demonstrated that women are more likely to report cigarette smoking and use of alcohol than to admit to marijuana use, even when they are told they will be tested. This variance in self-reporting is not surprising because marijuana is illegal. Given this consideration, the potentially detrimental effects of marijuana may be mistakenly attributed to alcohol or nicotine.

An illustration of possible mistaken causation is reported in a large study (1,690 mother-child pairs) done at Boston City Hospital by Hingson and associates (1982), which looked at the impact of maternal drinking and marijuana use on fetal development. In this study, 234 women reported using marijuana. When confounding variables were controlled, the researchers were surprised to find that women who used marijuana during pregnancy were five times more likely to deliver an infant with a combination of features compatible with fetal alcohol syndrome (FAS). This finding suggests that the development of FAS, which was previously attributed solely to excessive maternal alcohol use, may also be associated with marijuana use or a combination of marijuana and alcohol use during pregnancy.

Neurobehavioral and Developmental Effects

Increased tremors, often accompanied by exaggerated startles, and poorer habituation to visual stimuli have been observed in neonates prenatally exposed to marijuana. In addition, the infants were less successful at self-quieting (Fried, Watkinson & Willan 1984). However, these findings are not consistent with other studies (Zuckerman 1991).

Long-term Effects

In long-term studies, Fried and Watkinson (1990) and Fried, O'Connell, and Watkinson (1992) have followed a group of children prenatally exposed to marijuana, cigarettes, and alcohol up to 72 months. Up to the age of 36 months there were no negative effects of marijuana on cognitive, motor, or language development. In fact, a surprising observation at 36 months was a positive relationship between maternal marijuana use and superior motor performance among the children. Conversely, at 48 months the children demonstrated poor performance on memory and verbal tests after adjusting for confounding variables. At 5 and 6 years of age, no differences were noted in the children prenatally exposed to marijuana and the children not exposed. Fried, O'Connell, and Watkinson (1992) suggest that as the children reach school age, some of the more subtle differences may be overridden by the common factor of formal schooling.

The researchers, (Fried, O'Connell & Watkinson 1992) state that three additional factors must be considered before extrapolating the absence of findings in the children at ages 5 and 6 to other populations of children prenatally exposed to marijuana. First, the strength of marijuana has increased significantly since this study was started in the late 1970s and the early 1980s (Zuckerman 1988). Second, the mothers were from a

low-risk sample, which eliminated the potentiating factor of poverty and poor nutrition. Finally, the assessment tools used may not have detected the subtle neurobehavioral differences between children prenatally exposed to marijuana and those children not exposed. At this time, there are no consistent findings clearly associating maternal marijuana use with long-term behavioral/cognitive deficits.

Some studies, however, report long-term adverse physiologic effects. In a case-control study of 204 pairs of children, the investigator found a tenfold increased risk of leukemia in the children exposed to marijuana in utero. No other drug use, including alcohol, tobacco, or pain killers, was associated with such a risk (Robinson, Buckley & Daigle 1989).

Another area of concern is vision. Ophthalmologic exams of children (3 to 6 years old) who were prenatally exposed to marijuana have revealed an increased risk of myopia (nearsightedness), strabismus (crossed eyes), and abnormal oculomotor (movement of eye) functioning (Fried 1985). Thus, there may be some long-term adverse effects, but there are too few studies to draw any firm conclusions.

Narcotics (opiates)

The term narcotics refers to opium and opium derivatives or semisynthetic substitutes.

Origin and Pharmacology

The poppy, *Papaver somniferum*, is the source of opium, which is broken down into morphine and codeine for medical use. Methadone, Percodan, Dilaudid, and Talwin are some of the semisynthetic narcotics derived by a modification of the chemicals contained in opium. In addition to these narcotics used in medicine, there are several illegal semisynthetic narcotics, notably heroin. Heroin was first synthesized in 1898 by Heinrich Dreser, the developer of aspirin (Zagon & McLaughlin 1992). Both aspirin and heroin were touted as painkillers, and heroin was also promoted as a powerful cough suppressant. However, heroin was soon recognized as a potent addictive drug and subsequently banned from legitimate use.

Even before the development of heroin, opium was known to have ill effects on the fetus. Clinical reports from as early as the 1870s describe unusual behavior in the neonate exposed to opium (Zagon & McLaughlin 1992). In fact, even Hippocrates related fetal distress to maternal opium use. Today, the symptoms of neonatal withdrawal from opiates are well defined as the neonatal abstinence syndrome (NAS) and will be discussed later in this chapter.

Maternal Effects

Common complications associated with maternal heroin use include first trimester spontaneous abortions, premature delivery, intrauterine growth retardation (IUGR), neonatal meconium aspiration syndrome, and maternal/neonatal infections, including venereal diseases (Finnegan, Kron & Connaughton 1975). The parenteral (injected) use of heroin also increases the risk of bacterial endocarditis, septicemia, cellulitis, and hepatitis types A, B, and C, and more recently, the transmission of the human immunodeficiency virus (HIV) (Kaltenbach & Finnegan 1992). These infections may have devastating effects on both mother and her unborn child if left untreated throughout pregnancy.

In the early 1970s, methadone maintenance was introduced as a means to reduce perinatal complications of maternal heroin addiction. Methadone satisfies the physical craving for opiates without providing the psychological high associated with heroin. In addition, methadone is effective orally and acts for a longer period of time than heroin or morphine (Finnegan & Kandall 1992). Participation in a methadone program usually brings some order to the mother's chaotic lifestyle. Generally, maternal nutrition improves and prenatal care is offered through the treatment program. In addition, the prescribed level of methadone prevents erratic maternal blood drug levels so the fetus is not subjected to repeated episodes of withdrawal. More importantly, the danger of infections from contaminated needles is avoided, a critical point in this age of AIDS.

Some controversy exists over the use of methadone during pregnancy, however, and some studies (Davis & Templer 1988; Annuziato 1971) have indicated that infants who go through methadone withdrawal have more severe abstinence symptoms and require a longer recovery period than infants going through heroin withdrawal. These effects have been shown to be dose-related. When the mother is placed on a low dose (20mg per day) of methadone maintenance, neonatal withdrawal is less severe and it is hoped the long-term effects will be diminished as well (Chasnoff 1988). Other researchers caution against lowering maternal methadone as low as possible (Finnegan & Kandall 1992). Instead, they advocate for maternal comfort and fetal well-being, which would put most women on a higher dose (35 - 80 mg) of methadone during pregnancy.

Unfortunately, the reduction of maternal methadone dosage during pregnancy may result in the mother seeking a substitute such as diazepam (Valium) (Sutton & Hinderliter 1990). The onset of withdrawal from diazepam may be delayed up to a week. Therefore, these infants need close follow-up if they are discharged before one week of age. Other mothers may seek even more harmful substitutes, or relapse to heroin if they are not adequately maintained on methadone. The final verdict on methadone maintenance is not in, but at this point it provides the best alternative to heroin dependence. Lifschitz and colleagues (1983) suggest that the lack of consistent improvement in fetal outcome with the use of methadone may be related to the wide variance in patient management.

Fetal/Neonatal Effects

As mentioned previously, infants born to mothers using opiates have a high incidence of neonatal withdrawal (abstinence syndrome) (Zuckerman 1991). However, prophylactic drug treatment for withdrawal is not recommended, because not all infants prenatally exposed to narcotics develop neonatal abstinence syndrome (NAS). For babies with mild withdrawal, techniques such as swaddling, demand feeding, and minimal environmental stimulation may be sufficient to overcome abstinence symptoms. An infant going through withdrawal may exhibit significant irritability, gastrointestinal dysfunction, tremulousness, respiratory difficulties, a high-pitched

cry, poor feeding, increased tone, and occasionally seizures (Finnegan, Kron & Connaughton 1975). The babies have difficulty getting comfortable and frequently develop abrasions on their extremities as they repeatedly move about, trying to get comfortable. These withdrawal symptoms may start at birth or as late as two weeks after birth, but the majority of symptoms appear within seventy-two hours (Desmond & Wilson 1975). The onset of abstinence is affected by many factors including the type, timing, and dose of the drug used by the mother before delivery; the analgesics and anesthetic given during labor; nutrition; and the maturity of the infant.

Premature infants may actually fare better than full-term infants as found in a study by Doberczak, Kandall, and Wilets (1991). Their data from 178 term and 38 preterm infants born to methadone-maintained mothers showed that preterm infants appeared to have less severe withdrawal symptoms. Furthermore, the peak severity of abstinence symptoms occurred one to two days later in preterm infants than in term infants. The authors concluded that this difference could be due to the preterm infant having shorter duration of in utero exposure or to the developmental immaturity of the preterm infants' central nervous system (CNS). That is, the CNS may have immature specific opiate receptors, a relative lack of dendrites, or immature neurotransmitters, thus altering the expression of abstinence symptoms. In addition, the delay of symptoms could be due to a slower rate of metabolism in the preterm infant resulting in persistently higher tissue levels of the drug, which would postpone the appearance of withdrawal symptoms. Another possibility would be that the abstinence scoring system for term infants is inappropriate and not sensitive enough to detect withdrawal in a preterm infant. This is an area needing further study to ensure that preterm infants exposed to opiates are treated with appropriate pharmacotherapy for the control of abstinence and for detoxification.

The abstinence score, developed by Finnegan, Kron & Connaughton (1975), is used to assess the passively addicted newborn for the onset, progression, and cessation of withdrawal symptoms. It is also used to gauge the infant's clinical response to pharmacotherapeutic intervention. Currently, the most commonly used drugs for the treatment of NAS are paregoric (tincture of opium) and phenobarbital (Zuckerman 1991).

In addition to the acute NAS, which usually lasts from two to eight weeks, some infants experience a subacute withdrawal syndrome that may last up to one year (Kaltenbach & Finnegan 1988). These symptoms include an irregular sleep pattern, irritability, and vomiting and usually do not require medical treatment. However, studies have shown that some infants exposed to narcotics continue to demonstrate delayed physical growth until approximately one year of age (Chasnoff, Burns & Burns 1986). This is believed to be due to a prolonged NAS.

Furthermore, NAS makes narcotic-exposed infants difficult to engage and console thus compromising the normal process of maternal-infant bonding. If the symptoms continue over an extended period of time, the infants are also at risk of neglect and abuse. Therefore, early diagnosis and appropriate intervention are important.

In addition to NAS, infants prenatally exposed to opiates have a significantly higher incidence of intrauterine growth retardation (IUGR) and smaller head circumference than comparison babies (Chasnoff 1988; Finnegan & Kandall 1992; Lifschitz et al 1983). Stimmel and associates (1982) found that infants born to women who use methadone have somewhat higher birth weights than do children born to women using heroin. Researchers also found that although the severity of the NAS did not vary depending on the type of narcotic abused, the infants exposed to methadone had significantly improved perinatal outcome (Kaltenbach & Finnegan 1992). Also, babies exposed to narcotics in utero usually do catch up in growth parameters by age three.

Neurobehavioral and Developmental Effects

Despite the severe NAS noted in some infants prenatally exposed to narcotics, research studies indicate they score within normal limits at two years of age (Chasnoff 1988; Finnegan & Kandall 1992; Strauss et al 1976). Follow-up studies of fifty-nine infants born to women maintained on methadone during pregnancy found no correlation between maternal drug intake or degree of NAS with Gesell profiles up to 24 months of age (Finnegan, Reeser & Ting 1974). Another study of twenty-five infants prenatally exposed to methadone compared favorably to a control group. All neurologic findings were within normal limits and there was no relationship between the severity of NAS and the children's IQ scores (Kaltenbach, Graziani & Finnegan 1978).

Long-Term Effects

Studies assessing children prenatally exposed to narcotics at four years of age or beyond are extremely limited. However, it is encouraging that some studies indicate a positive outcome for narcotic-exposed children. Strauss and associates (1975) assessed 5-year-old children using the McCarthy Scales of Children's Abilities and found no differences between the drug-exposed children and the controls. Kaltenbach and Finnegan (1989) replicated the study by Strauss and associates (1975). It is of note that the mean General Cognitive Index in both studies was slightly higher for the children exposed to drugs as compared to the controls.

Strabismus

Maternal drug abuse and increased methadone dosage may predispose infants to the development of strabismus (Nelson et al 1987). Nelson and colleagues (1987) followed twenty-nine infants born to mothers enrolled in a methadone maintenance program. Strabismus was diagnosed in 24% of the infants, in contrast to the general population where the prevalence of strabismus in childhood is between 2.8% to 5.3%. Although women in the group were polydrug users, there was a dose-related relationship between methadone and the development of strabismus. The specific mechanism causing the strabismus in unknown. However, this study indicates that infants born to drug-dependent women are at greater risk of developing strabismus. Thus, close follow-up is required so that appropriate treatment can be prescribed.

Sudden Infant Death Syndrome (SIDS)

The link between prenatal exposure to opiates and subsequent SIDS was made in 1969 as discussed by Kandall and Gaines (1991). Even though there is now a general consensus that maternal opiate use places the offspring at greater risk of SIDS, the exact mechanism is unknown. Kandall and Gaines (1991) stress the fact that no studies clearly separate opiate use from the complexities associated with a drug-using lifestyle that could independently increase the risk of SIDS.

Phencyclidine

Origin and Pharmacology

Phencyclidine (PCP) was originally developed in the mid-1950s as a short-acting anesthetic. However, it was taken off the market for human use in 1965 due to its unfavorable hallucinatory side effects (Zukin & Zukin 1992). PCP continued to be widely used in veterinary medicine until manufacturing of the drug was stopped in 1978 (L.A.W. Publications 1992).

Unfortunately, PCP can be made in home laboratories from common, inexpensive chemicals in a variety of forms to be inhaled, ingested, or injected. On the street, PCP is often mixed with other drugs or disguised as a variety of other drugs. The most common misrepresentation of PCP is as marijuana (Zukin & Zukin 1992). Thus a person seeking marijuana may be unknowingly exposed to PCP. Another risk is the unknown strength of PCP, which may vary from 5% to 100% pure depending on the form and preparation (Harry & Howard 1992). The variability of its purity, the substitution of PCP for other drugs, and the fact that PCP is usually used with a number of other drugs make researching the effects of PCP very difficult.

Phencyclidine is classified as a hallucinogen, but could also be categorized as a nonspecific CNS depressant, an anticholinergic (similar to atropine), an anesthetic, and tranquilizer or psychedelic (Holbrook 1983). The exact mode of action of PCP is unclear, but it is known that it alters several neurotransmitter systems and in this respect is similar to cocaine (Zukin & Zukin 1992). Since PCP is lipid-soluble, large quantities accumulate in tissues with high fat content. Consequently, the active drug can be gradually released from fatty stores over a period of time. In one study, the mothers had discontinued PCP use at least three months before delivery, yet PCP was detected in the urine of their infants one to seven days after birth (Ahmad 1987). This delayed release of PCP may also explain the disorder of cognitive function, memory, and behavior observed in chronic users months to years after their last use (Zukin & Zukin 1992).

The popularity of PCP has varied over the years since it was first offered for illicit use in California in the mid-sixties (Harry & Howard 1992). Use of PCP reached its first epidemic in 1978 and then declined in use for about three years.

In the mid-1980s most users were male (Zukin & Zukin 1992); yet in 1986, 12.5% of 915 newborns in Los Angeles County had positive urine toxicology screens for PCP (Durfee 1986). It has been, and still is, a drug used by women during pregnancy.

Maternal Effects

Use of PCP during pregnancy places the mother at risk for tachycardia (fast heart rate), agitation/panic, muscular rigidity, nystagmus (jerking movement of eyes), seizures, and hyperthermia. In addition, mild hypertension may occur with even minimal use of PCP. Severe hypertension resulting in CNS complications has been reported when high doses of PCP are taken (Zukin & Zukin 1992). Furthermore, PCP use may result in poor reflective thinking and poor problem-solving skills which may negatively influence the appropriation of consistent prenatal care (Harry & Howard 1992). There is very little published information on the effects of PCP use during pregnancy. However, it is known that PCP crosses the placental barrier and is also present in breast milk (Nicholas, Lipschitz & Schreiber 1982).

Fetal/Neonatal Effects

Limited information on the gestational effects of PCP does not allow solid conclusions to be drawn. Experimental studies in animals have demonstrated a variety of gross malformations following in utero exposure to PCP (Jordan et al 1979; Marks, Worthy & Staples 1980). However, most of these teratogenic effects occurred only at dose levels producing maternal toxicity. In two studies, which looked at a total of forty-nine newborns primarily exposed to PCP, almost 100% of the infants exhibited tremors and nearly 50% of the infants were irritable and hypertonic. Less than 20% of the infants had autonomic nervous system symptoms—diarrhea, vomiting, and/or temperature instability (Howard, Kropenske & Tyler

1986; Tabor, Smith-Wallace & Yonekura 1990). The long-term implications of these symptoms is unknown; they could be just withdrawal symptoms similar to those seen in adults.

Tabor, Smith-Wallace, and Yonekura (1990) noted that infants prenatally exposed to PCP were likely to be born less prematurely when compared to cocaine-exposed infants. In comparing the two groups, however, the infants exposed to PCP were more likely (32.4%) to be small for gestational age (SGA) than were the infants exposed to cocaine (18.9%).

Neurobehavioral and Developmental Effects

Few studies regarding the effects of prenatal PCP exposure on neurobehavioral functioning have been published. Animal studies indicate that gestational exposure to moderate amounts of PCP produce mild, if any, long-term alterations in the performance of offspring (Harry & Howard 1992). One research project comparing forty-one children with prenatal PCP exposure to a non-drug-exposed control group found that the drug-exposed children demonstrated poor fine motor coordination and delayed language skills, indicating evidence of neurological dysfunction (Harry & Howard 1992). This occurred despite early and ongoing intervention from social workers, public health nurses, and/or early childhood educators. As a result of this research, Harry and colleagues concluded, "that the majority of children do not escape the deleterious effects of prenatal substance exposure, despite comprehensive and consistent intervention" (Harry & Howard 1992). This finding contrasts

with that of other researchers (Coles et al 1992; Kronstadt 1991; Mayes et al 1991; Neuspiel & Hamel 1991) who suggest that the postnatal environment, including early intervention, is probably more important than prenatal substance exposure in predicting the developmental outcome of children exposed to substances in utero.

Tobacco

Origin and Pharmacology

Tobacco is native to Peru, but it has been cultivated in the Americas for centuries. Cigarette smoke contains more than 2,000 pharmacologically active substances, and many deleterious compounds in tobacco such as carbon monoxide, hydrogen cyanide, and nicotine are absorbed into the body through the lungs. Nicotine, the addictive ingredient in tobacco, is also considered the primary toxic agent. It is water- and liquid-soluble, which allows rapid distribution throughout the body including crossing into the placenta (Zuckerman 1988). Nicotine produces a wide array of physiologic actions, including the release of catecholamines such as acetylcholine, epinephrine, and norepinephrine. The excessive level of catecholamines results in a vasoconstriction of the peripheral vessels, a rise in blood pressure, increased heart rate, changes in fat and carbohydrate metabolism, and an increased tendency to thrombophlebitis (Pirani 1978).

The harmful effects of smoking have been recognized for hundreds of years. In fact, the earliest anti-tobacco campaign happened in 1604 when King James I imposed a tax on the tobacco imported from the New World in an attempt to limit the "custome loathesme to the Eye, hatefull to the Nose, harmeful to the Braine, dangerous to the Lungs" (Stebbins 1990). Although smoking is on the decline in this country, far fewer women manage to stop smoking during their pregnancies than drinking (Rubin et al 1986). This is true despite the fact that for the past twenty years research has demonstrated a dose-related response between maternal smoking and lower birth weight, and recent studies are adding to the list of deleterious effects of tobacco. At present, cigarette smoking and smokeless tobacco use are responsible for nearly 500,000 deaths per year. In contrast, heroin and cocaine combined produce only 6,000 deaths per year (Centers for Disease Control 1991).

Maternal Effects

Smoking during pregnancy places the mother at risk for the tobacco-related diseases, including coronary heart disease, chronic bronchitis, chronic obstructive pulmonary disease, lung and laryngeal cancer, and peripheral vascular disease. In addition, nicotine in the tobacco suppresses the appetite by stimulating the sympathetic nervous system (Hofstetter et al 1986). As a result of the chronic stimulation of the sympathetic nervous system, smokers have an increased metabolism. Both decreased appetite and increased metabolism contribute to the minimal weight gain often noted in pregnant women who smoke (Grunberg 1986).

Some studies have reported a link between smoking and the increased likelihood of spontaneous abortion (Kline et al 1977; Himmelberger, Brown & Cohen 1978). This increased risk could be explained by a recent study which

demonstrated placental alterations associated with heavy smokers, meaning more than twenty cigarettes per day (Jauniaux & Burton 1992). Another possible mechanism could be a dysfunction in the hormones that sustain pregnancy such as progesterone or prolactin (Zuckerman 1988).

Fetal/Neonatal Effects

Fetal Growth

Although nicotine crosses the placental barrier, most of the adverse effects on the fetus are indirect. For example, maternal vasoconstriction may reduce uteroplacental blood flow, thus reducing transplacental transport of oxygen and nutrients (Mactutus 1989). Pirani (1978) found that infants of mothers who smoked had an elevation in red cell volume (polycythemia) as if they were oxygen-deprived. Furthermore, the carbon monoxide in cigarette smoke combines with hemoglobin to form carboxyhemoglobin. Both vasoconstriction and carboxyhemoglobin reduce oxygenation to the fetus, thereby contributing to decreased birth weight, length, and head circumference. Babies born to mothers who smoke weigh an average of 275 grams less than babies of nonsmokers (Kline, Stein & Hutzler 1987). Conversely, Zuckerman (1988) cites studies that demonstrate an increase in birth weight and length for babies whose mothers quit smoking during pregnancy. These studies illustrate the need for early prenatal care associated with counseling intervention to enable the mother to quit smoking. The Surgeon General (U.S. Department of Health and Human Services 1990) has stated that smoking is probably the most important preventable cause of poor pregnancy outcome in the United States.

Congenital malformations

The association of smoking and congenital malformations is not established. Zuckerman (1988) reviewed several studies and found conflicting results. A large study in Britain (Fedick, Alberman & Goldstein 1971) linked cigarette smoking during pregnancy with congenital heart defects but an even larger study in the United States (Heinonen 1976) did not support this finding. However, the U.S. study did find a relative increased risk for malformations of the CNS, inguinal hernia, eye and ear malformations, and hypospadias among children of women who smoked during pregnancy. Andrews and McGarry (1972) reported an increased risk of cleft palate and/or cleft lip for infants of women who smoked during pregnancy.

Neurobehavioral and Developmental Effects

Smoking during pregnancy has been reported to have negative neurobehavioral consequences for the infant, such as increased tremors, increased hypertonicity (Fried et al 1987), delayed auditory responsiveness, and poorer habituation to sound (Fried et al 1987; Saxton 1978). However, in these studies, as well as in others not cited, tobacco was not established as the independent causative factor. Zuckerman (1988) concluded tobacco appears to have a mild effect on neurobehavioral functioning but there may be long-term consequences due to the impact on mother-infant interaction; or there may be a mild, static neurologic dysfunction.

Long-Term Effects

Several studies have looked at the possible effect of maternal smoking during pregnancy on subsequent child development. Rush and Callahan (1989) reviewed over thirty papers on this subject and concluded that there is indeed a consistent pattern of diminished reading, verbal, and math skills as well as overall lower IQ linked with maternal smoking during pregnancy. They also noted a relationship between maternal smoking and increased behavioral problems, attention deficit, poorer social skills, and hyperactivity. It must be noted that Rush and Callahan (1989) are careful to emphasize that smokers may differ from nonsmokers in terms of personality, behavior, and social status. Thus, it is difficult to separate the effect of smoking from the impact of parenting or environmental differences.

A long-term study on the effects of prenatal exposure to marijuana, cigarettes, and alcohol was done in Ottawa, Canada (Fried, O'Connell & Watkinson 1992). The researchers quantified environmental factors by use of the Home Observation for Measurement of the Environment (HOME) test (Caldwell & Bradley 1984). This prospective study was conducted with a low-risk, predominantly middle-class sample in which 97% of the women received prenatal care. The children were evaluated annually from 12 months to 72 months of age for cognitive and receptive language development. There was a consistent association betweeen prenatal exposure to cigarette smoke and lower cognitive and receptive language development scores. Although maternal temperament, lifestyle habits, and exposure to smoke after birth cannot be ruled out as contributing factors to the lower scores at ages 5 and 6, the fact that the findings at 5 and 6 years of age paralleled that at 12 months would support the belief that prenatal exposure to smoke was at least partially responsible for the lower scores.

Sudden Infant Death Syndrome (SIDS)

The relationship of maternal smoking and SIDS is clearly supported by several studies (Bergman & Wiesner 1976: Kandall & Gaines 1990; Lewak, Vanden-Berg & Beckwith 1979; Naeye, Ladis & Drage 1976). An epidemiologic study done by Haglund and Cnattingius (1990) in Oakland, California, between 1960 and 1967 found that maternal smoking during pregnancy doubled the risk of SIDS from 2.3 per 1,000 to 4.6 per 1,000. Furthermore, the risk appears to be dose-related. They found that if a pregnant woman smoked up to nine cigarettes a day, the risk of SIDS was doubled, and smoking ten or more cigarettes nearly tripled the risk. However, the studies have not clearly isolated the effects of intrauterine exposure from those of passive smoking after birth. Passive smoking involves inhaling the contents of side-stream smoke (the smoke that comes from the burning end of a cigarette, cigar, or pipe) as well as breathing the smoke that the smoker has exhaled. Because so many of the babies exposed in utero are also subjected to passive or involuntary smoke after birth, it is difficult to quantify the role of both exposures. Studies with a large number of children will be needed to allow control of this variable.

Poor infant/child health

Maternal smoking is associated with an increase in respiratory illnesses in infancy and early childhood (Fried, Watkinson & Willan 1984). Infants of mothers who smoked have a 27.5% greater hospital admission rate for bronchitis and pneumonia (U.S. Department of Health and Human Services 1990). Children of parents who smoke were found overall to have a 30% to 80% excess prevalence of chronic respiratory problems compared to the children of nonsmokers. In addition, these children had decreased lung function and an increased risk of chronic middle ear infection (U.S. Department of Health and Human Services 1986). Again, both prenatal and postnatal exposure are implicated as causative factors.

As early as 1958 prenatal exposure to maternal smoking was linked to childhood malignancies (Stewart, Webb & Hewitt 1958). Estimates indicate that 6% of all childhood cancers and 17% of acute lymphocytic leukemias at present may be a result of prenatal exposure to maternal smoking (John, Savitz & Sandler 1991). In some cancers, the risk is dose-related, as in Wilms' tumor, non-Hodgkin's lymphoma, and acute lymphocytic leukemia, where the risk is doubled with ten or more cigarettes per day. (Stjernfeldt et al 1986). Mothers who smoke during pregnancy usually continue to smoke; therefore, it is difficult to rule out the influence of passive exposure to smoke after birth.

Passive smoking

In addition to looking at the deleterious effects of active maternal smoking during pregnancy, some researchers have recently investigated the effects of passive smoking both in utero and post-natally. Makin, Fried, and Watkinson (1991) found that most studies on passive smoking considered paternal smoking as the only source of environmental smoke. However, in their study they considered all sources of involuntary smoking. They concluded that the consequences of passive smoking are similar to active maternal smoking, just smaller in magnitude. Consequently, we need to educate not only the mother-to-be, but also others in her life (spouse, coworker) who may be sources of second hand smoke, that their smoking may have harmful consequences for the developing fetus and child.

Conclusions

Substance abuse during pregnancy puts both the mother and baby at risk. However, the multiple risk factors associated with a drug-using lifestyle make research in this area very difficult. Although, in most cases, a direct link between certain drugs and specific outcomes is not established, published studies support the need for intervention beginning early in pregnancy. When mothers are motivated to quit using drugs as soon as possible, and when they receive prenatal care, adequate nutrition, family support, and early intervention for their infants, the number of risks beyond drug exposure are greatly reduced.

REFERENCES

Abel EL. *Marijuana, Tobacco, Alcohol, and Reproduction.* Boca Raton, FL: CRC Press, 1983.

Abel EL. Cannabis: Effects on hunger and thirst. *Behavioral Biology* 1975;15:255-8.

Acker D, Sachs B, Tracy K, Wise W. Abruptio placenta associated with cocaine use. *American Journal of Obstetrics and Gynecology* 1983;146:220-4.

Ahmad G. Abuse of phencyclidine (PCP); a laboratory experience. *Clinical Toxicology* 1987;25:341-6.

Andrews J, McGarry JM. A community study of smoking in pregnancy. *Journal of Obstetrics and Gynaecology* 1972;79:1057-62.

Annuziato D. Neonatal addiction to methadone. *Pediatrics* 1971;47:787-91

Bader PL, Lewis WJ. Holoprosencephalay in a cocaine-exposed infant. *American Journal of Human Genetics* 1990;47:A47.

Bauchner H, Zuckerman B, McClain M, Fried L, Kayne H. Risk of sudden infant death syndrome among infants with in utero exposure to cocaine. *Journal of Pediatrics* 1988; 113:831-4.

Beckwith L, Parmalee AH. EEG patterns of preterm infants, home environment, and later IQ. *Child Development* 1986;57:777-89.

Bergman AB, Wiesner LA. Relationship of passive cigarette smoking to sudden infant death syndrome. *Pediatrics* 1976;58:665-9.

Bingol N, Fuchs M, Diaz V, Stone RK, Gromisch DS. Teratogenicity of cocaine in humans. *Journal of Pediatrics* 1987; 110:93-6.

Bresnahan K, Brooks C, Zuckerman B. Prenatal cocaine use: Impact on infants and mothers. *Pediatric Nursing* 1991;17:123-9.

Caldwell BM, Bradley RH. *Administration Manual: Home Observation for Measurement of the Environment.* Rev ed. Little Rock: University of Arkansas, 1984.

Callahan CM, Grant TM, Phipps P, Clark G, Novack AH, Streissguth AP, Raisys VA. Measurement of gestational cocaine exposure: Sensitivity of infants' hair, meconium, and urine. *Journal of Pediatrics* 1992;120:763-8.

Carzoli RP, Murphy SP, Hammer-Knisely J, Houy J. Evaluation of auditory brain-stem response in full-term infants of cocaine-abusing mothers. *American Journal of Diseases of Children* 1991;145:1013-6.

Centers for Disease Control. Cigarette smoking among adults—United States, 1988. *Morbidity and Mortality Weekly Report* 1991;40:757-65.

Chandler LS, Andrew MS, Swanson MW. *Movement Assessment of Infants: A Manual.* Rolling Bay, WA: Movement Assessment of Infants, 1980.

Charlebois AJ, Fried PA. Interactive effects of nutrition and cannabis upon rat perinatal development. *Developmental Psychobiology* 1980;13:591-4.

Chasnoff IJ. Drug use in pregnancy: Parameters of risk *Pediatric Clinics of North America* 1988;35:1403-12.

Chasnoff IJ, Burns KA, Burns WJ. Prenatal drug exposure: Effects on neonatal and infant growth and development. *Neurobehavioral Toxicology and Teratology* 1986;8:357-62.

Chasnoff IJ, Griffith DR, Freier C, Murray J. Cocaine/polydrug use in pregnancy: Two-year follow-up. *Pediatrics* 1992;80:284-9.

Chasnoff IJ, Griffith DR, MacGregor S, Dirkes K, Burns KA. Temporal patterns of cocaine use in pregnancy: Perinatal outcome. *Journal of the American Medical Association* 1989;261:1741-4.

Chasnoff IJ, Hatcher R, Burns W. Polydrug and methadone addicted newborns: A continuum of impairment? *Pediatrics* 1982;70:210-3.

Chasnoff IJ, Lewis DE, Griffith DR, Willey S. Cocaine and pregnancy: Clinical and toxicological implications for the neonate. *Clinical Chemistry* 1989;35:1276-8.

Chavez CJ, Ostrea EM, Stryker JC, Smialek Z. Sudden infant death syndrome among infants of drug dependent mothers. *Journal of Pediatrics* 1979;95:407-9.

Cherukuri R, Minkoff H, Feldman J, Parekh A, Glass L. A cohort study of alkaloidal cocaine ("crack") in pregnancy. *Obstetrics and Gynecology* 1988;72:147-51.

Christmas JT. The risks of cocaine use in pregnancy. *Medical Aspects of Human Sexuality* 1992;26:36-43.

Christmas JT, Penz TC, Dinsmoor MJ. Recent cocaine use and complications of pregnancy. (Abstract) *American Journal of Obstetrics and Gynecology* 1991;164 (1 Pt 2):379-84.

Christoffel KK, Salafsky T. Fetal alcohol syndrome in dizygotic twins. *Journal of Pediatrics* 1975;87:963-5.

Coles CD, Platzman KA, Smith I, James ME, Falek A. Effects of cocaine and alcohol use in pregnancy on neonatal growth and neurobehavioral status. *Neurotoxicology and Teratology* 1992;14:23-33.

Cregler LL, Mark H. Medical complications of cocaine abuse. *New England Journal of Medicine* 1986;315:1495-9.

Davis DD, Templer DI. Neurobehavioral functioning in children exposed to narcotics in utero. *Addictive Behavior* 1988;13:275-83.

Davis E, Fennoy I, Laraque D, Kanem N, Brown G, Mitchell J. Autism and developmental abnormalities with perinatal cocaine exposure. *Journal of the National Medical Association* 1992;84(4):315-9.

Desmond MM, Wilson GS. Neonatal abstinence syndrome: Recognition and diagnosis. *Addictive Diseases* 1975;2:113-21.

Dixon S. Effects of transplacental exposure to cocaine and methamphetamine on the neonate. *Western Journal of Medicine* 1989;150:436-42.

Dominguez R, Vila-Coro AA, Slopis JM, Bohan TP. Brain and ocular abnormalities in infants with in utero exposure to cocaine and other street drugs. *American Journal of Diseases in Children* 1991;145:688-95

Doberczak TM, Kandall SR, Wilets I. Neonatal opiate abstinence syndrome in term and preterm infants. *Journal of Pediatrics* 1991;118:933-7.

Durfee M. *Los Angeles County Neonatal Withdrawal Reports.* Los Angeles County Child Abuse Prevention Program, January-December 1986.

Dusick AM, Covert RF, Schreiber MD, Yee GT, Browne SP, Moore CM, Tebbett IR. Risk of intracranial hemorrhage and other adverse outcomes after cocaine exposure in a cohort of 323 very low birth weight infants. *Journal of Pediatrics* 1993; 122:438-45.

Eckerman CD, Lynne AS, Gross SJ. Different developmental courses for very-low birthweight infants differing in early head growth. *Developmental Psychology* 1985;21:813-22.

Endicott J, Skipper P. Marijuana and upper aerodigestive tract malignancy in young subjects. *Internationales Symposium VPM*, 1991, pp 547-52.

Fedick J, Alberman E, Goldstein H. Possible teratogenic effect of cigarette smoking. *Nature* 1971;231:530-4.

Finnegan LP, Kandall SR. Maternal and neonatal effects of alcohol and drugs. In Lowinson JH, Ruiz RB, Millman RB, Langrod JG, eds. *Substance Abuse: A Comprehensive Textbook.* Baltimore: Williams & Wilkins, 1992, pp 628-56.

Finnegan LP, Kron RE, Connaughton JF. A scoring system for evaluation and treatment of the neonatal abstinence syndrome: a clinical research tool. In Morselli PL, Garattini S, Sereni F, eds. *Basic and Therapeutic Aspects of Perinatal Pharmacology.* New York: Raven Press, 1975, pp 223-7.

Finnegan LP, Reeser DS, Ting RY. Methadone use during pregnancy: effects on growth and development. *Pediatric Research* 1974;11:377-81.

Fried PA. Postnatal consequences of maternal marijuana use. *National Institute on Drug Abuse Research Monograph* (Rockville, MD: The Institute) 1985;59:426-30.

Fried PA, O'Connell CM, Watkinson B. 60- and 72-month follow-up of children prenatally exposed to marijuana, cigarettes and alcohol: Cognitive and language assessment. *Developmental and Behavioral Pediatrics* 1992;13(6):383-91.

Fried PA, Watkinson B. Thirty-six and 48 month neurobehavioral follow-up of children prenatally exposed to marijuana, cigarettes, and alcohol. *Developmental and Behavioral Pediatrics* 1990;11:49-58.

Fried PA, Watkinson B, Dillon RF, Dulberg CS. Neonatal neurological status in a low-risk population after prenatal exposure to cigarettes, marijuana and alcohol. *Journal of Developmental and Behavioral Pediatrics* 1987;8:318-26.

Fried PA, Watkinson B, Willan A. Marijuana use during pregnancy and decreased length of gestation. *American Journal of Obstetrics and Gynecology* 1984;150:23-6.

Fulroth R, Phillips B, Durand DJ. Perinatal outcome of infants exposed to cocaine and/or heroin in utero. *American Journal of Diseases in Children* 1989;143:905-10.

Gawin F, Ellinwood E. Cocaine and other stimulants. *New England Journal of Medicine* 1988;318:1173-82.

Gold MS. *Drugs of Abuse: A Comprehensive Series for Clinicians. Vol 3: Cocaine.* New York: Plenum Publishing, 1993.

Gomby DS, Shiono PH. Estimating the number of substance exposed infants. *Future of Children* 1991;1:17.

Good WV, Ferriero DM, Golabi M, Kobori JA. Abnormalities of the visual system in infants exposed to cocaine. *Ophthalmology* 1992;99:341-6.

Greenland S, Statish D, Brown N, Gross SJ. The effects of marijuana use during pregnancy. *American Journal of Obstetrics and Gynecology* 1982;143:408-13.

Griffith DR. Congressional Testimony. 1991.

Grunberg NE. Nicotine as a psychoactive drug: Appetite regulation. *Psychopharmacological Bulletin* 1986;22:875-81.

Hadeed AJ, Siegel SR. Maternal cocaine use during pregnancy: Effect on the newborn infant. *Pediatrics* 1989;84:205-10.

Haglund B, Cnattingius S. Cigarette smoking as a risk factor for sudden infant death syndrome: A population-based study. *American Journal of Public Health* 1990;80:29-32.

Harry GJ, Howard J. Phencyclidine: Experimental studies in animals and long-term developmental effects on humans. In Sonderegger TB, ed. *Perinatal Substance Abuse.* Baltimore: Johns Hopkins University Press, 1992, pp 254-78.

Heinonen OP. Risk factors for congenital heart disease: A prospective study. In Kelly S, Hook EB, Janerich DT, eds. *Birth Defects: Risks and Consequences.* New York: Academic Press, 1976, pp 221-64.

Himmelberger DU, Brown BW, Cohen EN. Cigarette smoking during pregnancy and the occurrence of spontaneous abortion and congenital abnormality. *American Journal of Epidemiology* 1978;108:470-5.

Hingson R, Alpert J, Day N, Dooling E, Kayne

H, Morelock S, Oppenmeimer E, Zuckerman B. Effects of maternal drinking and marijuana use on fetal growth and development. *Pediatrics* 1982;70:539-46.

Hingson R, Zuckerman B, Amaro H, Frank D, Kayne H, Sorenson JR, Mitchell J, Parker S, Morelock S, Timperi R. Maternal marijuana use and neonatal outcome: Uncertainty posed by self-reports. *American Journal of Public Health* 1986;76:667-71.

Hofstetter A, Schutz Y, Jéquier E, Wahren J. Increased 24-hour energy expenditure in cigarette smokers. *New England Journal of Medicine* 1986;314:79-82.

Holbrook JM. Hallucinogens. In Bennett G, Vourakis C, Woolf DS, eds. *Substance Abuse: Pharmacologic, Developmental, and Clinical Perspectives.* New York: J Wiley, 1983, pp 86-101.

Howard J, Kropenske V, Tyler R. The long-term effects on neurodevelopment of infants exposed prenatally to PCP. In Clouet DH, ed. *Phencyclidine: An Update.* National Institute on Drug Abuse Research Monograph Series 1986;64:623-30.

Hoyme HE, Jones KL, Dixon SD, Jewettt T, Hanson JW, Robinson LK, Msall ME, Allanson JE. Prenatal cocaine exposure and fetal vascular disruption. *Pediatrics* 1990;85:743-7.

Indanpaan-Heikkila J. Placental transfer of titrated-I-tetrahydrocannabinol. (Abstract) *New England Journal of Medicine* 1969;281:330.

Isenberg, SJ, Spiero A, Inkelis SH. Ocular signs of cocaine intoxication in neonates. *American Journal of Ophthalmology* 1987;10(3):211-4.

Jauniaux E, Burton GJ. The effect of smoking in pregnancy on early placental morphology. *Obstetrics and Gynecology* 1992;79:645-8.

John EM, Savitz DA, Sandler DP. Prenatal exposure to parent's smoking and childhood cancer. *American Journal of Epidemiology* 1991;133:123-32.

Jordan RL, Young TR, Dinwiddie SH, Harry GJ. Phencyclidine-induced morphological and behavioral alterations in the neonatal rat. *Pharmacological Biochemical Behavior* (Suppl) 1979;11:39-45.

Kaltenbach KA, Finnegan LP. Prenatal narcotic exposure: Perinatal and developmental effects. *Neurotoxicology* 1989;10:597-600.

Kaltenbach KA, Finnegan LP. The influence of the neonatal abstinence syndrome on mother-infant interaction. In Anthony EJ, Chiland C, eds. *The Child in his Family. Perilous Development.* Vol 8: *Child Raising and Identity Formation Under Stress.* New York: Wiley-Interscience, 1988.

Kaltenbach KA, Finnegan LP. Methadone maintenance during pregnancy: Implications for perinatal and developmental outcome. In Sonderegger TB, ed. *Perinatal Substance Abuse.* Baltimore: Johns Hopkins University Press, 1992, pp 239-53.

Kaltenbach KA, Graziani LJ, Finnegan LP. Development of children born to women who received methadone during pregnancy. *Pediatric Research* 1978;13:332-7.

Kandall SR, Gaines J. Maternal substance use and subsequent sudden infant death syndrome (SIDS) in offspring. *Neurotoxicology and Teratology* 1991;13:235-40.

Kleber HD. Cocaine abuse: Historical, epidemiological, and psychological perspectives. *Journal of Clinical Psychiatry* 1988;49:3-6.

Kline J, Stein Z, Hutzler M. Cigarettes, alcohol and marijuana: varying associations with birthweight. *International Journal of Epidemiology* 1987;16:44-51.

Kline J, Stein M, Susser M, Walburton D. Smoking: A risk factor for spontaneous abortion. *New England Journal of Medicine* 1977;297:793-6.

Kobori JA, Ferriero DM, Golabi M. CNS and craniofacial anomalies in infants born to cocaine abusing mothers. (Abstract) *Clinical Research* 1989;37:196A.

Kronstadt D. Complex developmental issues of prenatal drug exposure. *Future of Children* 1991;1:36-49.

L.A.W. *Let's All Work to Fight Drug Abuse.* (K. Gerew, ed.) Dallas: L.A.W. Publications, 1992.

Lewak N, Van-den-Berg BJ, Beckwith JB. Sudden infant death syndrome risk factors: Prospective data review. *Clinical Pediatrics* 1979;18:404-9.

Lewis KD. *Lewis Protocol: A Measure of Pre-natal Drug Exposed Infants Behavior.* (Unpublished Master's Thesis) San Francisco: University of San Francisco, 1990.

Lifschitz MH, Wilson GS, Smith EO, Desmond MM. Fetal and postnatal growth of children born to narcotic-dependent women. *Journal of Pediatrics* 1983;102:686-91.

Lifschitz MH, Wilson GS, Smith EO, Desmond MM. Factors affecting head growth and intellectual function in children of drug addicts. *Pediatrics* 1985;75:269-74.

Linn S, Schienbaum S, Monson R, Rosner R, Stubblefield PC, Ryan KJ. The association of marijuana use with outcome of pregnancy. *American Journal of Public Health* 1984;73: 1161-6.

Lipshultz SE, Frassica JJ, Orav EJ. Cardiovascular abnormalities in infants prenatally exposed to cocaine. *Journal of Pediatrics* 1991;118:44-51.

Little RE, Sing CF. Father's drinking and infant's birthweight: Report of an association. *Teratology* 1987;36:59-65.

Little BB, Snell LM. Brain growth among fetuses exposed to cocaine in utero: Asymmetric growth retardation. *Obstetrics and Gynecology* 1991;77:361-5.

MacGregor SN, Keith LG, Bachicha JA, Chasnoff IJ. Cocaine abuse during pregnancy: Correlation between prenatal care and perinatal outcome. *Obstetrics and Gynecology* 1989;74:882-5.

MacGregor SN, Keith LG, Chasnoff IJ, Rosner MA, Chisum GM, Shaw P, Minoque JP. Cocaine use during pregnancy: Adverse perinatal outcome. *American Journal of Obstetrics and Gynecology* 1987;157:686-90.

Mactutus CF. Developmental neurotoxicity of nicotine, carbon monoxide, and other tobacco smoke constituents. *Annals of the New York Academy of Sciences* 1989;562: 105-22.

Makin J, Fried PA, Watkinson B. A comparison of active and passive smoking during pregnancy: Long-term effects. *Neurotoxicology and Teratology* 1991;13:5-12.

Marks TA, Worthy WC, Staples RE. Teratoge-nic potential of phencyclidine in the mouse. *Teratology* 1980;21:241-6.

Mayes LC, Granger RH, Bornstein MH, Zuckerman B. The problem of prenatal cocaine exposure: A rush to judgment. *Journal of the American Medical Association* 1992;267:406-8.

Naeye RL, Ladis B, Drage JS. Sudden infant death syndrome. *American Journal of Diseases* 1976;130:1207-10.

Nahas GG. *Marijuana: Chemistry, Biochemistry and Cellular Effects.* New York: Springer-Verlag, 1976.

Nahas G, Latour C, eds. *First International Colloquium on Illicit Drugs: Advances in the Biosciences.* Oxford: Pergamon Press, 1991.

Nahas G, Latour C. The human toxicity of marijuana. *Medical Journal of Australia* 1992;156:495-7.

National Institute of Drug Abuse. *National Household Survey on Drug Abuse: Population Estimates 1988.* Washington, D.C.: U.S. Government Printing Office, 1989 (DHHS publication No.ADM 89-16363).

Neerhof MG, MacGregor SN, Retzky SS, Sullivan TP. Cocaine abuse during pregnancy: Peripartum prevalence and perinatal outcome. *American Journal of Obstetrics and Gynecology* 1989;161:633-8.

Nelson LB, Erlich S, Calhoun JH, Matteucci T, Finnegan LP. Occurrence of strabismus in infants born to drug-dependent women. *American Journal of Diseases in Children* 1987;141:175-8.

Neuspiel DR, Hamel SC. Cocaine and infant behavior. *Journal of Developmental and Behavioral Pediatrics* 1991;12:5-64.

Nicholas JM, Lipschitz J, Schreiber EC. Phencyclidine: Its transfer across the placenta as well as into breast milk *American Journal of Obstetrics and Gynecology* 1982;143:143-6.

Oro AS, Dixon SD. Perinatal cocaine and methamphetamine exposure: Maternal and neonatal correlates. *Journal of Pediatrics* 1987;111:571-8.

Ostrea EM Jr, Romero A, Yee H. Adaptation of the meconium drug test for mass screening. *Journal of Pediatrics* 1993;122(1):152-4.

Pirani B. Smoking during pregnancy. *Obstetrical and Gynecological Survey* 1978; 33(1):1-13.

Richardson GA, Day NL. Maternal and neonatal effects of moderate cocaine use during pregnancy. *Neurotoxicology and Teratology* 1992;13:455-60.

Ritvo ER, Jorde LB, Mason-Brothers A, Freeman BJ, Pingree C, Jones MB, McMahon WM, Petersen PB, Jenson WR, Mo A. The UCLA-University of Utah epidemiologic survey of autism; recurrence risk estimates and genetic counseling. *American Journal of Psychiatry* 1989;146:1032-6.

Robinson LL, Buckley JD, Daigle AE. Maternal drug use and risk of childhood nonlymphoblastic leukemia among offspring. *Cancer* 1989;63:1904-10.

Rubin DH, Craig GF, Gavin K, Sumner D. Prospective survey of use of therapeutic drugs, alcohol and cigarettes during pregnancy. *British Medical Journal* 1986;292:81-3.

Rush D, Callahan KR. Exposure to passive cigarette smoking and child development. *Annals of the New York Academy of Sciences* 1989;562:74-100.

Ryan L, Ehrlich S, Finnegan L. Cocaine abuse in pregnancy: Effects on the fetus and newborn. *Neurotoxicology and Teratology* 1987;9:295-9.

Salamy A, Anderson R, Eldredge L, Bull D. Brain-stem transmission time in infants exposed to cocaine in utero. *Journal of Pediatrics* 1990;117:627-9.

Saxton D. The behavior of infants whose mothers smoke in pregnancy. *Early Human Development* 1978;2:363-9.

Schneider JW, Chasnoff IJ. Motor assessment of cocaine/polydrug exposed infants at age 4 months. *Neurotoxicology and Teratology* 1992;14:97-101.

Schneider JW, Griffith DR, Chasnoff IJ. Infants exposed to cocaine in utero: Implications for developmental assessment and intervention. *Infants and Young Children* 1989;2:25-36.

Sexton M, Fox NL, Hebel JR. Prenatal exposure to tobacco. II. Effects on cognitive functioning at age three. *International*

Journal of Epidemiology 1990;19:72-77.

Shih L, Cone-Wesson B, Reddix B. Effects of maternal cocaine abuse on the neonatal auditory system. *International Journal of Pediatric Otorhinolaryngology* 1988;15:245-51.

Singer L, Arendt R, Minnes S. Neurodevelopmental effects of cocaine. *Clinics in Perinatology* 1993;20:245-62.

Slutsker L. Risks associated with cocaine use during pregnancy. *Obstetrics and Gynecology* 1992;79:778-89.

Sonderegger TB, ed. *Perinatal Substance Abuse.* Baltimore: Johns Hopkins University Press, 1992.

Stebbins KR. Transnational tobacco companies and health in underdeveloped countries: Recommendations for avoiding a smoking epidemic. *Social Science Medicine* 1990;30:227-35.

Stewart A, Webb J, Hewitt D. A survey of childhood malignancies. *British Medical Journal* 1958;1:1495-1508.

Stimmel B, Goldberg J, Reisman A, Murphy R, Teets K. Fetal outcome in narcotic-dependent women: The importance of the type of maternal narcotic used. *American Journal of Drug and Alcohol Abuse* 1982; 9:383-95.

Stjernfeldt M, Berglund K, Lindsten J, Ludvigsson J. Maternal smoking during pregnancy and risk of childhood cancer. *Lancet* 1986;1:1350-2.

Strauss M, Lessen-Fireston JK, Starr RH Jr, Ostrea EM. Behavior of narcotic-addicted newborns. *Child Development* 1975; 46:887-90.

Strauss ME, Starr RH, Ostrea EM, Chavez CJ, Stryker JC. Behavioral concomitants of prenatal addiction to narcotics. *Journal of Pediatrics* 1976;89:842-6.

Sutton LR, Hinderliter SA. Diazepam abuse in pregnant women on methadone maintenance. *Clinical Pediatrics* 1990;29:108-11.

Tabor BL, Smith-Wallace T, Yonekura ML. Perinatal outcome assisted with PCP versus cocaine use. *American Journal of Drug and Alcohol Abuse* 1990;16:337-48.

Tanaka H, Suzki N, Armina M. Experimental studies on the influence of male alcoholism on fetal development. *Brain Development* 1982;4:1-6.

Taylor FM. Marijuana as a potential respiratory tract carcinogen: A retrospective analysis of a community hospital population. *Southern Medical Journal* 1988;81:1213-6.

Turner CE. Marijuana research and problems: An overview. *Pharmacy International* 1980;l:93-5.

U.S. Department of Health and Human Services. *The Health Consequences of Involuntary Smoking. A Report of the Surgeon General.* Washington, D.C.: U.S. Government Printing Office, 1986.

U.S. Department of Health and Human Services. *The Health Benefits of Smoking Cessation. A Report of the Surgeon General.* Washington, D.C.: U.S. Government Printing Office, 1990.

Werner E. Children of the garden island. *Scientific American* 1989;106:111.

Wilson GS. Heroin use during pregnancy: Clinical studies of long-term effects. In Sonderegger TB, ed. *Perinatal Substance Abuse.* Baltimore: Johns Hopkins University Press, 1992.

Wolfe HM, Gross TL. Increased risk to the growth-retarded fetus. In Gross TL, Sokol RJ, eds. *Intrauterine Growth Retardation: A Practical Approach.* Chicago: Year Book Medical Publishers, 1989.

Yazigi RA, Odem RR, Polakoski KL. Demonstration of specific binding of cocaine to human spermatozoa. *Journal of the American Medical Association* 1991; 266:1956-9.

Yonekura ML. *The Impact of Crack Cocaine and Other Drugs on Mother and Children.* Presented at the Conference on Drug-Free Pregnancy. San Francisco: Far West Laboratories, 1989.

Young SL, Vosper HJ, Phillips SA. Cocaine: Its effects on maternal and child health. *Pharmacotherapy* 1992;12(1):2-17.

Zagon IS, McLaughlin PJ. The perinatal opioid syndrome: laboratory findings and clinical implications. In Sonderegger TB, ed. *Perinatal Substance Abuse.* Baltimore: Johns Hopkins University Press, 1992, pp 207-23.

Zuckerman B. Drug exposed infants: Understanding the medical risk. *Future of Children* 1991;1:26-35.

Zuckerman B. Marijuana and cigarette smoking during pregnancy: Neonatal effects. In Chasnoff IJ, ed. *Drugs, Alcohol, Pregnancy, and Parenting.* Hingham, MA: Kluwer Publishers, 1988, pp 73-86.

Zuckerman B, Frank DA, Hingson R, Amarao H, Levenson SM, Kayne H, Parker S, Vinci R, Aboagye K, Fried LE, Cabral H, Timperi R, Bauchner H. Effects of maternal marijuana and cocaine use on fetal growth. *New England Journal of Medicine* 1989;370:762-8.

Zukin SR, Zukin RS. Phencyclidine. In Lowinson JH, Ruiz P, Millman RB, Langrod JG, eds. *Substance Abuse: A Comprehensive Textbook.* Baltimore: Williams & Wilkins, 1992, pp 290-302.

ANNOTATED BIBLIOGRAPHY

Lowinson JH, Ruiz P, Millman RB, Langrod JG, eds. *Substance Abuse: A Comprehensive Textbook.* Baltimore: Williams & Wilkins, 1992.
This comprehensive book provides a detailed description of current thinking and new developments in research and clinical practice in substance abuse. Multiple aspects of substance abuse are presented, including historical perspectives of substance abuse, determinants of substance abuse, evaluation and early treatment, HIV infection and AIDS, management of associated medical conditions, prevention and education, medical education, and staff training and policy issues. In addition, seventeen chapters cover the effects of specific drugs.

Neuspiel DR, Hamel SC. Cocaine and infant behavior. *Journal of Developmental and Behavioral Pediatrics* 1991; 12:55-64.
This article reviews animal and human studies of the neurobehavioral effects of cocaine on offspring. The distinctions between direct effects and indirect effects are presented and the multiple variables

that confound the gestational effects of cocaine are discussed. The reference list has 129 entries.

Singer L, Arendt R, Minnes S. Neurodevelopmental effects of cocaine. *Clinics in Perinatology* **1993; 20:245-62.**
This journal article addresses itself to clarifying what is and what is not known about the neurodevelopmental effects of prenatal cocaine exposure. Difficulties in research and the influences of caregiving on infant development are also discussed. There is an extensive reference list.

Sonderegger TB, ed. *Perinatal Substance Abuse.* **Baltimore: Johns Hopkins University Press, 1992.**
This book presents the consequences of perinatal exposure to substances of abuse in separate chapters written by well-respected researchers and/or clinicians. Three chapters are devoted to alcohol, which has been studied extensively. The other chapters address the effects of marijuana, cocaine, phencyclidine, amphetamines, and tobacco.

3

Pregnancy and Chemical Dependency

Gay M. Chisum, B.A., R.N., C.D.
Keeta DeStefano Lewis, R.N., P.H.N., M.S.N.

This chapter provides nurses and other health care professionals with a foundation for understanding maternal chemical dependency. A model of chemical dependency, attitudes of health care providers, and contributing factors in maternal chemical dependency are explored. The chapter also focuses on nursing and interdisplinary interventions which can be implemented with the woman who is chemically dependent in the antepartum, intrapartum, and postpartum setting.

Chemical dependency in pregnant women is a major medical and social concern facing nurses and other health care professionals. Although clinical observations of maternal opiate use and pregnancy outcomes were published before the beginning of the twentieth century, research began to appear in the literature after World War II, in the 1950s (Goodfriend, Shey & Klein 1956). In 1973, Jones and Smith focused on the impact of maternal alcohol use and described fetal alcohol syndrome. During the 1980s, the focus had shifted to maternal polydrug, cocaine, and crack use. In a 1989 prevalence study of thirty-six hospitals across the United States, an 11% incidence of illicit drug use among pregnant women was found and a range of 0.4% to 27% was reported (Chasnoff 1989). With the increase in use of crack/cocaine the popular media have called society's attention to maternal addiction and the impact on the fetus, infant, and young child.

The phenomenon of crack/cocaine has now led to an increased demand for continuing education on maternal addiction. This chapter discusses maternal drug use/addiction, the implications for nursing interventions, and the use of a multidisciplinary approach to case management, with reports of professional experiences that can interfere with client management.

Estimates of Maternal Drug Use

Numerous reports and studies have shown that maternal drug use has reached into all communities, including urban, rural, and suburban settings, regardless of race, culture and socioeconomic levels (Chasnoff, Landress & Barrett 1990; Khalsa & Gfroerer 1991; Schutzman et al 1991; Horger, Brown & Condon 1990). Estimates from the Institute of Medicine of the National Academy of Sciences indicate that from 350,000 to 625,000 pregnant women use one or more illegal drugs during their pregnancies (Child Welfare League of America 1992).

Clinicians and researchers find it difficult to obtain reliable estimates of drug use among pregnant women because women underreport their use. The underreporting is due to fear of legal consequences and the stigma attached to female drug users. Multiple measures are most effective in providing estimates of prenatal drug use. Several medical institutions have developed policies and procedures which include combinations of the following measures: maternal self-reporting, observations of medical and obstetrical complications, urine toxicologies, and hair and meconium analysis. Reliance on one method identifies only a small percentage of pregnant women with a history of drug and alcohol use (Gomby & Shiono 1991; Schutzman et al 1991).

Research studies are most often conducted in facilities serving poor, minority populations making it crucial that medical institutions develop consistent policies and procedures for identification of all pregnant drug users. Without consistent guidelines, identification of women can be racially, culturally, or socioeconomically biased. Anecdotal reports by medical personnel confirm that hospital policies regarding drug assessments and follow-up referrals frequently do not apply to private-pay women. However, a similar prevalence rate among private (13.1%) and public (16.3%) clinic patients was found in a study in Pinellas County, Florida, using toxicology studies taken during the patient's first prenatal exam (Chasnoff, Landress & Barrett 1990).

Nurses' Reactions

Maternal chemical dependency can stimulate strong emotional reactions in nurses and other health care providers. Emotions range from anger to feelings of helplessness and disbelief. Nurses' negative judgmental reactions to chemically dependent women can interfere with the provision of empathic responses and quality nursing care (Wallace 1991; Adams, Eyler & Behnke 1990).

Nurses must first address their own feelings and attitudes as influenced by their personal and family histories of alcohol and drug use. Studies have shown that students entering health care fields have a greater incidence of being raised in alcoholic families (Murphy 1989). Being raised in a dysfunctional family system can lead to biases which affect nursing interventions and the teaching of self-care (Snow & Willard 1989).

In addition to internal sources of bias, nurses must confront professional and environmental experiences that may interfere with effective nursing practice. For example, past negative experiences with women who are chemically dependent and high relapse and poor compliance rates associated with persons with addiction can produce feelings of hopelessness in helping professionals. Additionally, nurses can experience negative feelings toward women who are addicted and are involved in prostitution or other illegal activities to support their drug habit. Finally, media portrayals of these women as abusive and/or neglectful mothers may challenge the nurses' ability to remain nonjudgmental.

Codependency among nurses can interfere with positive interactions with pregnant women who are chemically dependent. A simple definition of codependency is: the behavior that is a result of drug abuse or compulsive behaviors (gambling, overeating, undereating) of family members. Beattie (1987) defines a codependent as a person who has let someone else's behavior affect him or her and is obsessed with controlling other people's behavior. Codependent characteristics may emerge in childhood or adult life as coping mechanisms or reactions to stress, personal problems, and unsatisfactory interpersonal relationships.

Nurses with codependent characteristics may have poor communication with pregnant women who are chemically dependent. Certain communication styles can lead to further decreased self-esteem in the women and, as a result, avoidance of medical services. Nurses may use shame-based statements, provoke guilt, and use threats in an attempt to control a chemically dependent woman's behavior. The following are examples of codependent communication styles:

Shame-based statements—

"You knew you were pregnant. How could you continue using crack?"

Guilt—

"If something happens to your baby, you have no one to blame but yourself."

Threats—

"If you come late again next week, the doctor will not see you."

To meet the emotional and physical challenges of working with perinatal drug use, nurses need to address their personal issues through peer discussion, interaction with supervisors, support groups, and continued education. Discussions with peers and supervisors and support groups provide an opportunity to express frustrations, to receive from and provide support to colleagues, and to prevent burnout.

Nursing Education

A major barrier to identifying maternal alcohol/drug use is nurses' lack of education on perinatal drug use. Reports on lack of nursing education about addictive behaviors began in 1965 (Murphy 1989). Recent literature has confirmed that maternal-child health nurses need more information for handling maternal drug addiction (Murphy 1989). Nurses require professional preparation on the following topics: a model of chemical dependency and unique psychosocial factors contributing to a woman's drug use history, comprehensive treatment services, common maternal behaviors and defense mechanisms, and the impact of drug use in pregnancy.

Model for chemical dependency—In order to consistently identify and treat pregnant women, nurses must first have an understanding of chemical dependency. There are five basic models of chemical dependency: moral, learning, self-medication, social, and the disease model (Brower, Blow & Beresford 1989). Only the disease model is discussed here, as it has been accepted by many health care professionals and organizations as an appropriate framework. According to the disease model, the etiology of chemical dependency is unknown, although the individual may

have a genetic or biochemical predisposition to the disease. The disease is chronic and progressive and is characterized by compulsions, loss of control, and continued drug use in spite of adverse consequences (Ohlms 1983). The disease of addiction causes preoccupation with chemicals, and an inordinate amount of time is spent acquiring and using alcohol or other drugs.

If nurses accepted the disease concept of addiction, women with chemical dependencies could be treated as women with other chronic illnesses, such as diabetes and hypertension (Miller & Toft 1990). Women with chronic illnesses should not be blamed for their disease, although they must take responsibility for their treatment (Miller & Toft 1990).

A pregnant woman who is cocaine-dependent, when asked to describe her addiction, stated, "When I get a craving for cocaine, nothing else seems to matter. I don't care what I'm doing, that does not matter. All I can think about, all I can focus on, is using. How I'm gonna get it, when I'm gonna use it, how much I'm gonna do." The woman's description clearly describes the preoccupation, compulsion, and loss of control associated with the disease of addiction.

Many contributing factors may affect a woman's chemical dependency history regardless of her socioeconomic, racial, or cultural status. Finnegan (1978) reports at least 70% of chemically dependent women have experienced sexual abuse and 83% have one parent with a history of drug abuse. Additionally, these women report past and current histories of emotional and physical abuse.

Comprehensive treatment services—The pregnant woman who is chemically dependent requires comprehensive treatment for the disease of addiction. Treatment may include prenatal care, psychosocial case management, and chemical dependency recovery services. Nurses, as well as other health care providers, can support the woman's efforts to remain abstinent and encourage continuous prenatal and chemical dependency treatment.

Women entering chemical dependency treatment will be asked to make a commitment to complete abstinence and to accept the need to change the people, places, and things associated with past drug use behaviors. Most treatment programs require the women's participation in 12-step programs such as Alcoholics, Narcotics, or Cocaine Anonymous.

Common maternal behaviors and defense mechanisms—Nurses may find some common behavior patterns among women who are chemically dependent. The pregnant woman may respond to triggers, which are circumstances in her environment, that can lead to relapse or continued drug use. Common triggers for the pregnant woman include the physical and emotional stress of pregnancy, prenatal visits, marital conflict, fear, loneliness, isolation from family, and parenting responsibilities.

The following is an example of a discussion on triggers and relapse between a nurse and a woman addicted to heroin. With tears in her eyes the woman admitted, "I don't think I can stay clean until I deliver this baby." When the nurse asked the woman what triggers she was experiencing, she said, "My boyfriend keeps arguing with me and I'm scared about the baby's withdrawal." The nurse acknowledged the woman's concerns, encouraged her to request addi-

tional time with her counselor, and then spent time with her discussing withdrawal symptoms and comforting measures for the infant.

Drugs such as tobacco, alcohol, heroin, and cocaine are highly addictive. With chronic use tolerance to the drug develops, leading the person to use more of the chemical to produce the desired effect. Without the chemical, physiological and psychological withdrawal symptoms occur, causing craving and drug-seeking behaviors.

Defense mechanisms often prevent pregnant women from acknowledging their addiction and the impact of drug use on the expected infant. Many women use denial, minimization, underreporting or rationalization when questioned about their drug use patterns. The use of defense mechanisms often interferes with the early identification of pregnant women who are chemically dependent.

Impact of Drug Use in Pregnancy—The pregnant woman who uses, or is addicted to, drugs places her fetus at risk. Alcohol and many other drugs cross the placenta due to their small molecular weight and because they are fat-soluble (Zuckerman 1991). Many factors determine the direct or indirect impact of drugs on the fetus. These include poor maternal health and nutrition, maternal and fetal genetics, lack of prenatal care, poverty, drug combinations used, and timing and dosage of the drug (Lewis, Bennett & Schmeder 1989). The fetus is most susceptible to drugs taken between twenty to eighty days after gestation due to the process of organ development at this stage. After eighty days of gestation, the fetus is vulnerable to growth retardation and functional and behavioral abnormalities (Finnegan 1978).

Prenatal Nursing Intervention

Nursing intervention begins with the assessment process. Assessment focuses on the woman's physical appearance and behavior, drug use, history of infectious diseases (Chisum 1990), obstetric history, and any other pertinent medical history.

The woman's physical appearance and behavior may provide clues to active alcohol and other drug use. However, early recognition of substance abuse (among middle class or upper middle class women) may be missed when women do not exhibit physical or behavioral symptoms. Additionally, nurses and other health care professionals may overlook signs and symptoms due to bias and stereotypes which lead them to expect only women of color or low-income women to be substance abusers.

An awareness of signs and symptoms of intoxication and withdrawal from drugs most actively used in a geographical area is crucial (Table 1). For those women who use intravenous drugs, edema of hands, cellulitis, fresh abscesses, or old scarring and track marks may be noted. Recent drug use may be apparent in vital signs, such as high blood pressure, tachycardia, and elevated temperature, as observed when cocaine is ingested. Other physical signs of cocaine intoxication are tremors, anxiety, restlessness, excessive talking, and dilated pupils. Additionally, poor weight gain due to decreased appetite is sometimes seen in pregnant women using cocaine.

Medical history may reveal past or recent hospitalizations for infectious diseases. The diseases may include pneumonia, tuberculosis, bacterial endocarditis, pancreatitis (Finnegan 1979), hepatitis B, or human immunodeficiency virus (HIV) infection. The infectious illnesses are related to the lifestyle of chemical dependency, the drug of choice, or the route of drug administration or may be a direct result of being a sexual partner of an HIV- or hepatitis B-infected person(s).

Obstetric histories can reveal complications of past and current alcohol/drug use. Women may have experienced spontaneous abortions, stillbirths, preterm labor, and placenta abruptio (Chasnoff 1988). Nurses can inquire into the circumstances of obstetric complication and request past and current health records. Current complaints may include a hyperactive or hypoactive fetus, spotting, vaginal bleeding, and preterm labor.

Nursing Approach—The key to obtaining the most accurate chemical dependency evaluation is a nurse's approach. One example may be to give the woman a written statement explaining the need for a drug use evaluation. This statement should be discussed during the nurse-client meeting. This approach allows the nurse to facilitate understanding for the client with inadequate reading and comprehension skills. The following is an example of a written statement that can be used during registration of prenatal clients:

Table 1. Symptoms of Drug Intoxication and Withdrawal

	PHYSICAL SYMPTOMS	*WITHDRAWAL SYMPTOMS*
ALCOHOL (beer, wine, liquor)	Intoxication, slurred speech, unsteady walk, relaxation, relaxed inhibition, impaired coordination, slowed reflexes	6-48 hours - 10 days restlessness, irritability, anorexia, nausea, vomiting, sweating, tremors, tachycardia, hypertension, insomnia, nightmares, impaired concentration and memory
COCAINE AND OTHER STIMULANTS Cocaine (coke, rock, crack, base), Stimulants (speed, uppers, crank, crystal, ice), Amphetamines	Brief, intense euphoria; elevated blood pressure and heart rate; restlessness; excitement; feeling of well-being followed by depression; alertness; talkativeness; loss of appetite	Irritability, lethargy, depression, anxiety, suicidal thoughts, confusion
MARIJUANA (pot, dope, grass, weed, herb, hash, joint)	Altered perceptions; red eyes; dry mouth; reduced concentration and coordination; euphoria; laughing; hunger	Insomnia, hyperactivity, increased appetite
NARCOTICS Heroin (junk, dope, black tar, china white), Demerol, Dilaudid (Ds), Morphine, Codeine	Euphoria, drowsiness, insensitivity to pain	Drug craving, lacrimation, rhinorrhea, yawning, sweating, restless sleep, mydriasis, anorexia, vomiting, diarrhea, chills, flushing, muscle spasms and aches, tremors and irritability, hypertension, hyperventilation, tachycardia, piloerection
SEDATIVE/HYPNOTICS Sedative, Barbiturates, Tranquilizers (downers, tranks, ludes, reds, Valium, yellow jackets)	Depressed breathing and heartbeat, intoxication, drowsiness, uncoordinated movements	Anxiety, insomnia, agitation, tremors, delirium, anorexia, nausea, vomiting, tendon hyperreflexia, diaphoresis, postural hypotension, grand mal convulsions (between days 3 and 7)

Dear Ms _____ :

As a part of our prenatal history, we feel it's important to look at the use of tobacco, alcohol, and other drugs and how that could affect you, your pregnancy, and your unborn child. Many women are not aware of the impact tobacco, alcohol, and other drugs can have on their pregnancy. After the interview, you will be given educational materials to read which explain how drugs can impact pregnancy. You will also have an opportunity to discuss any questions you may have regarding your pregnancy. Any self-reports of prenatal, tobacco, alcohol and other drug use are held in strict confidence and will only be used to refer you to additional services. Our hospital is here to provide you with the best care possible for a safe pregnancy and a healthy baby.

An additional statement could be added to cover any existing prenatal or postnatal mandatory reporting of state and/or local laws. The state of Minnesota currently requires that prenatal drug use be reported to county social service agencies, with provision of prenatal care and drug treatment services, although there is an option to civil commitment to drug treatment if the pregnant woman refuses voluntary services (Stevens & Ahlstrom 1991).

Illinois law requires a mandatory postnatal report to the Illinois Department of Children and Family Services if an infant is born with a positive urine toxicology. Illinois hospitals, such as Northwestern Memorial Prentice Women's Hospital, have developed policies that require informing pregnant women who are chemically dependent of the mandatory postnatal reporting laws. Nurses and other health care providers may wish to consider developing statements that explain state reporting laws to pregnant women.

A second approach is to establish a rapport with the woman by directly explaining the purpose of the evaluation and expressing concern for her and the fetus. This approach decreases the woman's possible defensive posture during the interview.

Chemical Dependency Evaluation—
The interview will flow more smoothly if a consistent format is used. The format takes into account the drugs used and the frequency, amount, and route of drug use. Drug use categories to be explored begin with the most acceptable drugs in society and end with the illicit drugs of abuse (Table 2).

Nurses often report a feeling of anxiety during chemical dependency evaluations. The anxiety seems to stem from formulating the interview questions. Often the questions are not open-ended or they are asked as if the interviewer does not really wish to know the answer. For example,

"Do you use drugs?"
"You don't use drugs, do you?"

This interview technique will not elicit an accurate history.

Open-ended questions have been suggested by clinicians experienced in chemical dependency assessments. The ten-question drinking history and the T-ACE have been used successfully with pregnant women who use alcohol (Weiner & Morse 1988; Sokol et al 1989). Table 3 presents the original version of the ten-question drinking history.

Table 2. Drug Use Categories*

1. Cigarettes
2. Alcohol - all forms
   (beer, wine, mixed drinks, hard liquor, wine coolers)
3. Over-the-counter drugs
   (diet pills, cough medicines, sleeping aids)
4. Prescribed medications
   (analgesics with opiates, minor and major tranquilizers, and sedative/hypnotics)
5. Illicit drugs
   (cocaine, crack, marijuana, heroin, PCP, methamphetamine [ICE] and drug combinations)

*Drugs are listed from the most socially acceptable to illicit drugs of abuse.

Modified versions of this tool have been used to assess pregnant women who are polydrug abusers (Chisum 1990; Starr & Chisum 1992).

Psychosocial Assessment—After completing the chemical dependency evaluation, a brief psychosocial assessment is crucial. Open-ended questions to assess psychosocial status are also useful. The assessment can include the woman's overall emotional state, determining if the pregnancy was planned and inquiring into the woman's support systems, current living arrangements, and involvement with child welfare agencies or the legal system. The nurse then becomes aware of the level of prenatal attachment and investment in prenatal care. Some women may wish to discuss

Table 3. Ten Question Drinking History

Beer:	How many times per week? How many cans each time? Ever drink more?
Wine:	How many times per week? How many glasses each time? Ever drink more?
Liquor:	How many times per week? How many drinks each time? Ever drink more?

Has your drinking changed during the past year?

Adapted, with permission, from Rosett, Weiner, and Edelin. Strategies for prevention of fetal alcohol effects. *Obstetrics and Gynecology* 1981; 57(1): 1-7.

termination of the pregnancy, foster care, or adoption services. This brief assessment determines the direction of nursing care, case management, and social service interventions.

Health Education—Education is critical following the completed assessment. The woman's denial system can be empathically confronted through the education process. Information concerning the legal implications of prenatal drug use is helpful for the pregnant woman. Nurses need to be knowledgeable about existing state laws which mandate prenatal or postnatal reporting of urine toxicologies for mother or infant. This discussion requires sensitivity to the woman's fears and possible thoughts of avoiding prenatal care. Emphasis can be placed on understanding the legal implications of prenatal drug use, benefits of early abstinence, importance of prenatal care, and the availability of existing chemical dependence services.

Additional discussions and educational materials can cover the impact of drug use and implications for fetal development, neonatal behavior, and breast-feeding. The woman also should understand the risk of passive drug exposure (crack) for infants and young children and the risk of HIV. Written materials must meet the woman's literacy level and should be culturally sensitive.

Current research supports education that stresses the benefits of drug abstinence early in pregnancy. Weiner and Morse (1988) reported improved neonatal outcome when mothers reduce heavy drinking before the third trimester. Improved infant weight gain also has been noted for mothers who stop smoking early in gestation (Cook, Peterson & Moore 1990). Research on cocaine use in pregnancy indicates improved intrauterine growth if drug abstinence occurs prior to the third trimester (Chasnoff et al 1989). Early intervention efforts through education and treatment referrals have the potential to decrease maternal and neonatal morbidity if women understand the benefits of early abstinence.

Intervention and Referral—Pregnant women addicted to opiates (heroin) can be referred to a methadone clinic. These women should be counseled against abstinence due to the potential of maternal and fetal withdrawal, as well as risks of spontaneous abortion, stillbirth, and premature labor. Methadone, a narcotic, is used as a legal alternative to heroin and can be given daily to pregnant women who are opiate-dependent. Methadone provides mother and fetus with a safe dose of opiates. As a result of receiving methadone, pregnant women can decrease their use of illicit drugs. Women who are receiving an adequate dosage of methadone appear more available for prenatal care; therefore, the risk of a poor perinatal outcome is decreased. Comprehensive treatment for these pregnant women involves obstetrical care and appropriate referrals to methadone services.

During the nurse-client interview the nurse can conclude by reviewing the findings of the assessment with the woman. Nurses can describe the impact of drugs and alcohol on the woman's physical appearance and behavior, medical and obstetric history, and psychosocial functioning. This process helps the woman face her denial if the interviewer presents specific examples from the woman's history (Jessup & Green 1987). The following is an example of an intervention:

"Ms Smith, we have completed your prenatal assessment and I'm very concerned about you and your baby. From your history I see that use of cocaine and other drugs has led to hospitalization for hypertension, a stroke, and the loss of two pregnancies. You have also discussed feelings of depression, separation from your family, and your involvement with child protection services. These are my concerns; what concerns do you have about this pregnancy? I would like to make a referral to our social worker and a chemical dependency program."

After the woman has stated her concerns, she can be referred to a social worker or a chemical dependency program. If the woman is open to a chemical dependency referral, the telephone call can be made during the interview. A release of information should be signed so the medical facility can communicate openly with the program and assist in case management. Providing the woman with brochures on the community or in-house chemical dependency programs can be helpful in familiarizing her with the location, services, and admission requirements. Hospitals and clinics must have easy access to referral manuals, brochures, and names of direct contact persons in order for the professional to facilitate an appropriate referral.

Some women will refuse a referral to a chemical dependency program because of denial, lack of self-esteem, fear or ambivalent feelings, and previous experiences with withdrawal and drug treat-

ment programs. These women require close case management services that may include intensive social service intervention, nutritional counseling, random urine toxicologies, close follow-up for infectious diseases, prenatal education classes, parenting education, and psychiatric evaluation. Continued evaluation and therapeutic confrontation of drug use patterns at each subsequent prenatal visit are critical. It is important to support these women's efforts for any decreased drug use, participation in chemical dependency programs, and continued prenatal care. In many cities and counties there are few, if any, chemical dependency residential programs or facilities for pregnant women or women and their children. And in many areas such facilities most likely will have a long waiting list and possibly no placement until the end of the pregnancy. It is unfair not to make this information known to women if these situations occur.

Subsequent prenatal care for women who are chemically dependent requires monitoring for sexually transmitted diseases, pre- and post-test counseling for HIV status, HIV testing with proper consent, hepatitis and tuberculosis screening, and urging use of condoms to prevent becoming HIV- and/or hepatitis B-infected during pregnancy. Some medical facilities also monitor closely for intrauterine growth retardation and fetal distress through extra ultrasounds and weekly non-stress testing after 32 weeks of gestation (Keith, MacGregor & Sciarra 1988). Additional time must be taken to explain the necessity for extra testing and procedures to increase compliance and decrease heightened levels of anxiety.

Continued nursing intervention evaluates drug use patterns at each follow-up visit with thorough history taking. Women may decrease drug use for the primary drug of choice, but increase use for a secondary or tertiary drug. Due to poor self-reporting of drug use patterns, some hospitals and clinics also use random urine toxicologies to evaluate current drug use patterns. Urine toxicologies may require a woman's consent or medical facilities may feel the urine toxicology is part of standard care. To prevent discriminatory practices, consistent policies for urine toxicologies should be developed with the assistance of legal counsel.

Nursing intervention also includes prenatal education. Women require basic education on normal pregnancy, nutrition, emotional adjustment to pregnancy, and the labor and delivery process. Some chemically dependent women assume physical discomforts are an indication of the need for additional drugs; therefore, common discomforts of pregnancy and early signs of preterm labor should be reviewed.

Women may also fear not receiving pain medication during labor, so they need an explanation of anesthesia and analgesia procedures, as well as information on the dangers of self-medication prior to or during labor. Prenatal education classes can incorporate the physiologic impact of cigarettes, alcohol, and other drug use in pregnancy, early care of newborns prenatally exposed, withdrawal symptoms, neurobehavioral functioning, and comforting measures.

A comprehensive prenatal education program is essential due to the brief postpartum hospitalization and the shortage of postpartum home health care services. The education program can be offered individually during the prenatal visit or in a classroom setting following the appointment.

The nutrition counselor is a valued member of the interdisciplinary team and may be the first to discover a pregnant woman's excessive use of alcohol or other drugs. A nutritional assessment can evaluate caloric intake, understanding of proper nutrition, possible eating disorders, and interest in breast-feeding, and a referral can be made to WIC (Women, Infants and Children program).

Social Service and Case Management—Social service consultation and case management are essential due to the pregnant woman's complex psychosocial issues. In many institutions, the social worker or nurse is responsible for hospital or clinic case management. Case management is initiated by an in-depth evaluation to facilitate internal and community referrals and to begin early discharge planning. The evaluation looks at the immediate basic needs for food, clothing, shelter, financial status, support systems, legal involvement, and child protection services. A mental status exam can determine the need for a psychiatric consultation due to existing psychopathology.

Women who are chemically dependent have a high incidence of physical, emotional, and sexual abuse (Finnegan 1991). These women may need referrals for domestic violence and sexual abuse counseling. Professional counselors must be knowledgeable about and willing to accept women who are chemically dependent and women receiving methadone treatment.

Early hospital discharge planning usually involves preparation for delivery, care of the newborn, and aftercare refer-

Table 4. Timetable for Detecting Drugs in Urine

Alcohol	12 hours
Barbiturate	10-30 days
Cocaine	24-72 hours
Heroin	24 hours
Marijuana	3-30 days
Methaqualone	4-24 days
Phencyclidine (PCP)	3-10 days
Valium	4-5 days

rals. However, women who are chemically dependent may also need assistance with financial matters, housing, health, and safety issues for older children.

Perinatal/Postnatal Nursing Intervention

Labor and Delivery—If a woman is admitted to labor and delivery without prenatal care, a thorough assessment should include medical and obstetric history and chemical use/dependence, which is difficult to obtain at this time. The laboring woman should be encouraged to cooperate with a chemical use/dependence evaluation to ensure proper use of analgesia/anesthesia and management of possible obstetric and neonatal complications. Researchers found that urine toxicologies were more reliable than self-reporting although urine toxicologies detect only the most recent drug use by pregnant women. Testing pregnant women for cocaine metabolites will detect only those women who have used cocaine within the last three days (McCalla et al 1992). Table 4 outlines the timetable for drug detection in urine.

Numerous obstetric complications are related to the specific drug of choice. Cocaine has been associated with spontaneous abortions, abruptio placentae, premature rupture of membranes, and preterm labor and delivery (Zuckerman 1991). A recent study to predict cocaine use in laboring women through historical and clinical data with positive urine toxicologies identified 60% of women who had used cocaine (Chasnoff 1987). Complications of maternal alcohol use have been noted to include spontaneous abortions, abruptio placentae, precipitate labor, and fetal distress (Weiner & Morse 1988). Studies have linked premature rupture of membranes, toxemia, placenta previa, abruptio placentae, and stillbirths with maternal heroin use (Finnegan 1978). As a consequence the woman's vital signs and physical status must be monitored more closely. Continuous electronic fetal monitoring is indicated once labor begins. The nursery staff should be alerted well in advance of birth in order to plan appropriate neonatal care, to provide equipment, and to assure that a pediatric or neonatal physician and nurse are present for the delivery.

In anticipation of a painful labor and

delivery experience and mistrust of hospital staff, some women use illicit drugs prior to admission. Intoxicated women present a medical and behavioral challenge to the staff. Nurses must be aware of safety issues due to the woman's altered mental status and poor judgment. Injuries from falls and cigarette burns can occur without close monitoring of the woman (Starr & Chisum 1992).

Pain management for women who are chemically dependent should be determined on the basis of evidence of intoxication, but analgesia should not be withheld due to a history of drug use. Physicians have found that short-acting narcotics have been effective for pain. However, nurses should be aware of possible increased tolerance to narcotics and observe women carefully for pain relief. Regional or local anesthesia has been successfully used with women who are chemically dependent (Hoegerman & Schnoll 1991; Starr & Chisum 1992; Keith, MacGregor & Sciarra 1988). Epidural anesthesia is particularly effective because of few systemic effects and may be used in many women who have used drugs before coming to labor and delivery.

Pregnant women on methadone presenting in labor should be assessed for their most recent dosage of methadone. The dosage and time of last dose can be confirmed by contacting the local methadone clinic. If the woman requires a dose of methadone during labor, it can be given orally or intramuscularly. If a dose is given intramuscularly, the oral dose should be decreased by 50% (Hoegerman & Schnoll 1991). It should be remembered, however, that methadone does not eliminate the woman's need for analgesia. Epidural anesthesia

is often preferred over use of narcotic analgesics in women receiving methadone.

Women who are chemically dependent should be observed for withdrawal symptoms. Narcotic agonist-antagonists, such as Talwin or Stadol, which are often used in labor, should not be used in pregnant, opiate-addicted women due to the potential it creates for acute withdrawal. Maternal withdrawal may potentiate fetal withdrawal and result in fetal hypoxia. The potential for fetal distress due to maternal intoxication or withdrawal requires close observation of the fetal monitor. Cocaine can cause fetal hyperactivity, tachycardia, and late or variable decelerations. Cocaine and opiates have been associated with fetal distress and meconium aspirations (Chasnoff 1987).

In addition to biochemical complications during labor, the chemically dependent woman may have poor coping and communication skills. Nursing interventions must focus on establishing an atmosphere of genuine concern and emotional support. Positive communication is enhanced by making direct eye contact, using clear and direct statements, showing empathy for feelings of fear, anxiety and pain, and avoiding verbal confrontations with clients (Byrne & Lerner 1992).

Women may blame or be uncooperative or communicate with abusive language, angry outbursts, or expressions of paranoid thought. The behaviors may be drug-induced or aggravated by withdrawal. Women may also be afraid of neonatal outcome, have underlying psychopathology, and/or have had prior experiences that led them to distrust and fear medical personnel. Nurses can rec-

Table 5. Signs and Symptoms of Neonatal Narcotic Abstinence

Convulsions	Loose stools
Dehydration	Mottled skin
Excoriation of knees and elbows	Nasal stuffiness
Fever <101°	Rapid respiration
Frantic fist sucking	Regurgitation
Frequent yawning	Sleeplessness
High-pitched cry	Sneezing
Hyperactive reflexes	Tremors
Increased muscle tone	Vomiting

ognize their own feelings of anger, resentment, and fear in response to the women's behavior. If clinical staff members become overwhelmed by the behavior of these women, they can seek support from peers, supervisors, or social services.

After delivery, during the recovery phase, women who are chemically dependent may need additional assistance with bonding and early attachment behaviors. As with all new mothers, encourage them to hold infants skin to skin, using enface position and touching and talking to the newborns when the neonate's condition is stable. Early detachment behaviors may be an indicator of poor maternal attachment and possible abuse and neglect after discharge (Byrne & Lerner 1992). Indications of poor maternal-infant interactions can be documented, and interventions can be planned with social services and the postpartum staff.

Postpartum Interventions—The postpartum woman who is chemically dependent may require emotional support, extensive teaching, and interdisciplinary discharge planning services. A major challenge to nurses, and other health care professionals, is providing the emotional support these women need. The mother may require emotional support

due to feelings of guilt regarding her newborn's behavior or physical condition, such as possible transmission of HIV from mother to child or atypical infant behaviors due to drug use (Table 5). She may also feel inadequately prepared to parent and may fear that the infant's needs will be overwhelming, although many infants do not require special care. These mothers also experience fear when neonates have a positive urine toxicology and are reported to child protection services.

Women referred to child protection services require extensive staff time, patience, and understanding from the health care team. The new mother may react with denial, minimization of the problem, or angry outbursts. Often the nursing and social service staff become the target of the mother's anger. The anger may be an external response to the shame and pain the woman feels as a consequence of her prenatal drug use and not a personal attack on the nursing staff. The postpartum woman will need to express her anger before she is able to discuss her emotional pain.

Nurses are also challenged to meet the educational needs of these chemically dependent women. Like other women, these women should be assessed for their knowledge regarding maternal self-care and basic newborn care. Extra time may be required to address any special needs the neonate may have, for example, HIV seropositivity, hepatitis B, neonatal abstinence syndrome, neurobehavioral symptoms, possible disruptions in mother-infant interactions, or physical abnormalities which may require long-term follow-up.

In some settings the infant may remain in the nursery due to physical complications related to prenatal drug exposure, or because a "policy hold" has been initiated by social services or the courts. The mother should be encouraged to come to the nursery to feed her infant and provide as much care as possible. An "open door" policy should be instituted which conveys a positive attitude toward the woman and encourages frequent visits to the infant.

Discharge Planning—The nursing staff is challenged to provide comprehensive interdisciplinary discharge planning. This planning should include a social service assessment, referral for community health services and a date the nurse will visit, and any other appropriate social service agency referrals, and should address chemical use and relapse prevention.

Relapse prevention is a critical part of discharge planning. Drug use or return to drug use after a period of abstinence is unchanged by delivery. The high rates of relapse for women who abuse cocaine, opiates, or poly-drugs occur during the first eight weeks post-delivery. The first eight weeks postpartum is crucial for all women due to the physiological and psychological recovery period and adjustment to parenting. Relapses in women who are chemically dependent

are often triggered by the physical and emotional discomforts, as well as a difficult or unresponsive newborn.

Considering the indicators of high risk for return to drug use and the potential for abuse and neglect, a social service assessment is critical. The social service consultation can identify maternal/family concerns and provide psychological support, linkage to community services and parenting classes and, if needed, coordination with child protection services. The assessment includes the woman's desire to parent, any history of abuse and neglect of other children, preparation for the newborn, family support, history of alcohol/drug use, appropriate living environment, and knowledge of community services.

A social worker may initiate the postpartum mother's first contact with alcohol or other drug treatment services. The birth may serve as the impetus for voluntary chemical dependency treatment. Women may be referred to intensive or regular outpatient chemical dependency services. One stop shopping models and interagency agreements have proven more effective in providing comprehensive and integrated services.

In Illinois, Northwestern Memorial Hospital's Perinatal Wellness Program is an example of a one-stop shopping model. The program provides chemical dependence services, maternal and child health care, parenting education, funds for transportation, and children's play therapy. The Perinatal Wellness Program also has interagency agreements regarding case management with the Illinois Department of Children and Family Services and Family Guidance Center's methadone treatment programs. As social workers or nurses make chemical dependency referrals, they should consider programs which meet the complex needs of a mother and infant.

Some states are beginning to initiate services for mothers and children who are in need of comprehensive residential chemical dependency treatment. The first priority of the Women's Treatment Center in Illinois is to provide residential rehabilitation for pregnant women. The Women's Treatment Center and Haymarket/Maryville, also in Illinois, provide residential treatment services for postpartum women and children. The length of treatment varies between three months up to one year. A safe residential setting provides the mother with an opportunity to address her dependence on chemicals, learn how to effectively parent, and pursue vocational or employment training.

In some states, women may be reported to child protection services and mandated to have treatment because the newborn's positive toxicology is considered child abuse (Jenkins & Westhus 1981). Child protection agencies are overwhelmed by the numbers of infants with prenatal drug exposure. Women can be assured that reports to child protective services do not always result in foster care placement. In some states, the trend is to discharge the infants to a mother's care with court-mandated supervision by child protection services. A private or state-funded child welfare agency may then provide case management according to the mandate of the courts. Individualized treatment plans may include treatment for chemical dependency, compliance with medical services for the infant, random urine toxicologies, and parenting education (Marshall 1992).

Discharge planning also includes linking the mother and infant dyad to other health services. A referral to home health services can encourage mothers to follow up on discharge planning. The staff of home health services can then assess the home environment, identify disturbances in maternal/infant interactions, assess maternal/infant health, and provide emotional support for early newborn care. Home health staff also can detect early relapse signs which could lead to a failure of adequate care and possible child abuse or neglect.

Prior to discharge, an interdisciplinary team can meet with the new mother and her support system (family) to discuss the total discharge plan. If the mother relapses shortly after discharge, ideally a support person will understand and meet the needs of the infant and mother. During this meeting, the parent and support person should be encouraged to ask questions about the immediate and long-term needs of the infant. The team should emphasize the mother's need to obtain chemical dependence services, ongoing medical care for the child, and support for parenting.

SUMMARY

Maternal chemical dependency continues to challenge nurses and other health care providers. It is essential for nurses to understand the biopsychosocial implications of chemical dependency and the complex needs of women and their infants who have been prenatally exposed to alcohol and other drugs.

Nurses and other providers can develop the skills needed to assess their personal views of chemical dependency. Education about new models of addiction, changes in knowledge about drugs commonly abused, and implications for maternal/neonatal morbidity and mortality is needed.

An interdisciplinary approach to case management opens communication among nurses, nutritionists, social workers, chemical dependency counselors, and physicians. This approach also ensures coordination of medical, nursing, psychosocial, and chemical dependency interventions for families with addiction problems.

REFERENCES

Adams C, Eyler F, Behnke M. Nursing intervention with mothers who are substance abusers. *Journal of Perinatal and Neonatal Nursing* 1990;3(4):43-52.

Beattie M. *Codependent No More*. Center City, MN: Hazelden Foundation,1987.

Brower K, Blow F, Beresford T. Treatment implications of chemical dependency models: an integrative approach. *Journal of Substance Abuse Treatment* 1989; 6:147-57.

Byrne M, Lerner H. Communicating with addicted women in labor. *Maternal Child Nursing* 1992;17:22-6.

Chasnoff I. Cocaine: effects on pregnancy and the neonate. In Chasnoff IJ, ed. *Drugs Alcohol, Pregnancy and Parenting*. Hingham, MA: Kluwer Academic Publishers, 1988, pp 97-104.

Chasnoff I. Drug use and women: Establishing a standard of care. *Annals of the New York Academy of Science* 1989;562: 208-10.

Chasnoff I. Perinatal effects of cocaine. *Contemporary Obstetrics and Gynecology* 1987;27:163-79.

Chasnoff I, Griffith D, MacGregor S, Dirkes K, Burns K. Temporal patterns of cocaine use in pregnancy. *JAMA* 1989;271: 1741-4.

Chasnoff I, Landress H, Barrett M. The prevalence of illicit-drug or alcohol use during pregnancy and discrepancies in manda-tory reporting in Pinellas County, Florida. *New England Journal of Medicine* 1990;322:1202-6.

Child Welfare League of America. *Children at the Front*. Washington, DC: Child Welfare League of America, 1992.

Chisum GM. Nursing interventions with the antepartum substance abuser. *Journal of Perinatal and Neonatal Nursing* 1990; 3(4):26-33.

Cook P, Peterson R, Moore D. *Alcohol, Tobacco and Other Drugs May Harm the Unborn*. Washington, D.C.: U.S. Department of Health and Human Services, 1990.

Finnegan L, ed. Drug Dependence in Pregnancy: Clinical Management of Mother and Child. Rockville, MD: National Institute on Drug Abuse, 1978 (NIDA Service Research Series).

Finnegan L. Perinatal substance abuse: Comments and perspectives. *Seminars in Perinatology* 1991;15(4):331 -9.

Gomby D, Shiono P. Estimating the number of substance-exposed infants. *Future of Children* 1991;1(1):17-24.

Goodfriend MJ, Shey IA, Klein MD. The effects of maternal narcotic addiction on the newborn. *American Journal of Obstetrics and Gynecology* 1956;71:29-36.

Hoegerman G, Schnoll S. Narcotic use in pregnancy. *Clinics in Perinatology* 1991;18(1):51-76.

Horger E, Brown S, Condon C. Cocaine in pregnancy: Confronting the problem. *Journal of the South Carolina Medical Association* 1990;86(10):527-31.

Jenkins R, Westhus N. The nurse's role in parent-infant bonding. *Journal of Obstetric and Gynecologic Nursing* 1981;l0:114-8.

Jessup M, Green J. Treatment of the pregnant alcohol dependent woman. *Journal of Psychoactive Drugs* 1987;19(2).

Jones KL, Smith DW. Recognition of the fetal alcohol syndrome in early infancy. *Lancet* 1973;2:999-1001.

Keith L, MacGregor S, Sciarra J. Drug abuse in pregnancy. In Chasnoff IJ, ed. *Drugs, Alcohol, Pregnancy, and Parenting*. Hingham, MA: Kluwer Academic Publishers, 1988, pp 17-46.

Khalsa JH, Gfroerer J. Epidemiology and health consequences of drug abuse among pregnant women. *Seminars in Perinatology* 1991;15(4):265-70.

Lewis KD, Bennett B, Schmeder NH. The care of infants menaced by cocaine abuse. *Maternal Child Nursing* 1989;14(5):324-9.

McCalla S, Minkoff H, Feldman J, Glass L, Valencia G. Predictors of cocaine use in pregnancy. *Obstetrics and Gynecology* 1992;79(5 Pt 1):641-4.

Marshall A. *1992 Legislative Review.* Perinatal Addiction Research and Education Update. 1992.

Miller N, Toft D. *The Disease Concept of Alcoholism and Other Drug Addiction.* Center City, MN: Hazelden Foundation, 1990, pp 1-35.

Murphy A. The urgency of substance abuse education in schools of nursing. *Journal of Nursing Education* 1989;28(6):247-51.

Ohlms DL. *The Disease Concept of Alcoholism.* Belleville, IL: Whiteaker, 1983.

Schutzman D, Frankenfield-Chernicoff M, Clatterbaugh H, Singer J. Incidence of intrauterine cocaine exposure in a suburban setting. *Pediatrics* 1991;88(4):825-7.

Snow C, Willard D. *I'm Dying to Take Care of You.* Redmond, WA: Professional Counselor Books, 1989, pp 1-26.

Sokol AJ, et al. The T-ACE questions: Practical prenatal detection of risk drinking. *American Journal of Obstetrics and Gynecology* 1989;160:863-8; Discussion, pp 868-70; Comments 1990;163:684-5.

Starr K, Chisum GM. The chemically dependent woman. In Mandeville LK, Troiano NH, eds. *NAACOG High Risk Intrapartum Nursing.* Philadelphia: JB Lippincott, 1992, pp 115-45.

Stevens S, Ahlstrom A. Perspective from a Minnesota County Attorney's office. *Future of Children* 1991;1(1):93-9.

Wallace B. Chemical dependency treatment for the pregnant crack addict: Beyond the criminal sanctions perspective. *Psychology of Addictive Behavior* 1991;5(Nov 1):2335.

Weiner L, Morse B. FAS: Clinical perspectives and prevention. In Chasnoff IJ, ed. *Drugs, Alcohol, Pregnancy, and Parenting.* Hingham, MA: Kluwer Academic Publishers, 1988, pp 127-48.

Zuckerman B. Drug exposed infants: Understanding the medical risk. *Future of Children* 1991;1(1):26-36.

ANNOTATED BIBLIOGRAPHY

Brower K, Blow F, Beresford T. Treatment implications of chemical dependency models: An integrative approach. *Journal of Substance Abuse Treatment* 1989; 6:147-57.

This article describes five basic models of chemical dependency and their treatment implications. The five models described include: moral, learning, disease, self-medication, and social. The article provides a foundation for understanding chemical dependency. The intended audience includes therapists or other clinicians working with chemically dependent persons.

Chasnoff I, ed. *Drugs, Alcohol, Pregnancy, and Parenting.* Hingham, MA: Kluwer Academic Publishers, 1988.

Health care professionals have been faced with increasing numbers of pregnant women and mothers and their infants affected by chemical dependency. However, few of these professionals have received extensive training in the area of perinatal addiction. This book integrates a multidisplinary view of the crucial issues facing professionals who work with chemically dependent women and their infants.

Starr K, Chisum GM. The chemically dependent woman. In Mandeville LK, Troiano NH, eds. *NAACOG High Risk Intrapartum Nursing.* Philadelphia: JB Lippincott, 1992, pp 115-45.

This chapter was written for perinatal nurses and other health care professionals who work with chemically dependent mothers and their at-risk infants. Emphasis is placed on the etiology of chemical dependency, the assessment process, nursing diagnoses, interventions, and expected outcomes. Several tables are used to provide detailed guidelines for daily clinical practice.

Angelini DJ, Gives RH, eds. Substance abuse and environmental toxins. *Journal of Perinatal and Neonatal Nursing* **1990; 3(4): 1-87.**

This issue focuses on issues of substance abuse and environmental toxins. Three articles focus on maternal substance abusers, implications for treatment, and nursing interventions. Other articles cover cocaine, fetal and neonatal effects, fetal alcohol syndrome, and medications commonly used during pregnancy and their effects on the fetus and newborn.

Nursing Care of the Newborn with Prenatal Alcohol and Drug Exposure: The Immediate Postnatal Period

Laura Mahlmeister, R.N., Ph.D.

One of the most critical periods for the infant with prenatal drug exposure (PDE) is in the immediate post-birth and neonatal period. A multidisciplinary approach is essential for the initial assessment and stabilization of the newborn. While some newborns with PDE are born without obvious problems related to drug exposure and maternal life-style, it is necessary for the nurse and other health professionals to be prepared for significant, and life-threatening complications to the neonate and the mother. The nurse needs current knowledge for effective management about the most common problems regarding the neonate with PDE such as asphyxia, congenital infections, and low birth weight, necessary equipment and personnel requirements. These specific nursing activities which are described in this chapter require the highest level of nursing skill and expertise to promote physiologic stability of the newborn. Recommendations are made for specific nursing interventions including discharge planning, parent education and timely referrals to achieve realistic outcome goals. The latest research findings are incorporated throughout the text to validate recommended strategies for assessment, planning, implementation, and evaluation of the nursing care plan.

Preparing for the Birth of the Infant Prenatally Drug Exposed

An aura of uncertainty often surrounds the birth and subsequent condition of the neonate because many women using illicit drugs fail, or are unable, to seek prenatal care. Factors that adversely affect fetal growth and development—such as the type and frequency of drugs used—are often unknown. Other variables such as prenatal infection and inadequate maternal nutrition, which contribute to poor intrauterine growth, the development of congenital anomalies, and perinatal asphyxia, cannot be easily evaluated in the short period before birth. There may not even be time to estimate the gestational age of the infant prior to delivery.

Identifying the Chemically Dependent Woman

Foreknowledge of a woman's prenatal substance use and chemical dependence permits mobilization of appropriate personnel and equipment for the birth. Labor and delivery and nursery personnel should be skilled in the early identification of these women.

Demographic factors frequently observed in women with substance abuse problems include:
- Lack of prenatal care
- Homelessness
- Prostitution
- History of:
    Psychiatric problems
    Domestic violence
    Past drug abuse
    Incarceration

In addition, obvious signs of disorientation, alteration in mentation, inadequate weight gain, poor nutrition, a diagnosis of sexually transmitted disease, or the presence of track marks, skin ulcerations, or cellulitis at the time of admission should alert caregivers to the strong possibility of chemical dependence.

More difficult to identify are middle-class women with substance abuse problems. Little research has been conducted to date to elucidate the most common signs and symptoms of drug use in this population of pregnant women. Kaplan (1992) notes that the middle-class, privately insured patient does not fit the stereotype of the "hard core" substance abuser. Her infant may also initially appear to be normal and free from the major complications frequently observed at birth in urban indigent women. The drugs most often abused by middle class women also may be different. Lake and associates (1992) found that African-American women giving birth in a county hospital in Florida had a higher rate of cocaine use, whereas Caucasian and Hispanic women delivering in a private facility were more likely to use cannabis.

However, Chasnoff, Landress, and Barrett (1990) discovered very little difference in the rate of positive urine tests for cocaine among another group of Florida women receiving prenatal care in either public clinics or private obstetricians' offices.

Other groups of women often overlooked are those living in rural or suburban communities, even though the rate of illicit drug use has approached 10% in recent investigations (Sloan et al 1992;

Kaplan 1992). Further study is clearly indicated before definitive answers can be provided to assist maternal neonatal nurses.

When substance abuse is unidentified or unexpected before delivery, the neonatal nurse is often the first health care provider to suspect prenatal drug exposure. If non-opiates are abused, the classic neonatal abstinence syndrome may not be observed. Many infants reveal subtle neurobehavioral cues, which can be missed by an unskilled clinician. Research findings support the critical role of the neonatal nurse in early recognition of behavioral abnormalities in the newborn (Budreau & Kleiber 1991). Thorough and ongoing assessments of the infant in the immediate postnatal period are essential for the nurse to identify aberrant neurobehavioral responses or early neonatal abstinence syndrome (NAS). Characteristic signs of prenatal drug exposure are discussed later in the chapter.

Notifying Nursery Personnel

Adequate preparation for immediate postbirth care of the prenatally drug exposed infant is based on close collaboration between obstetric and neonatal health care providers so staff and equipment can be mobilized before the infant's birth. In a facility where women with problems related to substance abuse frequently give birth, the nursery charge nurse should periodically touch base with the labor and delivery unit throughout the shift. A close working relationship between the two units permits timely preparation and a smooth response when the birth is imminent. If time and the woman's condition permit, nursery personnel should introduce themselves prior to delivery and discuss the anticipated placement and care of the infant after birth.

Many nurses working in private, suburban, and rural community hospitals feel their hands are tied when they attempt to report and act upon suspicions of maternal substance abuse (Mahlmeister 1992). Attempts to confirm reasonable suspicions of prenatal drug use have been met with physician resistance at times. Chasnoff, Landress, and Barrett (1990) note that a significant discrepancy currently exists in the reporting of maternal substance abuse or positive urine screens in the neonate. African-American women with positive urine screens were ten times more likely to be reported.

Kaplan (1992) discovered that obstetricians in private practice were not referring clients for drug treatment programs available in suburban communities. Possible reasons for underutilization of treatment facilities included lack of awareness regarding the extent of substance abuse problems in middle-class women and concerns about the legal ramifications of reporting.

In Level I facilities or in hospitals where "hard core" substance abusers infrequently give birth, labor and delivery nurses should be guided by formal policies when they suspect substance abuse. Recent research supports the critical role of the nurse in recognizing more subtle signs of drug use, even in the middle-class client (Wiley et al 1991). The primary health provider should be notified as soon as possible, and nursery personnel should be kept apprised of the situation.

An in-depth discussion of problems related to identification and reporting of suspected drug use in private patients is beyond the scope of this chapter. However, it is essential that labor and delivery and neonatal nurses be aware of strategies that can be used to enlist the cooperation of the obstetrician or private pediatrician in the initial assessment and follow-up process. Enlisting the full cooperation of the medical team in a private institution is often facilitated when nurses form an alliance with neonatologists and health care professionals working in local drug treatment programs for pregnant women. Once formal policies and procedures are established and information regarding treatment programs is available, consistent identification, assessment, and treatment of women and infants may be accomplished.

Identifying Major Neonatal Risks and Complications

The neonatal nurse is responsible for preparing essential equipment and supplies required to care for the infant prenatally drug exposed. When little or no information regarding the woman's prenatal course is available, neonatal nurses must rely on general knowledge about lifestyle problems related to substance abuse which can affect the fetus and newborn. Table 1 lists the major maternal and neonatal problems related to substance abuse during pregnancy. In addition, the nurse should possess a thorough understanding of the complications associated with specific drugs and substances abused in the prenatal period. If the woman has received even limited prenatal care, the neonatal nurse will have some information upon which to plan care. As additional information is obtained by the obstetric team, and if new problems develop during labor, the neonatal staff should be updated.

Providing Immediate Postbirth Care

Because perinatal asphyxia is a common sequela of prenatal substance abuse, all nurseries should be prepared for initial resuscitation and stabilization of the infant who has been prenatally drug exposed. Both medical and neonatal nursing staff should be present at the birth when substance abuse is confirmed or strongly suspected. If possible, sufficient forewarning should be provided so that nursery personnel can prepare special equipment which is needed, such as intubation equipment, meconium aspirator, or mechanical ventilator, and summon additional assistive personnel.

The goals of care immediately following birth include:

- Providing a neutral thermal environment
- Establishing a patent airway
- Supporting cardiorespiratory function
- Establishing the one- and five-minute Apgar scores
- Verifying pH and umbilical cord gas status
- Estimating gestational age
- Identifying obvious congenital anomalies
- Obtaining tissue and fluid samples for culture and sensitivity when infection is suspected
- Informing parents about the infant's initial status
- Encouraging early parent-infant interaction when the infant's condition permits

In addition to the activities just listed, the nurse often administers eye prophylaxis (erythromycin ophthalmic ointment) and parenteral vitamin K to reduce the risk of hemorrhagic disease in the

Table 1. Problems Related to Maternal Substance Abuse and Associated Neonatal Complications.

Maternal Factors	Neonatal Complications
Poor maternal weight gain Maternal malnutrition	Low birth weight - Small-for-gestational age - Prematurity
Multiple sex partners Prostitution Sexually transmitted diseases	Congenital infections - Chlamydia - Syphilis - Gonorrhea - Herpesvirus type II - Hepatitis B - Human papillomavirus - HIV
Urinary tract infections	Prematurity
Domestic violence	Fetal/neonatal trauma
Criminal violence	Prematurity
Inadequate housing, homelessness • Communicable diseases • Respiratory infections	Congenital rubella or varicella Parvovirus - Fetal hydrops - Neonatal anemia Congenital tuberculosis Cytomegalovirus
Use of other substances Nicotine	Low birth weight - Small-for-gestational age - Prematurity Polycythemia
Alcohol use	Low birth weight Congenital anomalies Mental retardation Neonatal abstinence syndrome

newborn. Recent guidelines from the Centers for Disease Control and Prevention regarding the prevention of hepatitis B (Centers for Disease Control 1991) recommend the universal vaccination of infants (whether or not the mother is HBsAg-Positive). The nurse administers the first dose of hepatitis B vaccine (Recombivax HB or Engerix B), 0.5 mL, intramuscularly within twelve hours of birth. Furthermore, if the mother is HBsAg-Positive, a one-time dose of Hepatitis B Immune Globulin (HBIG), 0.5 mL, is administered intramuscularly as soon as possible after birth at a site different from that used for the vaccine.

Admission and Initial Assessment

Once the condition is stabilized, the infant who has been prenatally drug exposed should be transferred to a nursery which can provide an increased level of assessment and care, such as an *observation, intermediate*, or *intensive care* unit. The infant's status, and the capabilities of medical and nursing staff as well as other ancillary departments to care for the neonate, will determine whether in-house care or transport is indicated. In the event transport is necessary the neonatal nurses must be skilled in providing appropriate care until the transport team arrives. Table 2 lists the major areas of support required and equipment necessary to monitor the neonate and implement care.

Assessment of the infant prenatally exposed to drugs should be accomplished shortly after birth. This is essential in order to:

1) Obtain baseline vital signs and assess physiologic status. The nurse must establish baseline parameters in order to identify significant problems in the infant precipitated by prenatal drug exposure, including asphyxia, meconium aspiration syndrome, respiratory distress syndrome (RDS) of prematurity, polycythemia, and infection. Alterations in vital signs and physiologic functioning will also occur with the development of neonatal abstinence syndrome.

2) Verify baseline neurobehavioral status. Both significant and subtle neurobehavioral aberrations can occur after prenatal drug exposure. Effective nursing care and appropriate parent education must be based on the unique neurobehavioral characteristics of the infant and the infant's capacity to adapt to both internal and external environmental stimuli. An initial nursing assessment of behavioral state and central nervous system status is often followed by a formal examination. The Brazelton Neonatal Behavioral Assessment Scale (BNBAS) is the most widely used behavioral assessment tool and has been adapted for use with premature infants (Als et al 1982). The BNBAS is administered by a trained examiner when the infant's condition stabilizes.

3) Confirm the birthweight. Prenatal substance abuse is associated with preterm birth and intrauterine growth retardation. Low birth weight requires adjustments in the nursing care plan to prevent complications such as hypothermia and hypoglycemia and to promote adequate weight gain. The nurse often performs an initial gestational age assessment using the Ballard Gesta-

Table 2. Essential Support of the High-Risk Infant Prenatally Exposed to Drugs

Areas of Support	Essential Monitors and Supplies
Maintain neutral thermal environment	Radiant warmer bed Incubator Heat shields Bubble wrap / Plastic wrap
Support cardiovascular function	Cardiorespiratory monitor Emergency drugs - Epinephrine 1:10,000 solution - Sodium bicarbonate - Calcium gluconate 10% - Atropine - Dopamine - Albumin Blood products IV therapy supplies Exchange transfusion equipment
Maintain adequate oxygenation	Pulse oximeter $TcPO_2$ / $TcPCO_2$ monitor Oxygen equipment - Blenders - O_2 analyzer - Oxygen hood U/A catheter Arterial blood gas supplies and analyzer
Support pulmonary function	Cardiorespiratory monitor Mechanical ventilator Suction equipment Chest physiotherapy cups Intubation supplies
Maintain blood glucose levels	10% dextrose in water solution 25% and 50% glucose solutions Glucose reagent strips

tional Age Assessment Tool (Ballard, Novak & Driver 1979). If more precise dating is required, a skilled examiner may perform a more detailed assessment using the Dubowitz scale (Dubowitz, Dubowitz & Goldberg 1970) after the infant's condition is stabilized.

4) Identify congenital anomalies. Some substances that are abused during pregnancy are known teratogens. Lifestyle factors which predispose the woman to malnutrition and infection also increase the risk of congenital anomalies. The nurse must perform a complete systems assessment after birth in order to identify both obvious and hidden congenital defects.

5) Obtain initial tissue and fluid samples for laboratory analysis.The nurse is generally responsible for obtaining specimens to evaluate neonatal well-being and identify specific problems frequently related to prenatal drug exposure, including:
   • CBC with differential
   • Serum electrolytes
   • Serum glucose level
   • Blood cultures

The nurse also often assists the physician in other diagnostic tests, such as a lumbar puncture for evaluation of cerebrospinal fluid.

An important aspect of the initial assessment is the collection of specimens for toxicology screening. The nurse is guided by the pediatrician's or pediatric nurse practitioner's order, hospital policy and procedure, and state laws governing collection of samples for toxicology tests in the newborn. Recent technological advances in drug screen-ing have led to the development of new tests.

Urine Toxicology Screen: One of the most widely used methods for detection of drugs and chemicals is the urine toxicology screen. Radioimmunoassay or thin-layer chromatography is most often used to detect cocaine metabolites, opiates, cannabinoids, amphetamines, barbiturates, benzodiazepines, ethanol, and phencyclidine (PCP). The possibility of false negatives is well documented (Mullen & Bracha 1988). Identification of specific drugs depends on the amount of drug used, the time lag between last use and collection of the specimen, and the clearance rate of the substance from the body. Approximately 30 ml to 60 ml of urine is needed for the test, and may require that the nurse reapply urine collection bags for twenty-four hours or more in the postnatal period. Even when meticulous care is taken to prevent dislodgement of the collection bag, urine may leak from it, reducing the accuracy of results. Because of the narrow "window of time" permitted with the urine toxicology screen, drugs taken by the mother as recently as two to three days before birth may not be detected in the urine.

Meconium Analysis: A newer method of drug detection involves the collection of neonatal meconium. A fluorescence polarizing immunoassay technique is used to screen for cocaine metabolites, cannabinoids, opiates, PCP, and amphetamines. Alcohol cannot be detected. Maximum sensitivity is increased when at least 2 grams of meconium is collected within three days of birth. The maximum window of drug exposure during pregnancy is widened by collecting and pooling all meconium passed during the first days of life (U.S. Drug Testing Laboratories 1991). Studies evaluating the sensitivity of urine and meconium screening tests indicate a significantly greater sensitivity when meconium analysis is performed (Ostrea et al 1992).

Hair Analysis: Another new technique, radioimmunoassay of hair samples, has been studied as a method to detect morphine (Valente, Cassini & Pigliapochi 1981) and cocaine (Baumgartner et al 1982; Graham et al 1989). Preliminary results suggest its usefulness as a tool to assess prenatal drug use during pregnancy. Since hair grows approximately 1 cm to 1.5 cm/month, hair analysis can reflect changes in the pattern of drug use over time (Graham et al 1989). Further evaluation of the technique is indicated. Current costs of the analysis also reduce its utility in most settings.

Regardless of the method of analysis ordered by the primary health care provider, the nurse is responsible in most cases for collecting the specimen. Documentation of the sample collection procedure, including the following aspects, should be entered in the infant's record:

1) Start of the sample collection period for urine or meconium
2) Accidental loss or discarding of urine or meconium during collection period
3) Time the collection process is concluded
4) Time the sample is sent to lab

Even if collection of the sample is mandated by state law, or can be obtained without the mother's permission, the nurse or primary health care provider should inform the mother of intent to sample and test the infant's urine, stool, or hair. If the mother is involved in providing infant care, the urine collection bag or special diaper used to collect meconium should be explained to her. She should be cautioned not to throw away soiled diapers, and to alert the nurse if she finds that the infant has voided or passed meconium.

Providing Ongoing Nursing Care of the Infant Prenatally Drug Exposed

Accurate planning of ongoing nursing care is based on the constellation of nursing diagnoses established during the admission assessment and subsequent evaluations. The most severe problems are often observed in the infant experiencing neonatal abstinence syndrome secondary to opiate withdrawal. However, the infant suffering from asphyxia, infection, or low birth weight secondary to maternal substance abuse will also experience major problems.

Establishing Nursing Diagnoses and Planning Care

The following are selected nursing diagnoses frequently identified in the infant exposed to drugs during the prenatal period.

High risk for:
• Altered growth and development related to intrauterine growth retardation and/or premature birth
• Injury, potential for perinatal asphyxia related to meconium aspiration
• Ineffective breast-feeding related to ineffective and uncoordinated sucking and swallowing reflexes

- Altered nutrition, which is less than body requirements, related to ineffective and uncoordinated sucking and swallowing reflexes
- Fluid volume deficit related to diarrhea, diaphoresis, and decreased fluid intake
- Ineffective thermoregulation related to low birth weight, prematurity, or extrauterine transition
- Impaired skin integrity related to generalized diaphoresis, diarrhea, agitation, and uncontrolled tremors
- Infection related to altered immune function or exposure to pathogens during pregnancy or birth
- Sensory-perceptual alteration related to neurobehavioral disorganization
- Sleep pattern disturbance related to neurobehavioral disorganization and aberrant state control

In addition, collaborative problems are also evident and influence the plan of care.

Collaborative problems:
- Anemia
- Sepsis
- Asphyxia
- Seizures
- Dehydration
- Hypothermia
- Polycythemia
- Hypoglycemia
- Respiratory distress
- Electrolyte imbalances
- Neonatal abstinence syndrome

Providing Individualized Nursing Care

Nursing care must be tailored to meet the special needs of the infant who has been prenatally exposed to drugs. Research findings clearly indicate that the differences observed in postnatal problems are in large part based on the type, amount, and frequency of prenatal drug exposure. Today, polysubstance abuse is probably the norm in women who experience chemical dependency. However, the following section attempts to delineate the primary differences in neonatal adaptations when maternal addiction to one of the following categories of substances occurs:

- Opiates
- Alcohol
- Cocaine and amphetamines
- Nicotine and cannabinoids

Care of the Infant Exposed to Opiates—Estimates indicate that approximately 9,000 infants are born to narcotic-addicted women in the United States each year (Hoegerman & Schnoll 1991). Although this statistic has been overshadowed by the current crack cocaine epidemic, the problems related to neonatal narcotic addiction and abstinence syndrome can be life-threatening.

While heroin is the most commonly used opioid, women may abuse a wide variety of narcotics during pregnancy, including morphine, codeine, fentanyl, dilaudid, meperidine, and oxycodone. Methadone, a synthetic opioid used in the treatment of addiction, also results in neonatal abstinence syndrome. Outcomes are generally more positive for infants whose mothers receive prenatal care, food supplements, and counseling within the context of a methadone maintenance program during pregnancy than infants whose mothers do not receive supportive care during pregnancy.

Narcotic addiction during pregnancy is strongly associated with intrauterine growth retardation, preterm birth, and small-for-gestational-age infants. Teratogenic effects are much more difficult to pinpoint because of the impurity of street drugs and the pattern of polysubstance abuse observed in narcotic addicts. Heroin, for instance, is often "cut," or mixed, with quinine, a known teratogen. Congenital infection is common and increasing in incidence with the growing practice of trading sex for drugs. The rate of syphilis, for example, has risen 500% in some communities (Tillman 1992). With the advent of the human immunodeficiency virus, infection with a sexually transmitted disease creates potentially lethal problems for the infant.

The most obvious problems that the nurse must respond to in the postnatal period are development of the neonatal abstinence syndrome and specific neurobehavioral characteristics which may persist well beyond the phase of acute narcotic withdrawal. Slow excretion of opioids and structural anomalies in brain growth and development have been suggested as reasons for prolonged behavioral aberrations (Chasnoff 1988). Withdrawal has been noted to be more severe with polydrug abuse (opiates, plus cocaine or amphetamines) and with methadone (Oro & Dixon 1987).

Assessment. The neonatal nurse is responsible for initiating a withdrawal scoring sheet (Figure 1) whenever maternal narcotic use is confirmed or suspected. Nursing staff periodically evaluate the neonate for signs and symptoms of neonatal abstinence syndrome (Table 3). Signs of withdrawal usually begin within 24 to 48 hours after birth but the onset, severity, and duration will be influenced by the time of last drug exposure before birth. Withdrawal from methadone poses unique problems for the nurse. Signs may appear shortly after birth, improve, and then recur at 2 to 4 weeks postbirth, or may not become evident at all until 2 to 3 weeks of age (Flanagan-Everett 1991). Length of hospitalization may therefore be prolonged when methadone has been administered during pregnancy.

Vital signs should be taken, and assessment of physiologic integrity performed at more frequent intervals—at least every 2 to 4 hours, depending on the infant's condition and severity of withdrawal. A cardiorespiratory monitor and pulse oximeter should be applied during the acute phase of withdrawal because respiratory distress and apnea are common occurrences. A $TcPO_2/CO_2$ monitor is indicated in infants with evidence of hypoxemia. The nurse must be alert for seizure activity. This is made more difficult because many of the abnormal CNS signs that occur with neonatal abstinence syndrome *mimic* seizure activity. Meticulous monitoring of weight loss and intake and output is essential to identify fluid imbalances and dehydration. Finally, the nurse is responsible for monitoring specific laboratory tests that may be performed to assess for evidence of infection, polycythemia, and electrolyte imbalances. Blood glucose levels should also be evaluated periodically as hypoglycemia is a common complication.

An ongoing evaluation of the behavioral responses and interactive abilities

(text continues on page 94)

Table 3. Signs of Neonatal Abstinence Syndrome

Central Nervous System
Tremors
Agitation
Irritability
Seizures
Hyperreflexia
Myoclonic jerks
High-pitched cry
Hypertonia and rigidity
Hyperactive Moro reflex
Sleep disturbances
Excessive sucking/hypertonic suck
Discoordinate suck/swallow reflexes

Autonomic System
Yawning
Sweating
Sneezing
Skin mottling
Nasal stuffiness
Low-grade fever

Respiratory System
Tachypnea
Nasal flaring
Apnea episodes

Gastrointestinal System
Diarrhea
Loose stools
Vomiting
Poor feeding
Regurgitation

Integumentary System
Skin excoriation
Behavioral responses
   Intolerance to cuddling
   Irritability
   Rapid state changes
   Difficulty initiating/maintaining eye contact
   Gaze aversion

Figure 1.   Neonatal Abstinence Syndrome Scoring System

DATE: _____

SYSTEM	SIGNS AND SYMPTOMS	SCORE	AM	PM	COMMENTS
CENTRAL NERVOUS SYSTEM DISTURBANCES	Excessive High-pitched (OR Other) Cry	2			Daily weight:
	Continuous High-pitched (OR Other) Cry	3			
	Sleeps <1 Hour After Feeding	3			
	Sleeps <2 Hours After Feeding	2			
	Sleeps <3 Hours After Feeding	1			
	Hyperactive Moro Reflex	2			
	Markedly Hyperactive Moro Reflex	3			
	Mild Tremors Disturbed	1			
	Moderate-Severe Tremors Disturbed	2			
	Mild Tremors Undisturbed	3			
	Moderate-Severe Tremors Undisturbed	4			
	Increased Muscle Tone	2			
	Excoriation (Specify Area): _____	1			
	Myoclonic Jerks	3			
	Generalized Convulsions	5			
METABOLIC/VASOMOTOR/RESPIRATORY DISTURBANCES	Sweating	1			
	Fever <101)99-100.8° F./37.2-38.2° C)	1			
	Fever >101 (38.4°C. and Higher)	2			
	Frequent Yawning (>3-4 times/interval)	1			
	Mottling	1			
	Nasal Stuffiness	1			
	Sneezing (>3-4 times/interval)	1			
	Nasal Flaring	2			
	Respiratory Rate >60/Min.	1			
	Respiratory Rate >50/Min. with Retractions	2			

Guidelines for the use of neonatal abstinence scoring system

1. Record time of scoring (end of observation interval).

2. Give points for all behaviors or symptoms observed during the scoring interval, even though they may not be present at the time of recording. (For example, if the baby was diaphoretic at 11 A.M. and is "scored" at noon, when he or she is not, the baby still gets the "sweating" point.)

3. Awaken the baby to test reflexes. Calm before assessing muscle tone, respirations, or Moro reflex. Many of the signs of hunger can appear the same as withdrawal. Appearance after feeding gives a good idea of muscle activity.

4. Count respirations for a full minute. Always take temperature at the same site. The temperatures on the sheet are *rectal* levels; an axillary temperature that is 2 degrees cooler may also indicate withdrawal.

5. Do not give points for perspiration if it occurs due to swaddling.

6. A startle reflex should not be substituted for the Moro reflex.
7. Record doses administered (dose/time/initials) on sheet. One hour leeway is acceptable in dosing a fairly stable baby.
8. Record daily weight on graphic sheet.
9. Do not hesitate to get your experienced colleagues' opinions.

GASTROINTESTINAL DISTURBANCES		
Excessive Sucking	1
Poor Feeding	2
Regurgitation	2
Projectile Vomiting	3
Loose Stools	2
Watery Stools	3
TOTAL SCORE	
INITIALS OF SCORER	

NO.	PHARMACOTHERAPY REGIMEN	STATUS OF PHARMACOTHERAPY	RX	STATUS	DOSE	TIME	STATUS	DOSE	TIME	STATUS	DOSE	TIME	STATUS
1	TITRATION REGIMENS Diluted Tincture of Opium (DTO)	Indicate exact dose, time of administration & coded dosing status in the following blocks Dosing Code	#1										
			#2										
2	Phenobarbital (PB)	Initiation (+) Maintenance (m) Increase (↑) Decrease (↓) Discontinuation (–)	#3										
			#4										

SEROLOGIC QUANTITATION OF PHARMACOLOGIC AGENTS

Drug Administered:		AM PM	AM PM	AM PM	AM PM
* BEFORE BIRTH	METHADONE				
– AFTER BIRTH	BENZODIAZEPENES (Specify): _____				
	BARBITURATES (Specify): _____				
	OTHERS (Specify): _____				

Adapted, with permission, from Finnigan LP et al. A scoring system for evaluation and treatment of neonatal abstinence syndrome: A new clinical and research tool. In: Morselli PL, Garattini S, Sereni F, eds. Basic and Therapeutic Aspects of Perinatal Pharmacology. New York: Raven Press, 1975.

of the infant is an integral part of the assessment. Inadequate state control, poor auditory and visual orientation, hyperactivity, muscle rigidity, frequent startles, and disturbed sleep patterns interfere with parent-newborn interactions and the bonding process. The nurse must help parents read the infant's cues and respond appropriately to them (Lewis, Bennett & Schmeder 1989; Caron & Maguire 1990).

Planning and Organizing Care. A critical aspect of care is determining the most appropriate setting for the infant experiencing neonatal abstinence syndrome. A dark, quiet environment is often best, and provides a therapeutic milieu during the acute phase of withdrawal by limiting external stimuli. If it is not possible to isolate the infant, it may be most appropriate to place the infant in an incubator and to cover the top of the unit with a blanket to reduce the light intensity. Efforts should be made to minimize handling and care and to organize activities into clusters, to avoid disturbing the infant unnecessarily.

Efforts should be made to involve parents in the planning of specific infant care activities, so that they may provide as much care as possible. The social worker, community health nurse, foster parents, or other professionals involved in follow-up or long-term care should also be integrally involved in discharge planning. Because of the association between narcotic exposure in infants and sudden infant death syndrome (SIDS) (Davidson et al 1990), infant caretakers should be taught cardiopulmonary resuscitation (CPR) before discharge.

Nursing Care. Care of the infant during the acute phase of narcotic withdrawal is one of the most challenging, and at times difficult, nursing assignments. Intensive physical and emotional support is essential to prevent rapid deterioration in the infant's condition. Specific nursing actions are related to aberrations in each body system and are described in the following section.

CENTRAL NERVOUS SYSTEM

As noted, the nurse attempts to reduce environmental stimuli which exacerbate irritability, agitation, and sleep disturbances observed with neonatal abstinence syndrome. Tight swaddling of the infant is indicated to reduce self-perpetuating tremors, startles, and myoclonic jerks (Lewis, Bennett & Schmeder 1989). "Nesting" the infant with several rolled blankets curved around the body is also useful in controlling disorganized motor activity. This strategy is also indicated when the infant's temperature is elevated and swaddling with blankets is not feasible. Others have achieved positive results with waterbeds (Oro & Dixon 1987). Some nurses have experimented successfully with the use of elastic "fishnet" materials to reduce limb movement when hyperthermia contraindicates the use of blankets. Noise and light intensities should be reduced to their lowest possible level. A cardiorespiratory monitor and pulse oximeter can be applied to reduce the frequency of taking vital signs. When acute withdrawal leads to deterioration in the infant's condition, central nervous system depressants may be ordered to reduce the *intensity of neonatal abstinence syndrome*. The goal is to reduce symptoms so that the infant is com-

Table 4. Drugs Commonly Used in the Treatment of Neonatal Abstinence Syndrome

Drug	Dose	Therapeutic Effect Advantages	Side Effects Disadvantages
Neonatal Opium Solution	0.05 ml/kg Q 4 - 6 hrs PO	Controls symptoms of NAS	Impairs suck May cause sleepiness and constipation Narcosis occurs with overdose Requires slow withdrawal Short shelf life
Paregoric Solution (contains 0.4% opium)	0.05 ml/kg Q 4-6 hrs PO	Controls symptoms of NAS Long shelf life	Mixed in an alcohol base Contains benzoic acid and camphor with unknown effects
Pheno-barbital	5-8 mg/kg/day IM or PO	Drug of choice if infant withdrawing from phenobarbital May be used for sedation in cases of non-narcotic withdrawal	Requires blood level be drawn Causes sedation, poor suck, increased sensitivity to pain Does not control diarrhea in NAS Elixir may contain 20% alcohol
Valium	0.1 -0.3 mg/kg IM until symptoms controlled. Then the dose is halved, then given Q 12 hrs	Controls symptoms of NAS	May cause respiratory depression Sodium benzoate in the parenteral solution may interfere with binding of bilirubin

fortable and able to achieve physiologic stability, but is not sedated (Flanagan-Everett 1991). The drug is then slowly tapered until it is discontinued. The nurse administers the drug parenterally or by the oral route, according to the physician's order. The drugs most commonly used in the treatment of neonatal abstinence syndrome are listed in Table 4.

RESPIRATORY SYSTEM

Some degree of respiratory dysfunction characterized by tachypnea, nasal flaring, or decreased SaO2 level is common, and nursing care is focused on reducing agitation and concomitant energy requirements. Research indicates that opiates may accelerate fetal lung maturation, reducing the incidence and severity of respiratory distress syndrome of prematurity (Finnegan 1988). However, oxygen may be required as a result of extreme prematurity, infection, or meconium aspiration. With marked tachypnea (rates greater than seventy breaths per minute) oral intake is contraindicated. Intravenous fluids and parenteral nutrition are used to avoid stomach distention and reduce the risk of regurgitation and aspiration during acute withdrawal. Positioning should facilitate lung expansion (side-lying versus prone). The supine position is not recommended due to the likelihood of vomiting and regurgitation observed with neonatal abstinence syndrome. The infant is also at increased risk of aspiration due to discoordinate sucking and swallowing reflexes, and risk is increased with vomiting and regurgitation. Efforts should be made to prevent hyperthermia, which increases the respiratory rate and oxygen consumption. Removing extra blankets, reducing agitation, and maintaining adequate fluid intake will help maintain a normal temperature.

GASTROINTESTINAL SYSTEM

Regurgitation, vomiting, decreased intake, and diarrhea all combine to create significant fluid and electrolyte imbalances. If oral intake is initially contraindicated, the infant is maintained on total parenteral nutrition and intralipid infusions. When the infant is permitted to bottle-feed, patience and skill are required of the nurse to promote adequate intake. A small volume of breast milk or formula is introduced every two to three hours. A soft nipple should be attached to a small plastic container which permits accurate measurement of fluid intake. Due to the discoordinate sucking and swallowing reflexes, the infant cannot be rushed, and extra time must be permitted at each feeding and for burping. Breast-feeding may be permitted in some instances. Factors which may contraindicate the use of breast milk include maternal methadone use which exceeds 20 mg per 24 hours (American Academy of Pediatrics 1989) or positive human immunodeficiency virus (HIV) status (Hoegerman & Schnoll 1991). When the mother can breast-feed, initial efforts to nurse may be supplemented with formula to ensure adequate caloric intake.

INTEGUMENTARY SYSTEM

The neonate is at increased risk for skin breakdown, diaper rash, and perianal candidiasis due to diaphoresis, diarrhea, and friction-induced excoriations secondary to agitation.

Meticulous skin care is essential to prevent trauma and infection. Swaddling and "nesting" techniques, which reduce tremors, agitation, and restlessness, are effective strategies. Frequent diaper changes, exposure to light and air, and use of zinc-oxide-based ointments on the perianal area are also indicated. Antifungal agents will be ordered when candidiasis occurs.

NEUROBEHAVIORAL RESPONSES AND SOCIAL INTERACTIONS

The nurse facilitates neurobehavioral adaptations by controlling environmental stimuli and altering the intensity and pace of care. The care plan should identify activities and environmental factors that hamper smooth state transitions or exacerbate irritability and agitation and they should be avoided. The number of people providing care should be limited as much as possible (primary nurses and parents). Parents should be given ample time and opportunity to identify their infant's special needs and learn ways to meet those needs. They should have a clear understanding and appreciation of the infant's abilities to participate in social interaction. Appropriate referrals for ongoing evaluation, follow-up care, and early interventions should be arranged well in advance of discharge.

Evaluation. The purpose of the evaluation process is to determine if stated outcomes have been achieved and include:

- Achieving physiologic and neurobehavioral stability
- Demonstrating resolution of acute withdrawal symptoms
- Establishing adequate fluid and ca-

loric intake
- Maintaining an acceptable level of growth (weight gain)
- Achieving skin integrity
- Receiving all prophylaxis (Vitamin K, HBIG, and so on)
- Demonstrating freedom from infection
- Confirming parent (or foster parent) readiness for infant care

Care of the Infant Exposed to Alcohol—Alcohol is one of the most commonly abused drugs during pregnancy. Estimates indicate that at least 20% of pregnant women continue to drink during pregnancy, and the rate is higher (37%) among women who smoke (Serdula et al 1991). A recent study found that pregnant women who continue to drink may switch from hard liquor to beer or wine, but do not reduce the absolute amount of alcohol consumed (Serdula et al 1991; Barbour 1990). These findings are critical, because while the severity of fetal and neonatal problems resulting from alcohol use appears dose-related, a recent study by Rostand and associates (1990) found significant craniofacial anomalies in infants of women who were classified as "light" drinkers (fewer than six glasses of beer per week).

There is a massive body of evidence regarding the teratogenic effects of alcohol, and the development of fetal alcohol syndrome (FAS). Fetal alcohol syndrome is a combination of physical and mental birth defects (The characteristic stigmata of FAS are listed in Table 5.) Its incidence is estimated to be 3 cases per 1,000 live births in the United States. This may, however, underrepresent the problem. Little and associates (1990)

Table 5. Characteristics of Fetal Alcohol Syndrome

Abnormal Growth
Intrauterine growth retardation
Small-for-gestational age
Microcephaly
Failure to thrive

Central Nervous System
Hypotonia
Irritability
Hyporeflexia
Tremors
Poor coordination
Poor habituation
Disturbed sleep-wake cycles
Developmental delays
Mental retardation

Cardiovascular System
Cardiac defects
    Ventricular septal defect
    Atrial septal defect
    Patent ductus arteriosus
    Tetralogy of Fallot
    Dextrocardia
    Anomalous great vessels

Respiratory System
Pulmonary atresia
Atelectasis

Gastrointestinal System
Gastroschisis
Hepatic fibrosis
Childhood cirrhosis
Extrahepatic biliary atresia
Hyperbilirubinemia in childhood

Genitourinary System
Hydronephrosis
Aplastic/hypoplastic kidneys
Cystic diverticula
Hypospadias
Cryptorchidism
Labial hypoplasia

Musculoskeletal System
Pectus excavatum
Bifid xiphoid
Inguinal/abdominal hernia
Diastasis rectum
Polydactyly/Syndactyly
Talipes equinovarus
Hip dislocation
Scoliosis
Klippel-Feil syndrome

Integumentary System
Aberrant fingerprint and palm creases
Hemangiomas
Scalp hirsutism in childhood
Nail hypoplasia

Craniofacial Anomalies
Head
    Microcephaly/Anencephaly
    Dandy-Walker malformation
Face
    Midface hypoplasia
Eyes
    Ptosis
    Strabismus
    Short palpebral fissures
    Microphthalmia
    Cataracts
    Glaucoma
    Coloboma retinae
Ears
    Abnormal position (posterior rotation)
    Eustachian tube dysfunction
    Microtia
    Sensorineural hearing loss
Nose
    Short, upturned nose
    Hypoplastic philtrum
Mouth
    Dental malalignments
    Small teeth/defective enamel
    Retrognathia
    Cleft lip/Cleft palate
    Thin upper vermilion
Maxilla
    Hypoplastic maxilla

discovered in a retrospective review of infant medical records at a large medical center that physicians consistently failed to recognize classic signs of FAS.

In addition to FAS, the neonate who has been exposed prenatally to alcohol may suffer from a variety of complications frequently observed among women who drink during pregnancy, including prematurity, anemia secondary to placental abruption, and birth asphyxia (Pietrantoni & Knuppel 1991). Acute alcohol intoxication has also been documented in the infant immediately after birth as well as in infants who have been breast-fed by women who have ingested alcohol shortly before nursing the baby (Marx & Stoukides 1991). Neonatal abstinence syndrome can occur and is exacerbated by withdrawal from other drugs.

Assessment. While identification of the infant with fetal alcohol effects (FAE) would appear to be relatively straightforward based upon current knowledge of the syndrome, research suggests that many cases may not be recognized (Little et al 1990). When initial assessment indicates the possibility or likelihood of FAS, the nurse should collaborate with the physician or nurse practitioner to confirm the diagnosis. Evaluation of cardiac, pulmonary, and renal function is critical because anomalies in these systems are common but not usually obvious at birth. Careful documentation of abnormal physical findings is essential; the nurse should also initiate a withdrawal scoring sheet to determine the presence and severity of the abstinence syndrome.

Planning and Organizing Nursing Care. The plan of care is formulated on the basis of specific nursing diagnoses identified during the course of assessments. Evidence of specific congenital anomalies or development of withdrawal symptoms requires significant alterations in care of the newborn. Whenever possible, parents should be consulted and encouraged to actively participate in setting goals and providing as much hands-on care as possible. Early consultation with experts in the diagnosis and treatment of FAS and with other professionals who will provide follow-up and ongoing care is essential for discharge planning.

Nursing Care. Management of care depends on the specific problems evident in the infant. The potential for injury related to neurologic aberrations or deficits is a major concern. Alterations in CNS functioning related to FAS or precipitated by withdrawal require the following interventions:

- Airway maintenance
- Prevention of aspiration
- Support of respiratory function
- Reduction in irritability and agitation
- Promotion of sleep and quiet alert states
- Facilitation of interaction with caregivers

Another major area of concern is gastrointestinal function. Generalized hypotonia, poor feeding reflexes, and regurgitation may interfere with adequate fluid and caloric intake. Use of a soft nipple and a plastic bottle which permits accurate measurement of intake is essential. Extra time may be required to complete the feeding, and careful burping and positioning are essential to prevent regurgitation and aspiration. Breast-feeding is

Table 6. Neurobehavioral Abnormalities Associated With Prenatal Cocaine Exposure

Lethargy

Hypotonia

Hypertonia

Irritability

Tremulousness

Abnormal reflexes

Increased startles

Impaired habituation

Decreased consolability

Rigidity/ Decreased cuddliness

Disorganized feeding patterns

Poor state control or regulation

Increased time spent in dull alert period

Decreased social responsivity and interaction

Poor auditory and visual orienting skills

not advisable if the woman continues to use alcohol, and may not be possible in infants with hypotonic feeding reflexes and poor growth.

Intake and output should be monitored closely, and the infant assessed for evidence of dehydration and inadequate intake, including weight loss, poor skin turgor, decreased urine output, and increasing urine specific gravity. The presence of anomalies such as cleft lip or palate will require additional nursing measures to prevent fluid and electrolyte imbalances (Eliason & Williams 1990).

Whenever possible the nurse should establish a close working relationship with the parents. Guilt is a common response to the diagnosis of FAS and may initially hinder the parents' ability to interact with and care for the infant (May & Mahlmeister 1990). Parents should be permitted to ask questions, explore the impact of alcohol use on the infant's current condition and prognosis, and be allowed to express their grief, which may include verbalizations of denial or anger. Increased alcohol use also may occur, seriously reducing the parent's ability to participate in decision making and care. Appropriate referrals should be initiated in the early phases of discharge planning.

Evaluation. A major focus of the nursing evaluation centers on indicators of physiologic stability. Signs of acute withdrawal should be resolved, and evidence of adequate fluid and caloric intake for growth and development must be documented before the infant is ready for discharge. The parents (or foster parent) must demonstrate the ability to meet the infant's special needs, which will vary depending on the type and severity of FAS characteristics present at birth. They should also be able to implement strategies that promote neurobehavioral adaptations.

Care of the Infant Exposed to Cocaine and Amphetamines—The epidemic of crack cocaine use has posed a crisis for the American health care system of unprecedented proportions. It is estimated that between 90,000 to 240,000 infants are born each year to women who have used cocaine during pregnancy (Phibbs, Bateman & Schwartz 1991). Studies have documented a number of significant neonatal problems related to prenatal substance abuse, including intrauterine growth retardation, cerebral infarcts and lesions (Dixon & Bejar 1989), prematurity, anemia and asphyxia secondary to placental abruption, and urogenital malformations (Kelley, Walsh & Thompson 1991). Investigators have been unable to document the development of classic withdrawal signs observed with neonatal abstinence syndrome when the neonate has been exposed to cocaine in utero. However, neurobehavioral sequelae have also been documented and are listed in Table 6.

While amphetamines are less widely used than cocaine, the physiologic effects are similar, and research findings demonstrate adverse sequelae for the neonate including higher rates of intrauterine growth retardation and prematurity (Little, Snell & Gilstrap 1988; Oro & Dixon 1987). Current studies, however, are limited by the inability to control for the effects of other drugs commonly used by methamphetamine abusers, including nicotine, cocaine, and marijuana.

Assessment. Cocaine and/or amphetamine use may often be suspected or confirmed in the prenatal period; however, studies indicate that many women deny its use (Ostrea et al 1992). If labor and delivery personnel do not encounter problems often associated with these stimulant drugs, the neonatal nurse is often the first health care professional to suspect their use. Abnormal neurobehavioral signs are the most common alerting cues observed (Peters & Theorell 1991; Schneider, Griffith & Chasnoff 1989). Careful documentation of these characteristics will assist in the diagnosis of cocaine or amphetamine exposure.

Use of a traditional withdrawal scoring sheet may not be helpful, since the classic signs of neonatal abstinence syndrome are usually absent. The development of newer assessment tools such as the Lewis Protocol (1990) which describe neurobehavioral abnormalities as well as specific physiologic dysfunction appear promising. Collection of urine or meconium samples for drug screening may be part of the assessment process. The majority of states now permit the physician or nurse practitioner to order newborn urine toxicology screens without parental consent when evidence of cocaine use is obtained through the assessment process.

Planning and Organizing Care. When cocaine use is confirmed, nursing care is planned to support neurobehavioral adaptations and assist parents in identifying the infant's special needs. Because obvious congenital anomalies and signs of acute withdrawal are often absent, the parents may deny the adverse effects of drug use. Early consultation with experts in cocaine use and treatment is an essential aspect of discharge planning. Referrals for follow-up evaluation and care should also be initiated well before discharge, including communication with programs specifically designed for early intervention and long-term care of infants and children prenatally exposed to cocaine. Parents should be integrally involved in identifying goals for parent education and participating in newborn care.

Nursing Care. While many infants exposed to cocaine require intensive nursing care in the postnatal period due to prematurity, low birth weight, or asphyxia, a significant number appear essentially normal. Care can be provided in the normal newborn nursery, and the infant may room in with parents if they so desire. In some cases, rooming in may not be permitted because of concerns regarding parental abduction if the infant has been placed on a police hold. In this case, parents should be encouraged to come to the nursery frequently to visit with and care for the infant.

Critical nursing interventions focus on providing a nurturing environment that reduces unnecessary stimuli and enhances neurobehavioral adaptations. The nurse must be alert for stress cues and alter or cease activities that promote them. Swaddling, rocking, bathing, or holding the infant may produce positive responses. Use of a waterbed, oscillating crib, or swing may be helpful in the initial postnatal period. Parents should, however, be advised to avoid walkers later in infancy, because they have been associated with abnormal posturing, increased rigidity, and other musculoskeletal problems (Lewis, Bennett & Schmeder 1989).

Alterations in coping and parenting and ongoing substance abuse problems often make it impossible for the cocaine addict to assume care for the newborn. A significant aspect of discharge teaching often involves preparing foster parents and grandparents to care for the infant. Efforts should be made to incorporate the newest information regarding infant care and specific strategies that can be used when neurobehavioral aberrations are evident. Demonstrating specific techniques that reduce irritability, agitation, and inconsolable crying can greatly reduce the stress involved in caring for the infant exposed to cocaine. Providing sufficient time for the caretaker to become comfortable with these skills is essential for success. As noted earlier, because of the association of apnea and SIDS with prenatal drug exposure, caretakers should be taught CPR before discharge (Donaher-Wagner & Braun 1992; Long 1992).

Evaluation. The primary goal of ongoing evaluation is to determine infant and parent readiness for discharge. When major complications of cocaine use necessitate intensive care, the infant must show physiologic stability, establishment of an effective feeding pattern, and appropriate growth. When the infant's primary problems revolve around neurobehavioral aberrations, the infant's caretakers must demonstrate appropriate skill in identifying stress cues and providing supportive care. Stated outcomes must be achieved and when specific problems are not resolved, appropriate referrals must be completed before the infant is discharged.

Care of the Infant Exposed to Other Drugs: Nicotine and Cannabinoids— In the past, few people considered nicotine a drug, and the compulsive desire to smoke, a form of addiction. It is now known that nicotine is an extremely addictive substance, and cessation of smoking is extremely difficult for many people without adequate treatment and support. The deleterious effects on the fetus and neonate are now also well established. Estimates indicate, in fact, that 25% of all perinatal morbidity is due to cigarette smoking (Wen et al 1990).

Smoking has been associated with a fivefold increase in the risk of intrauterine growth retardation (Kline, Stein & Hutzler 1987), placental infarcts and abruption (Abel 1980), preterm labor and birth, fetal distress, and low Apgar scores (Johnson, McCarter & Ferencz 1987). Evidence of a neonatal abstinence sydrome in infants of women who continued to smoke heavily throughout pregnancy also exists (Abel 1980).

Marijuana is the most commonly used illicit drug in the United States today (MacGregor et al 1990). The effect of cannabinoids on fetal growth and development, as well as neonatal consequences, is a matter of some controversy. In several studies there have been reports of congenital anomalies (Abelson & Miller 1985), decreased birth weight (Fried, Watkinson & Dillon 1987), and prematurity (Gibson, Baghurst & Colley 1983). Other investigators have found no association between marijuana use and birth defects. A stronger correlation has been established between the use of marijuana and neurobehavioral disorders ((Fried & O'Connell 1987; Fried & Makin 1987).

Assessment. With the high prevalence of smoking and marijuana use today, the neonatal nurse should inquire if the infant has been exposed to nicotine or cannabinoids. The prenatal record may provide information about recreational drug use, but when there is no notation of substance use, the neonatal nurse can ask about patterns of drug use as discharge teaching is initiated. Current research findings have established that infants exposed to secondhand smoke have a greater incidence of respiratory infections and childhood asthma (Martinez, Cline & Burrows 1992). This information can be employed as an introduction to the topics of smoking and marijuana use and nonjudgmental inquiries can then be made about their use.

Ongoing and systematic assessments of physiologic status and neurobehavioral responses may help to determine the nature of the problem. As noted, some infants exposed to high levels of nicotine may exhibit signs of withdrawal, and initiation of a scoring sheet is appropriate when indicators of neonatal abstinence syndrome are evident. A urine or meconium sample may be obtained for toxicology screening for detection of cannabinoid metabolites, and many facilities now have written policies to guide nurses in the initiation of specimen collection.

When a woman has denied drug use, it is critical to provide informed consent and explain the reasons for any special neonatal assessments, examinations, or tests performed. Even when the woman does not give permission for the collection of urine or meconium samples and the drug screening process, efforts should be made to provide explanations and enlist her help in the diagnosis and treatment of problems that develop in the neonatal period.

Planning and Organizing Care. In most cases, the infant exposed to nicotine or cannabinoids will not require specialized care. Alterations are made if low birth weight or prematurity complicate the postnatal period, but the majority of infants can be placed in the normal newborn nursery or may room in with their mother. If neurobehavioral abnormalities are noted, parents should be involved in decisions that are made regarding additional diagnostic tests performed to rule out other causes of CNS dysfunction. Research indicates that women who smoke and use marijuana are also more likely to use alcohol or other drugs (Johnson, McCarter & Ferencz 1987). Appropriate planning for evaluation of family functioning and the home environment should be made well before discharge to identify significant problems.

Nursing Care. The major goal of nursing care is to support physiologic and neurobehavioral adaptations. Manipulation of the environment to reduce external stimuli is often effective in decreasing irritability, agitation, and sleep pattern disturbances. The nurse should be alert for negative responses during care or interactions with the infant, and alter or cease activities which appear to cause distress. If withdrawal signs become evident, the nurse can employ specific strategies described earlier in the chapter, including swaddling, rocking, and "nesting" the infant.

Breast-feeding is generally contraindicated when women plan to continue smoking cigarettes or using marijuana. Nurses should emphasize the deleterious

aspects of passive smoke inhalation for the infant, and can refer parents to smoking cessation programs. Some infants exposed to cannabinoids demonstrate discoordinate feeding reflexes or regurgitation after feeding. Discharge teaching should include ample opportunities for parents to become comfortable with feeding the infant. Referrals for follow-up care and evaluation should also be initiated before discharge.

Evaluation. The nurse completes the evaluation process to determine if stated outcomes have been achieved. An important aspect of this process is to assess the degree of neurobehavioral aberrations. Limitation in the ability to interact with parents and respond positively to touch or other soothing behaviors may contribute to alterations in parenting. When continuing difficulties are evident, the nurse must initiate appropriate referrals for in-home follow-up and parental support before discharge. If foster parents or grandparents will assume responsibility for infant care, the nurse must also evaluate their readiness for this role.

CONCLUSION

Maternal neonatal nurses face an unprecedented crisis in health care today. Substance abuse now results in the birth of over 300,000 infants prenatally exposed to drugs each year (NIDA 1991). Research indicates that nurses in most maternity settings will be called upon to care for infants whose mothers have abused drugs and other substances during pregnancy (Chasnoff, Landress & Barrett 1990; Kaplan 1992). Research also clearly shows that some of the problems faced at birth by the infant prenatally exposed to drugs may be resolved before discharge, but others will continue throughout childhood.

The initial nursing care provided to infants prenatally exposed to drugs is critical to their future potential for growth and development. All maternal and neonatal nurses must therefore develop the knowledge and skill required to identify and care for these infants. Regardless of the setting in which care is provided, the nurse should be guided by clearly delineated hospital policies and procedures when substance abuse is suspected. Nurses should have the freedom to discuss the issue of drug use and substance abuse with families and feel confident that physicians will respond positively when they report findings which strongly suggest drug use. An essential aspect of care is collaboration with health care professionals skilled in diagnosis and treatment of problems related to perinatal substance abuse. Discharge teaching should focus on strengthening parent-infant ties and building confidence in parents as they attempt to provide infant care. Timely referrals must be initiated to prepare for the infant's discharge to the home or into the care of foster parents.

REFERENCES

Abel E. Smoking during pregnancy: A review of effects on growth and development of offspring. *Human Biology* 1980; 52: 593-626.

Abelson HI, Miller JD. A decade of trends in cocaine use in the household population. *National Institute of Drug Abuse Research Monograph Series* 1985; 61: 35-49.

Als H, Lester B, Tronick E, Brazelton TB. Manual for the assessment of preterm infants' behavior (APIB). In: Fitzgerald HE, Lester BM, Yogman MW, eds. *Theory and Research in Behavioral Pediatrics* New York: Plenum Press, 1982: 65-132.

American Academy of Pediatrics, Committee on Drugs. Transfer of drugs and other chemicals into human breast milk. *Pediatrics* 1989; 84 (4): 924-36.

Ballard JL, Novak LK, Driver M. A simplified score for assessment of fetal matura-

tion of newly born infants. *Journal of Pediatrics* 1979; 95(5): 769-74.

Barbour B. Alcohol and pregnancy. *Journal of Nurse-Midwifery* 1990; 35(2): 78-85.

Baumgartner W, Black C, Jones P, Blahd W. Radioimmunoassay of cocaine in hair. *Advances in Biology of Skin and Hair Growth* 1982; 23(2): 790-3.

Brazelton TB. *Neonatal Behavioral Assessment Scale. Monograph* 88 (revised edition). Philadelphia: JB Lippincott, 1984.

Budreau G, Kleiber C. Clinical indicators of infant irritability. *Neonatal Network* 1991; 9(5): 23-30.

Caron E, Maguire D. Current management of pain, sedation, and narcotic physical dependency of the infant on ECMO. *Journal of Perinatal and Neonatal Nursing* 1990; 4(1): 63-74.

Centers for Disease Control. *Hepatitis B Virus: A Comprehensive Strategy for Eliminating Transmission in the United States Through Universal Childhood Vaccination.* Atlanta: Centers for Disease Control, 1991.

Chasnoff IJ. Drug use in pregnancy: Parameters of risk. *Pediatric Clinics of North America* 1988; 35:1403-12.

Chasnoff IJ, Landress H, Barrett M. The prevalence of illicit-drug or alcohol use during pregnancy and discrepancies in mandatory reporting in Pinellas County, Florida. *New England Journal of Medicine* 1990; 322(17):1202-6.

Davidson Ward S, Bautista D, Chan L, Derry M, Lisbin A, Durfee M, Mills K, Keens T. Sudden infant death syndrome in infants of substance-abusing mothers. *Journal of Pediatrics* 1990; 117(6): 876-81.

Dixon S, Bejar R. Echoencephalographic findings in neonates associated with maternal cocaine and methamphetamine use: Incidence and clinical correlates. *Journal of Pediatrics* 1989; 115(5): 770-8.

Donaher-Wagner B, Braun D. Infant cardiopulmonary resuscitation for expectant and new parents. *MCN* 1992; 17(1): 27-9.

Dubowitz L, Dubowitz V, Goldberg B. Clinical assessment of gestational age in the newborn infant. *Journal of Pediatrics* 1970; 77(1): 1-10.

Eliason M, Williams J. Fetal alcohol syndrome and the neonate. *Journal of Perinatal and Neonatal Nursing* 1990; 3(4): 64-72.

Finnegan L. In: Chasnoff IJ, ed *Drugs, Alcohol, and Parenting*. Norwell, MA: Kluwer Academic Publishing, 1988.

Flanagan-Everett M. Drug abuse and withdrawal. In: Cloherty J, Stark A, eds. *Manual of Neonatal Care*. Boston: Little, Brown, 1991.

Fried PA, Watkinson B, Dillon RF. Cigarettes, alcohol and marijuana: Varying associations with birthweight. *International Journal of Epidemiology* 1987; 16: 44-7.

Fried PA, Makin JE. Neonatal behavioral correlates of prenatal exposure to marijuana, cigarettes, and alcohol in a low-risk population. *Neurotoxicology and Teratology* 1987; 9 (1): 1-7.

Fried PA, O'Connell. A comparison of the effects of prenatal exposure to tobacco alcohol, cannabis and caffeine on birth size and subsequent growth. *Neurotoxicology and Teratology* 1987; 9: 79-85.

Gibson GT, Baghurst P, Colley D. Maternal alcohol, tobacco and cannabis consumption and the outcome of pregnancy. *Australian and New Zealand Journal of Obstetrics and Gynecology* 1983; 23: 15-8.

Graham K, Koren G, Klein J, Schneiderman J, Greenwald M. Determination of gestational cocaine exposure by hair analysis. *Journal of the American Medical Association* 1983; 262(23):3328-30.

Hoegerman G, Schnoll S. Narcotic use in pregnancy. *Clinics in Perinatology* 1991; 18(1): 51-75.

Johnson S, McCarter R, Ferencz C. Changes in alcohol, cigarette, and recreational drug use during pregnancy: Implications for intervention. *American Journal of Epidemiology* 1987; 126(4): 695-702.

Kaplan BA, Idelson R, Sachs W, Weiner L, and Kaplan L. Pediatrician's perspectives on fetal alcohol syndrome. *Journal of Substance Abuse* 1992; 4 (2): 187-95.

Kelley S, Walsh J, Thompson K. Birth outcomes, health problems, and neglect with prenatal exposure to cocaine. *Pediatric Nursing* 1991;17(2):130-6.

Kennard M. Cocaine use during pregnancy: Fetal and neonatal effects. *Journal of Perinatal and Neonatal Nursing* 1990; 3(4): 53-63.

Kline J, Stein Z, Hutzler M. Cigarettes, alcohol and marijuana: Varying associations with birthweight. *International Journal of Epidemiology* 1987;16: 44-8.

Lake M, Jefrey A, Murphy J, Poekert G. Patterns of illicit drug use at the time of labor in a private and public hospital. *Journal of Perinatology* 1992; XII(2): 134-6.

Lewis KDeS. Lewis Protocol: *A Measure of Prenatal Drug Exposed Infants Behavior*. Unpublished master's thesis. San Francisco: University of San Francisco, 1990.

Lewis KDeS, Bennett B, Schmeder NH. The care of infants menaced by cocaine abuse. *MCN* 1989; 14(5): 324-9.

Little B, Snell L, Gilstrap L. Methamphetamine abuse during pregnancy: Outcome and fetal effects. *Obstetrics and Gynecology* 1988; 72(4):541-4.

Little B, Snell L, Rosenfeld C, Gilstrap L, Gant N. Failure to recognize fetal alcohol syndrome in newborn infants. *American Journal of Diseases of Childhood* 1990;144(10):1142-6.

Long C. Teaching parents infant CPR — lecture or audiovisual tape? *MCN* 1992; 17(1):30-2.

MacGregor S, Sciarra J, Keith L, Sciarra J. Prevalence of marijuana use during pregnancy. *Journal of Reproductive Medicine* 1990; 35(12):1147-9.

Mahlmeister L. *Dispelling the Myth: Substance Abuse in Middle Class Women*. Paper presented at Contemporary Forums Perinatal Dilemmas Conference, Jackson, WY, 1992.

Martinez F, Cline M, Burrows B. Increased incidence of asthma in children of smoking mothers. *Pediatrics* 1992; 89(1):21-6.

Marx C, Stoukides C. Drug use by nursing mothers. In: Cloherty J, Stark A, eds. *Manual of Neonatal Care*. 3rd ed. Boston: Little, Brown, 1991.

May K, Mahlmeister L. *Comprehensive Maternity Nursing*. 2nd ed. Philadelphia: J.B. Lippincott, 1990.

Mullen J, Bracha S. Toxicology screening. *Postgraduate Medicine* 1988;84(1):141-7.

National Institute on Drug Abuse (NIDA). Methodological issues in controlled studies on effects of prenatal exposure to drugs. *National Institute on Drug Abuse Research Monograph Series*. Washington, DC: US Department of Health and Human Services, 1991.

Oro A, Dixon S. Perinatal cocaine and methamphetamine exposure: Maternal and neonatal correlates. *Journal of Pediatrics* 1987; 111: 571-8.

Ostrea E, Brady M, Gause S, Raymundo A, Stevens M. Drug screening of newborns by meconium analysis: A large-scale, prospective, epidemiologic study. *Pediatrics* 1992; 89(1): 107-13.

Peters H, Theorell CJ. Fetal and neonatal effects of maternal cocaine use. *Journal of Obstetric, Neonatal, and Gynecologic Nursing* 1991; 20 (2): 121-6.

Phibbs C, Bateman D, Schwartz R. The neonatal costs of maternal cocaine use. *Journal of the American Medical Association* 1991; 266(11):1521-6.

Pietrantoni M, Knuppel R. Alcohol use in pregnancy. *Clinics in Perinatology* 1991; 18(1): 93-109.

Rostand A, Kaminski M, Lelong N, Dehaene P, Delestret I, Bertrand C, Querlue D, Crepin G. Alcohol use in pregnancy, craniofacial features, and fetal growth. *Journal of Epidemiology and Community Health* 1990; 44: 302-6.

Serdula M, Williamson D, Kendrick J, Anda R, Byers T. Trends in alcohol consumption by pregnant women. *Journal of the American Medical Association* 1991; 265(7): 876-9.

Schneider J, Griffith D, Chasnoff I. Infants exposed to cocaine in utero: Implications for developmental assessment and intervention. *Infant and Young Children* 1989; 2(1): 25-36.

Sloan L, Gay J, Snyder S, Bales W. Substance abuse during pregnancy in a rural population. *Obstetrics and Gynecology* 1992; 79(2): 245-7.

Tillman J. Syphilis: An old disease, a contemporary perinatal problem, *Journal of Obstetric, Neonatal, and Gynecologic Nursing* 1992; 21(3): 209-13.

Wiley K, Gibbs B, Kahn S, Karlman R, Tse A, Perez-Woods R. Prevalence of illicit drug use among prenatal patients and predictive validity of nurses' judgments. *Journal of Perinatology* 1991; XI(4): 330-4.

United States Drug Testing Laboratories. *Mecstat Collection Instructions*. Chicago: US Drug Testing Laboratories, 1991.

Valente D, Cassini M, Pigliapochi M. Hair as the sample in assessing morphine and cocaine addiction. *Clinics in Chemistry* 1981; 27(10):1952-3.

Wen S, Goldenberg R, Cutter G, Hoffman H, Oliver S, Davis R, DuBard M. Smoking, maternal age, fetal growth, and gestation age at delivery. *American Journal of Obstetrics and Gynecology* 1990; 162 (1): 53-8.

ANNOTATED BIBLIOGRAPHY

Hamel S, Neuspiel D. Cocaine and infant behavior. *Journal of Developmental and Behavioral Pediatrics 1991;12(1):55-64.* The authors present a comprehensive review of the research literature regarding behavioral sequelae of cocaine use during pregnancy. A summary of current statistics emphasizes the widespread use of cocaine, which now crosses socioeconomic, ethnic, and geographical lines. Studies cited indicate that between 10% to 15% of women use drugs while pregnant, with rates as low as 4% and as high as 17%, depending on the characteristics of the population sample.

The pharmocology of cocaine is discussed, with peak plasma levels defined for nasal (15 to 16 minutes) and intravenous or inhalation (5 to 11 minutes) routes. The ability to detect cocaine metabolites in urine is noted to be time-limited, possibly three days after use in nonpregnant adults. Data is not available on the changes in detection over time which occur with the physiologic changes of pregnancy. Newer methods of screening (hair and meconium analysis) are briefly discussed.

Both animal and human studies examining the physical and behavioral effects of cocaine are reviewed, and offer growing evidence of the long-term neurobehavioral impact on infant growth and development. The authors note that the existence of a true neonatal abstinence syndrome is questionable, although it has been observed and is possibly exacerbated in cases of concomitant narcotic use. A major weakness of several studies attempting to identify the behavioral effects of cocaine was, in fact, the use of opiate withdrawal scoring sheets. The Neonatal Behavioral Assessment Scale (NBAS) was used in several investigations and was able to discern behavioral anomalies including state liability, tremulousness, increased startles, and decreased consolability compared with non-drug-exposed infants. In addition to behavioral effects, several studies have discovered brain lesions in cocaine-exposed infants, including intracranial hemorrhages, brain lesions, and skull defects.

The authors conclude the review with recommendations for future research including, but not limited to, the study of women who are not patients in drug treatment programs, investigations of the infant's social environment, and development of new tools to assess neurobehavioral outcomes. A strong selection bias was discovered when the authors reviewed a group of abstracts submitted for one research conference on the effects of perinatal drug use. Of the fifty-eight abstracts submitted for review, only 11% of studies showing "no effect" were accepted for presentation, compared with 57% of studies demonstrating adverse outcomes, although the "no effects" group reported better methodology. Greater objectivity is encouraged in the selection of reports on this topic.

Schneider J, Griffith D, Chasnoff IJ. Infants exposed to cocaine in utero: Implications for developmental assessment and intervention. *Infants and Young Children* **1989; 2(1): 25-36.**

Findings of developmental assessments in the newborn and during early infancy are presented in this review paper. The difficulty of identifying the specific contribution of an isolated drug is noted in light of polysubstance abuse in the general population and during pregnancy. The authors elaborate on developmental implications of exposure to cocaine. In the neonatal period, aberrations in sleep-wake patterns and social interactions make it difficult or impossible for the infant to respond appropriately to caregivers. Reciprocity normally present in the bonding process may be absent, and can interfere with effective parenting. Negative infant responses will suppress positive parental reactions and efforts to nurture the newborn.

In the older infant (4 months), neuromuscular function is altered. Rigidity in posture and movement and predominance of extensor muscle tone decrease the ability of the infant to explore the environment and develop eye-hand coordination. They also inhibit appropriate balance control. Interventions are proposed which support developmental progress, and are outlined in detail. In the newborn phase specific strategies are recommended to reduce rigidity and extension including positioning the infant on its side, maintaining the spine in a state of flexion, and bringing the arms and legs toward the midline of the body. Swaddling to encourage the flexed position is also recommended. Vestibular-proprioceptive stimulation is essential for normal development and includes rocking or other slow rhythmical input. Hydrotherapy is also recommended as a method for encouraging smooth limb movements, flexion, and proprioception. The use of these developmental strategies should be withdrawn gradually as the infant's condition improves in order to facilitate self-control and self-state regulation.

The paper concludes with a discussion of parent education considerations. Assisting parents to recognize common distress signs from overstimulation, which include yawning, sneezing, hiccuping, gaze aversion, regurgitation, color change, and crying, will improve caretaking abilities and reduce infant frustration. Parents are taught to engage the infant during the quiet, alert state, and to offer one form of stimulation at a time so the infant is not overwhelmed. Play activities which improve flexion and reduce antigravity extensor strength should be demonstrated. Specific guidelines for play, and ongoing positioning techniques to reduce extensor thrusting, are delineated. A major prevention strategy includes bending the infant at the waste when thrusting occurs and carrying the infant in a position which encourages flexion.

Wiley K, Gibbs B, Kahn S, Karlman R, Tse A, Perez-Woods R. Prevalence of illicit drug use among prenatal patients and predictive validity of nurses' judgments. *Journal of Perinatology* 1991; XI(4): 330-4.

This study was conducted to determine the prevalence of illicit drug use within the prenatal population of a midwestern suburban ambulatory care center. Further study aims were to explore the relationship between nurses' judgments of patient illicit drug use and urine toxicology results, and to determine if differences existed between nurses' judgment of drug use by private patients and clinic patients. The investigation was motivated by research findings which indicate that substance abuse is often undetected by health care providers, and that drug users commonly underreport their drug use. Furthermore, there were no studies in the literature which evaluated the validity of nurses' judgment regarding which patients were most likely using drugs.

The sample in this study consisted of 189 new patients seeking prenatal care in a suburban medical center. Of this sample, 78 were seen by private physicians and

111 by residents in training. The groups differed significantly in demographic characteristics. The majority of private patients were Caucasian (87%) and married (85%) and began prenatal care at 10 weeks gestation. Women seen by residents were primarily African-American, Hispanic (60%), and single (70%), and began prenatal care at 21.5 weeks gestation.

Staff nurses in the clinic were trained to conduct a drug-use history with each patient. All patients enrolled in the study were interviewed by the nurses about drug use, and urine samples were obtained for toxicology screening. Nurses' judgments of illicit drug use were measured using a Likert-type scale.

The prevalence rate of positive urine toxicologies for the study sample was 7.4%; 10.3% of the urine samples were positive for the residents' group and 5.4% for the private patient group. The two groups also differed in the type of drug detected. Only one of the specimens in the private patient group was positive for cocaine; the remainder of the samples tested positive for cannabinoids (marijuana). In the residents' group, two urine samples were positive for cocaine, one positive for opiates, and one for phencyclidine. Cannabinoids were detected in only 50% of the specimens.

The nurses were significantly more likely to suspect residents' patients of illicit drug use. The relationship between the nurses' judgment and actual patient drug use based on positive toxicology results was, however, low (r= .28). Other studies have identified biases in reporting of drug use. Poor women, African-American, and Hispanic women are more likely to be reported. In one study African-American women were ten times more likely to be reported, although cocaine use was almost identical in Caucasian women.

Recommendations stemming from the study include developing an educational program for patients regarding marijuana use, because it was the most commonly detected drug, and providing ongoing education for nurses regarding identification of substance abusers. Finally, the authors encouraged nurses to develop an awareness of their attitudes and discover the factors that influence their decision-making about suspecting women of illicit drug use. The researchers could not recommend universal drug screening based on the prevalence of 7.5% in this study.

Rostand A, Kaminski M, Lelong N, Dehaene P, Delestret I, Bertrand C, Querleu D, Crepin G. Alcohol use in pregnancy, craniofacial features, and fetal growth. *Journal of Epidemiology and Community Health* **1990; 4:302-6.** The aim of this investigation was to examine the relationship between the level of alcohol consumption in pregnancy and craniofacial characteristics of the neonate. The study was motivated by knowledge that partial forms of fetal alcohol syndrome (FAS) are not clearly understood; in particular, their relationship to the amount of alcohol consumed during pregnancy. Furthermore, recent research indicates that the diagnosis of FAS may be missed by health care providers when partial forms present at birth. The study hypothesis was that no clinical effects of light or moderate drinking during pregnancy would be detectable. A second hypothesis was that clinical features of heavy drinking (not alcoholic) would be in a minor form of FAS with specific craniofacial abnormalities.

During an eight month period, 684 women were interviewed at the first prenatal visit regarding alcohol consumption. Three hundred forty-seven women identified as drinkers were divided into three groups: heavy drinkers (at least 21 drinks per week), moderate drinkers (7 to 20 drinks per week), and light drinkers (0 to 6 drinks per week). The majority of women drank beer. Abstinent women were not considered separately as a control group. A subsample of infants (202 infants) was examined for a standardized neonatal morphological examination after delivery.

Both hypotheses were rejected. Craniofacial anomalies were found in all three groups of infants. No differences existed in the number or type of aberrations found in the infants of light and moderate drinkers. The greater number of craniofacial anomalies was found in heavy drinkers. Infants of heavy drinkers who reduced their alcohol consumption during pregnancy had fewer craniofacial features. Two infants whose mothers were heavy drinkers were diagnosed with FAS. Additionally, infants of mothers who were classified as heavy drinkers during pregnancy had a shorter gestation. A significant finding was the contributing effect of smoking on the incidence of craniofacial anomalies. However, in the statistical analysis, the proportion of infants with craniofacial aberrations reached significance only in the infants of heavy drinkers.

The authors conclude that craniofacial anomalies can be sensitive indicators of alcohol use and fetal effect during pregnancy. Health care professionals must become alert to subtle signs of facial dysmorphology. The number of craniofacial anomalies could also be a useful outcome measure in evaluating the effectiveness of intervention aimed at reducing alcohol consumption during pregnancy.

5

Alcohol-Related Effects on the Infant, Child, and Adult

Helen Bosson Thomson, R.N., B.S.N., P.H.N.
Keeta DeStefano Lewis, R.N., P.H.N., M.S.N.

Fetal alcohol syndrome (FAS) lies at the extreme end of the spectrum of disabilities caused by the use of alcohol during pregnancy. Common characteristics of the syndrome are facial, growth, and central nervous system anomalies. Every organ system can be affected depending on the time of fetal exposure to alcohol, the amount of alcohol taken, and genetic susceptibility. Research shows FAS causes lifelong physical, mental, and behavioral disabilities. The amount of alcohol a pregnant woman can drink and not cause harm to her unborn baby is still unclear; therefore, abstinence from alcohol during pregnancy is the primary prevention. Early identification of harmful drinking patterns and a humanistic approach to intervention are critical in the effort to prevent FAS and enable those affected to attain their fullest potential.

Ample historical evidence is available that use or abuse of alcohol during pregnancy can harm fetal development and outcome. In the Old Testament, an angel warned Samson's mother, "Behold, thou shall conceive and bear a son; and now drink no wine or strong drink." (Judges 13:7)

Greek and Roman mythology suggested the same phenomenon led to an ancient Carthaginian practice which forbade any drinking by bridal couples on their wedding night (Jones & Smith 1973). The British House of Commons in 1834 noted that infants born to alcohol-using mothers had a "strained, shriveled, imperfect look" (Jones 1986). Yet it was years later that the scientific community identified a distinctive pattern of physical and behavioral abnormalities in infants and children of alcoholic mothers for which we now use the term fetal alcohol syndrome (FAS) (Jones & Smith 1973; Jones et al 1973).

Fetal alcohol syndrome has been identified as the leading known cause of mental retardation in the United States, surpassing spina bifida and Down's syndrome (Streissguth et al 1991). *Healthy People 2000* (1990) denotes FAS as the leading preventable cause of birth defects in the United States. Estimates of FAS are 1.9 per 1,000 births in the United States and about 25 per 1,000 infants born to women who are alcoholics (Abel & Sokol 1987).

Alcohol-related birth defects are variable and the average minimal occurrence is about 3.1 per 1,000 births and 90 per 1,000 for women who are alcoholic (Abel 1984). Prenatal alcohol exposure may account for 5% of all congenital anomalies (Sokol 1981). If this estimate is substantiated, numerous infants with congenital anomalies attributed to an unknown etiology may actually have been caused by use and abuse of alcohol (Sokol & Abel 1992).

It is not known why some children are severely affected by prenatal exposure to alcohol while others exhibit only subtle fetal alcohol effects. Research has demonstrated a number of mediating factors, including maternal chronicity of alcohol use and dose levels of alcohol, duration of exposure and sensitivity of fetal tissue, gestational stage (Weiner & Morse 1988), increased maternal age/parity, and genetic susceptibility (Sokol & Abel 1992).

Alcohol is a teratogen. Like many teratogens the effects of prenatal exposure to alcohol can have a continuum of outcomes for the fetus, including no effects, subtle or severe effects and, at the far end of the continuum, a nonviable fetus (Figure 1). Alcohol is known to cross the placenta from maternal circulation to fetal circulation, rapidly reaching the same concentration in the fetus as in the mother (Zuckerman 1991). The mechanism of how the fetus is adversely affected by alcohol is as yet unclear. It may be due to the alcohol, or it may be related to the toxic effects of acetaldehyde within the mother and/or the fetus.

Acetaldehyde is the first metabolite of alcohol which is cytotoxic and teratogenic (Tranmer 1985). Acetaldehyde dehydrogenase is the enzyme that metabolizes acetaldehyde. This enzyme develops early in the fetus and is able to metabolize acetaldehyde as early as 10 to 16 weeks gestation (Sippel & Kesaniemi 1975). This suggests that the fetus can be protected from small amounts of acetaldehyde diffusing from maternal circulation to fetal circulation

(Abel 1984).

It is hypothesized that genetic determination for acetaldehyde metabolism can alter fetal susceptibility (Goodman & Gorlin 1983). Some humans are missing the enzyme acetaldehyde dehydrogenase, which breaks down and absorbs alcohol, thereby making alcohol less toxic to the human system. This may be an explanation as to why even after modest alcohol intake, some pregnant women with genetically determined or acquired liver function problems could have acetaldehyde levels well over the danger limit for the fetus (Dunn et al 1979). Furthermore, this may also partially explain why some women who drink large amounts of alcohol may have an unaffected infant whereas a woman who drinks only socially may have a seriously involved infant (Ladewig, London & Olds 1990).

Even with abundant literature available about FAS, infants are not consistently identified and diagnosed at birth or even in early childhood by practitioners. Characteristic features are not easily discerned in the newborn period, since facial dysmorphia and developmental abnormalities tend to become more distinct between three and six years of age (Martin 1992). Further, if maternal alcohol abuse is suspected, there is often a reluctance to question the mother regarding her drinking habits, particularly if the mother is of an upper- or middle-class status.

During the period from 1981 to 1986 the Centers for Disease Control (CDC) collected data on the rates of major congenital malformations in the United States by race/ethnicity. The surveillance was conducted by the Birth Defects Monitoring Program (BDMP), and FAS was one of the eighteen congenital malformations monitored. Data showed the prevalence of

Figure 1. Continuum of Pregnancy Outcome of Women Who Drink Alcohol

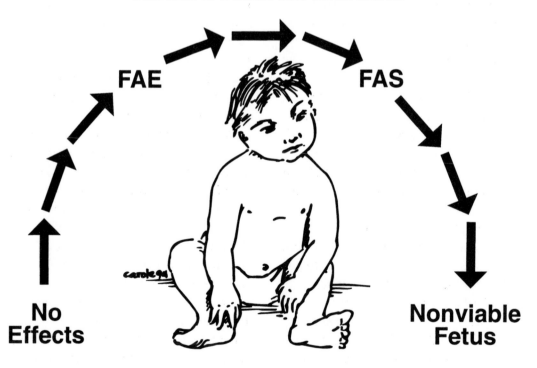

FAE

FAS

No
Effects

Nonviable
Fetus

FAS per 10,000 births by race/ethnicity was as follows: American Indians 29.9, African-Americans 6.0, whites 0.9, Hispanics 0.8, and Asians 0.3 (Chavez, Cordero & Becerra 1988).

The Centers for Disease Control recognizes the need to improve surveillance methods for gathering data on the prevalence of FAS. Fetal alcohol syndrome is underreported, and this may be due to failure on the part of the primary practitioner to discern the syndrome in the newborn period, failure to diagnose and document FAS in the medical record, and/or reluctance to "label" the child or mother. An accurate surveillance system depends on a diagnosis being made and documented in medical records for case data inclusion (Martin 1992).

This chapter focuses primarily on the characteristics of FAS as observed in the infant, child, adolescent, and adult. The individual diagnosed with FAS represents only the most severe effects of prenatal alcohol exposure. Even more prevalent than FAS are those individuals who are referred to as having fetal alcohol effects (FAE). Though not as easily recognized as FAS, FAE can cause life-long motor, mental, and behavioral difficulties. A portion of this chapter addresses this often undiagnosed condition. The last section discusses the nurse's role in the identification of prenatal alcohol abuse and the utilization of nursing skills in providing services to the child and family affected by the abuse.

Characteristics of Fetal Alcohol Syndrome

A diagnosis of fetal alcohol syndrome is appropriate when there is a history of maternal alcohol abuse and (1) facial anomalies, (2) growth deficiency, both prenatal and postnatal, and (3) central nervous system abnormalities (Rosett, Weiner & Edelin 1981). Children who are exposed to alcohol in utero, but do not have sufficient characteristics for a diagnosis of FAS, are referred to as having fetal alcohol effects. Numerous research studies now provide information on the long-term effects of prenatal alcohol exposure and the characteristics of FAS from infancy into adulthood.

The following discussion focuses on the main diagnostic criteria of FAS: (1) facial anomalies, (2) growth deficiency, and (3) central nervous system involvement (Figures 2 and 3). Characteristics of the syndrome are presented as they apply to the infant, child, adolescent, and adult.

Infant

FACIAL ANOMALIES

Clarren and Smith (1978) believe it is the facial similarities that unite FAS into a discernible entity. Their observations show the key facial features of FAS to be short palpebral fissures (eye openings), a hypoplastic upper lip with thinned vermilion (thin upper lip), flattened to absent philtrum (underdevelopment of the two ridges between the nasal septum and upper lip), and mid-facial and mandibular growth deficiency (flat look to the face with small chin).

A number of other physical anomalies are found in the literature which can occur in the areas of the eyes, ears, nose, and mouth. These include: *eyes —* epicanthal folds (vertical fold of skin at inner canthus of eyes), hypertelorism (wide-spaced eyes), microphthalmia (small eyes), blepharophimosis (narrowing of slit between eyelids at external angle of eye), ptosis (drooping eyelids), strabismus (deviation of eyes), myopia (nearsightedness); *ears*—low-set, poorly formed conchae (hollow of external ear); abnormal pinna (external ear); posterior rotation of the helix (margin of external ear); *nose*—short, low bridge, anteverted (upturned) nostrils; *mouth*—prominent lateral palatine ridges, cleft lip, cleft palate, small teeth with faulty enamel (Clarren & Smith 1978; Abel 1984; Jones 1986).

GROWTH DEFICIENCY

Growth deficiency in the infant with fetal alcohol syndrome begins in utero. Its occurrence is differentiated from prematurity, since growth deficiency caused by maternal alcohol use persists with advancing age (Weiner & Morse 1988).

Jones (1986) reports birth length, weight, and head circumference are approximately two to three standard deviations below the mean for gestational age. When microcephaly occurs, it generally is of prenatal onset and reflects deficient brain growth. However, a normal head size after intrauterine alcohol exposure is not necessarily accompanied by normal brain structure or function (Clarren & Smith 1978).

Children with FAS grow very slowly even with good nutrition and a good environment, and failure to thrive is often the primary complaint when the infant is presented for the initial diagnostic evaluation. Many cases of growth failure are the result of alcohol's effect on cell growth and division and not a reflection of poor parenting care (Weiner & Morse 1991).

CENTRAL NERVOUS SYSTEM ABNORMALITIES

Damage to the central nervous system

(CNS) is the most serious consequence of fetal exposure to alcohol. The effects of prenatal exposure are manifested in a number of ways and to varying degrees, and are mediated by many factors, including time of gestational exposure, the length and severity of the exposure, genetic susceptibility, and maternal nutrition and health.

Staisey and Fried (1982) found that newborns who had been prenatally exposed to alcohol displayed decreased muscle tone at nine days of age, but also noted that the decreased muscle tone had attenuated by thirty days. In another study, researchers observed particular characteristics in newborns of mothers who were moderate to heavy social drinkers during their pregnancy as compared to newborns whose mothers had consumed less or no alcohol. The characteristics observed in the newborns of the moderate to heavy drinkers included: less vigorous body activity, more time with eyes open, increased body tremors, more hand-to-face behavior, and more turning of the head to the left, which is an atypical behavior for term infants (Landesman-Dwyer, Keller & Streissguth 1978).

A neonate prenatally exposed to alcohol may be jittery and restless, cry excessively, have a poor suck, and have disturbed sleep patterns, all of which persist beyond the neonatal period. The jitteriness is not due to withdrawal, because withdrawal is not common in the newborn exposed to alcohol as it is in the newborn exposed to opiates.

The infant with FAS may also have feeding problems due to neuromuscular delay or structural abnormalities. These difficulties include uncoordinated sucking and swallowing movements coupled

(text continues on page 119)

Figure 2. Possible Facial Effects of Fetal Alcohol Syndrome.

Common Facial Features:

1) Mandibular deficiency
2) Flat midface
3) Eyes: Short palpebral fissure
4) Mouth: Poorly developed philtrum and thin upper vermilion

Possible Facial Features:

Head: Microcephaly
Eyes: Epicanthal folds
      Hypertelorism
      Ptosis
      Blepharophimosis
Nose: Short, upturned
      Low nasal bridge
Ears: Low-set
      Poorly formed conchae
      Abnormal pinna
      Posterior rotation

Figure 3. Possible Effects of Fetal Alcohol Syndrome.

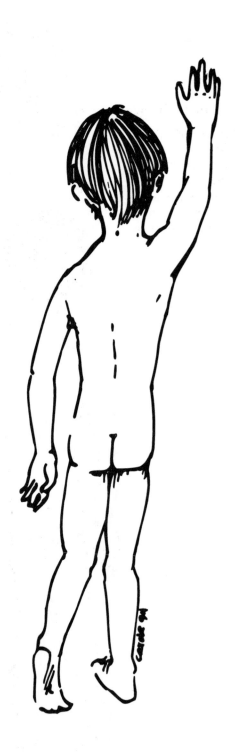

Cardiac defects

Skeletal anomalies

Organ damage

Genital anomalies

Hearing deficiencies

Growth deficiencies

Central nervous system
    abnormalities

Motor and mental delays

Behavioral problems

with thrusting of the tongue and decreased endurance. During the first year of life, a single feeding can possibly take as long as two hours (Weiner & Morse 1991). Another characteristic of FAS in early infancy is poor habituation to repetitive stimulation, which means it takes these infants longer to become accustomed to and stop overresponding to external stimulation (LaDue 1993).

There is a definite correlation between maternal alcohol use during pregnancy and an infant's mental and motor development. A study by Golden and coworkers (1982) shows Bayley Motor and Mental Development scores to be significantly lower in infants with heavy prenatal exposure to alcohol. Retardation tends to be more severe and the possibility for improvement decreased in those infants who have severe dysmorphology and very low birth weights (Weiner & Morse 1988).

Excessive use of alcohol interferes with growth throughout the pregnancy. Brain growth and organization of the central nervous system are particularly disrupted by alcohol in the third trimester. Though frequently not evident at birth, developmental delays become apparent when milestones are not reached at the expected time (Weiner & Morse 1991).

One study reported motor concerns in several infants, between four and eight months of age, whose mothers used alcohol during pregnancy. The concerns cited included low tone of the trunk and extremities, persistence of primitive reflexes, tremulousness, delays in development of head control, and delays in fine and gross motor skills (Harris et al 1993).

ADDITIONAL INFORMATION

In addition to growth, facial, and central nervous system anomalies, a number of other major and minor congenital defects are associated with FAS. Heart defects and skeletal problems are frequently observed at birth. Giunta and Streissguth (1988) report approximately one-third of the population with FAS has congenital heart defects. Atrial and ventricular septal defects, tetralogy of Fallot, and patent ductus arteriosus are some of the heart anomalies that can occur (Weiner & Morse 1988).

The following are listed by Jones (1986) as possible skeletal anomalies: joint alterations including camptodactyly (permanent flexion of fingers or toes), congenital hip dislocations, flexion contractures at elbows, cervical spine abnormalities, tapering terminal phalanges with hypoplastic fingernails and toenails (defective development), radioulnar synostosis (union of radius and ulna), foot positional defects, and altered palmar crease pattern. Jones links many of the skeletal defects to the effect of alcohol on brain development. Normal joint development depends on fetal activity, and when normal activity is decreased, contracture of joints can occur. Similarly, altered palmar crease patterns occur due to decreased fetal hand movement, which, again, is secondary to the effect of alcohol on early development of the brain.

The list of anomalies associated with prenatal alcohol exposure is extensive. As with other teratogens, every organ system is vulnerable to damage. The severity and chronicity of the mother's drinking, the gestational age at time of exposure, and genetic susceptibility all play a part in determining the extent of occurring anomalies (Weiner & Morse 1991). Other factors which may contribute to the abnormal development of the alcohol-exposed fetus are poor maternal diet, low socioeconomic status, and drugs such as diazepam, caffeine, and nicotine (Chasnoff 1986).

Child

FACIAL ANOMALIES

As the child grows, some of the facial anomalies of FAS can become less distinctive. A study was done of children with FAS to determine if there was an association between hearing disorders and prenatal alcohol exposure. High incidences of both recurrent serous otitis media and bilateral sensorineural hearing loss were observed. The researchers believed the results of the study made good theoretical sense, because hearing disorders have been commonly associated with craniofacial anomalies (Church & Gerkin 1988).

GROWTH DEFICIENCY

In a 1978 article by Clarren and Smith, they report having observed decreased adipose tissue as a nearly constant feature of children with FAS. Weiner and Morse (1991) find children with FAS often remain short and skinny in comparison to other children, though thyroid tests, bone scans, and nutritional assessments are normal.

CENTRAL NERVOUS SYSTEM ABNORMALITIES

Developmental delays and neurobehavioral disorders become increasingly apparent during early childhood and when the child with FAS enters school or other learning and social situations. As in infancy, CNS damage related to fetal alcohol exposure manifests itself during childhood in a variety of ways and degrees of severity.

In a study by Barr and associates (1990), both gross and fine motor development were negatively affected in children four years of age whose mothers drank moderate amounts of alcohol during pregnancy. These 457 children tested had difficulty with balance and their fine motor skills were slower and less accurate.

Research by Weiner and Morse (1990) shows childhood cognitive function can be impaired and, consequently, difficult to accurately assess because of hyperactivity, poor attention span, and processing and perceptual problems. Hyperactivity is the most persistent symptom and greatest inhibitor to school performance. Language delays (expressive being more proficient than receptive), memory deficits, and an inability to follow directions or complete tasks are also characteristic of children with FAS.

In a more recent article, Weiner and Morse (1991) report average IQ scores of children with FAS as being between 70 and 89. Some children may have an IQ above 115, but their development is impaired by neurobehavioral disorders due to brain damage. Children with FAS, regardless of IQ ability, have difficulty picking up cues that allow generalization of information from one situation to another. These children are also reported to be socially inappropriate, unresponsive to subtle social cues, unable to consider the consequences of their actions, excessively friendly, fearless, and to have poor judgment. Often they lack impulse control and have poor response inhibition. In addition, these children react strongly to smells, sound, and touch due to sensory integration deficits.

Adolescent and Adult

FACIAL ANOMALIES

Streissguth and associates (1991) report that abnormalities of the philtrum, lips, and palpebral fissures often remain useful diagnostic features in the adolescent and adult with FAS. However, as the child with FAS grows into an adolescent and adult, the facial phenotype of childhood changes. Four observable areas of facial change are (1) continued growth in the height of the nasal bridge and in nasal length from root to tip, (2) continued growth in the midfacial region, which corrects the earlier midfacial flattened profile, (3) continued growth of the chin, and (4) improvement in the soft-tissue modeling of the philtrum and upper lip. In some adults it is necessary to obtain childhood photographs to confirm a diagnosis because the face has become so normalized.

GROWTH DEFICIENCY

Research by Streissguth and colleagues (1991) shows head circumference and height to be two standard deviations from the mean in adolescents and adults with FAS. The weight deficiency which is so typical earlier in childhood becomes less noticeable.

CENTRAL NERVOUS SYSTEM ABNORMALITIES

The following information on the long-term effect of fetal alcohol exposure on the central nervous system has been taken from the research of Streissguth and associates (1991) who conducted a systematic follow-up study on adolescents and adults with FAS. The sixty-one participants in the study ranged in age from 12 to 40 years. None of the patients was known to be independent in terms of income and housing.

Common behavior problems were attentional deficits, poor judgment and comprehension, and difficulty with abstractions.

Arithmetic skills were low, which the researchers believed reflected the participants' extreme difficulty with abstract concepts, for example: cause and effect, time and space, and generalization from one situation to another. The overall level of adaptive functioning was also low (around seven years on the Vineland Adaptive Behavior Scale). Often verbal skills masked disabilities.

The average academic functioning of the adolescents and adults with FAS studied was at the early grade-school level. The mean IQ was 66, and none of the patients studied was age-appropriate in terms of socialization and communication skills. Failure to take into consideration consequences of actions, lack of reciprocal friendships, lack of appropriate initiative, and unresponsiveness to subtle social cues were typical problems of even those participants whose IQ scores fell within the normal range.

The most frequently noted maladaptive behaviors were poor attention and concentration, social withdrawal, stubbornness or sulkiness, crying or laughing too easily, teasing or intimidating, periods of anxiety, dependency, and impulsiveness. Maladaptive behaviors were singled out as presenting the greatest challenge to treatment.

Though much more long-term research needs to be done, it is evident that FAS is not a disorder of infancy and childhood alone. Gestational exposure to alcohol in utero can cause physical, mental, and behavioral disabilities which are lifelong and difficult to treat.

Characteristics of Fetal Alcohol Effects

A large number of children affected by alcohol in utero do not meet the criteria for a diagnosis of FAS but have many of the same problems and needs. The term fetal alcohol effects (FAE) is used when referring to this population of children. Some professionals prefer the term alcohol-related birth defects (ARBD).

Fetal alcohol effects is difficult to diagnose at birth. Some neonates born to women who are heavy drinkers demonstrate functional disturbances, such as problems with sleep-wake regulation, but there are no observable morphologic anomalies (Rosett, Weiner & Edelin 1981). The effects of prenatal exposure to alcohol can be very subtle during the child's early years, then emerge as real-life problems during the early school years.

Havey (1991) describes children with FAE as often marginally retarded, hyperactive, difficult to discipline, emotionally unstable, and they may demonstrate problems with motor skills. Children with FAE tend not to learn from experience, whether it be skills like learning multiplication tables and how to tell time, or in a behavioral situation. Inappropriate behaviors are continually repeated, even though they have been cautioned about them in the past. In school, children with FAE demonstrate poor memory skills, short attention spans, lower IQs, and behavioral problems. The behaviors and disabilities are a reflection of central nervous system damage and, therefore, are difficult to remediate.

A long-term prospective study was done on the development of a group of basically normal children who had a history of moderate prenatal alcohol exposure. Subtle alcohol-related neurobehavioral deficits were observed between birth and seven years of age. At the age of seven years these children showed difficulty in mastering academic skills and demonstrated the need for special programming (Streissguth, Barr & Sampson 1990).

Research is scarce regarding the effects of mild to moderate intake of alcohol on the developing fetus. Great numbers of children, adolescents, and adults do not meet the criteria for the full fetal alcohol syndrome. However, they and their families face enormous problems and are in need of a number of medical, educational, and social services.

As there is no determined safe amount of alcohol a pregnant woman can drink and still be assured that her baby is not going to be affected, it is advisable that a woman abstain from the use of any amount of alcohol during her pregnancy. A woman attempting to become pregnant also should stop the use of alcohol or postpone becoming pregnant until an existing alcohol problem is controlled.

Identification and Intervention

It is crucial that nurses and other health professionals be knowledgeable about the effects of prenatal alcohol abuse. Additionally, a systematic approach for recognizing the problem and providing services must be developed (Leonard, Boettcher & Brust 1991)

Russell and Skinner (1988) stress the importance of identifying harmful drinking patterns as early as possible, because a woman who drinks heavily will very likely practice the same drinking habits during a pregnancy. This is particularly true early in the first trimester before conception is known.

Often intervention is not possible prior to pregnancy, and Rosett, Weiner, and Edelin (1981) report that the obstetrician's office and prenatal clinic become the potential site for recognition of a drinking problem. Health professionals working with pregnant women need to adopt new attitudes toward women who drink and rid themselves of traditional pessimism regarding treatment of alcoholics. Rosett and colleagues believe that pregnancy is a time when most women become concerned about their own bodies and the well-being of their unborn children. Strong feelings of responsibility for their babies motivate these women to deal with their drinking problem.

Rosett, Weiner, and Edelin (1981) caution that the problem drinker cannot be identified by appearance or socioeconomic characteristics, and a systematic drinking history is essential when taking the initial prenatal history. The Ten-Question Drinking History (TQDH)

used at the Boston City Hospital prenatal clinic is a recommended brief means of determining heavy drinking patterns. This tool takes less than five minutes to administer when the respondent is not drinking at a risk level. The TQDH provides information about the frequency, quantity, and variability of the use of beer, wine, and liquor and is a good method for beginning a dialogue between nurse and patient (Figure 4).

Weiner and Morse (1988) also recommend a drinking history be part of every initial prenatal evaluation. Alcohol, they write, has the capacity to affect each stage of fetal development, and the earlier in the pregnancy heavy drinking ceases, the greater the potential for improved outcome. Abnormalities and growth retardation that develop in later stages are prevented. Weiner and Morse support the use of the TQDH and believe most patients respond honestly if the questions are asked in a direct, nonjudgmental fashion, and are preceded by simple introductory statements which reassure the pregnant woman that

Figure 4. Ten-Question Drinking History (TQDH)

Beer: How many times per week _____

How many cans/bottles each time _____

Ever drink more? _____

Wine: How many times per week _____

How many glasses each time _____

Ever drink more?_____

Liquor: How many times per week _____

How many drinks each time _____

Ever drink more?_____

Has your drinking habit changed during the past year?

Developed by Henry Rosett, M.D. and Lyn Weiner, M.P.H.
Taken, with permission, from Rosett H, Weiner L, Edelin KC. Strategies for prevention of fetal alcohol effects. *Obstetrics and Gynecology* 1981; 57: 1-7.

she is being asked the questions as part of an effort to improve the outcome of the pregnancy.

Another brief and easy method of identifying pregnant women who are heavy drinkers is the T-ACE screen. Risk-drinkers in this screening are defined as those who drink more than one ounce of absolute alcohol per day, which is the equivalent of two standard drinks. The key feature of the screening is the question regarding tolerance (T). To determine the woman's tolerance to alcohol, she is asked how many drinks it takes to feel high (tolerance increases with drinking). Researchers believe that the woman who wants to minimize the extent of her problem is less likely to perceive the question as a means of determining her drinking habits and is more apt to answer honestly. The three remaining questions ascertain if the woman is annoyed (A) when people criticize her drinking, if she has felt she should cut down on her drinking (C), and if she ever has a drink first thing in the morning to steady her nerves or get rid of a hangover (Eye opener, or E). The screening requires less than a minute and is appropriate for routine use in the office of the obstetrician-gynecologist and the prenatal clinic (Sokol, Martier & Ager 1989).

As soon as a drinking problem is identified in a pregnant woman, supportive counseling needs to be initiated, and therapy directed toward attaining and sustaining abstinence (Weiner, Rosett & Mason 1985). When encouraging the mother to seek counseling regarding her use of alcohol, the nurse should use a positive and tactful approach. Weiner and Morse (1988) find women respond positively to a hopeful message of po-

tential benefits from reduction of drinking, and provocation of guilt and self-criticism may lead to the consumption of increased amounts of alcohol. They suggest accentuating the positive and avoiding the negative. For example, one might say, "You have a better chance of having a healthy baby if you stop drinking," rather than "Your baby has already been damaged by your drinking."

Eliason and Williams (1990) have observed that in many cases a mother's alcohol abuse is not identified prenatally, and nurses working with neonates are seen as having the added responsibility of identifying infants affected by alcohol. A thorough prenatal history is necessary if maternal alcohol abuse is to be identified and an accurate diagnosis made. Early identification of FAS can lead to better utilization of medical and educational resources, and it also provides an opportunity for parent education to prevent future siblings from being affected.

Eliason and Williams (1990) emphasize the purpose of gathering a history is not to place blame on the mother for her actions during pregnancy. The focus should be on acquiring information needed to understand the child's problems and obtain appropriate treatment and resources. They suggest questions be asked in a nonjudgmental and sensitive manner, and the history include information on (1) when alcohol was consumed, (2) how much alcohol was consumed, and (3) what kind of alcohol was used. They recommend that the nurse start with nonthreatening questions such as the use of prescription medication when pregnant or questions regarding illnesses during the pregnancy. When interviewing a parent regarding amounts of alcohol used, Eliason and Williams recommend suggesting an amount that seems high, such as, "Did you drink a bottle of wine a day?" The mother should also be asked if she recalls specific times, such as during a celebration or crisis, when she consumed more alcohol than usual.

When a neonate with FAS has been identified, the nursing role expands. Nursing responsibilities, according to Eliason and Williams (1990), include planning for discharge and continuity of care for the infant and family. Assessment of nutrition, parenting skills and needs, and feeding practices are also part of nursing activities. Close monitoring of the home environment is particularly important. Giunta and Streissguth (1988) report children with FAS as being at a higher than average risk for physical abuse, sexual abuse, and neglect, because the mothers often are in a struggle for sobriety and have few resources and little support.

Earlier in the discussion a number of congenital anomalies were listed as associated with FAS, including heart defects, skeletal anomalies, sensorineural hearing losses, and central nervous system problems. Many of these anomalies present lifelong problems. Nurse practitioners, public health nurses, clinic nurses, school nurses, and other community-based nurses must frequently use their physical assessment skills to determine the health needs of the child with FAS. Community health nursing skills are then utilized to ensure these health needs are met through appropriate referral to physicians and other professionals or agencies.

In addition to the long-term physical problems, many psychosocial and emotional needs of the child with FAS must be addressed if optimal development is to be attained. A total assessment of the child and family by the nurse may indicate a referral is needed to one or several of the following resources: (1) public health department, (2) health clinic, (3) educational facility, (4) social service agency, (5) Child Protective Services, (6) Alcoholics Anonymous, (7) Women, Infants, and Children Program (WIC), (8) welfare department, (9) nutritionist, (10) parent support group, (11) parenting classes, (12) mental health, (13) physical and occupational therapy, (14) counseling. The list of community services and resources is long, and the nurse who is familiar with their functions and availability plays a crucial role in the lives of children with FAS and their families.

A referral for educational assessment should be discussed with the parent or care provider and initiated as soon as possible. Special education services are mandated in the United States for children 3 to 5 years of age. In addition, many states offer programs for infants 0 to 3 years with special needs. These infant and preschool programs provide structured and individualized services in a supportive environment. A nurse is part of the multidisciplinary team which plans and implements the child's program, following up with the infant/preschooler's developmental progress, health, and home environment. Parents receive education and support and work with the team in planning their child's educational program. Because of these early intervention services, many children exposed to alcohol in utero are able to attend and fully participate in regular school programs with little or no additional support services.

Conclusion

Prenatal alcohol exposure resulting in fetal alcohol syndrome is now identified as the leading known cause of mental retardation in the United States (Abel & Sokol 1987) and one which is totally preventable. Alcohol use by a pregnant woman can cause her newborn to have physical, mental, and behavioral disabilities which persist into adulthood. Occasionally a child with prenatal alcohol exposure may have an IQ which falls within the normal range; however, behaviors such as lack of response to subtle social cues, failure to take into account the consequences of actions, lack of self-initiated activity, and inability to develop reciprocal friendships hinder the development of age-appropriate living and social skills (Streissguth et al 1991). The wide spectrum of disabilities can create obstacles to employment, positive relationships, independence, and quality of life.

Early identification and intervention is vital for the child with alcohol-related disabilities to attain optimal growth and development. Furthermore, the intervention needs to be delivered within the context of the child's family, culture, and community.

REFERENCES

Abel EL. *Fetal Alcohol Syndrome and Fetal Alcohol Effects.* New York: Plenum Press, 1984.

Abel EL, Sokol RJ. Incidence of fetal alcohol syndrome and economic impact of FAS-related anomalies. *Drug Alcohol Dependency* 1987; 19:51-70.

Barr H, Streissguth A, Darby B, Sampson P. Prenatal exposure to alcohol, caffeine, tobacco, and aspirin: Effects on fine and gross motor performance in 4-year-old children. *Developmental Psychology* 1990; 26:339-48.

Birth Defects and Developmental Disabilities. Program summary Atlanta: National Center for Environmental Health, 1992, pp. 57-61.

Chasnoff IJ. *Drug Use in Pregnancy: Mother and Child.* Boston: MTP Press, 1986.

Chavez GF, Cordero JF, Becerra JE. Leading major congenital malformations among minority groups in the United States, 1981-1986. *Morbidity Mortality Weekly Report* 1988; 37 (SS3).

Church MW, Gerkin KP. Hearing disorders in children with fetal alcohol syndrome: Findings from case reports. *Pediatrics* 1988; 82:147-53.

Clarren SK, Smith DW. The fetal alcohol syndrome. *New England Journal of Medicine* 1978; 298: 1063-7.

Day NL, Jasperse D, Richardson G, Robles N, Sambamoorthi U, Taylor P, Scher M, Stoffer D, Cornelius M. Prenatal exposure to alcohol: Effect on infant growth and morphologic characteristics. *Pediatrics* 1989; 84: 536-41.

Dunn PM, et al. Metronidazole and the fetal alcohol syndrome. *Lancet* 1979; 2:144.

Eliason MJ, Williams JK. Fetal alcohol syndrome and the neonate. *Journal of Perinatal and Neonatal Nursing* 1990; 3(4): 64-72.

Giunta CT, Streissguth AP. Patients with fetal alcohol syndrome and their caretakers. *Social Casework: Journal of Contemporary Social Work* 1988; (Sept):453-9.

Golden NL, Sokol RJ, Kuhnert BR, Bottoms S. Maternal alcohol use and infant development. *Pediatrics* 1982; 70: 931-4.

Goodman RM, Gorlin RJ. *Malformed Infant and Child: An Illustrated Guide.* New York: Oxford University Press, 1983.

Hanson JW, Streissguth AP, Smith DW. The effects of moderate alcohol consumption during pregnancy on fetal growth and morphogenesis. *Pediatrics* 1978; 92: 457-60.

Harris SR, Osborn JA, Weinberg J, Loock C, Junaid K. Effects of prenatal alcohol exposure on neuromotor and cognitive development during early childhood: A series of case reports. *Physical Therapy* 1993; 73: 608-17.

Havey EA. Fetal alcohol syndrome. *Pediatrics for Parents* 1991; (Jul-Aug): 6.

Healthy People 2000. Washington, D.C.: U.S. Government Printing Office, 1990 (DHHS publication No. PHS91-50213).

Jones KL. Fetal alcohol syndrome. *Pediatrics* 1986; 8:122-6.

Jones KL, Smith DW. Recognition of the fetal alcohol syndrome in early infancy. *Lancet* 1973; 2:999-1001.

Jones KL, Smith DW, Ulleland CW, Streissguth AP. Pattern of malformation of chronic alcoholic mothers. *Lancet* 1973; 1(7814): 1267-71.

Ladewig PW, London ML, Olds SB. *Essentials of Maternal Newborn Nursing* 2nd ed. Menlo Park, CA: Addison-Wesley Nursing, 1990.

LaDue RA. Psychosocial needs associated with fetal alcohol syndrome and fetal alcohol effects. Seattle: University of Washington, School of Medicine, Department of Psychiatry and Behavioral Science, Fetal Alcohol and Drug Unit, 1993, February 4.

Landesman-Dwyer S, Keller LS, Streissguth AP. Naturalistic observations of newborns: Effects of maternal alcohol intake. *Alcoholism: Clinical and Experimental Research* 1978; 2:171-7.

Leonard BJ, Boettcher LM, Dwyer Brust J. Alcohol-related birth defects. *Minnesota Medicine* 1991; 74: 23-5.

Martin L M. Possible state approaches to surveillance for fetal alcohol syndrome. Prepared for the Maternal Infant Child Health Program (MICHP) Data Analysis Tracking Approaches (DATA) Conference. Atlanta, Georgia, Jan. 6-8, 1992.

O'Connor MJ, Brill NJ, Sigman M. Alcohol use in primiparous women older than 30 years of age: Relation to infant development. *Pediatrics* 1986; 78: 444-50.

Rosett H, Weiner L, Edelin KC. Strategies for prevention of fetal alcohol effects. *Obstetrics and Gynecology* 1981; 57: 1-7.

Russell M, Skinner JB. Early measures of maternal alcohol misuse as predictors of adverse pregnancy outcomes. *Alcoholism: Clinical and Experimental Research* 1988; 12: 824-30.

Sippel HW, Kesaniemi YA. Placental and foetal metabolism of acetaldehyde in the rat. II. Studies on metabolism of acetaldehyde in the isolated placenta and foetus. *Acta Pharmacologia et Toxicologica* 1975; 37: 49-55.

Sokol R. Alcohol and abnormal outcomes of pregnancy. *Canadian Medical Association Journal* 1981;125:143-8.

Sokol RJ, Abel EL. Risk factors for alcohol-related birth defects: Thresholds, susceptibility, and prevention. In Sonderegger TB, ed. *Perinatal Substance Abuse* Baltimore: Johns Hopkins University Press, 1992, pp. 90-104.

Sokol RJ, Martier SS, Ager JW. The T-ACE questions: Practical prenatal detection of risk-drinking. *American Journal of Obstetrics and Gynecology* 1989; (April): 863-8.

Staisey NL, Fried PA. Relationships between moderate maternal alcohol consumption during pregnancy and infant neurological development. *Journal of Studies on Alcohol* 1982; 44: 262-9.

Streissguth AP, Aase JM, Clarren SR, Randels SP, LaDue RA, Smith DF. Fetal alcohol syndrome in adolescents and adults. *Journal of the American Medical Association* 1991; 265: 1961-7.

Streissguth AP, Barr HM, Sampson PD. Moderate prenatal alcohol exposure: Effects on child I.Q. and learning problems at age 7 1/2 years. *Alcoholism: Clinical and Experimental Research* 1990; 14:662-9.

Tranmer JE. Disposition of ethanol in maternal venous blood and the amniotic fluid. *Journal of Obstetric, Gynecologic, and Neonatal Nursing* 1985;14(6): 484-90.

Weiner L, Rosett HL, Mason EA. Training professionals to identify and treat pregnant women who drink heavily. *Alcohol Health and Research World 1985; (Fall): 32-6.*

Weiner L, Morse BA. Recommended interventions for fetal-alcohol syndrome children. *Brown University Child Behavior and Development Letter* 1990;1(2): 6.

Weiner L, Morse BA. Facilitating development for children with fetal alcohol syndrome. *Brown University Child and Ado-*

lescent Behavior Letter (Special Supplement) 1991; S1(4): 7.

Weiner L, Morse BA. FAS: Clinical perspectives and prevention. In Chasnoff IJ, ed. *Drugs, Alcohol, Pregnancy, and Parenting*. Hingham, MA: Kluwer Academic Publishers, 1988, 127-48.

Zuckerman B. Drug-exposed infants: Understanding the medical risk. *Future of Children* 1991; 1(1): 26-35 (Available from the Center for the Future of Children, David and Lucille Packard Foundation, Los Altos, California).

ANNOTATED BIBLIOGRAPHY

Eliason MJ, Williams JK. Fetal alcohol syndrome and the neonate. *Journal of Perinatal and Neonatal Nursing* **1990; 3 (4): 64-72.**
This article provides a summary of the effects of prenatal alcohol exposure on the developing embryo and fetus. Also included is a discussion on the amount and timing of alcohol use during pregnancy and the relationship to fetal damage. Identification and management of infants affected by prenatal use of alcohol are viewed as a crucial role for nurses.

Harvey EA. Fetal alcohol syndrome. *Pediatrics for Parents* **1991; (July-August):6.**
The harmful effect of alcohol on the developing fetus is stressed in this article. Recommendations are made for complete abstinence from alcohol during pregnancy. Characteristics are given of children who have fetal alcohol syndrome (FAS) and those who have fetal alcohol effects (FAE).

Streissguth AP, Aase JM, Clarren SR, Randels SP, La Due RA, Smith DF. Fetal alcohol syndrome in adolescents and adults. *Journal of the American Medical Association* **1991; 265: 1961-7.**
This article discusses one of the first systematic follow-up studies which examines adolescent and adult manifestations of FAS. Results of this research show FAS to have a long-term progression into adulthood. Some of the long-term societal implications of the disorder are discussed.

Weiner L, Morse BA. Facilitating development for children with fetal alcohol syndrome. *Brown University Child and Adolescent Behavior Letter* **(Special Supplement) 1991; S1(4):7.**
An overview of FAS in infants and children is presented. Several manifestations, i.e., sleep disturbances, and their effect on caregiver-infant interaction are discussed and intervention strategies are provided. Other sections address neurobehavioral disorders associated with FAS and the affected child's variation in learning ability. Results of studies on the long-term prognosis are given, and the importance of early intervention using a family approach.

6

Physical Health Concerns of the Infant and Child with Prenatal Alcohol and Drug Exposure

Barbara Bennett, M.D.
Keeta DeStefano Lewis, R.N., P.H.N., M.S.N.
Helen Bosson Thomson, R.N., B.S.N., P.H.N.

Infants and young children prenatally exposed to legal or illegal drugs represent an emerging population who may have numerous physical health needs which challenge the nurse, the physician, and the educator. The conditions and concerns discussed in this chapter may occur prenatally, perinatally, or postnatally and may leave significant neurologic, developmental, or sensory deficits requiring special treatment or early intervention services. This chapter presents the current knowledge base about the physical health care needs of these infants and children.

Drug addiction or use during pregnancy is a major medical, societal, and economic concern. Drugs readily pass through the placenta and can directly and indirectly affect the fetus. The ensuing health issues are both complex and interwoven.

It is known that use of drugs by the mother can have a harmful effect on the fetus. However, the exact dosage necessary to cause problems is still unclear. Other factors also play a significant role in the potential for fetal damage, such as gestational age when exposure to the drug occurred, the type of drug taken, and the susceptibility of the mother and fetus to the drug.

In addition to drug use during pregnancy, maternal lifestyle and behaviors can contribute to health problems for the mother which may inadvertently affect the fetus, and ultimately the infant and child. Pregnant women who are chemically dependent are often homeless, without a spouse or support system, and physically abused and use their resources and energy to obtain drugs rather than to care for their unborn child. Furthermore, their diet is likely to be of little nutritional value and there may be no or very little prenatal care.

Studies are in progress to more clearly delineate the possibility of an association between paternal drug use and the health outcome of the fetus. One study demonstrates the binding of cocaine to human spermatozoa. Thus a new concept emerges implying the possibility of preimplantation embryopathy, which suggests that cocaine use by fathers may lead to damage of the embryo (Yazigi, Odem & Polakoski 1991).

The neonate with prenatal drug exposure is at high risk for one or more medical conditions, some of which occur in neonates who are non-drug-exposed. Not all neonates prenatally drug exposed manifest the same problems or degree of severity. Certain conditions/symptoms exhibited by the neonate are often associated with particular drugs; however, the polydrug abuse that is now common clouds the known specific effects of a particular drug on the neonate.

This chapter addresses medical and health aspects of prenatal drug exposure as they relate to the fetus, newborn, infant, and young child. Only conditions and concerns more commonly associated with prenatal drug exposure are addressed.

Pregnancy and Birth Complications

Adequate prenatal care is one of the most specific predictors of positive maternal and neonatal outcome. Women who are chemically dependent often do not seek prenatal care or they have infrequent visits to the physician or nurse practitioner. There are many reasons for this, including fear of a punitive approach, rather than the treatment approach, as practiced in many segments of society. In addition, the woman with chemical dependency may be so consumed by the need for drugs that little attention is given to her health needs or the health needs of her unborn baby.

The pregnant woman who is chemically dependent, particularly one without adequate prenatal care, is prone to the following health concerns: anemia, mineral and vitamin deficiency, and infections which include HIV, sexually transmitted diseases, hepatitis, and tuberculosis. These concerns are frequently the result of poor nutrition, unprotected sex, multiple sex partners, and use of dirty needles during drug use. Many obstetrical complications related to the use of drugs can occur and include: abruptio placentae, preeclampsia, placental insufficiency, infections, and premature labor and delivery. All of these maternal complications can negatively affect the fetus and neonate and reduce the infant's opportunity for optimal growth and development.

Prematurity

Prematurity and its many related health issues is a major concern with infants who are prenatally drug exposed. Neonates with prenatal drug exposure to cocaine and methamphetamines have a high incidence of preterm delivery (Dixon 1989). Additional studies site maternal use of cocaine associated with preterm birth (Chasnoff et al 1989; Cherukuri et al 1988; Christmas 1992). However, studies associating particular drugs with prematurity are inconsistent (Hadeed & Siegel 1989; Richardson & Day 1991). This may be due in part to the fact that some women who use drugs or have a history of drug abuse receive good prenatal care and nutritional counseling during pregnancy, are in a managed recovery program, or are receiving other support.

With current medical technology newborns are now surviving at 24 to 26 weeks gestation. A large number of these preterm newborns are at an increased risk of having medical complications which can lead to long-term disabilities.

Respiratory distress syndrome (RDS) is a leading cause of death among premature infants, whether or not they are exposed to drugs in utero. Infants with this syndrome are not yet producing a naturally occurring crucial lubricant, surfactant, which gives the lungs the elasticity needed to expand and not collapse when the infant exhales ("The tiniest" 1990; "More help" 1990). Mechanical ventilators can be used to deliver high pressure oxygen to the infant's lungs. The infants that survive may have severe complications, including blindness, cerebral palsy, retardation, and permanent lung damage ("The tiniest" 1990). Exogenous surfactant can now be given to premature infants to decrease their problems with this condition, as well as perhaps to decrease problems with bronchopulmonary dysplasia (BPD). Bronchopulmonary dysplasia is a complication of prematurity and can be a long-term lung condition. It is a result of damage to the alveolar epithelium secondary to oxygen toxicity, ventilator pressures, and lung immaturity (Bernbaum & D'Agostino 1986).

A premature infant may experience patent ductus arteriosus (PDA). In PDA there is persistence of a blood vessel in the heart between the pulmonary artery and aorta which normally contracts and its lumen is obliterated 10 to 15 hours after birth (Mott, Fazekas & James 1985). This can be treated with medication (indomethacin) or sometimes surgery is indicated.

Prematurity predisposes the newborn to many types of infections because of decreased immunity. Gastrointestinal problems include necrotizing enterocolitis (NEC) where portions of the bowel are damaged due to decreased blood flow secondary to shock or prolonged hypoxia (Ladewig, London & Olds 1990). Additionally, intraventricular hemorrhages can cause neurologic manifestations in the premature newborn and a shunt may need placement for hydrocephaly. Apnea, bradycardia, retinopathy of prematurity (ROP), anemia, difficulty maintaining body temperature, hearing impairment, and feeding problems add to the wide spectrum of difficulties associated with prematurity.

Intrauterine Growth Retardation

Intrauterine growth retardation (IUGR) is a relatively common finding for infants who are exposed to drugs in utero (Chasnoff et al 1989; Hadeed & Siegel 1989; Oro & Dixon 1987; Zuckerman 1991). The etiology of this problem is multifactorial. Inadequate maternal nutrition and decreased utero placental blood supply are associated with IUGR and poor fetal development. Drugs such as cocaine have anorectic effects on the user and can contribute to inadequate maternal nutrition. Cocaine and marijuana are known to cause sudden hypertension and cardiac arrhythmias and induce uterine vasoconstriction, all of which can interrupt the maternal fetal blood supply to various fetal tissue, thereby potentiating fetal hypoxia (Woods, Plessinger & Clark 1987) and inadequate nutritional supply. In addition, moderate to heavy use of nicotine during pregnancy is known to increase the risk for IUGR (Naeye 1981).

Intrauterine growth retardation is occasionally used as a descriptive term for the small-for-gestational-age (SGA) infant. The acronyms IUGR and SGA are not totally synonymous, but both terms include assessment of size and maturity. Intrauterine growth retardation is a reflection of poor fetal growth. With a diagnosis of IUGR the fetus is noted to

ceiling or decrease in growth pattern or to be smaller in size when compared to the population norm (Allen 1992). Generally SGA can be defined as an infant with a slowed rate of intrauterine growth and whose birth weight is below the tenth percentile on intrauterine growth charts (Whaley & Wong 1991) for a given gestational age. Both IUGR and SGA are of grave concern, since low birth weight (LBW) is a primary factor associated with infant mortality in the United States (Zuckerman 1991). Low birth weight is defined as an infant whose birth weight is less than 2,500 grams (5 pounds).

Intrauterine growth retardation is an indicator that an abnormality or insult to the fetus occurred. The insult can cause damage to various organ systems. Damage to the central nervous system (CNS) can be particularly devastating because it can lead to long-term problems such as mental retardation, developmental disabilities, hearing and vision impairment, speech and language difficulties, hyperactivity, and attention deficit disorder (Allen 1992). A wide range of developmental disabilities are related to IUGR, but it is unclear which one may affect the infant/child with prenatal drug exposure, as these studies are not available. Long- and short-term infant developmental outcome is related to the etiology and timing of the insult and associated perinatal complications.

Close pediatric follow-up of these infants is recommended. Parents can be counseled as to the cause of the growth retardation as well as the significance and the prognosis as it relates to their child. Developmental evaluation and assessment can be arranged prior to discharge from the hospital (Allen 1992).

Neonatal Abstinence Syndrome

Neonatal abstinence syndrome (NAS) is the term generally used to indicate withdrawal from opiates such as heroin and methadone. Dependence develops in the fetus much like in the mother. The neonate passively addicted to opiates in utero may display signs of withdrawal shortly after birth and up to two weeks of age. Usually symptoms appear within seventy-two hours. Onset is influenced by a number of factors, including type and dosage of the drug used by the mother, timing of the drug in relationship to delivery, fetal maturity, maternal nutrition during pregnancy, and whether the neonate has an intrinsic disease (Chasnoff 1988).

Symptoms of NAS can persist for a few weeks with some residual symptoms lasting for months. There may be some withdrawal symptoms in infants who are non-opiate exposed, but these are not as striking in their appearance as those who are opiate-exposed when observed in the nursery. There is a question as to whether these are neurobehavioral changes rather than withdrawal (Zuckerman & Bresnahan 1991). Neonatal abstinence syndrome consists of physiologic symptoms such as sweating, stuffy nose, diarrhea, and vomiting. Behaviorally, infants are irritable, jittery, overstimulated easily, and difficult to console. Finnegan (1986) developed the NAS scale to identify withdrawal of the neonate and to monitor the progress and effectiveness of treatment.

Supportive measures such as swaddling, small feedings, and a pacifier make up the primary treatment of NAS. Pharmacologic intervention is used in some centers for those infants who have long-lasting or severe symptoms. The most commonly used drugs for neonate withdrawal from narcotics are paregoric, diazepam, and phenobarbital (Chasnoff 1986). Paregoric is considered by many to be the drug of choice for neonates exhibiting symptoms attributable only to narcotics and who require pharmacologic treatment. Infants treated with paregoric have better sucking response than those treated with phenobarbital or diazepam (Kron et al 1976). If pharmacotherapy is used, it should be gradually titrated and carefully controlled.

Congenital and Neonatal Infections

Neonates born to women who use drugs are at risk for certain congenital and neonatal infections. Infections particularly associated with maternal drug abuse are syphilis, cytomegalovirus, chlamydia, human immunodeficiency virus (HIV), herpes, and hepatitis B, C, and D. These conditions are prevalent among women who are chemically dependent for two primary reasons: 1) they may use dirty needles to inject drugs, and 2) persons who are involved in the use of drugs often exchange sex for drugs or money. The high-risk behavior which increases the number of sexual encounters and partners places the woman and fetus at risk for sexually transmitted diseases (STD) and congenital infections, including HIV and syphilis.

Syphilis

The one sexually transmitted disease that is closely linked to behavioral practices of drug users is syphilis. Syphilis is caused by the spirochete *Treponema pallidum*. Congenital syphilis is acquired transplacentally.

In 1993 there were 1,493 reported

cases of congenital syphilis (age below one year) in the United States (Centers for Disease Control 1994). At one point, congenital syphilis was almost unheard of but now is on the increase. Between the years 1980 and 1986 fewer than sixty cases of congenital syphilis were reported annually in New York City. In 1989 New York reported 1,017 cases of congenital syphilis. During the same period the number of women who were known to have used cocaine or crack during pregnancy increased dramatically (Greenberg et al 1991a). Similar increases in the number of syphilis cases were reported in Philadelphia. In that city the number of early syphilis cases increased 551 percent during the years 1985 through 1989. The increase was attributed to the use of crack cocaine and the exchange of drugs for sex (Centers for Disease Control 1991a).

The diagnosis of congenital syphilis can be difficult to make because a neonate may have no clinical signs and the mother may be undiagnosed. Accurate blood tests for syphilis are available, yet it is possible for an infected infant to slip by undetected. This can occur when an infected pregnant woman tests negative during initial testing and then becomes infected at a later date. Additionally, a newborn may be tested before antibodies to the syphilis pathogen have developed or a blood test at birth may not be included in routine hospital procedures (Centers for Disease Control 1991a).

A significant number of newborns with congenital syphilis will have no clinical symptoms (Centers for Disease Control 1988). The disease can escape detection until the infant is weeks or months old.

Clinical signs of syphilis during infancy vary and can include: a diffuse maculopapular skin rash with peeling of the skin on the palms of the hands and soles of the feet; rhinitis, which is mucopurulent or blood-tinged and highly infectious; swollen glands in the neck, axilla and groin; and pallor due to anemia. At times a newborn may have nonspecific findings of infection which can include: intrauterine growth retardation (IUGR), anemia, jaundice, hepatosplenomegaly, and thrombocytopenia (Williamson & Demmler 1992) and failure to thrive (Berkow & Fletcher 1992). The skeletal system may be affected, and malformations may occur (Emmett 1992). Syphilis can affect numerous organ systems in the body, and if left untreated extensive and permanent damage can occur (Centers for Disease Control 1991a; Emmett 1992; Williamson & Demmler 1992).

Later manifestations of congenital syphilis can occur. These include: bowing of the lower extremities (saber shins), a broadening of the bones in the nose (saddle nose), peg-shaped and notched upper central incisors (Hutchinson's teeth), interstitial keratitis, and deafness (Benenson 1990; Emmett 1992; Chow et al 1979).

Even with appropriate treatment after birth, a newborn with congenital syphilis can develop late manifestations secondary to inflammatory and hypersensitivity reactions. These manifestations include dental abnormalities (lower first molars and irregular shaped upper central incisors), clouding and inflammation of the cornea, and neural deafness (Williamson & Demmler 1992).

A neonate is at highest risk for having congenital syphilis if the mother experiences primary or secondary syphilis during pregnancy. Infants should be tested if their mothers have untreated syphilis or evidence of relapse or reinfection after treatment. Affected neonates are usually treated with appropriate antibiotic therapy and have ongoing serologic studies. Ophthalmologic, audiologic, neurodevelopmental, and early intervention assessments are also appropriate.

Cytomegalovirus

Cytomegalovirus (CMV) is a ubiquitous organism found throughout the world and is a member of the herpes virus family. Cytomegalovirus is transmitted through direct contact with urine, saliva, semen, blood, other body fluids, and transplanted organs. An infected pregnant woman can transmit the virus to the fetus transplacentally, connatally (during or shortly following delivery), and through breast milk. It is the most frequent cause of congenital infections in humans (Hanshaw, Dudgeon & Marshall 1985).

Congenital CMV disease is a serious viral infection among newborns in the United States—and the most common (Hanshaw, Dudgeon & Marshall 1985). Congenital infection with CMV occurs in approximately 40,000 newborns, or 1% of all births each year. About 3,000 to 4,000, or 10%, of these congenitally infected newborns have sufficient signs and symptoms to fit the case definition for congenital CMV disease. Of the newborns who were asymptomatic at birth, 4,000 to 6,000, or 10% to 15%, develop symptomatic problems in the first few months of life (Yow 1989).

Cytomegalovirus postnatal infections transmitted to the fetus from the mother may be either primary (first time infection) or secondary recurrent (reactiva-

tion of a previous infection). Congenitally infected newborns have a greater probability of being symptomatic at birth if the mother experiences primary CMV infection some time during pregnancy. Information is becoming available suggesting that infants without symptoms at birth, but who have long-term sequelae such as hearing loss, may be born to mothers who had either a primary or secondary CMV infection during pregnancy (Williamson et al 1991).

In the newborn the classic symptoms associated with congenital CMV infection include: petechiae, hepatomegaly, splenomegaly, jaundice, hemolytic anemia, intracranial calcifications, microcephaly, and chorioretinitis (Williamson & Demmler 1992). The newborn may also exhibit seizures, IUGR, low platelet count, elevated bilirubin level, and elevated alamine aminotransferase (ALT) (Dobbins, Stewart & Demmler 1991).

Almost all symptomatic newborns have some long-term neurologic, developmental, or audiologic sequelae (Williamson et al 1982). Mental retardation and sensorineural hearing loss are the two most frequent sequelae found and occur in half of all symptomatic infants with CMV (Williamson & Demmler 1992). The hearing loss can be progressive.

Treatment for congenital CMV infections includes both symptomatic and supportive measures. Experimental therapies with antiviral medications such as ganciclovir are being conducted for symptomatic infants at birth. No CMV vaccine is currently available for widespread use; however, clinical trials are in progress (Williamson & Demmler 1992).

The infant and young child with CMV both symptomatic and asymptomatic are at risk for developmental delays, language disorders secondary to the sensorineural hearing loss, learning disabilities, and mental retardation. Medical and educational assessments and follow-up are important throughout infancy, toddlerhood, and the school-age years for successful developmental experiences.

Herpes simplex

Another serious infection that affects infants with prenatal drug exposure is herpes simplex virus (HSV). Herpes simplex virus can be congenital; however, the majority of neonatal HSV infections are contracted during birth, and approximately 70% are due to HSV-type II (Arvin & Prober 1992). Herpes simplex type I is often thought of as oral herpes, the virus which causes cold sores, and type II is thought of as genital herpes. Both types can infect either the mouth or genital sites and both types can cause damage to the fetus. A high incidence of mortality and morbidity is associated with the virus.

A pregnant woman is more likely to infect her infant during birth if she is experiencing a primary HSV infection. Following an initial infection with HSV, the virus lies dormant and can be reactivated. In contrast to neonates infected during a primary maternal infection, those who contract HSV from a woman with a recurrent infection constitute a small percentage (Arvin & Prober 1992).

An acquired neonatal HSV infection manifests one to two weeks following birth, and may occur as late as the fourth week of life. The most recognized symptom of HSV is skin vesicles; however, in a large percentage of infected neonates these are not present. Other signs of neonatal infection are temperature instability, lethargy, respiratory difficulty (apnea or pneumonia), hypotonia, seizures, hepatitis, and disseminated intravascular coagulation. These symptoms may present alone or in combination (Berkow & Fletcher 1992).

Neonatal HSV infections are sometimes classified in one of three categories: (1) disseminated, (2) central nervous system, and (3) skin, eye, and mouth. In the disseminated form of the disease, symptoms are suggestive of severe bacterial sepsis and several organs are usually involved, including the liver, lungs, skin, brain, and adrenal glands. Specific manifestations reflect the organ affected. Fever, lethargy, seizures, apnea, and loss of rudimentary reflexes are common manifestations of central nervous system infections. With skin, eye, and mouth infections, skin lesions are usually on an erythematous base. These lesions evolve from macules to vesicles in one to two days. Conjunctivitis frequently occurs and occasionally the oral mucosa is involved. Of the three categories, the neonate with a disseminated infection has the highest probability of death occurring (Arvin & Prober 1992).

The neonate who acquires HSV in utero presents with more devastating manifestations than the one with an acquired infection. These manifestations include skin lesions and scars evident at birth, chorioretinitis, microcephaly, intracranial calcifications, microphthalmia (abnormally small eyes), and hydranencephaly (complete or almost complete absence of cerebral hemispheres) (Arvin & Prober 1992).

It is generally agreed that treatment for the HSV-infected neonate should be started as early as possible (Whitley et al 1991; Berkow & Fletcher 1992; Arvin & Prober 1992). Though not a cure, early therapy with vidarabine or acyclovir decreases neonate morbidity caused by HSV infection and may increase the number of neonates who develop normally (Berkow & Fletcher 1992). Infants exhibiting symptoms associated with delayed development will benefit from a discussion between the parent and health caregiver regarding early referral for developmental assessment and intervention.

HIV Seropositivity

Human immunodeficiency virus seropositivity is a major health concern for infants born to women who use drugs. Women who use drugs are more at risk for acquiring human immunodeficiency virus (HIV) due to their high-risk behavior. They may be partners of intravenous (IV) drug users, use IV drugs themselves, trade drugs for sex, and not practice safe sex.

The passage of HIV from mother to child may occur in utero, during childbirth, or as the result of breast-feeding (Goldfarb 1993). There is controversy as to when passage of the virus to the fetus actually occurs (Adeos, Newell & Peckham, 1991; Van de Perre et al 1991). A pregnant woman with HIV does not always pass the virus to her unborn infant. Some studies report maternal infant transmission rates ranging from 13% to 39% (Blanche et al 1989; Hutto et al 1991).

The Centers for Disease Control (CDC) has defined HIV/AIDS for children somewhat differently than for

adults. The CDC (1987) classification divides children into three groups:

PO - Indeterminate infection: Infants less than 15 months old whose HIV status is unknown.

Pl - Asymptomatic infection: Divided into three subclassifications according to immune system functioning.

P2 - Symptomatic HIV infection: Divided into six various subclassifications according to symptoms and/or clinical findings.

A surveillance definition for pediatric AIDS, identifying specific diagnoses as AIDS indicators, has been developed by the CDC (1987). Such indicators are similar to those in adults with the exception of lymphoid interstitial pneumonitis (LIP) and recurring multiple bacterial infections being applicable only to children less than thirteen years old.

There are usually no significant symptoms for the neonate with HIV seropositivity. Infants and children infected with HIV may remain healthy for long periods of time or they may become ill within months of birth. Unlike the adult, infants and children experience shorter lengths of incubation and shorter times between the symptomatic phase and death. Signs and symptoms of advanced infection develop in many infants in the first eighteen months of life (Connor 1991).

Early diagnosis of HIV infection in infants at risk is complicated by the presence of high maternal IGG anti HIV which is passively transferred to the fetus in utero. Also, identifying HIV in the blood mononuclear cells is difficult before eight weeks. In the past a diagnosis of HIV infection could not be made until the age of nineteen months; however, it is now possible to diagnosis HIV by the age of six months (Landesman et al 1991). A new approach to the diagnosis of HIV during infancy is the identification of serum IGA anti-HIV antibody which reflects an infant's own immune response to the virus. Early diagnosis still poses problems which include possible sequestration of the virus in the central nervous system. Additionally, the timing of transmission is important because in perinatal transmission the IGA antibody formation is delayed (Wara 1992).

Hepatitis

Hepatitis is another medical risk factor for infants who are born to mothers who use drugs. Hepatitis can be transmitted to the infant from the affected mother during birth, and occasionally in utero. Viral hepatitis now includes hepatitis A virus (infectious), hepatitis B virus (serum), hepatitis C virus (non- A non- B), hepatitis D virus (delta), and hepatitis E virus. These virus types differ in both etiology and epidemiology.

Pregnant women with hepatitis A virus (HAV) usually do not transmit the virus to their fetus, since it is transmitted via the fecal-oral route. Hepatitis C virus (HCV) is transmitted primarily through blood, and intravenous drug users are at an increased risk for infection (Emmett 1993). Maternal fetal transfer has been inferred. Hepatitis D virus (HDV) causes infection only in the presence of active hepatitis B. Hepatitis E virus (HEV), like hepatitis A, is spread by the fecal-oral route and fecal-contaminated water. The mortality rate for pregnant women who have hepatitis E is 10% (Marx 1993). A chronic carrier state can develop in HBV and HCV. To date perinatal transmission of HAV, HCV, HDV, and HEV has not been well documented. There is a vaccine for HBV.

Newborn infants born to infected HBV women are at risk for developing hepatitis B. Hepatitis B virus is transmitted primarily through infected blood, saliva, and semen. Women who use drugs often contract the virus by using dirty needles and having unprotected sex. The Centers for Disease Control estimates that from 200,000 to 300,000 cases of HBV infection occur annually. It is not known how many newborns are infected. Preventing neonatal HBV infection is important because the possibility of becoming a carrier is high in infants who contract the virus. Carriers in turn are prone to chronic HBV infection and the associated risk of cirrhosis and liver cancer. Prevention measures by the CDC have targeted pregnant women, infants, and children (Centers for Disease Control 1991b).

The American Academy of Pediatrics (1992) recommends that all neonates receive vaccinations in the newborn nursery; however, if the mother tests positive for HBV (HBsAg+) the newborn is given the initial HBV vaccine along with hepatitis B immunoglobulin (HBIG) within twelve hours of birth, followed by HBV vaccine at one month of age and at six months of age. Infants born to mothers who tested seronegative at birth can begin the three-dose HBV vaccine schedule within two months of birth. A modified schedule can be followed, with the second dose given within two months of the first dose and the third dose given between six and eighteen months of age. Testing may follow to determine if the vaccine was effective.

If any of the HBV vaccines are missed, the infant will not have adequate protection. Parent education regarding the importance of this medical compliance and follow-up by the nurse is extremely important.

Chlamydia

Chlamydia is still another serious infection that can occur in the neonate as a result of passing through an infected birth canal. Almost two-thirds of infants born vaginally to women who have a chlamydial infection become infected during delivery (Centers for Disease Control 1993).

Neonates prenatally exposed to drugs are particularly prone to exposure due to the fact that chlamydia is a sexually transmitted disease, and women who are chemically dependent may have frequent sex with multiple partners. Expectant mothers with untreated chlamydia infections have an increased incidence of premature rupture of membranes, premature labor, intrauterine growth retardation, and stillbirths (McGregor & French 1991). Neonates who acquire this infection during birth can come down with inclusion conjunctivitis and/or pneumonia.

Conjunctivitis caused by chlamydia usually occurs within several weeks of delivery, and pneumonia can develop from six weeks to six months (McGregor & French 1991). The prophylactic antimicrobial medication for conjunctivitis required in many states is silver nitrate, which is instilled in neonates' eyes after birth. Some states, such as California, permit other agents to be used (Isenberg 1990).

If the incidence of chlamydial infec-

tions in neonates is to be reduced, there must be early identification and treatment of maternal infections. When risk factors are present, the woman needs to be tested for sexually transmitted diseases, including chlamydia, during the first visit to the physician or nurse practitioner and again in the third trimester of her pregnancy. Oral erythromycin or oral amoxicillin is often prescribed.

Early Childhood Concerns

HIV Seropositivity

Children with HIV seropositivity need good ongoing pediatric care with available new therapies. The therapies that are now used with children include zidovudine (ZDV), Dideoxyinosine (ddI), and intravenous immunoglobulins (National Institute of Child Health and Human Development 1991). Future directions for therapeutic trials include a combination trial of medications. These therapies are used in various combinations depending on the child's health status. Because *Pneumocystis carinii* pneumonia is the most common, serious HIV-related opportunistic infection among children, prophylaxis guidelines, specifically for children, have been developed (Centers for Disease Control 1991b).

Children should receive childhood immunizations if they are asymptomatic, following the same protocol as for other children, with the exception that inactivated polio vaccine (IPV) is administered instead of oral polio vaccine (OPV). When children are HIV symptomatic it is recommended that they also receive Pneumovax and influenza vaccines.

One of the primary manifestations of

HIV infection acquired in utero or at birth may be progressive encephalopathy. It is likely to develop slowly, but worsen proportionately as immunodeficiency increases, marked by progressive or plateau courses. In the progressive course, the motor, language, and adaptive functions exhibit a gradual but progressive decline. The infant or young child may show deterioration in play and acquired language skills as well as increased motor dysfunction, such as changes in gait, toe walking, or even inability to walk (Belman 1990). Rigidity, dystonic posturing, or extrapyramidal tremor may occur. Cerebellar signs may even develop in some, with serial head circumference measurements indicative of poor brain growth with acquired microcephaly. Many children may have an episodic course with periods of neurologic stability between periods of deterioration (Belman et al 1988). Other children may experience more rapid deterioration over a few months. Older children may initially demonstrate loss of interest in school, as well as psychomotor slowing, attention deficits, and increased emotional lability (Belman 1990).

The plateau course may be marked by little or no further gain in developmental skills or milestones. Any milestone gained or skill acquired occurs at a markedly slow rate, noticeably deviating from the child's previous rate of progress. Severity or progression of motor function deficits may vary. However, as the HIV disease process advances, those following the plateau course will experience further neurologic as well as motor dysfunction.

Some children appear to have a static encephalopathy characterized by cognitive and motor deficits that are nonprogressive, functioning in the moderate to mild to borderline ranges of mental retardation. Verbal proficiency appears to be the predominant problem, although they continue to acquire other developmental skills and maintain a stable IQ. Children may exhibit hyperactivity and attention deficits. Although head circumferences fall below the fiftieth percentile, they remain in the same percentile, confirming stable brain growth (Nozyce et al 1989).

Failure to Thrive

Failure to thrive (FTT) is another issue that may exist for children who are exposed to drugs in utero or who are living in a drug environment. Failure to thrive is a term used to describe children who fail to achieve normal linear and weight growth. There can be many organic etiologies for this problem, including fetal alcohol syndrome, nutritional deprivation, and AIDS. Some children are normal but small due to hereditary factors; therefore, growth patterns should be carefully examined using appropriate growth curves to make this diagnosis.

Failure to thrive may also be nonorganic, or a combination of both. The most common etiology for FTT in children with PDE is nonorganic. This may be due to poverty, ignorance, and inappropriate dietary and/or feeding practices. An infant with prenatal drug exposure who has disorganized suck-swallow patterns is an example of a combination of organic and nonorganic FTT. These disorganized suck-swallow patterns may contribute to feeding difficulties and, without intervention, may persist. Parents caring for a child with feeding difficulties may become frustrated and impatient, which in turn creates a stressful environment for the infant, thereby potentiating the feeding problem.

Child Abuse and Neglect

Child abuse and neglect can occur in families where substance abuse is a problem (Bays 1990). Estimates indicate that at least one in ten children in the United States is born into a chemically dependent family. Parental addiction can have significant effects on children. Parents are not as available to provide for the care of their children if they are addicted. "Drug" becomes all to them when they are using, and the needs of their children are often not adequately met. In some families where chemical dependency is a problem, there is violence within the family unit and physical abuse of the children. Those who are identified as having the disease of addiction also have a higher rate of having experienced poor parenting themselves. They may have experienced sexual and/or physical abuse and the pattern of abuse often continues into the next generation. A positive relationship between childhood physical abuse and use of illicit drugs is documented in one study (Dembo et al 1988). Parental drug use has been identified as one of the markers of fatal child abuse.

It is mandated by law that all cases of suspected child abuse or neglect be referred to the appropriate child protective agency. Family violence is also a mandated reportable incidence by health professionals in some states. The nurse should be familiar with signs and symptoms that may be indicative of child abuse or neglect and family violence, and the mandated reporting laws in their state.

Other concerns

The child prenatally drug exposed is directly or indirectly susceptible to several other physical problems. Some parents who are addicted to drugs also smoke tobacco. Passive inhalation of smoke can cause a susceptibility to upper respiratory infections. Children who meet the criteria for fetal alcohol syndrome have a tendency to have frequent ear infections and/or hearing loss due to their craniofacial anomalies. Passive inhalation of crack or cocaine in an enclosed environment is reported to cause seizures.

CONCLUSION

The possible physical health concerns of the child prenatally drug exposed cover a wide range of conditions with varying degrees of severity. Many of the same problems, such as prematurity, are also seen in other children. Children with PDE, however, often have psychosocial and environmental factors at play which can hinder attainment of their fullest potential. The multifactorial concerns surrounding the issues of prenatal drug exposure can present enormous challenges to the service provider. Health professionals can learn how to meet the obvious health needs of these children; however, the acceptance, perseverance, caring, and hope needed to meet the challenge of the child with PDE must come from within.

REFERENCES

Adeo AE, Newell ML, Peckham CS, and European Collaborative Study. Children born to women with HIV-a infection: Natural history and risk of transmission. *Lancet* 1991; 337(8736): 253-60.

Allen M. Developmental implications of intrauterine growth retardation. *Infants and Young Children* 1992; 5(2):13-28.

American Academy of Pediatrics. *Hepatitis B: What Parents Need to Know*. Elk Grove Village, IL: American Academy of Pediatrics Department of Publications, 1992.

Arvin AM, Prober CG. Herpes simplex virus infections: The genital tract and the newborn. *Pediatrics in Review* 1992; 13(3): 107-11.

Bays J. Substance abuse and child abuse, impact of addiction on the child. *Pediatric Clinics of North America* 1990; 87(4): 881-904.

Belman AL. AIDS and pediatric neurology. *Neurology Clinics* 1990; 8(3): 571-603.

Belman SL, Diamond G, Dickson D, Horoupian D, Llena J, Lantos G, Rubenstein A. Pediatric acquired immunodeficiency syndrome: Neurologic syndromes. *American Journal of Diseases in Children* 1988; 142: 29-39.

Benenson A, ed. Control of communicable diseases in man. *American Public Health Association Journal* 1990; (15): 421.

Berkow R, Fletcher AJ. *The Merck Manual of Diagnosis and Therapy*. 16th ed. Merck Research Laboratories, 1992, pp 2037-8, 2043.

Bernbaum J, D'Agostino J. The NICU graduate managing the major complications. *Contemporary Pediatrics* 1986; (Aug): 69-82.

Blanche S, Rouzioux C, Moscato M, Veber F, Mayaux M, Jacomet C, Tricoire J, Deville A, Vial M, Firtion G. A perspective study of infants born to women seropositive for HIV type I. HIV infection in newborns. *New England Journal of Medicine* 1989; 25: 1643-8.

Centers for Disease Control. Revision of the CDC surveillance case definition for acquired immunodeficiency syndrome. *Morbidity and Mortality Weekly Report* 1987; 36 (Supplement l-S): IS-155.

Centers for Disease Control. Guidelines for the prevention and control of congenital syphilis. *Morbidity and Mortality Weekly Report* 1988: 37(1): 1-13.

Centers for Disease Control. Alternative case-finding methods in a crack-related syphilis epidemic — Philadelphia. *Morbidity and Mortality Weekly Report* 1991a; 40(5): 77-80.

Centers for Disease Control. Guidelines for prophylaxis against *Pneumocystis carinii* pneumonia for children infected with human immunodeficiency virus. *Morbidity and Mortality Weekly Report* 1991b; 40 (RR2): 1-3.

Centers for Disease Control. Recommendations for the prevention and management of chlamydia trachomatis infections. *Morbidity and Mortality Weekly Report* 1993; 42 (August 6).

Centers for Disease Control. Summary — cases of specified notifiable diseases, United States, cumulative, week ending January 1, 1994. *Morbidity and Mortality Weekly Report* 1994; 42(5):1002.

Chasnoff IJ. Newborn infants with drug withdrawal symptoms. *Pediatrics in Review* 1988; 9 (9): 273-7.

Chasnoff IJ. *Drug Use in Pregnancy: Mother and Child*. Boston: MTP Press Limited, 1986; pp 52-63.

Chasnoff IJ, Griffith DR, MacGregor S, Dirkes K, Burns KA. Temporal patterns of cocaine use in pregnancy: Perinatal outcome. *Journal of the American Medical Association* 1989;261:1741-4.

Chasnoff IJ, Lewis DE, Griffith DR, Willey S. Cocaine and pregnancy: Clinical and toxicological implications for the neonate. *Clinical Chemistry* 1989; 35: 1276-8.

Cherukuri R, Minkoff H, Feldman J, Parekh A, Glass L. A cohort study of alkaloidal cocaine (crack) in pregnancy. *Obstetrics and Gynecology* 1988; 72: 147-51.

Chess S. Developmental theory revisited. *Canadian Journal of Psychiatry* 1987; 24 (2): 101-12.

Chow M, Durand B, Feldman M, Mills M. *Handbook of Pediatric Primary Care* New York: John Wiley, 1979, pp 941-2.

Christmas JT. The risks of cocaine use in pregnancy. *Medical Aspects of Human Sexuality* 1992; 26: 36-43.

Connor E. Advances in early diagnosis of perinatal infection. *Journal of the American Medical Association* 1991; 266: 3474-5.

Dembo R, Williams L, Berry E, Sulain J, Brick K. The relationship between physical and sexual abuse and illicit drug use: A replication among a new sample of youths entering a juvenile detention center. *International Journal of Addiction* 1988;11:1101.

Dixon S. Effects of transplacental exposure to cocaine and methamphetamine on the neonate. *Western Journal of Medicine* 1989; 150: 436-42.

Dobbins J, Stewart, Demmler G. Surveillance of congenital cytomegalovirus diseases, 1990-1991. *Morbidity and Mortality Weekly Report* 1992; 41(2): 35-44.

Emmett P. Syphilis update. *Nurse Week* 1992; 5(28): 12-3.

Emmett P. Hepatitis C: Recognizing the risks to patients and healthcare workers. *Nurse Week* 1993; 6(21): 14-5.

Feretich S. Focus on psychometric internal consistency estimates of reliability. *Research in Nursing and Health* 1990;13: 437-40.

Finnegan L. Neonatal abstinence syndrome: Assessment and pharmacotherapy. In Rubatelli F, Granati B, eds. *Neonatal Therapy: An Update.* New York: Elsevier and Science Publishers, 1986.

Goldfarb J. Breast feeding—AIDS and other infectious diseases. *Clinics in Perinatology* 1993; 20(1): 225-43.

Greenberg S, Singh T, Htoo M, Schultz S. The association between congenital syphilis and cocaine/crack use in New York City: A case control study. *American Journal of Public Health* 1991;81(3): 1316.

Hadeed AJ, Siegel SR. Maternal cocaine use during pregnancy: Effect on the newborn infant. *Pediatrics* 1989; 84: 205-10.

Hanshaw JB, Dudgeon JA, Marshall WC. *Viral Diseases of the Fetus and Newborn.* 2nd ed. New York: Saunders Publishing, 1985.

Howard J, Kropenski V, Tyler R. The long-term effects on neurodevelopment of in-

fants exposed to PCP. In Coulet DH, ed. *Phencyclidine: An Update.* Rockville MD: The Institute, 1985, pp 623-30 (National Institute on Drug Abuse Research Monograph Series, 64).

Hutto C, Parks W, Lai S, Mastrucci M, Mitchell M, Mitchell C, Munoz J, Trapido E, Master I, Scott G. A hospital-based prospective study of perinatal infection with HIV type I. *Journal of Pediatrics* 1991;18(3): 347-53.

Isenberg S. The dilemma of neonatal ophthalmic prophylaxis. Important advances in clinical medicine: Ophthalmology. *Western Journal of Medicine* 1990; 153 (2):190.

Kron R, Litt M, Phoenix M, Finnegan L. Neonatal narcotic abstinence: Effects of pharmacologic agents and maternal drug usage on nutritive sucking behavior. *Journal of Pediatrics* 1976; 88: 637.

Ladewig PW, London ML, Olds SB. *Essentials of Maternal-Newborn Nursing.* 2nd ed. Menlo Park, CA: Addison-Wesley Publishing, 1990, pp 683-4.

Landesman S, Weiblan B, Mendez H, Sullivan H, Gregor G. Clinical utility of HIV IGA immunoblot assay in the early diagnosis of perinatal HIV infection. *Journal of the American Medical Association* 1991; 266: 3443-6.

Le Blanc DE, Parekh AJ, Naso B, Glass L. Effects of intrauterine exposure to alkaloidal cocaine (crack). *American Journal of Disabilities in Children* 1987; 141: 937-8.

McGregor J, French J. Chlamydia trachomatis infection during pregnancy. *American Journal of Obstetrics and Gynecology* 1991;164 (8):1782.

Marx JF. Hepatitis: Unscrambling the alphabet. *Nursing* 1993; 93: 34-41.

Mott SR, Fazekas NF, James SR. *Nursing Care of Children and Families* Menlo Park, CA: Addison-Wesley Publishing, 1985, pp 666, 1191.

Naeye RL. Influence of maternal cigarette smoking during pregnancy on fetal and childhood growth. *Obstetrics and Gynecology* 1981; 57(1):18.

National Institute of Child Health and Human Development. Intravenous Immunoglobulin Study Group. Intravenous immuno-globulin for the prevention of bacterial infections in children with symptomatic human immunodeficiency virus. *New England Journal of Medicine* 1991; 235 (2): 73-80.

Nozyce M, Diamond G, Belman A. Neurodevelopmental impairment during infancy in offspring of IVDA and HIV seropositive mothers. *Pediatric Research* 1989; 25: 359A.

Nozyce M, Diamond G, Belman A, Cabot T, Douglas C, Hopkins K, Cohen H, Rubinstein A, Willoughby A. Neurodevelopmental impairments during infancy in offspring of NDA and HIV seropositive mothers. *Pediatric Research* 1989; 25(2): 359A.

Oro AS, Dixon SD. Perinatal cocaine and methamphetamine exposure: Maternal and neonatal correlates. *Journal of Pediatrics* 1987;111(4): 571-8.

Richardson GA, Day NL. Maternal and neonatal effects of moderate cocaine use during pregnancy. *Neurotoxicology and Teratology* 1991;13:455-60.

Schmitt B, Seeger J, Kreu W, Enenkel S, Jacobi G. Central nervous system involvement of children with HIV infection. *Developmental Medicine and Child Neurology* 1991; 33(6): 535-40.

The tiniest babies: Breathing easier. *In Health* 1990;4 (1):16.

More help for preemies. *FDA Consumer* 1990; 24 (1):3.

Congenital syphilis makes a comeback. *Pediatric Report's Child Health Newsletter* 1991; 7 (2): 82.

U.S. Department of Health and Human Services. *Healthy People 2000: National Health Promotion and Disease Prevention Objectives.* Washington, D.C.: U.S. Government Printing Office, 1993 (DHHS publication No. PHS 91-50213).

Van de Perre P, Simonon A, Msellati P, Hitamara D, Vaira D, Bazubagira A, Van Goethens C, Stevens A, Karita E, Sondag-Thull D, Davis F, Le Page P. Postnatal transmission of human immunodeficiency virus from mother to infant. *New England Journal of Medicine* 1991; 325 (9): 593-8.

Vega WA, Noble A, Kolody B, Porter P, Hwang J, Bale A. Profile of alcohol and drug use during pregnancy in California, 1992 Sacramento, CA: California Department of Alcohol and Drug Programs, 1993.

Wara D. Pediatric AIDS. *U.C.S.F. Advances and Controversies in Pediatrics Conference,* San Francisco, 1992.

Whaley LF, Wong DL. *Essentials of Pediatric Nursing* 4th ed. St. Louis: C.V. Mosby, 1991.

Whitley R, Arvin A, Prober C, Corey L, Burchett S, Plotkin S, Starr S, Jacobs R, Powell D, Nahmias A, Sumaya C, Edwards K, Alford C, Caddel G, Soong S. Predictors of morbidity and mortality in neonates with herpes simplex virus infections. *New England Journal of Medicine*, 1991;324(5):450.

Williamson WD, Demmler GJ. Congenital infections: Clinical outcome and educational implications. *Infants and Young Children* 1992;4(4):1-10.

Williamson WD, Demmler G, Percy AK, Catlin F. Asymptomatic congenital CMV infection: Association of congenital and progressive sensorineural hearing loss (SNHL) with recurrent as well as primary maternal CMV infection. (Abstract) *Pediatric Research* 1991; 29:167A.

Williamson WD, Desmond MM, La Fevers N, Taber L, Catlin FI, Weaver TG. Symptomatic congenital cytomegalovirus: Disorders of language, learning, and hearing. *American Journal of Diseases in Children* 1982; 136: 902-5.

Woods FR, Plessinger M, Clark K. Effect of cocaine on uterine blood flow and fetal oxygenation. *Journal of the American Medical Association* 1987; 257: 957-61.

Yazigi RA, Odem R, Polakoski KL Demonstration of specific binding of cocaine to human spermatozoa. *Journal of the American Medical Association* 1991; 266: 1956.

Yow MD. Congenital cytomegalovirus disease: A now problem. *Journal of Infectious Disease* 1989;159:163-7.

Zuckerman B. Drug exposed infants: Understanding the medical risk. *Future of Children* 1991; 1(1): 26-35.

Zuckerman B, Bresnahan K. Developmental and behavioral consequences of prenatal drug and alcohol exposure. *Pediatric Clinics of North America* 1991; 38 (6): 1387-1406.

ANNOTATED BIBLIOGRAPHY

Williamson DM, Demmler GJ. Congenital infections: Clinical outcome and educational implications. *Infants and Young Children* **1992;4(4): 1-10.**
This comprehensive article discusses the most frequently occurring congenital infections including cytomegalovirus, herpes, and syphilis. The article provides epidemiology of the infections, prevention and treatment modalities, clinical outcome and educational implications. It is written for nurses as well as others working with infants and young children.

Emmett P. Syphilis update. *Nurse Week* **1992; 5(28):12-3.**
This article identifies the etiologic agent of syphilis, and classifies the stages of the disease. Testing for the disease is discussed and the nurse's role in interpretation of test results. Recommendations are provided for the nurses' personal protection and suggestions are made for the education of the client. One section of the article provides information on congenital syphilis.

Marx JF. Hepatitis: Unscrambling the alphabet. *Nursing* **1993; 93: 34-41.**
The five types of viral hepatitis are presented and information is given on how to distinguish each from the other. Those affecting the pregnant women, fetus, and neonate are identified. Information is provided on the hepatitis B vaccine, and precautions for preventing transmission of all five infectious diseases are listed. A case study is given for hepatitis A, B, and C. Of great value to the nurse is a chart which compares various aspects of the five forms of hepatitis.

McGregor J, French JI. Chlamydia trachomatis infection during pregnancy. *American Journal of Obstetrics and Gynecology* **1991;164 (8):1782.**
Prenatal and neonatal conditions associated with a maternal chlamydia infection are presented. Recommendations are given from the Centers for Disease Control for identification of infected mothers. Information is provided for two forms of antibiotic treatment.

Greenberg M, Singh T, Htoo M, Schultz S. The association between congenital syphilis and cocaine/crack use in New York City: A case control study. *American Journal of Public Health* **1991; 81 (3): 1316.**
This article presents the results of a study done in New York City to determine if an association exists between congenital syphilis and cocaine/crack use. Data collected suggests a possible relationship.

7

Nursing Interventions and the At-Risk Infant and Child with Prenatal Alcohol and Drug Exposure

Keeta DeStefano Lewis, R.N., P.H.N., M.S.N.
Bonnie M. Bear, R.N., B.S.N., P.H.N.

Nurses have provided services to children in schools for 100 years. School nurse specialists today provide primary health care to all children in the school setting, including those with special health needs.

School nurses are serving increasing numbers of children who have risk factors associated with prenatal drug exposure that may interfere with their school performance and success. This chapter discusses the physical influences (vision, hearing, growth and clinical measurements, immunizations, and nutrition) as well as the environmental (child abuse and neglect) and cultural influences on the child's development. Home visiting, staff safety issues, and individualized developmental plans are also included.

The suggestions in this chapter can help the school nurse specialist to assess the child in order to improve the child's health care and his or her educational day and provide the school staff with knowledge about the child's need in order to empower families in the management and care of their children.

Nurses in the United States have worked with children in the school and home since the eighteenth century. They have served infants and children with a variety of health problems that affect their academic, social, and behavioral development. Infants and children with special needs due to prenatal drug exposure (PDE) are not a new phenomenon to the school health nurse. However, the increasing numbers of infants and children with multiple complex needs related to their mothers' drug use require particular knowledge and expertise of the nurse who practices in school and community settings.

The exact number of infants and children with prenatal drug exposure is unknown, as is the number who are at risk for health, developmental, or educational deficits due to PDE. All infants and children, whether they are at-risk or have disabilities with known etiologies, need to have the same assessment, treatment, and referral as other children with special needs in the education system. They need to be served in the least restrictive environment, which might be day care, preschool, early intervention program or regular or adapted classroom with a small teacher-child ratio. All special needs and at-risk children are entitled to primary health care in the school setting. School nurses and school nurse practitioners provide primary, secondary, and tertiary health care within the school environment.

Primary health care is defined in *School Nursing Practice: Roles and Standards* (Proctor, Lordi & Zaiger 1993) as: access to care, availability of care, service delivery, community involvement, remediation of the causes of health inequities such as poverty, unem-

ployment, and the right of all United States citizens to appropriate health care. Secondary health care is defined as early diagnosis and prompt intervention to limit disabilities, and tertiary health care is defined as rehabilitation activities.

This chapter will focus on the school nurse and school nurse practitioner role in the schools as it relates to current legislation, developmental school health assessments, physical and environmental risk factors that influence school performance and learning ability, home visiting, safety issues during home visits, and individualized developmental plans.

Federal Legislation

Since 1975, PL 94-142, the Education of All Handicapped Act, has mandated free, appropriate public education to all children with special needs ages five through twenty-one years of age in the least restrictive environment. This legislation was reauthorized in 1990, and retitled Individuals with Disabilities Education Act (IDEA).

In 1986, PL 99-457 (part H) Education of the Handicapped Amendments provided opportunity for states to extend services for special needs children down to birth. This legislation (reauthorized in 1991 as PL 102-119, part of IDEA) requires family-focused, interagency, interdisciplinary collaboration in developing early intervention services. Programs provided from birth to three years may vary from state to state, as each state has had flexibility in developing its own comprehensive plans. Some children with prenatal drug exposure may not qualify for services, since each state determines at-risk status eligibility for intervention. All services must be identified and written in an Individualized Family Service Plan (IFSP) by an inter-disciplinary team with the child's family as active participants.

Developmental School Health Assessment

Assessments are a significant part of the school nurse/school nurse practitioner's role opportunities. Assessment is an important way to delineate strengths and needs of school children. For example, vision and hearing concerns are known as the "quiet debilitators" (Lewis & Thomson 1986). Abnormalities in these areas can go unnoticed until educational, social, or behavioral problems occur or serious medical implications are diagnosed (Lewis & Thomson 1986).

Vision

Anatomical structures of the visual system are present at birth even though they are not completely developed or well coordinated (Aslin 1987). Infants with prenatal drug exposure may have delayed visual maturation, difficulty tracking, gaze aversion, or poor initiation and maintenance of eye contact. Difficulties in any one of these areas can negatively affect parental attachment and development of appropriate visual skills. Thus vision assessment in the neonatal period, along with helpful intervention techniques for the caregiver, are critical.

Every infant, toddler, and child prenatally drug exposed should be screened for visual functioning and defects upon referral to an early intervention program, day care center, or special education. Vision is an important sensory modality for learning, and learning begins at birth.

Thus, early detection of visual problems is critical for optimal development of the infant, toddler, or child (Lewis & Thomson 1986). Visual screening can be performed by the school nurse/school nurse practitioner or a trained paraprofessional. However, when done by a paraprofessional, the responsibility of interpretation and referral belongs to the school nurse/school nurse practitioner.

It is recommended that all children have an eye examination by a licensed specialist (ophthalmologist or optometrist) prior to beginning regular school (kindergarten). However, numerous constraints interfere with the successful completion of this examination, such as the lack of insurance or parental finances, different parental priorities, lack of knowledge of the importance of visual functioning, or nonavailability of clinical resources. Due to these constraints the availability of school nurses to perform visual screening, make referrals, and conduct successful follow-up is critical. Factors that increase the likelihood of visual abnormalities are displayed in Table 1.

RESEARCH FINDINGS

Research studies regarding maternal use of alcohol reveal a number of physical anomalies that can occur in the areas of the eyes, including: microphthalmia, (unusually small eyes), ptosis (drooping eyelids), blepharophimosis (narrowing of the slit between the eyelids at the external angle of the eye), epicanthal folds (vertical folds of skin at the inner canthus of the eye), strabismus (deviation of eyes, and myopia (nearsightedness). However, certain risks are associated with particular drugs as described in the literature. Maternal polydrug use makes it difficult to ascertain a direct correlation between a particular drug and specific visual anomalies.

Prenatal exposure to marijuana places a child at increased risk for strabismus, myopia, and abnormal oculomotor functioning (movement of eye) (Fried 1985). In utero exposure to methadone increases the risk for strabismus (Nelson et al 1987). Visual impairments associated with in utero exposure to cocaine include strabismus, nystagmus (rapid movement of the eye), optic nerve hypoplasia (incomplete development) (Dominguez et al 1991), abnormal dilatation of iris blood vessels (Isenberg, Spiero & Inkelis 1987), delayed visual maturation, and prolonged eyelid edema (Good et al 1992). These studies support the need for early visual screening, detection, and referral.

VISUAL MEASUREMENT

Visual functioning can be measured in the neonate by use of visual evoked response (VER). In the early months the corneal light reflex test can be used as well as the infant screening procedure for amblyopia. In later months, the cover-uncover test or the corneal light reflex test is used to determine deviation of the eyes, and the preferential looking test may be utilized to obtain approximate visual acuity. The Snellen Illiterate E Chart or Blackbird Preschool Vision Screening Systems (Sato-Viacrucis 1994) can be used with preschool and older children to determine visual acuity.

Hearing

Early identification of a hearing impairment is a national health care priority (*Healthy People 2000* 1990). Early identification in children is critical in order to begin medical and educational treatment for developing appropriate communication and social skills.

Hearing experience begins in utero because the cochlea is completely developed and fully functional by twenty weeks gestational age. At birth, the infant is capable of recognition and response to various frequencies and intensities of sound (Kearsley et al 1982). The acuity of the neonate's hearing improves after birth as the amniotic fluid is

Table 1. Risk factors for visual abnormalities in the newborn.

A. Prenatal	B. Postnatal
Syphilis	Oxygen toxicity (retinopathy of prematurity)
Toxoplasmosis	
Maternal rubella	Cerebral palsy
Cytomegalovirus	Histoplasmosis
Congenital herpes	Lead poisoning
Congenital malformations/conditions, e.g. albinism, microphthalmia	
Positive family history, e.g. strabismus, myopia	
Drug exposure: alcohol, marijuana, cocaine, methadone	

absorbed (Hecox & Deegan 1985).

Children with cranial malformations have a higher incidence of hearing impairment as compared to nonaffected children (Berry & Eisenson 1956). The facial anomalies associated with fetal alcohol syndrome may be indicators of children with an increased risk of conductive and sensorineural hearing loss due to either anatomical malformations or frequent ear infections, or both. Some newborns with PDE are premature and/or have low birth weight; both of these conditions are risk factors for sensorineural hearing loss.

An undetected hearing loss may deprive an infant of meaningful auditory input necessary for the acquisition of speech and language, since hearing is the primary mode for the development of speech and social attachment. Ideally hearing tests begin at birth and are repeated to detect onset of hearing loss that can occur later or to monitor the level of hearing that can change over time. Infants and children should be screened upon referral to early intervention, school entry, and at appropriate grade levels as recommended by the American Speech and Hearing Association (ASHA) (Turner 1990). Risk factors that increase the likelihood of hearing loss are found in Table 2.

RESEARCH FINDINGS

Children with fetal alcohol syndrome frequently have conductive and sensorineural hearing losses (Church & Gerkin 1988). Clinical experience makes us aware of the high incidence of polydrug use, which most often includes alcohol, placing many children with prenatal drug exposure at risk for hearing loss.

Exposure to tobacco smoke, both in utero and postnatally, is associated with an increased incidence of chronic middle ear infections. This places the exposed child at risk of conductive hearing loss (Surgeon General 1990).

Research findings regarding the impact of prenatal cocaine exposure on hearing are not conclusive. Abnormal auditory brainstem responses (ABR) were found in infants PDE (Shih, Cone-Wesson & Reddix 1988; Salamy et al 1990). The ABRs in both of the studies were normal by three to six months after birth. Another larger study by Carzoli and associates (1991), looking at infants PDE to cocaine, found no increased incidence of hearing deficits as measured by ABRs.

HEARING MEASUREMENT

Hearing can be measured by the use of the Crib-O Gram in neonates and children with special needs by the use of auditory evoked potentials. Measurements of auditory evoked potentials are known by several different acronyms, including: ABR (auditory brainstem response), BER or BSER (brainstem evoked response), and BAER (brainstem auditory evoked response). These tests have been reliable in the auditory assessment of infants and young children by providing an electrophysiologic, objective measure of hearing threshold. A new test, otoacoustic emission testing (OAE), is another tool that can be used with those whose age or disabilities prevent communication. The test is useful with both infants, children, and adults whose hearing test results are difficult to obtain or are inconclusive ("High-tech" 1993). All of the above tests require a prescription and are usually provided in the hospital or clinic setting by audiometric professionals and otorhinolaryngologists.

Table 2. Risk factors for hearing loss in the newborn.

A. Prenatal	**B. Postnatal**
Syphilis	Premature birth
Toxoplasmosis	Asphyxia
Rubella	Difficult or prolonged birth
Cytomegalovirus	Very low birthweight <1,500 gms (about 3.3 lbs.)
Herpes	Hyperbilirubinemia at a level exceeding indication for blood transfusion
Maternal alcoholism	
Diabetes mellitus	Bacterial meningitis
Ingestion by mother of ototoxic drugs during pregnancy, e.g. antibiotics (gentamicin, tobramycin, kanamycin, streptomycin), quinine, salicylates	Ototoxic medications used for more than 5 days
	Severe depression at birth: e.g. Apgar scores of 0-3 at 5 minutes, neonates who do not initiate spontaneous respiration in 10 minutes, hypotonia persisting to 2 hours of age
Maternal anoxia	
Preeclampsia/eclampsia	
Positive family history: congenital or delayed onset of childhood sensorineural impairment	Prolonged mechanical ventilation: duration 10 days or longer
	Craniofacial: e.g. abnormalities of pinna and ear canal, absent philtrum, low hairline
	Stigmata associated with syndromes known to include sensorineural hearing loss: e.g. Usher's or Waardenburg's syndrome, Marfan syndrome
	Congenital malformation: cleft palate/lip
	Lead poisoning
	Neurodegenerative disorders: neurofibromatosis, myoclonic epilepsy, Werdnig-Hoffmann disease, Tay-Sach's disease, infantile Gaucher's disease, Niemann-Pick disease, any metachromatic leukodystrophy, or any infantile demyelinating neuropathy
	Childhood infectious diseases identified with sensorineural hearing loss, such as measles and mumps

Screening tools that can be used by the nurse include the HEAR kit (Downs 1984), which can provide a gross behavioral estimate of hearing ability in infants and young children from birth through twenty-four months. If deficits in hearing ability are identified, referral for a complete audiological evaluation should be made. Preschool children can be screened with play audiometry and older children with school screening audiometry, both of which are called pure tone screening.

Reward or reinforcement tests are usually done in the clinic setting but some school districts provide sound-conditioned rooms where these tests are performed by nurse audiometrists or audiologists. Visual reinforcement audiometry (VRA) or conditioned orientation reflex (COR) provide the infant/child with an incentive to look at something, such as a dancing monkey or colored light, to the right or left where a test noise is sounded at differing levels. Both tests provide an evaluation of the level of hearing in at least the better ear but cannot provide ear specific information. Further testing with head phones when the child is older is needed to obtain ear-specific information.

Impedance audiometry provides an efficient and noninvasive method to measure middle ear pressure and compliance/mobility of the tympanic membrane. It can be used with children as young as two years of age and throughout the school years.

Growth and Clinical Measurements

Height, weight, head circumference, temperature, pulse, respirations, blood pressure, and laboratory studies such as hemoglobin and lead levels are considered routine measurements conducted by nurses and their assistants as part of regular health maintenance. These measurements are important to establish a baseline for the infant or child as well as to provide early detection of disease or abnormalities affecting learning or development. Table 3 displays risk factors which increase the likelihood for growth deficits detected in infancy.

RESEARCH FINDINGS

Research reveals that children prenatally drug exposed are at risk for decreased height, weight, and smaller head size at birth and during early development (Chasnoff et al 1989; Finnegan & Kandall 1992; Kline, Stein & Hutzler 1987). The smaller head circumference is of particular concern because it may reflect a smaller brain, which is an indicator of developmental and learning problems. The importance of continued measurement of the head circumference is supported by a study that found head growth after birth may be a more powerful predictor of developmental outcome than the circumference at birth (Eckerman, Lynne & Gross 1985).

Since prenatal drug exposure places a child at increased risk of infectious diseases secondary to a deficient immune system and/or cardiovascular or urinary defects, assessments such as pulse, respiratory rate, blood pressure, and urinalysis are important. Children with PDE are also at risk for HIV and, if frequent infections occur, referral for an immunological assessment may be warranted. Hemoglobin and lead levels are useful measurements since some children with PDE may have poor nutrition and live in older, dilapidated buildings. Blood levels of lead concentration greater than 100 ug/dl are usually asso-

Table 3. Risk factors for growth deficits.

Prenatal	Postnatal
Drug exposure: alcohol, cocaine, tobacco, heroin, methamphetamines	Prematurity
	Small for gestational age (SGA)
Poor maternal nutrition	Low birth weight (LBW)
Homelessness	Poverty
Poverty	HIV infection/AIDS
Diabetes	Metabolic disorders
Syphilis	Syphilis
Prescription or nonprescription drugs	Failure to thrive (FTT)
	Prescription or nonprescription drugs
	Chemically dependent breast-feeding mother
	Family's emotional climate, i.e. psychosocial dwarfism

ciated with lead encephalopathy. Lead encephalopathy involves blindness, paralysis, convulsions, mental retardation, and ultimately culminates in death. Even at lower blood lead levels, lower than 100 ug/dl, children can experience distractibility, impulsivity, impaired hearing, hyperactivity, and mild cognitive deficits (Whaley & Wong 1991).

Immunizations

Immunizations are central to providing good primary care to children. Inconsistent preventive health care due to frequent changes in caregivers interferes with immunization routines. The recommended routine immunization schedule should be followed with the following precautions.

Children with PDE are at increased risk for congenital HIV. If they are HIV-positive, inactivated vaccines should be used regardless of whether symptoms are present. When the child is HIV-

seronegative or the HIV status is unknown, the American Academy of Pediatrics (AAP) recommends use of enhanced inactivated polio virus (IPV) vaccine if the child is living with an immunocompromised caregiver because there is a potential for transmission of the virus to the immunocompromised individual. If the immune status of the caregiver is unknown, the IPV vaccine is the wiser choice.

Mothers who are chemically dependent are at an increased risk for hepatitis B (HBV) and of transmitting HBV to their infant either prenatally or postnatally. The adherence to AAP recommendations for administration of HBV vaccine is especially important for infants with PDE. If the series is not completed, the infant will not have adequate protection. A laboratory test is done to determine if the series was effective. Revaccination is possible for those infants who did not respond to the first series. It is unclear if boosters will be needed in the future.

The Advisory Committee on Immunization Practice (ACIP) recommends measles, mumps, and rubella (MMR) be seriously considered for children with symptomatic HIV infection. Severe measles have been reported in these children but there are no reports of serious or unusual adverse effects of MMR vaccine in children with symptomatic HIV infection.

The AAP recommends diphtheria, tetanus, and pertussis (DTP) immunization at two months after birth regardless of gestational age. Prematurity and low birth weight are risk factors associated with maternal drug use. With very low birth weight infants, their neurologic status, stability, and muscle mass should be considered. Weight above 1,500 grams by two months of age would be reasonable for giving DTP. If the neurologic status is unclear, administration of DTP should be delayed until the diagnosis is clarified even if the delay is up to one year. The incidence of diphtheria and tetanus in the United States is low and it is better to defer the immunization than give the DT to an infant who may be able to receive the DTP later.

Nutrition

Infants and young children with PDE are often premature or have intrauterine growth retardation (IUGR) which indicates the need for close supervision of caloric intake and an awareness of any feeding problems (Oro & Dixon 1987). The birth-retarded growth rate can continue through infancy and into early childhood. Infants with PDE can have difficulty with suck-swallow coordination, tongue tremors and thrusting, and

oral hypersensitivity (Lewis, Bennett & Schmeder 1989) which can lead to inadequate nutritional intake. The neurobehaviors such as increased heart and respiratory rate, hyperirritability, inconsolability, and tremors increase the need for kilocalories and nutrient requirements. Anomalies of the genitourinary tract or digestive system secondary to fetal hypoxia can decrease absorption of nutrients (Harsham, Hayden & Disbrow 1993). These difficulties all place the infant at risk for poor nutrition.

Families with limited means, homelessness, and drug-seeking behaviors often do not make nutrition a priority. Children living in families with irregular meal patterns and limited food selection due to parental lack of knowledge, developmental level, preferences, or lifestyle are in jeopardy of being inadequately nourished (Pearson 1977). Some children are placed in state licensed foster homes which require that children receive adequate nutritional intake. However, when children are moved from foster home to foster home this can produce social and emotional disturbances in the child which can adversely affect their appetite and weight gain.

RESEARCH FINDINGS

The few published study findings are not conclusive regarding growth retardation extending into childhood. One study found that infants exposed to cocaine had caught up in all growth parameters by twelve months of age (Weathers et al 1993). Another study found catch-up growth in height and weight but not in head circumference (Chasnoff et al 1992).

A small study of infants in foster care found catch-up growth in weight but not in length by six to eight months of age. This same group of infants displayed a drop-off of weight after foster home transfers. This study should not be generalized to stable foster home environments or the infants' natural homes (Harsham, Hayden & Disbrow in press).

NUTRITIONAL MEASUREMENT

Assessment of nutritional adequacy can be performed both directly and indirectly. Direct methods include a food intake diary (from twenty-four hours to one week), assessment of eating styles, and clinical observation of eating behaviors (Wold 1981). Indirect methods include assessment of growth and development (height, weight, and head circumference), physical examination (skin, hair, teeth, and eyes), laboratory tests, and x-rays. A variety of nutritional questionnaires or checklists are available for use with infants and children. Regardless of the methods used to evaluate a child's nutritional status, it is more conclusive to look at the data gathered over a period of time rather than individual time-limited assessments.

The Nursing Child Assessment Satellite Training (NCAST) feeding scale can be used to assess the parent-infant interaction and emotional patterns during feeding, which can negatively or positively affect the infants' absorption and nutritional intake (Barnard 1979). This tool can be used for ages birth through twelve months. Risk factors for inadequate nutrition for infants and children are found in Table 4.

Child Abuse

Infants with prenatal drug exposure are also likely to be susceptible to physical, emotional, social and sexual abuse and neglect. This is due in part to the infant/child's neurobehavioral characteristics such as irritability, frequent state changes, sleep-wake disturbances, and hyperactivity. These disorganized neurobehavioral characteristics of the infant place the infant and caregiver attachment process at risk, thus predisposing the infant/child to a variety of abuses.

Table 4. Risk factors for inadequate nutrition.

Postnatal

Parental lack of knowledge of infant cues

Uncoordinated suck-swallow reflex

Metabolic disorder

Chronic diarrhea

Prune-belly syndrome

Gastroesophageal reflux

Failure to thrive

Food intolerance

Intestinal parasite

Constipation

The second part of the abuse pattern is the parent's background and well-being. Adults with depression or drug-seeking and addictive behaviors may not be emotionally available to meet the needs of their infant, especially if the infant has nonnormative behaviors. Parents with a background of intergenerational abuse do not have appropriate parenting models and may lack the skills to care for the physical, emotional, and social needs of another person.

Research findings

The extent of abuse in children with PDE is unknown, and few research studies pertain to this question. There are, however, some studies about child neglect and abuse in general that include descriptions of the child's temperament and behavior, abusive parental characteristics, and childhood adversities of the parents. The descriptions of the general population of abused children and their parents are similar to the characteristics of children with PDE and their parents.

Maccoby and Martin (1983) report parents who abuse their children characterize their children as irritable and difficult to handle. Egeland and Sroufe (1981) describe abused children as significantly more frustrated, noncompliant, and aggressive and as displaying less positive affect than children in a control group. Risk factors for child neglect and abuse are found in Table 5.

Home Visiting

School nurses have a legacy of home visiting beginning in 1893, and this service now includes serving children with PDE. The home is the most natural environment for working with an infant and child. The art of home visiting lies in the nurses' ability to recognize their own

Table 5. Risk factors for infant/child neglect and abuse.

Infant/Child

Infant withdrawal symptoms

Nonnormative behavioral characteristics

Chronic illness

Parent/Caregiver

Numerous partners of caregiver

Homelessness

Single parent

Low socioeconomic environment

Chemically dependent caregivers

Lifestyle stress factors

Intergenerational neglect and abuse

values and belief systems and how this influences their work with families. Recognition and understanding of an individual's cultural and ethnic background is part of this process.

Nurses have used the home visiting model for many years and this design is now being integrated into early intervention services throughout the United States. This model's widespread appeal is based on the opportunity to provide individual services within the family domain and allows a view of the family life circumstances, values, and beliefs. Home visiting is also a way to reach children of families in rural areas who are isolated from services, those children whose families are unable physically, emotionally, or financially to bring their child to services, or fragile children unable to travel or be around other people.

The home is an appropriate place to gather health information and provide health care, perform a developmental assessment, assess the child's strengths and weaknesses, share information with the family, and provide developmental services to the child and family. Home visiting is most effective when the family needs and priorities are preeminent. The home visitor's agenda may need to be refocused if family members demonstrate or express other concerns, needs, or wishes.

Families of children with PDE, whether natural or foster parents, often have multiple professionals coming into their home. For example, a nurse, social worker, developmental specialist, physical/occupational therapist, teacher, or mental health worker may schedule home visits during a one-month period. The stress of multiple home visits can be relieved if professionals

from various agencies collaborate to minimize this intrusion into family life and recognize that the family may have its own previously established support systems and resources.

Some families may be in conflict regarding acceptance of the child with special needs and expectations for the future. The mother and father may have different views regarding their child's current and potential level of development. These differences require understanding and support from the home visitor so that the family can cope with the variances of the child and the different expectations among family members.

Cultural Competence

Awareness of cultural and ethnic diversity is necessary while working with families and their communities. Cultural competence involves practical knowledge of one's own beliefs, values, and biases; openness to learn about various cultural differences; and setting aside preconceived attitudes and assumptions. Cultural competence is the opposite of ethnocentric behavior. It is a dynamic process that changes as one gains knowledge and acceptance of differences through personal experience and is essential to developing effective partnerships with individuals and families.

The use of drugs is commonly referred to as a culture. Women and men of all colors, socioeconomic groups, and racial/ethnic backgrounds may use drugs and be part of the drug culture. Within this drug culture, behaviors are dictated more by addiction to drugs than ethnic or social backgrounds. Children within the drug culture may be living with their natural parent(s), extended family members, or in foster homes. Each of these environments in turn has its own cultural characteristics which may be very different from each other as well as that of the nurse.

The culture associated with ethnicity has its own unique characteristics. Nurses working with various ethnic groups would benefit from acquiring knowledge concerning: how the families regard the use of drugs within the culture, the acceptance or rejection of members who use drugs, and perceptions of how to solve problems associated with addiction.

A bilingual, bicultural translator is an important addition to the assessment and intervention process. The family relationship will benefit from the nurse spending time with the translator prior to the home visit or scheduled meeting to outline the purpose of the meeting and alert the translator to the necessary medical terms. Knowing a few words or phrases in the family's native language and pronouncing family's names correctly are important ways for the nurse to show and gain respect. Positive experiences foster trust by the family, which is necessary for the family to successfully interface with other agencies — whether they be health, education, or social services. Health practice questions for families of all culture groups (such as drug, ethnic, religious, contemporary families, and foster families) are listed in Table 6. The answers to these questions are significant for a constructive family-nurse relationship.

Personal Safety Issues

When visiting a multiproblem, high-risk family, the nurse is exposed to the real-life condition of the family unit, such as drug negotiations in the home, intoxicated or hostile family members, or a dangerous neighborhood. It is impossible to anticipate all high-risk situations, but it is possible to use common sense ideas to increase personal safety by reducing excessive risks. Particular safety precautions can be followed for the home visit.

Table 6. Family health questions.

How is health defined?

What are the family health practices?

Does the family rely on cultural healers, Western medicine, or both?

Is there a sense of intimidation when working with health professionals?

Who are the significant people the family seeks and relies on for health care and information?

Which family member is the primary contact?

Is illness considered a punishment?

Who is the primary caregiver?

Preparation in the office

1. Leave a schedule of visits and expected time of return.
2. Call and confirm visit with parent, when possible.
3. Have current directions, map, and sufficient gas.
4. Take a cellular phone when available.

Awareness in the neighborhood

1. Don't make home visits on paydays (usually the first of the month).
2. Restrict home visits to daylight hours, schedule during mornings when possible.
3. Avoid leaving valuables within sight in the car.
4. Lock the car.
5. Park close to home or apartment to avoid walking long distances.
6. When returning to the car have keys ready for easy access.
7. Be aware of gang activity in the neighborhood.
8. If it is a dangerous area or home, it may be appropriate to meet at another location, i.e., school, a friend's home, park, local family resource center, or church.

Personal preparation

1. Wear clothes appropriate for the visit.
2. Leave purse and valuables locked in the trunk or the office.
3. Conduct home visits in pairs.
4. Wear a nametag.
5. Display a sense of confidence by walking briskly with your head up.
6. Be alert to the immediate surroundings.

7. Trust your sixth sense — if you have a feeling of impending danger, get out of the situation.

Development of Individualized Plans

A requirement of PL 99-457, Part H, stipulates the use of the Individualized Family Service Plan (IFSP). This law mandates that services be provided to children from birth, be focused on parents as full partners with professionals, and be provided through collaboration among multiple agencies and professionals.

The IFSP is the framework for development of family-focused goals as well as child-directed goals based on multidisciplinary assessments. The family, the major influence on a child, plays a significant role in the design, implementation, and evaluation of all services received by their child. Another important issue is the selection of only one case manager even when numerous agencies and professionals are involved. Ideally one IFSP is developed by all involved agencies, though single agency IFSPs may be done.

The emphasis of the IFSP process is on enabling and strengthening families as well as encouraging and maintaining the family support already in place. This demands a change of attitude, feelings, and thought patterns of all staff serving young children and their families.

Many infants prenatally drug exposed are living in poverty, homeless situations, in single or multigenerational homes, or foster care. Those living in upper-or middle-class homes may not be identified as prenatally drug exposed and may receive services based on needs rather than diagnosis (as all children should). Due to the dissimilar living circumstances of these families, implementation of the law may require patience, sensitivity, and perseverance of the multiprofessional staff involved with the family.

The family-oriented multiagency approach used in early intervention services may be perceived as intrusive into family life. Furthermore, it is difficult to implement with families in disorganized or chaotic circumstances. There may also be conflict with some cultural and ethnic family values. Due to the diverse manner in which the law is being implemented it may be years before it's known if the law is useful to families or an unattainable federal mandate.

Health services are listed as a related service in PL 99-457 to the extent necessary to enable the child to benefit from early intervention services. The health assessment is part of the overall developmental assessment and is included in the team assessment written report.

It is useful to have health care objectives in the IFSP because this provides a descriptive baseline of the child's health strengths and needs, engages support of parents and staff regarding nursing care goals, and documents school health care delivered and health outcomes achieved (Silkworth & Haas 1993). Health objectives are directed toward the parent or other caregiver since the infant and young child cannot perform the activities. The school health nurse uses the nursing process while working with children, their families, school staff, and other professionals in a variety of circumstances and environments. (Luehr 1993).

SUMMARY

Families vary in structure, values, beliefs, and coping strategies. Regard for this diversity is essential in family-centered early intervention. Family-centered services begin with the acknowledgment that the family is the constant in the child's life whereas agencies, and personnel within those agencies, change over time. Accordingly, the health assessment plan should be shaped by family priorities and needs as well as diagnostic concerns. In situations where critical health needs are not a priority for the family, the nurse has a professional and ethical obligation to advocate for the child by bringing these issues to the attention of the caregivers so they can make informed decisions. Empowering the family may stretch the nurse's vision of traditional nursing roles and practices, but this enabling approach encourages family ownership of the plans and ultimately results in more effective, efficient follow-up.

REFERENCES

Aslin RN. Visual and auditory development in infancy. In Osofsky JP, ed. *Handbook of Infant Development.* 2nd ed. New York: Wiley, 1987.

Barnard KE. *Instructor's Learning Resource Manual.* Seattle: N-CAST Publication, University of Washington, 1979.

Berry M, Eisenson J. *Speech Disorders.* New York: Appleton-Century-Crofts, 1956.

Carzoli RP, Murphy SP, Hammer-Knisely J, Houz J. Evaluation of auditory brain-stem response in full-term infants of cocaine abusing mothers. *American Journal of Diseases in Children* 1991; 145: 1013-6.

Chasnoff IJ, Griffith DR, Freier C, Murray J. Cocaine/polydrug use in pregnancy: Two-year follow-up. *Pediatrics* 1992;89:284-9.

Chasnoff IJ, Lewis DE, Griffith DR, Willey S. Cocaine and pregnancy: Clinical and toxicological implications for the neonate. *Clinical Chemistry* 1989;35:1276-8.

Church MW, Gerkin KP. Hearing disorders in children with fetal alcohol syndrome: Findings from case reports. *Pediatrics* 1988;82:147-54.

Dominguez R, Vila-Coro AA, Slopis JM, Bohan TP. Brain and ocular abnormalities in infants with utero exposure to cocaine and other street drugs. *American Journal of Diseases in Children* 1991; 145: 688-95.

Downs M. *Hearing-Screening Guide.* Denver: Bam World Markets, 1984.

Eckerman CD, Lynne AS, Gross SJ. Different developmental courses for very low birthweight infants differing in early head growth. *Developmental Psychology* 1985; 21: 813-22.

Egeland B, Sroufe LA. Developmental sequelae of maltreatment in infancy. *New Directions for Child Development* 1981; 11: 77-92.

Finnegan LP, Kandall SR. Maternal and neonatal effects of alcohol and drugs. In Lowinson JH, Ruiz P, Millman RB, Langrod, JG eds. *Substance Abuse: A Comprehensive Textbook.* Baltimore: Williams & Wilkins, 1992, pp 628-85.

Fried PA. Postnatal Consequences of Maternal Marijuana Use. Rockville, MD: The Institute, 1985, pp 426-30 (National Institute on Drug Abuse Research Dynograph Series 59).

Good WV, Ferriero DM, Golabi M, Kobori JA. Abnormalities of the visual system in infants exposed to cocaine. *Ophthalmology* 1992; 99: 341-6.

Harsham J, Hayden J, Disbrow D. The nutritional implication of intrauterine cocaine exposure to the infant: A review of the literature. Unpublished manuscript, 1993.

Harsham J, Hayden J, Disbrow D. Growth patterns of babies exposed to cocaine and other drugs in utero (In Press).

Hecox K, Deegan DM. Methodological issues in the study of auditory development. In Gottlieb G, Krasnegor NA, eds. *Measurement of Audition and Vision in the First Year of Postnatal Life: A Methodological Overview.* Norwood, NJ: Ablex Publishing, 1985.

High-tech hearing test: A boon for difficult-to-diagnose patients. *Medsounds 1993;* 8 (1).

Isenberg SJ, Spiero A, Inkelis SH. Ocular signs of cocaine intoxication in neonates. *American Journal of Ophthalmology* 1987;10(3): 211-4.

Kearsley R, Snider M, Richie R, Crawford JD, Talbot NB. Study of relations between psychological environment and child behavior: A pediatric procedure. *American Journal of Diseases in Children* 1982; 146: 104-6.

Kline J, Stein Z, Hulzler M. Cigarettes, alcohol and marijuana: varying associations with birthweight. *International Journal of Epidemiology* 1987;16:44-51.

Lewis KD, Bennett B, Schmeder NH. The care of infants menaced by cocaine abuse. *Maternal Child Health* 1989;14:324-9.

Lewis KD, Thomson HB. *Manual of School Health* Menlo Park, CA: Addison-Wesley Publishing, 1986, pp 19-53.

Luehr RE. Using the nursing process in the school setting. In Haas MB, ed. *The School Nurse's Source Book of Individualized Healthcare Plans.* North Branch, MN: Sunrise River Press, 1993, pp 1-21.

Maccoby EE, Martin JA. Socialization in the context of the family: Parent-child interaction. In Hetherington EM, ed. *Handbook of Child Psychology.* Vol. 4. New York: Wiley, 1983.

Nelson LB, Erlich S, Calhoun JH, Matteusci T, Finnegan LP. Occurrence of strabismus in infants born to drug-dependent women. *American Journal of Diseases in Children* 1987;141:175-8.

Oro AS, Dixon SD. Perinatal cocaine and methamphetamine exposure: Maternal and neonatal correlates. *Journal of Pediatrics* 1987;111(4):571-8.

Pearson GA. Nutrition in the middle years of childhood. *Maternal Child Nursing* 1977; 2 (6): 378-84.

Proctor ST, Lordi SL, Zaiger DS. *School Nursing Practice: Roles and Standards.* Scarborough, ME: National Association of School Nurses, 1993.

Salomy A, Anderson R, Bull D, Eldredge L. Brainstem transmission time in infants exposed to cocaine in utero. *Journal of Pediatrics* 1990;117: 627-9.

Sato-Viacrucis K. Personal communication, February 1994.

Shih L, Cone-Wesson B, Reddix B. Effects of maternal cocaine abuse on the neonatal auditory system. *International Journal of Pediatric Otorhinolaryngology* 1988; 15: 245-51.

Silkworth C, Haas M. *Individualized Health Care Plans*. Paper presented at the Annual Conference of the National Association of School Nurses, Minneapolis, June 1993.

Surgeon General, U.S. Department of Health and Human Services. *The Health Benefits of Smoking Cessation. A Report of the Surgeon General* Washington, D.C.: U.S. Government Printing Office, 1990.

Surgeon General, U.S. Department of Health and Human Services. *Healthy People 2000: National Health Promotion and Disease Prevention Objectives*. Washington, D.C.: U.S. Government Printing Office, 1993 (DHHS publication No. PHS 91-50213).

Turner RG. Analysis of recommended guidelines for infants hearing screening. *ASHA* 1990; 32(9):57-61.

Weathers WT, Crane MM, Sauvain KJ, Blackhurst DW. Cocaine use of women from a defined population: Prevalence at delivery and effects of growth in infants. *Pediatrics* 1993; 91:350-4.

Whaley LF, Wong DC. *Nursing Care of Infants and Children*. 4th ed. St. Louis: Mosby Yearbook, 1991.

Wold SJ. *School Nursing: A Framework for Practice*. North Branch, MN: Sunrise River Press, 1981.

ANNOTATED BIBLIOGRAPHY

Haas MK, ed. *The School Nurse's Source Book of Individualized Healthcare Plans*. **North Branch, MN: Sunrise River Press, 1993.**
Written primarily for school health nurses, this book provides a systematic, organized way to use the nursing process in the development of specific individualized healthcare plans (IHPs). It includes assessment tools, checklists, and questions fashioned to ensure the development of comprehensive IHPs for forty of the most common health issues observed in the school environment. It provides a framework for the nurse to plan, describe, document, and evaluate the nursing care provided to the school-age child.

Lewis KD, Thomson HB. *Manual of School Health*. **Menlo Park, CA: Addison-Wesley Publishing, 1986.**
This comprehensive manual provides the school nurse with a quick reference when working with children with acute and chronic health conditions, birth through age twenty-one. It summarizes growth and developmental characteristics and assessment of hearing and vision. An entire chapter is devoted to special education including a brief description of commonly used developmental assessment tools and special health care procedures.

Proctor ST, Lordi SL, Zaiger DS. *School Nursing Practice: Roles and Standards*. **Scarborough, ME: National Association of School Nurses, 1993.**
This document represents the application of the American Nurses' Associations' Standards of "Clinical Nursing Practice" (1991) to a national speciality of school nursing. Standard concepts discussed include the nurse as: provider of client care, communicator, planner and coordinator of client care, client teacher, and investigator, and the role within the discipline of nursing.

Wold SJ. *School Nursing: A Framework for Practice*. **North Branch, MN: Sunrise River Press, 1981.**
Written primarily for school nurses, this book defines school nursing as a specialty practice and provides the philosophical and theoretical framework for practice. Realistic roles, goals, and expected contri-

butions of the nurse within a school system are discussed within a systematic process. It also includes chapters on school nursing tools, helping relationships, and children with special needs.

Cognitive Development of Children Prenatally Exposed to Alcohol, Tobacco, and Other Drugs

Dan R. Griffith, Ph.D.

The cognitive development of children prenatally exposed to alcohol, tobacco, and other drugs is not determined by the prenatal exposure alone. The lifestyle led by substance-abusing parents exposes children to many additional prenatal and postnatal risk factors. Damage done to the developing nervous system by prenatal exposure to drugs and/or other biological risk factors combines with factors such as chaotic, inconsistent, and sometimes abusive parenting; multiple placements; poverty; and urban violence to place this population at risk for a variety of developmental difficulties. The evidence to date indicates that a small percentage of children prenatally exposed to drugs may suffer damage to their nervous systems which results in identifiable cognitive deficits ranging from severe mental retardation to subtle learning problems. By far, the greater damage to cognitive achievement and performance seems to come from the effects the drug-using lifestyle has on other areas of development. Children with insecure attachments and/or behavioral problems fueled by insecurity, fear, anger, or a sense of learned helplessness are often emotionally and cognitively unable to engage in efficient learning or to demonstrate what they already know. Interventions to promote optimal cognitive development with this group of children must therefore include emotional and behavioral development.

Cognitive development depends on and is affected by a myriad of biological and environmental factors. Anything that disturbs the balance of the prenatal environment, thereby disrupting brain growth and development, may have lasting consequences for cognitive development. Any factor that detracts from an optimal postnatal environment may also contribute to long-term cognitive impairments.

A potential risk factor which has received a great deal of attention from researchers and the media over the last several years is in-utero exposure to alcohol and other drugs. Contrary to reports in the media, researchers are far from a clear definition of the effects prenatal exposure to any particular drug (with the possible exception of alcohol) has on the fetus. This is due largely to the fact that perinatal substance abuse does not occur in a vacuum. The average infant born to a substance-abusing woman is usually exposed to combinations of drugs, making it difficult to isolate the effects attributable to a specific drug. The drug-using lifestyle of the chronic substance abuser further confuses the picture by exposing the fetus/infant/child to numerous biological and environmental risk factors in addition to in-utero drugs. Only by studying the effects of those factors which coexist with perinatal substance abuse can researchers begin to understand the relative contribution of in-utero exposure to alcohol and other drugs.

Developmental Tasks

Just as prenatal drug exposure does not occur in a vacuum, cognitive development does not occur in isolation. During the first several years of life the infant/child is engaged in a variety of developmental tasks, all of which are interrelated. These tasks include physical growth and maturation, attachment, cognitive development, motor development, and the development of a sense of self. Successful completion of each of these tasks is aided by successful completion of the others. Conversely, factors that impede the completion of any task may adversely affect the others. Every child naturally strives toward the completion of all of these tasks but requires biological and environmental support for successful task completion.

Optimal physical growth and maturation from conception through delivery depend on the pregnant women receiving good prenatal care and adequate nutrition. Optimal postnatal growth and maturation require good nutrition; routine pediatric care; consistent, nurturing caretakers; and safe housing.

Secure attachment is essential for optimal cognitive growth in that it provides children with the security and social confidence to explore their environments. To develop secure attachments children must have consistent, nurturing caretakers.

Cognitive development requires opportunities to explore developmentally appropriate playthings and engage in developmentally appropriate social interactions. Levels of stimulation should not exceed the child's threshold for stimulation. Consistent, structured, predictable environmental routines and appropriate levels of stimulation allow children to learn the rules of their environments. Secure knowledge of the familiar frees up cognitive energy for exploration of the unknown. Conversely, chaotic, inconsistent, overstimulating environments force the child to expend cognitive energy coping with the present environment. Children living under such circumstances often develop methods for avoiding rather than engaging stimulation.

Motor development is optimized by environments that elicit and support first visual and later motor exploration. Such environments must be free from physical hazards so that the child can engage in successful exploration in safety and with a sense of security.

Development of a sense of self depends on the successful completion of each of the other developmental tasks. When presented with consistent, structured, predictable environments, children with healthy, fully functioning nervous systems are able to exercise and develop their abilities to self-regulate. Children's definitions of their worlds and their abilities to differentiate themselves from those worlds are determined by the qualities of their surroundings and of the people who determine the settings to which the children are exposed (Rivlin 1990). Through playful interactions with the people and objects in these settings children strive for mastery of skills and competency in dealing with their environments (Blasco, Hrncir & Blasco 1990; Fenson & Schell 1985; Tittnich et al 1989). When caretakers and/or environmental circumstances restrict children's opportunities to explore their environments and to develop mastery of their physical and intellectual skills, children develop confused, inadequate definitions of their self and worlds, which further hampers social, emotional, and cognitive developmental progress.

Developmental Risk Factors Associated With Substance Abuse Lifestyles

Children exposed prenatally to drugs, in particular those exposed to cocaine, have received a great deal of media coverage over the last several years. Although this attention has served to alert the general public to the potential harmful effects of substance abuse during pregnancy, the presentation of worse-case scenarios of children prenatally drug exposed as the norm has created an oversimplified, inaccurate, stereotypical view of the problem. Television and newspaper accounts of so-called crack babies describe and/or display tiny, premature, low birthweight, tube- and wire-laden infants screaming and trembling uncontrollably. Older children are reported to be hyperactive, hyperaggressive, antisocial, and unteachable. The conclusions usually implied, and frequently stated in media reports, are that 1) all children exposed prenatally to alcohol and/or other drugs are impaired, 2) very little can be done to help these children recover, and 3) all of the medical, behavioral, and learning problems observed in these children are caused directly and completely by exposure to alcohol and/or other drugs.

Children fitting the media descriptions do exist, but such severely impaired children are the exception rather than the rule. With few exceptions, children experiencing severe difficulties have been exposed to so many different risk factors it is impossible to attribute their problems to prenatal drug exposure alone. Lack of or poor quality prenatal care, inadequate maternal nutrition, intrauterine growth retardation, prematurity, the drug user's lifestyle, poverty, homelessness, abuse, neglect, and multiple caretakers and/or foster placements are just a few of the major risk factors that have an impact on the social, emotional, and intellectual development of many children who have been exposed prenatally to alcohol and/or other drugs. Research has linked each of these risk factors to increased rates of attachment difficulties, behavioral and/or emotional difficulties, and cognitive deficiencies in the absence of prenatal exposure to drugs.

Inadequate nutrition and lack of or poor quality prenatal care are associated with increased risks for premature delivery and intrauterine growth retardation even in the absence of prenatal exposure to alcohol and/or other drugs. Premature and/or low-birth-weight babies (whether prenatally drug exposed or not) are more likely to display cognitive problems with visual motor skills, spatial skills, and receptive language (Brooks-Gunn, Liaw & Klebanov 1992), to repeat grades in school and/or require special education (McCormick, Gartmaker & Sobol 1990), and to display behavioral problems associated with hyperactivity (McCormack, Gartmaker & Sobol 1990; Robertson, Etches & Kyle 1990). Children born small for gestational age are more likely to have significantly smaller head sizes than children born at an appropriate size for gestational age (Robertson, Etches & Kyle 1990). Small head size at birth (less than the fifth percentile), especially when accompanied by subnormal head growth over the first few months of life, is predictive of a greater incidence of mental and motor delays over the first two years of life (Eckerman, Sturm & Gross 1985) and lower IQ and receptive

language scores, speech and reading difficulties, and hyperactivity in school-age children (Hack et al 1991).

After birth, children exposed prenatally to drugs may be at greater risk due to the postnatal risk factors associated with their caregivers' substance-abusing lifestyle than to the direct effects of prenatal exposure. One of the greatest risk factors facing children prenatally exposed to alcohol and other drugs may be the continued drug use by one or both parents in the home. Parents actively engaging in substance abuse and drug-seeking behavior are at best more likely to be inconsistent in their positive and negative interactions with their children and at worst more likely to abuse and/or neglect their children (Mitchel & Savage 1991). Maternal inconsistencies in behavior may be responsible at least in part for attachment difficulties reported in some children prenatally exposed to drugs (Rodning, Beckwith & Howard 1989). Continued maternal substance abuse also has been linked to withdrawn, depressed, and/or anxious behavior in children (Brown et al 1991), lower developmental scores (Coles, Smith & Falek 1987), and lower IQ scores at age three years, especially in the area of verbal reasoning (Griffith, Azuma & Chasnoff 1994).

Beyond the effects on parental behavior, continued drug use in the home increases the likelihood of the child receiving repeated dosages of the drugs through passive inhalation, accidental ingestion, and/or breast-feeding. Although a few case studies concerning the immediate effects of such postnatal exposures have been reported in the literature (Neuspiel & Hamel 1991), there is no information to date on the long-term consequences.

Multigenerational poverty is a potent risk factor often associated with, but certainly not limited to, families affected by substance abuse, which impedes the developmental progress of a growing number of children in this country. Poverty can be associated with parenting styles that interfere with children's optimal cognitive development. Mothers of low socioeconomic status vocalize less often to their infants than do mothers from middle socioeconomic backgrounds (Field 1980) and become even less interactive with their children as they grow into toddlers, whereas middle-class mothers tend to increase the rate of interactions as children get older (Farran & Ramey 1980). Poverty also has been linked to a higher incidence of behavioral problems in children (Wasserman et al 1990) and lower scores on tasks measuring cognitive functioning (Dietrich et al 1991; Greene et al 1991).

One cannot, however, posit a direct cause/effect relationship between the parenting style of poor parents and the developmental outcomes of their children. Poverty includes multiple risk factors which individually and/or interactively have a negative impact on the resources, personalities, and behavioral patterns of parents and on the physical growth and maturation as well as the social, emotional, and cognitive development of children. Children raised in poverty, for example, often receive inadequate postnatal nutrition and inconsistent and/or inadequate health care. Poor postnatal nutrition impedes physical growth and maturation and is linked to behavioral and cognitive difficulties. Poor postnatal nutrition may also make children more susceptible to disease and

when combined with poor health care lead to chronic illnesses in some children. Without adequate pediatric care available many women of poverty use hospital emergency rooms as their children's pediatricians and may not seek treatment until illnesses become severe. Chronic illness and frequent use of hospital emergency services are both predictive of behavioral and attention problems in children as they reach school age (Larson, Pless & Miettinen 1988).

Children of lower socioeconomic status are more likely to be raised in inadequate overcrowded, poorly maintained housing. Such circumstances increase the likelihood that children will be exposed to toxic levels of lead and suffer resultant deficits in cognitive functioning (Deitrich et al 1991; Cordero 1990). Missing screens, poor lighting, and poorly maintained elevators in their housing units increase the chances of accidental physical harm coming to children and increase the chance of children and/or parents becoming victims of crimes as well (Dubrow & Garbarino 1989). Inner-city parents fearing the physical dangers presented by poorly maintained buildings and the social dangers of gang- and drug-related violence often develop severely restrictive and punitive discipline styles in an effort to keep their children from harm (Kimball et al 1980; Garbarino, Kolstelny & Dubrow 1991). Restrictive parenting styles are in turn linked to an increased rate of behavioral problems in children (Larson, Pless & Miettinen 1988).

In spite of inner-city parents' best efforts to isolate their children from the violence of their neighborhoods, the majority of inner-city children are well acquainted with violence. A group of researchers interviewing families from Chicago housing projects found that 25% of the children surveyed had witnessed a homicide first hand (Garbarino, Kolstelny & Dubrow 1991) and 100% of the children aged five years and under had direct experience with shootings, ranging from hearing shots at night to witnessing the deaths of relatives (Dubrow & Garbarino 1989). According to Garbarino and associates (1991) the effects of living under chronic danger may include alterations in personality and major behavioral changes. Children may develop hyperaggressive patterns that protect them on the streets but are inappropriate in a classroom, or they may become withdrawn and distrustful of any social contact (Garbarino et al 1991). Patterns of lashing out or withdrawing physically and/or emotionally when physically challenged may carry over into the realm of cognitive challenges. Such behavioral patterns may then interfere with children's abilities to demonstrate their cognitive skills, or even worse interfere with their acquisition of same. In addition to the emotional trauma suffered when children are exposed to chronic danger, the restrictions placed on children for their own safety may limit cognitive development by reducing the opportunities to explore their environments and to engage in peer interactions.

The behavioral problems manifested by some inner-city and/or substance-exposed children further hamper cognitive development if misinterpreted by teachers. Teachers may interpret aggressive and/or impulsive behavior as indicative of severe emotional/behavioral or attention deficit/hyperactivity disorders. The children perceived as problems are then likely to be placed in restrictive educational environments which emphasize behavioral management, often at the expense of cognitive endeavors. Withdrawn children may be interpreted as mentally delayed and/or disinterested in learning. Such labeling, when combined with the overcrowding prevalent in classrooms across the country, is likely to cause self-fulfilling prophecies for many children. Overwhelmed teachers spend less time teaching children and view the children as less capable or less interested in learning, and the children in turn learn less.

Homelessness is a developmental risk factor associated with poverty which has increased dramatically over the past several years. Recent estimates indicate that families account for approximately 30% of the homeless population (Rivlin 1990). Homeless children are more likely to receive inadequate nutrition and health care and be exposed directly to the social threats of the city. The inconsistencies created in children's lives by moving from shelter to shelter or from one relative's house to another may cause long-term socio-emotional damage in addition to severely restricting the type of experiences that would promote healthy cognitive development. The lack of consistent places of residence for many children may also severely limit the ability of the schools to provide consistent instruction. Those children who are identified may be moved frequently from school to school. Such frequent disruptions and readjustments not only interfere with the learning process but may aggravate existing emotional/behavioral problems in some homeless children. Still other children may fall through the cracks of the child welfare and educational systems and go for extended periods receiving no formal educational interventions.

Having a consistent home plays a crucial role in development of the child's self-identity (Rivlin 1990). As children develop their sense of self they need to engage their environments, but they also need to be able to disengage when the level of stimulation becomes too great. A home serves as a means to disengage periodically from the greater society, but within the home children require a personal place where they can disengage periodically from the family (Rivlin 1990). Homelessness, therefore, deprives children and their families of the means to regulate their interactions with society and members of the family to regulate interactions within the family. Over time this powerlessness may force children and families to withdraw emotionally from society and from each other in an effort to survive (Rivlin 1990), further limiting children's opportunities to engage in activities that foster cognitive development.

Concerned about the difficulties that many substance-abusing parents face in providing appropriate environments for their children, the response of many people has been to punish the parents and protect the children by removing the children from the parents' custody. Placing many additional children in an already overcrowded, understaffed, undertrained foster care system, however, also puts them at significant risk. Although children are usually removed from the homes of their natural parent(s) for good reason (Wightman 1991), not enough foster families are available for their children. Once removed from the home, the children may be left in

boarder nurseries or sent to emergency shelters for months at a time. Those placed may be sent to homes hours away from their natural parent(s), making it difficult for the natural parents to establish and/or maintain a relationship with the children. Consequently, when the child(ren) is (are) returned to the natural parents both they and the child(ren) have to start their relationship from scratch. The child in particular has to begin a new relationship with total strangers while grieving over the loss of previous caretakers. Perhaps the greatest danger to children within the foster system is when this pattern of loss, grief, and adaptation is repeated again and again as the child goes through multiple placements. This is particularly likely to occur with multi-risk children who are more likely to exhibit difficult temperaments and behavioral problems. Such children are more likely to "burn out" foster parents who are given inadequate training or support. Multiple placements deprive the child of the consistent, nurturing caregiver, the predictable environments, and the personal spaces that are essential for normal social, emotional, and intellectual development. The absence of secure attachment secondary to multiple placements severely undermines the emotional security of children and as a direct result the depth and breadth of their exploratory play. The concepts children learn through exploratory play serve as the basic building blocks of cognitive development. Consequently, anything that restricts exploratory play impedes cognitive development. For some children, multiple changes in caretakers may cause the development of a sense of learned helplessness. As these children move from place to place caretaking styles and household rules change, sometimes dramatically. Behaviors that were rewarded at one place may be ignored or even punished at the next. Under such circumstances, some children give up trying to master their environment.

Developmental Consequences of Prenatal Exposure to Alcohol and Other Drugs

In spite of some inconsistencies from study to study, research, which controls for the presence of risk factors other than prenatal exposure to alcohol and/or other drugs, has demonstrated some specific group effects for prenatal exposure to alcohol in particular and to a number of other drugs (most notably cocaine, marijuana, opiates, and nicotine). In interpreting these findings, however, it is important to stay mindful that researchers are looking at *group* effects. When large numbers of children who have been prenatally exposed to alcohol and/ or other drugs are compared to large numbers of children who have not been exposed, a group effect for the drug(s) under study would be any effect that occurs more often in the exposed group than in the nonexposed group. The specific effect will not occur in every child within the exposed group, nor to the same degree in those children who display the effect. The effect will also be displayed albeit less frequently in some children of the nonexposed group. Finally, considering the myriad of variables which impact the developmental outcome of children, it is likely that any group effect is due in part or at least moderated by factors other than exposure to the particular drug(s) under study, which may not have been adequately controlled for in the study.

Studies controlling for prenatal care and nutrition reveal that prenatal exposure to alcohol and cocaine are related to smaller height, weight, and head circumference at birth and decreased growth rates (Day & Richardson 1991; Zuckerman & Bresnahan 1991; Chasnoff et al 1992). Prenatal exposure to tobacco has been linked to smaller infants at birth in terms of length and weight and to continued small stature in a number of exposed children (Rush & Callahan 1989). The long-term effects of exposure to tobacco on stature may be due at least in part to continued postnatal exposure through passive inhalation of smoke.

Any factor that leads to intrauterine growth retardation, especially with regard to head circumference, is likely to interfere with the growth and development of the central nervous system. Although no perfect relationship exists between head circumference and subsequent cognitive development, children with head circumferences below the fifth percentile are at significant risk for cognitive deficiencies ranging from mental retardation to subtle learning problems. When prenatal exposure to alcohol and other drugs is combined with poor prenatal care and/or nutrition and possible postnatal exposure to the drug(s) under study, the effects on prenatal growth and development will likely be greater than exposure to any one risk factor. More research is needed, however, to study the independent and interactive effects of these variables when they occur simultaneously.

Disturbances in the neurobehavioral organization of the neonate have been linked to prenatal exposure to alcohol

(Day & Richardson 1991), cocaine (Chasnoff, Burns & Schnoll 1985; Chasnoff et al 1989; Lester et al 1991; Zuckerman & Bresnahan 1991), opiates (Jeremy & Hans 1985; Hans 1989), marijuana (Fried 1989), and nicotine (Rush & Callahan 1989). The behavioral disorganization observed in some infants exposed prenatally to alcohol, tobacco, and/or other drugs may be manifested through difficulties in state regulation, irritability, problems with motor control, and problems with social interactions. Infants displaying such characteristics have been referred to by some as "low-threshold" infants. Such infants expend so much of their energy regulating internal stimuli and bodily systems that they have little energy left to engage and learn about their external environments. Therefore relatively low levels of external stimulation are required to push these infants beyond their thresholds for overstimulation. The threshold for overstimulation is the point at which infants either lose the ability to regulate themselves (disintegrating into frantic, disorganized crying) or pull down into protective sleep states to avoid further external stimulation (Griffith 1988).

The most obvious characteristic of low-threshold infants is their difficulty in reaching and maintaining a calm alert state during which they would be processing external stimulation. This difficulty may have lasting consequences for low-threshold children's cognitive and social-emotional development. The quiet alert state is the state during which virtually all infant learning takes place concerning the external environment. Less quiet alert time means less learning. The difficulty low-threshold infants have in maintaining quiet alert states often is

most noticeable during social interactions. The demands that socially engaging caretakers make on infants' visual, auditory, and motor systems force many low-threshold infants to escape into unavailable sleep or cry states. Such behavior from their infants causes many caretakers to feel frustrated and often rejected. Caretakers may then respond to their infants with inappropriate behaviors that may further impair the infants' abilities to engage their environment.

For example, those parents who have fragile, low-threshold infants who respond to any attempts to hold, talk, or socially engage them by disintegrating into chaotic, uncontrollable cry states may learn very quickly to avoid interacting with their infants in an effort to avoid overstimulating them. At the extreme, these infants may be left in darkened rooms with minimal stimulation and little or no human contact. Such environmental deprivation if allowed to continue may cause severe motor and cognitive delays. On the other hand, those parents/caretakers of infants who seek to protect themselves from overstimulation by pulling down into deep sleep states are very likely to increase the levels of stimulation they provide to their infants in an effort to jar the infants out of sleep. Under these circumstances many infants learn to shut down even further. Over time these perpetually overstimulated infants may learn to shut down in response to every environmental challenge and become increasingly adept at doing so. Such cognitive withdrawal from the environment severely limits children's learning experiences.

It is important to note that high-risk

infants who have not been exposed prenatally to alcohol and/or other drugs (most notably premature and/or low birth weight infants) may be characterized as low threshold and often display the same patterns of behavior just described. Further, mothers of difficult, low-threshold infants tend to react to their infants' behavior by avoiding them or repeatedly overwhelming them with stimulation whether the mothers are substance abusers or not.

Interventions aimed at compensating for the neurobehavioral disorganization of low-threshold infants should be started at birth. Teaching parents/caretakers how to create environments that stimulate their infants but allow them to remain below their thresholds for overstimulation will enable the infants to develop and refine their self-regulatory skills (Griffith 1988). These skills allow infants/children to pace themselves during learning episodes, alternately engaging and withdrawing from stimulation as needed. Helping children stay below threshold requires caretakers to create consistent, predictable environments which are responsive to children's signs that they are becoming overstimulated.

The older children get, the more likely it is that prenatal events such as exposure to alcohol and/or other drugs will have been moderated by events in the postnatal environment. Consequently, evidence concerning the long-term effects of prenatal exposure to alcohol and/or other drugs is scarce and when it does exist is extremely difficult to interpret. Alcohol is the only drug of those commonly abused which consistently has been documented to have serious and lasting physical, behavioral, and cognitive consequences on infants and children. Heavy prenatal exposure to alcohol often results in fetal alcohol syndrome (FAS) which includes stunted prenatal and postnatal growth, facial and other physical anomalies, and central nervous system deficiencies (Burgess & Streissguth 1990; Day & Richardson 1991; Scott, Urbana & Boussy 1991). The central nervous system deficiencies of FAS are associated with a number of behavioral problems, including hyperactivity, irritability, distractibility, and stereotypical behaviors (Day & Richardson 1991) and with cognitive deficiencies often manifested as global mental retardation (Burgess & Streissguth 1990; Scott, Urbana & Boussy 1991). The average IQ scores of children with FAS fall in the mildly retarded range with some children displaying severe retardation and others attaining IQ levels in the average and above average ranges.

In spite of strong evidence linking FAS to alcohol during pregnancy, however, other factors must be considered. Not every woman who abuses alcohol during pregnancy has a child with FAS (Day & Richardson 1991; Jones, Smith & Ulleland 1973). If a woman has one FAS child she is much more likely to have another if she continues to drink in subsequent pregnancies. This suggests a potential genetic factor in the occurrence of FAS (Day & Richardson 1991). Some children who have been exposed to heavy levels of alcohol have the cognitive and behavioral difficulties associated with FAS without the physical abnormalities. These children are considered to have fetal alcohol effects (FAE) (Burgess & Streissguth 1990). The severity of cognitive and/or behavioral difficulties among children diagnosed as having FAS or FAE varies to a great deal from child to child. As a general rule children diagnosed as FAE have higher IQ scores than those with FAS, but there is considerable overlap between the two distributions (Day & Richardson 1991).

Research into the effects of light to moderate consumption of alcohol during pregnancy indicates more subtle cognitive and behavioral effects which do not occur consistently across research populations. Streissguth and associates (1989), for example, reported that the four-year-old children of mothers who drank as few as three drinks a day during their pregnancies scored an average of five IQ points lower than four-year-old children of mothers who did not drink during pregnancy. The children exposed to moderate levels of alcohol in Streissguth's study were also more likely to display attentional deficits at age four years. Fried and Watkinson (1990) found that low levels of maternal consumption of alcohol had negative effects on cognitive scores at twenty-four and thirty-six months on a group of middle-class children in their sample. These effects, however, were gone by the time the children reached forty-eight months of age. The sample of women and children followed by Fried and Watkinson were a low-risk sample predominantly from middle socioeconomic backgrounds and were receiving routine follow-ups from birth. These findings thus might suggest that low levels of prenatal alcohol exposure may produce cognitive deficits which are ameliorated under appropriate environmental circumstances. In fact, Greene and colleagues (1991) reported developmental outcomes through five years of age which indicated that exposure to alcohol in the absence of FAS or FAE is less im-

portant in predicting performance on cognitive measures than is the quality of the home environment.

Similarly, the long-term effects of their mothers' prenatal use of various combinations of cocaine, marijuana, tobacco, and/or opiates on children appear to be subtle and do not occur consistently across research populations. The most consistent findings include growth deficiencies (most notably in head circumference), behavioral and attentional difficulties, and cognitive deficits often in the form of learning disabilities. The disparate findings among these studies are particularly difficult to interpret owing to the extreme variability across research populations. In order to interpret these studies adequately one must examine carefully the specific characteristics of the population of women and children under study (i.e., Have all the major factors that affect the development of children been identified and controlled for so that existing differences may be legitimately attributed to the drug(s) in question?). One must further identify the differences across studies and within a particular study's comparison groups as to the number, types, quantities, frequencies, methods, and timing of drug use. Finally, the critical reader of research about the long-term effects of prenatal drug exposure must be aware that the subtle effects which certain drugs have on children may 1) be masked under certain testing conditions, 2) affect higher levels of selective cognitive functioning which are apparent as children get older, and 3) be attenuated by early interventions.

To date too few studies have been done to support conclusions about the long-term cognitive or behavioral effects of specific dosages of different drugs (except in the case of alcohol). The only long-term study on the effects of prenatal exposure to cocaine, for example, looked only at chronic, heavy users who were abusing multiple drugs (Chasnoff et al 1992; Griffith, Azuma & Chasnoff 1994). This research found that there were no differences in cognitive or motor developmental outcomes by age two years among children prenatally exposed to large doses of cocaine (usually in combination with light to moderate doses of alcohol, marijuana, and/or cigarettes) as compared to children with no prenatal history of drug exposure (Chasnoff et al 1992). The authors of this study, however, warned against the overgeneralization and interpretations of this finding. They reported that in spite of no differences in overall developmental scores, the polydrug-exposed children required more structuring and focusing by the examiner during testing and seemed to have difficulty with items that required self-organization and self-direction from the children. This reported difficulty with self-regulation which some children who were prenatally exposed to drugs have has been noted by other researchers in free-play situations (Rodning, Beckwith & Howard 1989). These findings suggest that many children prenatally exposed to drugs may have difficulty learning and/or performing in situations where they are required to organize environmental input and their responses to same. Some may have particular difficulty when placed in complex, constantly changing environments such as classrooms. Chasnoff and associates (1992) further warned that this research represented a best-case scenario for the developmental outcome of

children exposed prenatally to cocaine and other drugs. The women in this study received adequate prenatal nutrition and good prenatal care beginning in the first trimesters of their respective pregnancies. The children in this study received comprehensive medical and developmental screening, diagnosis, and intervention. There is still no data available on the outcomes for those children who in addition to receiving little or no intervention are exposed to multiple risk factors besides prenatal drug exposure.

The theory that the subtle effects of prenatal exposure to certain drugs may not surface until children get older has been supported by research on prenatal cocaine/polydrug exposure (Griffith, Azuma & Chasnoff 1994) and prenatal marijuana exposure (Fried & Watkinson 1990). Griffith and his colleagues found that their population of cocaine/polydrug-exposed children did not differ from the control group at age two, but by age three scored significantly lower on tasks of verbal reasoning than the nonexposed control group. Fried and Watkinson (1990) reported similar findings in their longitudinal study on the effects of prenatal exposure to marijuana. Through three years of age no differences were found in cognitive functioning between the group which had been prenatally exposed to marijuana and the nonexposed control group. By age four years, however, the group exposed prenatally to marijuana was receiving lower scores on tests of verbal abilities and memory.

The research to date has indicated that most drug-exposed children, with the exception of those diagnosed as FAS or FAE, do not display global learning problems. Even among those who score in the normal ranges on standardized measures of cognitive functioning, however, a number of children prenatally exposed to alcohol and/or other drugs have difficulties with impulse control and sustaining attention (Streissguth et al 1989; Griffith & Freir 1992). Research has demonstrated that these children are able to get normal scores in one-on-one testing situations but have difficulty attending to relevant information and regulating their behavior in more complex situations. These children can learn to regulate their behaviors but often require environmental and/or caretaker support to do so. Those children who never learn to self-regulate are in danger of becoming increasingly withdrawn or increasingly out of control. Either scenario is likely to disrupt social relationships at home and school and may impede cognitive development and interfere with school performance.

Interventions

The concept of a threshold for overstimulation is useful not only for infants but for clinical work with children displaying attentional and/or self-regulatory difficulties which interfere with attention, learning, and school performance. The cognitive deficiencies sometimes displayed by these children are not due to an inability to learn but to an inability to control behaviors which interfere with learning and/or performance. These interfering behaviors are most out of children's control when either internal (for example, fear, anxiety, anger, or faulty information processing) and/or external (for example, complex, chaotic environments and/or frequent, unstructured transitions) stimulation has combined to place the children's levels

of arousal above their respective thresholds for overstimulation.

The internal sources of arousal may be secondary to any of the many psychosocial risks which accompany the drug-using lifestyle. High levels of fear, anxiety, and/or anger may be present in children who have been the victims of and/or the witnesses to domestic or urban violence. These feelings would be further intensified in children with insecure attachments secondary to multiple placements and/or in homeless children who may never feel safe. Intervention for these children must include the development of nurturing, consistent relationships with one or more adults who can foster a basic sense of trust in the children. For those children with serious emotional disturbances, long-term therapy may be required to teach these children how to express and cope with their emotions.

Interventions to control excessive external stimulation are easier to implement and yield almost immediate benefits. When environments are well planned and provide in a consistent and predictable fashion levels of stimulation which are below children's thresholds, children are quite capable of utilizing their existing self-regulatory strategies and even learning new strategies. As children approach their thresholds for overstimulation, however, their usual methods for self-regulation are no longer effective and they have to adopt more intense strategies. Similar to the low-threshold infants discussed earlier in this chapter, low-threshold toddlers and preschoolers respond to excessive stimulation by withdrawing from the sources of stimulation or by becoming overwhelmed by the stimulation and losing all impulse control. These strategies are adaptive in the short run but may become chronic behavioral problems without intervention. When exposed to inconsistent, chaotic, unpredictable environments over extended periods of time (e.g., multiple caregivers, multiple placements, homelessness, continued substance abuse in the home) even the most adaptive children are likely to become apathetic and withdrawn in order to avoid being overwhelmed. Those children who cannot adapt may never learn to self-regulate at all and will display chronic patterns of acting out.

Improving the consistency and predictability of their environments, whether at home or in school, improves all children's abilities to self-regulate. Children with particularly low thresholds for overstimulation or who have already developed chronic patterns of withdrawing or acting out require individually prescribed interventions. Parents and teachers alike can intervene effectively with the behavioral problems of the children under their care by becoming better observers of their own and their children's behavior. Perhaps the best way to accomplish this task is by training caretakers to keep behavioral diaries of their children's problem behaviors. The first step in keeping a behavioral diary is to identify the target behavior which is to be tracked. Once the target behavior has been selected, the observer should record every occurrence of the behavior over a period of several days. Along with each occurrence of the target behavior the observer should record as much information as possible concerning the events which preceded the target behavior. The observer should include any environmental circum-

stances that may have triggered the target behavior and those behaviors of the child's that may be early warning signals of the target behavior. By discovering behavioral triggers, the caretaker can reduce the occurrence of the target behavior by either removing the triggers from the child's environment or desensitizing the child to same.

By identifying the early warning signals for the target behavior the caretaker can intervene with the child before he/she has lost control. For a child with self-regulatory difficulties, the loss of impulse control usually indicates that his/her arousal level has exceeded his/her threshold of self-regulation. Once this threshold has been exceeded most interventions will be unsuccessful and the child will be unable to learn from the caretaker's attempts to intervene. This sets both the child and the caretaker up for failure and frustration and may cause both to lose control. Conversely, when the caretaker intervenes at the first behavioral indications of the child's increasing arousal level more severe behavioral problems can be avoided and the child is still at an arousal level which is conducive to learning.

When keeping a behavioral diary caretakers should also document their own responses to the child's behaviors and the effectiveness of these responses in controlling the child's behavior. Caretakers will then be able to identify which of their responses are effective, which are merely ineffective, and which may actually further increase the child's arousal level.

One of the most frequent complaints voiced by teachers about low-threshold children concerns the apparent inconsistency in their behavior. Awareness of children's thresholds and keeping behavioral logs, however, enable caretakers to predict children's behavior and help those children learn to regulate their behavior over time. The following information is essential for creating appropriate learning environments which meet the individual needs of each high-risk/low-threshold child.

- What is the child's usual threshold for overstimulation?

- What are the child's warning signals in ascending order of increasing arousal?

- At what level of arousal does the child start a given activity or enter a particular situation?

- How stressful are different types of activities and/or situations to the child?

- What activities effectively reduce the arousal level of the child?

If, for example, a teacher recognizes that a particular student begins the school day at a level of arousal very near his/her threshold, the teacher can adjust the class schedule to compensate. Beginning a complex lesson with a child near threshold may at best result in poor learning and at worst in an uncontrollable behavioral outburst that may disrupt the entire class for much of the day. On the other hand, if the teacher first engages the student in activities that will decrease his/her arousal level, learning and behavioral problems can be avoided. The complex lesson that had been planned can be saved for a later time when the child's arousal level is more appropriate for learning.

CONCLUSION

The difficulties faced in explaining the cognitive development of and in designing interventions for children prenatally exposed to alcohol and/or other drugs lie not so much in the fact that they were exposed to a specific drug or combination of drugs but in the multiple factors that contribute to the emotional, behavioral, and/or cognitive problems they may be experiencing. Prenatal exposure to alcohol and/or other drugs, because of its association with so many other developmental risk factors, places children at greater risk for a variety of developmental problems. Problems sustaining attention and regulating behavior have been linked to prenatal exposure to alcohol and/or other drugs and are most likely exacerbated by other risk factors. Attachment and/or socialization disorders, emotional/behavioral disorders, learning deficiencies, and language disorders have been reported for high-risk children in general and in some reports on children exposed prenatally to alcohol and/or other drugs.

Separating out the relative contributions of the different risk factors, including prenatal exposure to alcohol and/or other drugs, to these developmental problems is a difficult if not impossible task that will require a great deal of study. In the meantime, however, it is clear that this country has large numbers of women, children, and families who are in trouble. Just as the causes of these problems are multiple, so must the plans for prevention and intervention be multifaceted. Focusing on drugs alone does not address the needs for safe, well-maintained housing; adequate nutrition; appropriate health care; training and support for caretakers of children; early screening, diagnosis, and intervention for high-risk children; and individualized educational programs for all children. Only by simultaneously addressing all of the major risk factors threatening the well-being of children can we expect to reduce the numbers of children with emotional, behavioral, and/or cognitive difficulties. Successful developmental outcome for each child, therefore, requires each professional or agency that normally deals with a specific facet of development to work together to improve the health of the whole child.

REFERENCES

Blasco PM, Hrncir EJ, Blasco PA. The contribution of maternal involvement to mastery performance in infants with cerebral palsy. *Journal of Early Intervention* 1990;14(2):161-74.

Brooks-Gunn J, Liaw F, Klebanov PK. Effects of early intervention on cognitive function of low birth weight preterm infants. *Journal of Pediatrics* 1992;120:350-9.

Brown RT, Coles CD, Smith IE, Platzman KA, Silverstein J, Erickson S, Falek A. Effects of prenatal alcohol exposure at school age. II. Attention and behavior. *Neurotoxicology and Teratology* 1991; 13: 269-376.

Burgess DM, Streissguth AP. Educating students with fetal alcohol syndrome or fetal alcohol effects. *Pennsylvania Reporter* 1990; 22(1):1-3.

Chasnoff IJ, Burns WJ, Schnoll SH. Cocaine use in pregnancy. *New England Journal of Medicine* 1985; 313: 666-9.

Chasnoff IJ, Griffith DR, MacGregor S, Dirkes K, Burns K. Temporal patterns of cocaine use in pregnancy. *Journal of the American Medical Association* 1989; 261 (12): 1741-4.

Chasnoff IJ, Griffith DR, Freier MC, Murray J. Cocaine/polydrug use in pregnancy: Two year follow-up. *Pediatrics* 1992; 89 (2): 284-9.

Coles CF, Smith IE, Falek A. Prenatal alcohol exposure and infant behavior: immediate effects and implications for later development. In: Beab-Bayog M, ed. *Children of Alcoholics*. New York: Haworth Press, 1987: 87-104.

Cordero JF. Effect of environmental agents on pregnancy outcomes: disturbances of prenatal growth and development. *Medical Clinics of North America* 1990;74(2): 279-90.

Day NL, Richardson GA. Prenatal alcohol exposure: A continuum of effects. *Seminars in Perinatology* 1991;15(4): 271-9.

Dietrich KN, Succop PA, Berger OG, Hammond PB, Bornschein RL. Lead exposure and the cognitive development of urban preschool children: The Cincinnati lead study cohort at age 4 years. *Neurotoxicology and Teratology* 1991; 13:203-11.

Dubrow NF, Garbarino J. Living in the war zone: Mothers and young children in a public housing development. *Child Welfare* 1989; LXVIII: 4-20.

Eckerman CO, Sturm LA, Gross SJ. Different developmental courses for very-low-birthweight infants differing in early head growth. *Developmental Psychology* 1985; 21(5): 813-27.

Farran DC, Ramey CT. Social class differences in dyadic involvement during infancy. *Child Development* 1980;51:254-7.

Fenson L, Schell RE. The origins of exploratory play. *Early Child Development and Care* 1985;19:3-24.

Field TM. Interactions of preterm and term infants with their lower-and middle-class teenage and adult mothers. In: Field T, Goldberg S, Stern P, Sostek A, eds. *High-Risk Infants and Children: Adult and Peer Interactions*. NewYork: Academic Press, 1980, pp 113-31.

Fried PA. Cigarettes and marijuana: Are these measurable long-term neurobehavioral teratogenic efforts. *Neurotoxicology* 1989; 10: 577-84.

Fried PA. Marijuana use during pregnancy: consequences for the offspring. *Seminars in Perinatology* 1991; 15 (4): 280-7.

Fried PA, Watkinson B. 36- and 48-month neurobehavioral follow-up of children prenatally exposed to marijuana, cigarettes, and alcohol. *Developmental and Behavioral Pediatrics* 1990;11(2): 49-58.

Garbarino J, Kolstelny K, Dubrow N. What children can tell us about living in danger. *American Psychologist* 1991; 46 (4): 376-83.

Griffith DR. The effect of prenatal exposure to cocaine on the infant and on early maternal-infant interactions. In: Chasnoff IJ, ed. *Drugs, Alcohol, Pregnancy and Parenting*. Lancaster, UK: Kluwer Academic Publishers, 1988.

Griffith DR, Azume SA, Chasnoff IJ. Three-year outcome of children exposed prenatally to drugs. *Journal of the American Academy of Child and Adolescent Psychiatry* 1994; 33(1):20-7.

Griffith DR, Freir MC. Methodological issues in the assessment of the mother/child interactions of substance abusing women and their children. In: Kilbey MM, Asghar K, eds. *Methodological Issues in Epidemiological, Prevention, and Treatment Research on Drug-Exposed Women and Their Children*. NIDA Research Monograph 1992; 117: 228-47.

Greene T, Ernhart CB, Ager J, Sokol R, Martier S, Boyd T. Prenatal alcohol exposure and cognitive development in the preschool years. *Neurotoxicology and Teratology* 1991;13 (1): 57-68.

Hack M, Breslau NB, Weissman B, Aram D, Klein N, Borawski E. Effect of very low birth weight and subnormal head size on cognitive abilities at school age. *New England Journal of Medicine* 1991; 325: 231-7.

Hans SL. Developmental consequences of prenatal exposure to methadone. *Annals of the New York Academy of Sciences* 1989; 562: 195-207.

Jeremy RJ, Hans SL. Behavior of neonates exposed in utero to methadone as assessed on the Brazelton scale. *Infant Behavior and Development* 1985; 8: 323-6.

Jones KL, Smith DW, Ulleland CN. Pattern malformations in offspring of alcoholic women. *Lancet* 1973;1:1267-71.

Kimball WH, Stewart RB, Conger RD, Burgess RL. In: Field T, Goldberg S, Stern P, Sostek A, eds. *High-Risk Infants and Children: Adult and Peer Interactions*. New York: Academic Press, 1980: 43-69.

Larson CP, Pless IB, Miettinen O. Preschool behavior disorders: their prevalence in relation to determinants. *Journal of Pediatrics* 1988;113:278-85.

Lester BM, Corwin MJ, Sepkoski C, Seifer R, Peucker M, McLaughlin S, Golub HL. Neurobehavioral syndromes in cocaine exposed newborn infants. *Child Development* 1991; 62(4):694-705.

McCormick MC, Gartmaker SL, Sobol AM. Very low birth weight children: behavior problems and school difficulty in a national sample. *Journal of Pediatrics* 1990;117:687-93.

Mitchel M, Savage C. The Relationship Between Substance Abuse and Child Abuse (Working Paper No. 854). Chicago: National Committee for the Prevention of Child Abuse, 1991.

Neuspiel DR, Hamel SC. Cocaine and infant behavior. *Journal of Development and Behavioral Pediatrics* 1991;12: 55-64.

Rivlin RG. Home and homelessness in the lives of children. *Child and Youth Services* 1990;14(1): 5-17.

Robertson CMT, Etches PC, Kyle JM. Eight-year school performance and growth of preterm, small-for-gestational-age infants: A comparative study with subjects matched for birth weight or for gestational age. *Journal of Pediatrics* 1990; 116 (1): 19-26.

Rodning C, Beckwith L, Howard J. Characteristics of attachment and play organization in prenatally drug-exposed toddlers. *Development and Psychopathology* 1989; 1: 277-89.

Rush D, Callahan KR. Exposure to passive cigarette smoking and child development: a critical review. *Annals of the New York Academy of Sciences* 1989; 562: 74-100.

Scott KG, Urbano JC, Boussy CA. Long-term psychoeducational outcome of prenatal substance exposure. *Seminars in Perinatology* 1991;15 (4): 317-23.

Singer LT, Garber R, Kleigman R. Neurobehavioral sequelae of fetal cocaine exposure. *Journal of Pediatrics* 1991; 119 (4): 667-72.

Streissguth AP, Barr HM, Sampson PD, Darby BL, Martin DC. IQ at age 4 in relation to maternal alcohol use and smoking during pregnancy. *Developmental Psychology* 1989; 25 (1): 3-11.

Tittnich E, Bloom LA, Johnson C, Muss CB, Frank M. The integrative nature of language development. *Journal of Children in Contemporary Society* 1989; 21 (1-2): 15-34.

Wasserman RC, DiBlasio CM, Bond LA, Young PC, Colletti RB. Infant temperament and school age behavior: 6-year longitudinal study in a pediatric practice. *Pediatrics* 1990; 85 (5): 801-7.

Wightman MJ. Criteria for placement decisions with cocaine-exposed infants. *Child Welfare* 1991; LXX (6): 653-63.

Zuckerman B, Bresnahan K. Developmental and behavioral consequences of prenatal drug and alcohol exposure. *Pediatric Clinics of North America* 1991; 38 (6): 1387-1405.

ANNOTATED BIBLIOGRAPHY

Griffith DR, Freir MC. Methodological issues in the assessment of the mother-child interactions of substance-abusing women and their children. *National Institute on Drug Abuse (NIDA) Research Monograph 1992;117:228-47.*
This article presents strategies for assessing mother-infant/child relationships in problem dyads for both clinical and research purposes. Problem behaviors in infants are described, along with potential causes for same, including prenatal exposure to drugs, prematurity and low birth weight, and infant temperament. Detailed descriptions of potential problems that may develop between substance-affected infants and their substance-abusing mothers are presented along with appropriate interventions.

Jones VG and Hutchins E. Finding Common Ground: A Call for Collaboration. Arlington, VA: National Center for Education in Maternal and Child Health, 1993.
This booklet discusses the challenges faced by various agencies in meeting the multiple service needs of women, children, and families affected by substance abuse. In the face of increasing numbers of affected families and dwindling resources, no single agency can service this population alone. This booklet presents a model for building a collaborative effort among agencies using collaborations between the Maternal and Child Health Bureau, Substance Abuse Services, and Child Welfare as an example.

Office for Substance Abuse Prevention. Identifying the needs of drug-affected children: public policy issues. *OSAP Prevention Monograph 11, 1992.*
This monograph presents balanced discussions by nationally known authors of both problems and solutions related to perinatal substance abuse. Summaries of research results on neonatal effects, cocaine, opiates, and alcohol are presented. Detailed discussions of social, cultural, and economic risk factors facing drug-affected children are presented. The effects that these "drug-affected" children are having on social agencies such as child welfare, education, and the legal system and on social policies are discussed.

Vincent L, Poulson M, Cole C, Woodruff G, Griffith D. Born Substance Exposed, Educationally Vulnerable. Reston, VA: Council for Exceptional Children, 1991.
This publication written for educators presents information from the scientific literature and successful educational programs, which indicates that many of the myths and stereotypes that have been presented about substance-exposed children are not accurate. The data presented support that there are a wide range of effects

of prenatal exposure to alcohol and other drugs and that the most severely affected children are those exposed to multiple risk factors. Educational strategies that focus on meeting the needs of the whole child and on developing a home-school partnership to foster educational achievement of children are presented. The need for transagency, transdisciplinary collaboration to meet the needs of substance exposed children is emphasized.

Zuckerman B, Bresnahan K. Developmental and behavioral consequences of prenatal drug and alcohol exposure. *Pediatric Clinics of North America* **1991; 38 (6): 1387-1406.**
This article provides a comprehensive review of the literature on the medical, neonatal, and long-term developmental effects of prenatal exposure to a variety of drugs. The effects of cocaine, opiates, alcohol, and marijuana are reviewed. An excellent discussion of the multivariate nature of the problem of identifying the effects of prenatal exposure to drugs and/ or alcohol is presented. The discussion of strengths and limitations of the research to date on this topic provides the reader with some of the tools he/she will need to critically evaluate future research.

9

Vulnerability and Resiliency Factors of the At-Risk Infant and Young Child with Prenatal Alcohol and Drug Exposure

Marie Kanne Poulsen, Ph.D.

A wide range of psychosocial and biological factors influences the social, emotional, and behavioral development of infants and children at risk due to prenatal substance exposure. The early identification of infant risk indicators, family needs, and available resources can lead to the preventive intervention services that are critical for building resilience in developmentally vulnerable children and their families.

The impact of prenatal alcohol and other drug exposure on a child's social, emotional, and behavioral development has caused considerable concern, if not hysteria, among parents, care providers, health professionals, educators, and policy makers.

There is no question that the impact of prenatal drug exposure *may* affect a child's behavior and development; however, countless studies have supported the notion that no one-to-one relationship exists between prenatal drug use and developmental/behavioral outcome. Yet, the popular press and other media have generated stereotypical images of *biologically damaged*, out-of-control, and aggressive children who will be "wreaking havoc on themselves and others." As a consequence, child care providers, Head Start teachers, and public school personnel are "gearing up" to deal with the onslaught of "out-of-control" children. Labeling, categorizing, and segregating children with labels such as "crack baby" or "drug child" still persist in many communities. The danger of labeling is that the concomitant misperception of the child as unteachable or unable to learn socially adaptable behaviors can become a self-fulfilling prophecy.

The perceptions are erroneous from several standpoints:

1. There is no single entity of "drug-exposed children." While some children may be compromised or at risk for behavioral and developmental problems, others are healthy, intact youngsters with no evidence of compromise or behavioral sequelae.
2. Stereotypical images and perceptions have been generated for the most part by anecdotal reports rather than by carefully documented study.
3. There is a dearth of long-term, methodologically sound research on the developmental/behavioral outcome of children prenatally drug exposed. Studies must address all psychological, environmental, and biological variables that contribute to outcomes. Variables such as temperament; maternal and child disease; neurologic intactness; cognitive potential; family resources, relationships, and management; community; and cultural context all play significant roles in the social, emotional, and behavioral development of a child.
4. Most of the children who are affected by drug exposure have the capacity to develop emotional health and prosocial behaviors if early intervention strategies are used to address the young child's neurodevelopmental, emotional, and psychosocial stressors and vulnerabilities.

While it is essential that children prenatally exposed to drugs are not labeled and stereotyped, it is equally important to recognize that maternal substance abuse *can* lead to vulnerabilities or disabilities that must be addressed in a timely, family-focused, child-centered fashion.

Early interventions are critical to protect those hypersensitive, poorly organized neonates who are at risk of becoming distressed, acting-out, nonadaptive preschool and school-age children. If children do not learn to deal adaptively with the biological and psychosocial stressors in their lives, they will most certainly be at risk in adolescence for school failure, teenage parenthood, and the perpetuation of an intergenerational cycle of substance abuse.

The purpose of this chapter is to clarify the roles that biological and psychosocial factors play in social-emotional development, the impact that maternal substance use may have on the healthy development of children, and strategies to develop resilience in children.

Social-Emotional Development: Vulnerability and Resilience

The variability in the developmental outcome of children born to drug-using women supports the notion of resiliency as a potent counterbalance to risk. The development of emotional health and social competence that contributes to resiliency involves the process of adaptive transactions between the individual child and the persons, objects, and events in his or her world. A wide range of psychosocial and biological factors influence the social and emotional development of young children. They include: neurodevelopmental characteristics and temperament of the child, the child/ caregiver relationship, developmental expectations, environmental stressors, and the cultural context in which the families live. Combined contributions of individual differences in infant behavior and the caregiving environment interact to create individual differences in social-emotional development along a continuum of vulnerability/resilience.

Neurodevelopmental intactness, mellow temperament, rich child/caregiver relationship, developmentally appropriate expectations, and low environmental stress tend to combine to build resilience in children which allows them to cope with the challenges that are a part of all children's lives and to recover from adversity. Competent children are better equipped to deal with internal and external stressors, and are more able to "bounce back" from traumatizing social and emotional events.

The emotionally and socially competent child is resilient because he/she has learned to:

- Develop and sustain relationships with peers and adults
- Understand peer and adult social expectations and social cues
- Use significant adults to have needs met
- Deal with an overwhelming environment
- Handle emotional events internally
- Express emotional state in socially adaptive ways
- Have the initiative to explore and learn
- Make choices
- Reflect before acting
- Control impulses and respond to limits
- Develop self-dependence in age-appropriate daily living activities
- Focus, persist, and finish tasks
- Problem solve
- Initiate, organize, and sustain work and play

Conversely, biological, psychosocial, and environmental factors may combine to produce a pattern of child vulnerability that results in negative transactions with the environment. The challenge for parents and health, educational, and social service providers is to help the vulnerable child to compensate for the negative factors and expand his/her zone of resilience through the development of emotional health and social competence. The at-risk child may need special attention to develop the coping skills necessary for a positive outcome.

Clearly, no single factor leads to developmental vulnerability, but the notion of cumulative risk asserts that the greater the number of negative factors in a child's life, the greater the risk for poor outcome. The child who has been prenatally drug exposed faces the possibility of biological *and* psychosocial influences that may negatively impact the development of emotional and social competence. The number and the severity of challenges confronting a drug-using woman and her newborn create the potential for significant child vulnerability.

Several factors contribute to resilience and vulnerability. They include: developmental/neurodevelopmental status, temperament, caregiver relationship, developmental expectations, family environment, and community/cultural context. Table 1 summarizes these factors.

Developmental/Neurodevelopmental Status

Intactness of developmental and neurodevelopmental functioning allows infants to engage with persons, objects, and events in ways that can expand their zone of resiliency. As children develop, they gradually learn how to call upon their internal capacity to organize, verbally mediate, guide, and direct their own behavior in the face of stressful life events. When a child's developmental or neurodevelopmental functioning is poorly organized, delayed, or compromised, maternal intervention is essential

to help the child learn to compensate for and/or cope with his or her vulnerabilities.

While it has been documented that prenatal exposure to alcohol can lead to significant developmental problems, it is not known whether maternal use of other drugs will have the same developmental consequences. However, the neurodevelopmental status of the newborn can be influenced by maternal substance use during pregnancy. Several other risk factors may contribute to the neurodevelopmental status of children born to drug-using mothers besides the potential deleterious effect of alcohol and drugs on the growing fetus. Poor maternal nutrition and general health, lack of prenatal care, maternal infection, sexually transmitted diseases, spousal abuse, birth complications, and the environmental concomitants of poverty all may contribute to neurodevelopmental vulnerabilities that place infants' emotional and social development at risk.

The neonatal period is particularly important because at this time the infant and mother learn to know one another and become attached. During infancy, young children learn that the world is a place to trust and that someone will be responsive to their needs. Several possible neurobehavioral characteristics that may affect mother-child attachment are seen in infants born to drug-using mothers (Chasnoff, Bussey & Sanich 1986; Kaltenbach 1981; Poulsen 1991), including poor feeding and sleep patterns, poor control of states of alertness, hypersensitivity to stimulation, difficulty in becoming soothed, muted interactive behavior, increased tone, and poor organization of behavior (see Table 2).

Table 1.   Factors Contributing to Resilience and Vulnerability

Factors	Contributors to Child Resilience	Contributors to Child Vulnerability
Developmental/ neurodevelopmental status	Intact	Delayed Disorganized Compromised
Temperament	Easy	Difficult
Caregiver relationship	Consistent primary caregiver over time Emotional availability Parental self-esteem Appropriate parental guidance	Mismatched Abusive Neglectful Emotionally unavailable Multiple caregivers
Developmental expectations	Matches child's emotional and social needs and developmental level	Parent is inappropriately • permissive • demanding • overprotective Not matched to developmental needs of child
Family environment	Stable housing Financial resources Adequate health care Stable family unit	Family poverty Homelessness Family separation Domestic violence Family illness Substance abuse Poor health care
Community/Cultural context	Identification with one's own cultural values Community acceptance Community support • to child • to family	Lack of identification with ethnic/cultural community Perceived discrimination Isolation Segregation

Temperament

Temperament is the mode of an individual's emotional response. It can be equated with disposition or behavioral style and includes such parameters as activity level, adaptability to new situations, intensity of reaction, quality of mood, distractibility, and persistence.

The seminal work of Thomas and Chess (1977) describes three temperamental constellations of functional significance: (1) The Easy Child tends to respond to new situations in a positive, adaptive manner. Frustration tolerance is high and the acceptance of rules presents no problems. The manner in which the easy child experiences and responds makes him or her less vulnerable to family environmental stress. An easy temperament may buffer a child from the ill effects of family instability; (2) In contrast, the Difficult Child has difficulty adapting to change, has prolonged periods of adjustment to new situations, and a low frustration tolerance that can easily produce tantrum behavior. Temperamentally difficult children are twice as likely as other children to be the target of parental criticism (Rutter 1979). The behavioral characteristics that describe the "difficult infant" and the infant prenatally drug exposed who experiences neonatal abstinence syndrome are remarkably similar. When a temperamentally difficult infant also is affected by prenatal drug exposure, his or her zone of vulnerability is expanded exponentially; (3) The Slow-to-Warm-Up Child also may show negative responses to new situations, but the reactions are mild in intensity, and the child adapts over time. This makes him or her less vulnerable to family stress. It is important to emphasize that the three constellations represent the wide range of behavioral style in children. The temperament of the difficult child is not a criterion of psychopathology, but rather increases that child's sensitivity to life events and vulnerability for negative experience.

Caregiver Relationship and Developmental Expectations

Infants with differing temperaments experience the world in very different ways and influence both the feelings and caregiving practices of their parents. An easy infant who smiles, gurgles, and cuddles can relax an anxious mother. The dyad most at risk is the difficult infant with an anxious, inexperienced, depressed, or emotionally unavailable mother (Escalona 1982).

It has been substantiated that the key factor in developmental resiliency among children at risk is a good mother-child relationship during the first year (Saylar, Tippa & Lee 1991). The postnatal social environment has been determined to be more significant to developmental outcome of the at-risk infant than is the occurrence of perinatal stress (Bradley et al 1989). The Kauai Longitudinal Study revealed that the one common characteristic of resilient individuals was that each one had had the opportunity to establish a close bond with at least one caregiver (Werner & Smith 1982). While it is extremely important that low threshold children are protected from an overload of sensory events, the critical elements of maternal caregiving are emotional availability, maternal responsiveness, and warmth.

Infants develop trust through a relationship with a consistent, responsive primary caregiver over time. Many mothers who use drugs have periods of

Table 2. Impact of Neurobehavioral Vulnerability on Mother-Infant Attachment

Neurobehavioral Vulnerability	Impact on Mother-Infant Attachment
• Poor feeding patterns	• Difficulties in sucking, accepting food, and retaining food can make this most primary mother-infant activity an aversive, anxiety-provoking event.
• Poor sleeping patterns	• The infant's inability to regulate sleeping patterns may keep the child (and mother) from sleeping through the night for the first year. The stress of perceived maternal failure and maternal or infant fatigue can lead to a decrease in positive dyadic time.
• Poor control of states of alertness	• The at-risk infant may have difficulty modulating sleep and agitated states to ones of calm, focused alertness. Thus, mother and infant lose important periods of time needed for bonding.
	• The hypervigilant infant may have periods of agitated alertness. However, the calmness needed for quality eye contact may be lacking.
• Hypersensitivity to stimulation	• Excessive crying may be the infant's response to being uncovered, touched, or moved. Parents may interpret this to mean the infant wants to be left alone rather than needing protection from overstimulation.
• Difficulty in becoming soothed	• The at-risk infant who cannot modulate his or her behavior may not be able to easily recover from normal whimpering but habitually escalate to loud cries of distress.
	The usual means of comforting the infant (repositioning, patting, rocking, singing, etc.) may not be effective. This leaves the mother and infant with growing feelings of incompetency.
• Muted interactive behaviors	• If the inborn behaviors of eye contact, smiling, and vocalizing are depressed, there will be an overall decrease in mutual gazing, responsive smiling, and vocalized dialogue, which are markers of human attachment.
• Increased tone	• Infants who stiffen when being cuddled experience less bodily contact opportunities than do infants who easily mold.
	• Inexperienced parents may interpret that the infant doesn't "need" or "like" to be cuddled.
• Poor organization of behaviors	• Infants who cannot coordinate self-calming, focused attention, and oculomotor/visual-motor behaviors will show diminished initiation of contact with mother.

unavailability, lack parenting models, are naive about how a child develops, and lack effective facilitating, soothing, and protective parenting strategies that are a part of many women's sociocultural heritage (Mondanaro 1977; Ambrose & Poulsen 1990).

Parenting styles observed in drug-using mothers that may work against a mother establishing a close relationship with her infant include:

1. Attributing negative intention to the infant's behavior. (He's hitting me because he knows I took drugs.)
2. Reading infant stress as, "leave me alone" signal, rather than "I need help."
3. Not waiting for the infant's readiness to engage in play.
4. Not noticing or responding to the infant's socially initiating behaviors.
5. Not using eye contact to engage the infant in interaction.
6. Not recognizing or responding to *muted* signals of approach or distress.

Naiveté about child development leads to a mismatch between parental expectations and a child's capacity to meet expectations. Children with low impulse control and a low frustration tolerance are at increased risk when parents' expectations are overdemanding, too permissive, or inappropriate for the child's developmental level.

Family Environment Stress Level

A child can handle stress to the extent the parents are not stressed beyond their own capacity to manage (Garbarino, Durbrow, & Kostelny 1989). Guaranteed shelter, food, and medical care are critical for the infrastructure of family life.

The assurance of any one of these elements is in jeopardy in the lives of many drug-addicted women who are poor, single, in recovery, and raising high-need children. Without family resources to ensure stability of the fundamental necessities for life, the social and emotional health of the child will remain at risk. In addition, the stresses of family chaos, violence, or instability significantly add to negative developmental outcome and therefore *must* be addressed in child intervention plans.

Community/Cultural Context

Social isolation, discrimination, and community segregation always have an influence on parental self-esteem and on the parent's capacity to help the child develop the strong cultural identification needed to support childhood resiliency and healthy emotional-social development. In addition, the Kauai Study underscores the importance of informal church or school programs that acknowledge child competencies and foster a sense of self (Werner & Smith 1982). These informal supports may contribute to the resiliency that serves as a protection from the effects of stressful experience.

Need for Preventive Intervention

A small percentage of infants who have been substance exposed will sustain permanent damage requiring long-term developmental and special education services. However, for the most part, children born to drug- or alcohol-addicted women are presented with a *potential* risk for emotional and social vulnerabilities or compromise. Neurodevelopmental immaturities combined with the emotional unavailability of a mother on drugs or of an overwhelmed caregiver can present formidable challenges to the development of the rich mother-infant relationship needed for healthy social and emotional development. Research has supported the notion that the significance of prenatal drug exposure as a risk factor is best understood within the context of the child caregiving environment (Johnson et al 1991).

If early intervention addresses the biological and psychosocial vulnerabilities inherent in a given mother-infant dyad, the infant *and* mother can have an opportunity to develop ways of coping that lead to enriched competency, self-esteem, and relationship. In this manner, vulnerable infants expand their zone of resiliency and mothers develop a sense of parental competency.

Conversely, when an infant experiences many negative emotional states arising from biological and/or psychosocial factors, he or she will become more vulnerable to the effects of later negative social-emotional events. However, vulnerability does not necessarily have to be a message of doom, since the child may have the capacity to achieve a significant level of resilience with appropriate interventions (Anthony 1987; Werner 1988).

Early intensive protective and facilitative intervention strategies that focus on consistent nurturing care can be effective in mediating the neurodevelopmental vulnerabilities of infants who have been prenatally drug exposed. With intervention, many infants who are significantly different from controls at birth develop relatively normally over the first year (Saylor, Lippa & Lee 1991).

Emotional development depends on how the child is experiencing the world and on how the child's social world re-sponds to his or her emotional states, emotional expressions, and the contexts in which they occur. A key socialization task is to learn the rules of acceptable emotional expression in particular situations. Significant adults who "tune into" and respond to a child's emotional experience, rather than focus only on how the child expresses emotions, will be able to help the child better interpret the world, integrate the experience, and express emotions in acceptable ways.

Children who continue to have difficulty in modulating their own states and temperamentally difficult children will be more sensitive to the world around them and may find particular experiences aversive that the temperamentally easy children find pleasurable. Parents and caregivers may need continued support to deal with the challenge of helping a difficult child learn to deal with the world. Both biological and socialization forces continue to play a role in emotional development.

Behavioral Characteristics

Some infants will continue to show atypical neurobehavioral characteristics that are unlike others in their age-group. As preschoolers and school-age children, persistent difficulties in attention, organization, and the modulation of behavior may place their learning as well as social/emotional development at risk. The exact biological basis of behavior resulting from prenatal substance exposure, low birth weight, maternal malnutrition, maternal infections, and so on, is difficult to differentiate. Behaviors observed in high-risk children who were prenatally drug exposed probably result from a constellation of biological, environmental, and psychosocial factors. If not resolved, there is a compounding effect of early neurobehavioral vulnerabilities *and* their impact on mother-child interaction, which then influences the development of attachment, learning, and coping strategies in the child. Children may exhibit nonadaptive behaviors because they have not yet learned to compensate for a less organized nervous system and/or have not learned to cope with the psychosocial stressors in the environment.

Those children with poorly organized nervous systems may be described as "low threshold children" who remain hypersensitive and hyperactive. They are easily overstimulated and may have difficulty modulating their responses. Their poorly organized nervous systems, which so acutely feel changes in the sensory and emotional environment, become a next source of stress. The consequences of negative biological and/or psychosocial factors affect two main areas of vulnerability that impair social/emotional and behavioral development: 1) disorganized behavior and 2) inadequate attachment/sense of self. Risk behaviors seen in children prenatally drug exposed follow a continuum of severe to mild. Children at risk may show an increase in behaviors that are inappropriate for their developmental age or may demonstrate an intensity of behavior that does not match the significance of the event. Table 3 describes behaviors that may place the healthy development of children at risk.

Specific strategies to help children at behavioral risk should be based on:

1. Attention to development of mean-

ingful adult-child relationship.
2. Consistency in expectations so the child can learn the social rules.
3. An environment that protects the child from overstimulation.
4. Opportunity for the child to make choices, be self-dependent, and practice self-mastery.
5. Proactive teaching of acceptable expressions of anger, fear, and frustration.
6. Preparation of the child for major and minor changes in daily routine.
7. Proactive teaching of social behaviors the nonrisk children learn incidentally, e.g., turn taking, peer conflict resolution, and so on.
8. Proactive teaching of problem-solving strategies to reduce task and peer-play frustration, for example, visual scanning skills, "stop-think-act" strategies, and so on.

Emotional-Social Factors Related to Foster Care Placement

When parents are unable to care for their children, out-of-home placement becomes necessary. Many children are cared for by extended family members without intervention of child protective services. However, countless others become part of the foster care system and are raised by foster families. Experienced, supported, loving foster parents can play an essential role in providing nurturance and care until a permanency plan is implemented. Many foster parents offer support to the families in recovery and contribute to the reunification process. However, except for those newborns who experience a single long-

Table 3.   Behaviors that may place the healthy development of children at risk

- **Disorganized behavior**
  - Behavioral extremes
  - Low tolerance for stress
  - Difficulty being consoled
  - Difficulty organizing own play
  - Limited attention/concentration on tasks
  - Difficulty responding to verbal limits
  - Decreased adaptive task persistence
  - Difficulty reading social cues
  - Impulsive behavior
  - Difficulty in peer relationships
  - Easily overstimulated
  - Sporadic mastery of spatial-motor tasks
  - Inconsistent use of problem-solving strategies
  - Difficulty handling changes in routine

- **Inadequate attachment/sense of self**
  - Decreased use of adults for solace, play, object attainment, and conflict resolution
  - Indiscriminate attachment to strangers
  - Decreased response to verbal direction of behavior
  - Regressive behavior
  - Difficulty making choices
  - Delay in imitation, language, and representational play
  - Decreased task persistence
  - Increased tantrums and oppositional behavior when faced with difficult tasks
  - Decreased self-dependence in daily living skills
  - Avoidance of new challenges
  - Increased clinging to adults
  - Decreased empathy and pro-social behaviors

term placement within the foster care system, all infants, toddlers, and children in the system are psychosocially vulnerable.

Children who are drug exposed tend to enter the foster care system earlier, stay longer, and have more changes in placement (Fanshel 1975; Feig 1990). Multiple placements, multiple caregivers, and overwhelmed emotionally unavailable parenting figures can negatively impact an infant's capacity to bond to a single significant person, to learn to modulate his or her behavior, and to develop the sense of self-effectiveness that leads to later self-esteem.

The separation of a child from his or her natural family and subsequent multiple placements within the system always serve to put the child in crisis. Since it is only through consistent relationships over time that attachment can occur, the trauma of separation and loss can interfere with the successful completion of the attachment process. The younger the child is, the more endangered is his or her capacity to develop trusting relationships.

A change of placement for the child may result in regressive, passive, or acting-out behaviors as a means of coping with loss. Despite foster parent efforts, the young child may not accept comforting or caregiving from a new parent figure. In addition, earlier relationships may have distorted the expectations of the child (e.g., the child may have learned *not* to initiate relationships due to a lack of earlier parental responsivity). The child's challenge is to face the anxiety of this frightening experience while adapting to comfort and caregiving from an unfamiliar adult.

The consequences of multiple placements can be even more serious. Loss of the psychological parent, the attachment figure, is the infant's experience, and the experience is repeated with each change

Table 4. Strategies to help children at risk due to family separation

1. Advocate to keep siblings together.
2. Develop a birth family contact plan whenever possible.
3. Prepare and encourage birth family contact with child, including use of photos, phone, audio and videotape recordings, letters, and visitations of parents and siblings.
4. Prepare child for change of placement.
5. Have child visit receiving parent prior to change within system whenever possible.
6. Provide opportunity for child to express sorrow, anger, and fear.
7. Provide child with information on rituals, rules, and expectations for receiving home.
8. Provide receiving home with information about the child and about bedtime, dressing, bathing, and playtime rituals that are important.
9. Have receiving parent visit child before change whenever possible.

of placement. Because of the significance of the primary relationship in supporting developmental progress, disruptions can undermine development, inducing general development delay, nonadaptive coping strategies, language delays, and a lack of willingness to form new relationships. The new caregiver's response to the child will have a critical impact on the child's capacity to emotionally resolve the prior loss. The young child will be able to resolve the crisis of separation only if the subsequent relationship is one that responds sensitively to the child's acute emotional needs (Yarrow & Goodwin 1965; Rutter 1979). Table 4 delineates strategies that can help children at risk due to family separation expand their zone of resilience.

Assessment and Intervention Issues and Case Management

Assessment of a child with social, emotional, and/or behavioral problems includes behavioral, learning, and developmental competencies (including language processing); neurologic and health history and status; psychosocial and behavioral history; family and environmental stressors; and sources of informal support. Parents, relatives, foster parents, child care providers, and/or teachers who have daily contact with the child should be part of the assessment team and help design interventions. Consistency in behavioral expectations and interventions among home, childcare, and school for the child is an essential process.

Service systems in place under Public Laws 94-142 and 99-457 provide assessment, intervention, and education for infants and young children with disabilities. The children likely to fall through the cracks of the developmental disability and special education service systems are those children who are *at risk* for developmental problems. While these children may not exhibit neurodevelopmental or psychosocial disabilities that qualify for services, their vulnerabilities *can* result in serious emotional, social, and/or behavioral problems if they go unaddressed. Therefore, preventive intervention programs are needed.

Mental health services are usually available for children with severe, pervasive, chronic behaviors, including:

- destruction of property
- hurting self
- hurting others
- extreme withdrawal
- extreme oppositional behavior
- distorted peer and personal relationships

Whereas children prenatally drug exposed can exhibit these behaviors, there is nothing to support that drugs *per se* are the direct cause. However, we do know that a child is subject to biological and psychosocial stressors and if the child does not learn to cope with these overwhelming circumstances, the child is vulnerable to the development of maladaptive ways of responding to the world.

Case management must address the needs of the child within the context of family needs. The interventions for the child can only *be* effective when there is a focus on stabilizing the family unit. Community support services for families need to be offered on the basis of a continuum of child-family needs.

Support and training
Family support groups
Foster family groups
Parent effectiveness training

Counseling and therapy
Parent counseling (individual and group)

Mother-child conjoint therapy
Family counseling
Child counseling/therapy (individual and group)

Children's programs
Child Guidance Clinic programs
Special education programs
Head Start
State preschools (same state)
Public school guidance programs
State child care programs
Therapeutic nursery schools

While studies suggest that children prenatally drug exposed are potentially vulnerable, studies on childhood resilience indicate that many children can be helped to learn adaptive ways of dealing with their world if the caregiving environment can offer enough protective factors.

REFERENCES

Ambrose S, Poulsen M. *Substance Abusing Mothers Whose Children Are in Out-of-Home Placements.* (Preliminary report). Los Angeles: Children's Institute International, 1990.

Anthony EJ. *The Invulnerable Child.* New York: Guilford Press, 1987.

Bradley RH, Caldwell BM, Rock SL, Ramey ET. Home environment and cognitive development in the first three years of life. *Developmental Psychology* 1989; 25: 217-35.

Chasnoff I, Bussey M, Sanich R. Perinatal cerebral infarction and maternal cocaine use. *Journal of Pediatrics* 1986;108:456.

Escalona S. Babies at double hazard: Early development of infants at biologic and social risk. *Pediatrics* 1982;70(5): 670-6.

Fanshel D. Parental failure and consequence. *American Journal of Public Health* 1975; 65: 604-12.

Feig L. Drug-exposed infants and children: Service needs and policy qualities. Washington, D.C.: Department of Health and Human Services, 1990.

Garbarino J. Durbrow N, Kostelny K. Progress Report. Chicago: Erikson Institute, 1989 May 5.

Johnson HL, Glassman MB, Fiks KB, Rosen RS. Resilient children: Individual differences in developmental outcome of children born to drug abusers. *Journal of Genetic Psychology* 1991; 151 (4): 523-39.

Kaltenbach K. Neonatal abstinence syndrome and interactive behavior. *Pediatric Research* 1981;15:64.

Mondanaro J. Women: Pregnancy, children and addiction. *Journal of Psychedelic Drugs* 1977: 9 (1).

Poulsen MK. *Schools Meet the Challenge: Educational Needs of Children at Risk Due to Substance Exposure.* Sacramento: Resources in Special Education, 1992.

Rutter M. Protective factors in children's responses to stress and disadvantage. In: Kent MW, Rolf JE, eds. *Primary Prevention of Psychopathology: Social Competence in Children.* Hanover: New England Press, 1979.

Saylor C, Lippa B, Lee G. Drug-exposed infants at home: Strategies and supports. *Public Health Nursing* 1991; 8 (1): 33-8.

Thomas A, Chess S. *Temperament & Development.* New York: Brunner/Mazel, 1977.

Werner EE. Individual differences, universal needs: A 30-year study of resilient high-risk infants. *Zero to Three,* 1988; 8 (April).

Werner EE, Smith RS. *Vulnerable but Invincible: A Longitudinal Study of Resilient Children and Youth.* New York: McGraw-Hill, 1982.

Yarrow L, Goodwin M. Some conceptual issues in the study of mother-infant interaction. *American Journal of Orthopsychiatry* 1965; 35: 473-81.

ANNOTATED BIBLIOGRAPHY

Garmezy N. Resilience in children's adaptation to negative life events and stressed environments. *Pediatric Annals* 1991; 20 (9): 459-66.
Discusses the significance of cumulative

stressors on child outcome and identifies critical protective factors that appear to correlate with positive adaptation under stressful circumstances. Significant protective factors include the dispositional attributes of the individual child, the affectional ties within the family, and the external support systems that provide a belief system by which to live.

Honig AS. Stress and coping in children (Part 1). *Young Children* **1986; May: 50-62.**
Describes how teachers and parents can create environments low in stress and how they can help young children cope better with stress. Preschool care providers can play a significant role in children's lives by building positive relationships with young children and by providing buffering social supports for high-need families.

Johnson HL, Glassman MB, Fiks KB, Rosen RS. Resilient children: Individual differences in developmental outcome of children born to drug abusers. *Journal of Genetic Psychology* **1991; 151 (4): 523-34.**
Supports the notion that there is a continuum of possible developmental outcomes for children born to substance-using mothers. Considerations concerning the interaction of environment and family characteristics with the needs of the drug-exposed child are crucial when looking at developmental outcomes. The importance of positive early caregiving to later developmental progress is affirmed.

Poulsen MK. *Schools Meet the Challenge: Educational Needs of Children at Risk due to Substance Exposure.* **Sacramento: Resources in Special Education, 1992.**
Discusses biological and psychosocial circumstances that influence the behavioral, learning, and developmental characteristics needed for kindergarten success. Early intervention and classroom strategies are identified. Service delivery issues are presented. The importance of family-centered service delivery, comprehensive coordinated care, early identification of psychosocial and developmental risks, and of preventive intervention is presented.

Trad PV. Regulation and the development of self. In: *Infant and Childhood Depression: Developmental Factors.* **New York: Wiley, 1987, pp 85-120.**
This chapter discusses cognitive, affective, and caregiver-infant interaction mechanisms influencing self-regulation and the development of self in the infant. Regulation refers to the comprehensive, all-embracing ability to function in a manner most likely to produce competency, mastery, and positive affect. The development of self-regulation is shaped by temperament, biological factors, and the responsiveness of the caregiver who is the infant's ally in establishing a sense of efficacy.

10

Motor Development of Neonates, Infants, Toddlers, and Children with Prenatal Alcohol and Drug Exposure

Lynette S. Chandler, B.S., P.T., B.A., M.Ed., Ph.D.

This article reviews the motor development of children who were prenatally exposed to legal and illegal drugs. The effects of prenatal exposure, as identified in controlled clinical trials, are reviewed for neonates (up to one month), infants and toddlers (up to two years), and children (up to nine years). There is sufficient evidence of drug effects on motor development and related domains of development to be concerned about prenatal exposure, though it must be acknowledged that considerable variation exists in the response to prenatal drug exposure, which has not yet been explained. Four models of care are suggested. Prevention is considered the best model of care. A synactive model and a neurodevelopmental model are proposed for neonates and infants who are affected by prenatal drug exposure. An eclectic approach is recommended for the care of toddlers and children. Treatment techniques are suggested for the specific drug effects that have been documented.

The focus of this chapter is on the motor development of neonates, infants and toddlers, and children who were prenatally exposed to drugs. Research on prenatal drug exposure (PDE) has been reviewed with a focus on motor development and related domains of development. Studies on the efficacy of treatment of motor delays caused by PDE have not been published and thus cannot be reported. Instead, four models of care for PDE are recommended. Prevention is the best model. However, the realities of PDE have made it necessary to discuss models for therapeutic intervention. A synactive model and a neurodevelopmental model are recommended for neonates and infants. An eclectic approach is then suggested for toddlers and children. Treatment strategies have been suggested, based on the models of care. The strategies have been applied to those developmental concerns that have been documented by clinicians and researchers.

Research on Prenatal Drug Exposure

In an attempt to distinguish between the impact of drugs and the impact of the many other biological and environmental factors commonly associated with the use of drugs, the concerns about the development of children prenatally exposed to legal and illegal drugs will be restricted to those developmental motor concerns documented by researchers. While acknowledging the value of the clinical observations of health care professionals, controlled clinical trials with more precise measures of drug use are key to unraveling the complex problems of prenatal exposure to drugs.

A clear picture of the effects of specific drugs has not surfaced from the diverse research interests, with the possible exception of maternal alcohol consumption at sufficiently high levels to cause fetal alcohol syndrome (FAS) or fetal alcohol effects (FAE) (Day 1992; Kyllerman et al 1985; Rotert & Svien 1993; Streissguth 1978). The effects on neonates, infants and toddlers, and children are less clear with the moderate use of alcohol and with the use of combinations of legal (e.g., caffeine and tobacco) and illegal (e.g., marijuana, cocaine, and so on) drugs. Figure 1 provides a listing of the studies that report on the effects of prenatal drug exposure on functional motor development and related domains. The effects of PDE and recommendations for treatment have been grouped for neonates (up to one month), for infants and toddlers (up to two years), and for children (up to nine years). The results are reported by study, rather than by drug, so that comparisons can be made across drugs within one sample of mother-infant dyads. Studies are also ordered by the age of the oldest children in the study. Thus longitudinal studies with the longest follow-up are discussed toward the end of a section. The exception to this is the final study (Aronson et al 1985), which presents the oldest children studied, but from the perspective of cross-sectional data.

Neonates

The findings of a number of studies on the newborn, using the Neonatal Behavioral Assessment Scale (NBAS) (Brazelton 1984) would seem to agree that there is, at minimum, a transient effect from prenatal drug exposure on the neonatal behaviors of infants. Fried and

Makin (1987) assessed 250 infants on the NBAS. They reported a significant increase in irritability as related to prenatal exposure to alcohol; an increase in startles, tremors, and irritability related to prenatal marijuana exposure; and an increase in tremors as well as a decrease in habituation to auditory stimuli related to prenatal tobacco exposure. Richardson, Day, and Taylor (1989) reported that second and third trimester alcohol use (N=372) predicted less optimal orientation responses on the NBAS. The same study reported conflicting data on the habituation measure for neonates who were prenatally exposed to drugs. However, third trimester use of tobacco predicted decreased habituation responses in the neonate.

A group of twenty-six term neonates, selected because of positive toxicology reports for cocaine, and sixteen matched controls were assessed on the NBAS by Eisen and associates (1991). Infants in the cocaine group were found to have abnormal reflex behavior, autonomic instability, and decreased ability to habituate to a variety of stimuli. It should be noted that the infants in this group, although selected because of their prenatal exposure to cocaine, were also more likely to be polydrug-exposed than the control group. Richardson and Day (1991) compared a group of twelve infants whose mothers used cocaine (often in conjunction with other legal and illegal drugs) with matched controls who did not use cocaine and found no behavioral differences on the NBAS. Mayes and colleagues (1993) noted that cocaine-exposed newborns (n=56) were significantly different than non-cocaine-exposed newborns (n=30) in birth weight and habituation scores on the

NBAS. The cocaine-exposed group had lower birth weights and depressed habituation scores. However, as in many of the studies on exposure to cocaine, these authors confirm that the cocaine-exposed group was more frequently exposed to alcohol, marijuana, and tobacco. Coles and coworkers (1992) reported on the outcome of the NBAS at two, fourteen, and twenty-eight days on 107 term infants. The specific groups established for the study were fifty infants who were prenatally exposed to cocaine as well as other drugs, seventeen infants prenatally exposed only to cocaine, seventeen infants prenatally exposed to alcohol only, and thirty infants whose mothers did not use illegal drugs. No clear pattern was present, though autonomic regulation was less optimal for the cocaine/polydrug and cocaine only groups at fourteen days. At the twenty-eight day assessment the cocaine/polydrug-exposed group was noted to have less optimal scores on reflexes than the non-drug-exposed infants.

In summary, some studies report no effects of prenatal drug exposure on the clinical behaviors of neonates. However, other studies report that behaviors, as assessed by the NBAS, are negatively affected by prenatal exposure to drugs. Autonomic instability has been reported. Abnormal reflexes, tremulousness, and an increase in startles have been identified. Infants prenatally exposed to drugs are also seen as irritable. A decreased ability to habituate and less optimal orientation responses have also been reported. Thus physiological, motor, and state behaviors have been identified as less than optimal in infants who have been prenatally exposed to drugs.

Infants and Toddlers

Schneider and Chasnoff (1992) compared a group of fifty non-drug-exposed infants with seventy-four cocaine/polydrug-exposed infants at four months of age using the Movement Assessment of Infants (MAI) (Chandler, Andrews & Swanson 1980). The authors reported a significant difference in total risk scores between the two groups, with the drug-exposed infants having a higher number of risk scores. An analysis of the items which distinguished the two groups seems to indicate that the risk behaviors for the cocaine/polydrug-exposed infants were most evident in high tone extension patterns. Examples of the patterns include a stiffness in neonatal standing and the failure of infants to use hip flexion patterns in kicking. Tremulousness was also significantly higher in the drug-exposed infants.

In a report on five infants exposed prenatally to alcohol, Harris and associates (1993) documented motor delays as identified on the MAI and the Psychomotor Developmental Index (PDI) of the Bayley Scales of Infant Development (BSID)(Bayley 1969). Motor developmental problems noted for several of the infants between four and eight months of age included low tone, which appeared to be generalized to trunk and extremities, primitive reflexes that were retained beyond the time that they should be integrated into more advanced motor skills; delays in the development of head control; tremulousness; and delay in fine and gross motor items. One infant was noted to have high tone in the adductor muscles (the muscles that pull the legs together). Variations were noted on the BSID scores, from one testing to another or from one child to another, but in general the scores on the BSID were in low normal or below normal range for all of the toddlers when last assessed. The examiners also noted ongoing eating problems (two of the toddlers were not on solids), inappropriate exploration of objects (throwing to the toys presented for the testing with the BSID), and ongoing behavioral concerns for three of the toddlers (unrealistic level of fear, hair pulling, and flat affect were given as examples).

Chasnoff and colleagues (1992) also used the BSID in their study. They found no drug effects at three months but reported a consistent pattern of motor delays on the Psychomotor Developmental Index (PDI) at six, twelve, and eighteen months of age for infants whose mothers used alcohol and marijuana during the pregnancy and a pattern of motor delays at six, twelve, and twenty-four months for infants whose mothers used cocaine/polydrugs during their pregnancy. The groups decreased in size as the study progressed from three month assessments to twenty-four month assessments (82 to 29 for the cocaine/polydrug group; 37 to 14 for the alcohol/marijuana group; 78 to 50 for the nonuser group).

In a study of alcohol effects on 462 eight month olds, Streissguth and associates (1980) reported significant delays on the motor scale of the BSID. Arendt, Singer, and Minnes (1993) compared a group of infants who were prenatally exposed to crack cocaine with a group of infants of similar socioeconomic and racial backgrounds who were not exposed to crack cocaine, using the BSID. Between six to eight months of age, fifty-one cocaine-exposed infants and twenty non-cocaine-positive infants were as-

(text continues on page 210)

Figure 1.   Studies That Examined the Impact of Prenatal Drug Exposure on Motor Development.

Figure 1a.   Studies which examined the impact of PDE on motor development.

Study	Year of Study	Authors	Assessment Used
1	1987	Fried & Makin	Neonatal Behavioral Assessment Scale
2	1989	Richardson, Day & Taylor	Neonatal Behavioral Assessment Scale
3	1991	Eisen et al	Neonatal Behavioral Assessment Scale
4	1991	Richardson & Day	Neonatal Behavioral Assessment Scale
5	1993	Mayes, Granger, Frank, Schottenfeld & Bornstein	Neonatal Behavioral Assessment Scale
6	1992	Coles, Platzman, Smith, James & Falek	Neonatal Behavioral Assessment Scale
7	1992	Schneider & Chasnoff	Movement Assessment of Infants
8	1993	Harris, Osborn, Weinberg, Loock & Junaid	Movement Assessment of Infants & Bayley Scales of Infant Development
9	1992	Chasnoff, Griffith, Freier & Murray	Bayley Scales of Infant Development
10	1980	Streissguth, Barr, Martin & Herman	Bayley Scales of Infant Development
11	1993	Arendt, Singer & Minnes	Bayley Scales of Infant Development
12	1993	Singer	Bayley Scales of Infant Development
13	1989	Rodning, Beckwith & Howard	Play
14	1993	Chandler, Richardson, Day & Gallagher	Balance & Ball Skills
15	1993	Janzen & Nanson	McCarthy Scales of Children's Abilities, Beery Test of Visual Motor Integration, Grooved Pegboard & Recognition Discrimination Task
16	1990	Barr, Streissguth, Darby & Sampson	Gross Motor Scale & Fine Motor (Battery)
17	1990	Fried & Watkinson	McCarthy Scales of Children's Abilities
18	1991	Coles, Brown, Smith, Platzman, Erickson & Falek	Vineland Adaptive Behavior Scale
19	1985	Aronson, Kyllerman, Sabel, Sadin & Olegard	Griffith Mental Developmental Scales & Developmental Test of Visual Perception

Figure 1b.   Details of the studies.

Study	N of PDE	N of Control	Drug Exposure	Age of Children	Drug Effects
1	250	*	A M T	Neonates	Increased irritability. Increased startles, tremors, and irritability. Increased tremors & decreased habituation to auditory stimuli.
2	372 92	* *	A T	Neonates	Less optimal orientation responses related to 2nd and 3rd trimester use. Decreased habituation related to 3rd trimester use.

Figure 1b continued on next page

Figure 1b. Details of the Studies (continued)

Study	N of PDE	N of Control	Drug Exposure	Age of Children	Drug Effects
3	26	16	C+PD	Neonates	Abnormal reflex behaviors, autonomic instability, & decreased ability to habituate.
4	12	12	C+PD	Neonates	None noted.
5	56	30	C+PD	Neonates	Depressed habituation.
6	50/17/10	30	C+PD & Ce & A	2 days / 14 days / 18 days	None noted. / Autonomic regulation less optimal for cocaine/polydrug & cocaine groups. / Reflexes less optimal for cocaine/polydrug group.
7	74	50	C+PD	4 Months	Increase in extension patterns of movement and tremulousness.
8	5		FAS & FAE	4 to 8 Months	Low tone, delayed integration of reflexes, delayed development of head control, tremulousness, delay in fine motor and gross motor development. Low PDI scores.
9	82/37 81/36 57/24 49/23 29/14	78 76 65 42 50	C+PD & A+M	3 Months 6 Months 12 Months 18 Months 24 Months	None noted. / Lower PDI scores & more scores <84 for PD Infants. / Lower PDI scores (A**); more PDI scores <84 (C**). / Lower PDI scores & more PDI scores <84 for A** Infants. / More PDI scores <84 for C** & MDI scores <84 for PD infants.
10	462	*	A	8 Months	Delays on PDI.
11	51 43	20 12	C	6-8 Months 12 Months	No significant differences on PDI. / Significant differences on PDI.
12	30	37	C	16 Months	Scored significantly lower on PDI. More 1 & 2 grade IVH.
13	18	57	PD	Toddlers	Less representational play.
14	650	*	A, M, & C	3 Years	None noted for alcohol, marijuana, & cocaine, though marijuana effects were unclear.
15	10	10	FAS	3.5-5	Delays in gross motor & those visual perceptual skills that required motor control. Fine motor delays not found.
16	457	*	A	4 Years	Decreased gross motor and fine motor (accuracy & timing) performance
17	16	18	PD	4 Years	Decreased performance on all subscales.
18	22 & 25	21	A	5 to 8 Years	No effects noted on motor skills by parent report.
19	13 17	13 17	A A	1.5 to 7 Years 5 to 9 Years	Lower locomotor & hand-eye coordination. / Perceptual problems.

*One set of numbers indicates that the authors studied a continuum of drug exposure and thus did not have two groups.

**(A) Prenatal Alcohol Exposed; (C) Prenatal Cocaine Exposed; (M) Prenatal Marijuana Exposed; (PD) Prenatal Polydrug Exposed; (Ce) Cocaine used early in pregnancy only.

sessed. At twelve months there were forty-three and twelve infants in the study. The authors reported that there were no significant differences at six to eight months between the groups. Significant differences were noted at twelve month testing on the PDI. It is important to note that the cocaine-exposed infants had mean PDI scores within normal limits though significantly lower than infants who were not exposed to cocaine. The mean PDI scores were 101.9.

In a comparison of forty-one cocaine-exposed very low birth weight (VLBW) infants and forty-one non-cocaine-exposed VLBW infants, the cocaine-exposed infants had a higher incidence of Grade I-II Intraventricular Hemorrhage (IVH) (Singer 1993). At follow-up, thirty of the cocaine-exposed infants were tested at a mean age of 16.5 months and thirty-seven of the non-cocaine-exposed infants were tested at a mean age of 18.5 months on the BSID. The cocaine-exposed infants had lower mean BSID scores (PDI=85) than the non-exposed infants (PDI=97), after controlling for the effects of IVH. However, according to the authors, the cocaine-exposed infants were also cared for in poorer caretaking environments. Control for polydrug exposure was not noted.

Rodning, Beckwith, and Howard (1989) used a play assessment to compare eighteen month olds who were prenatally exposed to drugs (N = 18) to high-risk preterm infants (N = 57) at eighteen months (age corrected for prematurity). Children who were prenatally exposed to drugs had significantly less representational play in a sixteen minute play session.

In summary, four-month-old infants who were prenatally exposed to cocaine/polydrugs were reported to exhibit unusual extension (apparent high tone) in their movement patterns, whereas infants prenatally exposed to alcohol, with one exception, appeared to have generalized low tone. Infants from both groups were seen as tremulous. Toddlers who had been prenatally exposed to varying, but substantial, amounts of alcohol also demonstrated delays in gross motor and fine motor development as well as eating and behavioral problems. A study which looked at play of eighteen month olds reported a lack of representational play in the repertoire of the toddlers prenatally exposed to drugs. Studies using the BSID to assess movements in larger cohorts of infants and toddlers exposed to varying amounts and classes of drugs often reported motor delays. It was not unusual to find that these infants and toddlers scored within normal limits, but that as a group they scored lower than the control group. The delays seen in the motor scales may not be clinically visible. Often the motor impairment was sufficiently mild so that it could only be accounted for in experimental designs for larger groups of infants. However, it should also be noted that in some of the well controlled studies the motor development of infants and toddlers prenatally exposed to drugs was apparently not affected by the exposure to drugs.

Children

The effects of prenatal substance use on the gross motor development of 650 three year olds were assessed by Chandler and associates (1993). The motor assessment, which included balance items and ball handling items, was adapted for three year olds from the Bruininks-Oseretsky Test of Motor Proficiency (Bruininks 1978). Prenatal exposure to alcohol, marijuana, and cocaine was not shown to have a negative impact on the gross motor skills of these children. This was true for exposure during each trimester of pregnancy. The study controlled for the potentially confounding variables of child characteristics, demographics, examiner, family configuration and preschool/daycare attendance, child medical characteristics, and current maternal substance use.

Ten children with a diagnosis of fetal alcohol syndrome (FAS) were compared with ten children with no known impairments or disabilities. Janzen and Nanson (in press) studied these 3.5 to 5 year olds using, among other tests, the McCarthy Scales of Children's Abilities (MSCA) (McCarthy 1972), the Grooved Pegboard (Trites 1987), the Beery Test of Visual Motor Integration (VMI) (Beery & Buktenica 1967), and the Recognition Discrimination Task (RDT)(Satz & Fletcher 1982). The children with FAS scored significantly lower than the control children on the motor and perceptual subscales of the MSCA. No differences were found on the Grooved Pegboard task (fine motor) between the two groups. Visual perceptual skills tested with the VMI noted significant differences between the two groups, but when visual perceptual skills were tested using the RDT (a nonmotor test), there was no difference between the groups. This raises the possibility that children prenatally exposed to alcohol may have difficulty in combining motor tasks with the visual tasks, that is, visual motor planning.

Gross motor and fine motor develop-

ment was reported to be affected by moderate prepregnancy alcohol use in a group of 457 children examined at four years three months of age (Barr et al 1990). The gross motor assessment was adapted from the Gross Motor Scale (Crippled Children's Division of the University of Oregon Medical School), the Gesell (Gesell & Amatruda 1941), and the BSID. These researchers reported that balance was negatively affected by alcohol consumption. Fine motor items assessed in this study included four tests from the Wisconsin Fine Motor Steadiness Battery (Matthews & Kløve 1978), the Tactual Performance Test for Young Children (TPT) (Trites & Price 1978), and Finger Tapping and Grip Strength (Reitan & Davison 1974). The fine motor items that were negatively influenced by prenatal alcohol consumption seemed to require accuracy of movements or speed. Thus the children who were prenatally exposed to alcohol were slower and less accurate in fine motor skills.

In a study of 133 three year olds assessed on the McCarthy Scales of Children's Abilities (MSCA), Fried and Watkinson (1990) noted marijuana effects on the motor scale. Children of mothers who were moderate users scored higher on the motor scale than the children born to either the heavy users or the light users. Possible reasons for this phenomenon could be the sample that this research drew or a dose-response effect. It deserves further study. There were no motor effects noted at forty-eight months on the 130 children tested. Alcohol and tobacco did not impact motor development.

Coles and associates (1991) reported their assessment of five to eight year olds whose mothers continued to drink alcohol throughout their pregnancy (N=25), whose mothers stopped drinking during the second trimester when advised of the risk (N=21), and whose mothers never drank (N=21). The children were assessed on many measures, among them the Vineland Adaptive Behavior Scales (Sparrow, Balla & Cicchetti 1987). The scales, administered through interview, provide measures of children's functional abilities in the area of communication, daily living skills, socialization, and motor skills. There were no differences among the three groups on the motor skills of the children.

Aronson and colleagues (1985) reported a retrospective study of the youngest children of alcoholic women. Twenty-one children and their matched controls were found to differ in a number of measurers of interest. Children's ages ranged from 1.5 to 9 years and thus different assessments were used on the distinct age groupings. The Griffiths Mental Developmental Scales (Griffiths 1954; Griffiths 1970) with locomotor and hand and eye coordination subscales were given to thirteen pairs of children between the ages of 1.5 and 7 years of age. The children of women who were alcoholics scored significantly lower than their matched controls. The Developmental Test of Visual Perception (DTVP) (Frostig, Lefver & Whittlesey 1973) was administered to the seventeen children and their matched controls who were five years of age or older. None of the control group demonstrated perceptual problems, whereas all of the alcohol-exposed children's scores were consistent with their delayed mental ages. The implication is that perceptual delay

as tested on the DTVP may be part of a global delay. However, these children, prenatally exposed to alcohol, had particular difficulties with the figure-ground and spatial relations subscales.

In summary, there is compelling evidence for alcohol effects on motor development for children of mothers who are alcoholics. General measures of gross motor development as well as visual perceptual scales that have a motor component are affected. Delays of motor development appear to be part of a picture of global delay, that is, motor and mental delays are comparable. There is conflicting data on the effects of moderate prenatal exposure to alcohol on balance. However, moderate prenatal exposure to alcohol appears to affect fine motor items demanding accuracy and timing. The effects of other legal and illegal drugs have not yet been clarified. Motor deficits as a result of minimal and moderate exposure to the drugs may not be detectable by functional measures of gross motor development. Tronic and associates (1991) suggest that application of new technology to the assessment of the more subtle soft signs may be needed in order to detect the neurologic dysfunction of infant and children exposed in utero to drugs. The effects of prenatal substance use on speed, timing, accuracy, balance, fine motor coordination, and perception need to be further assessed.

Intervention Models

Intervention with infants who are prenatally drug exposed will be addressed from several perspectives or frames of reference. The intervention models discussed at length include prevention as proposed by the Public Health Model

(Last 1980, cited in Bukoski 1991); assessment and intervention as suggested by the Synactive Theory (Als 1991); and treatment of immature motor patterns using neurodevelopmental techniques (Bobath & Bobath 1975; Finnie 1975). Finally, it is acknowledged that an eclectic approach is what is needed to address the diverse concerns raised by researchers.

The Public Health Model

Prevention of drug use would, of course, be the best treatment. The Public Health Model (Last 1980, cited in Bukoski 1991) provides a framework for treatment at three distinct levels of prevention. Primary prevention is viewed as the prevention of a disease. A program aimed at the school-age child who has not yet been tempted to use drugs is an example of primary prevention. Secondary prevention is focused on screening for a disease. When the signs and symptoms of a disease are first identified, treatment is initiated to prevent its progression. Secondary prevention would include the participation of parents and teachers in programs that prepare them to recognize the signs of drug use in their youths and the involvement of youths in alternative activities to those of the drug culture. The tertiary level of prevention acknowledges impairment caused by the disease; therefore, treatment is directed toward preventing side effects of drug addiction as well as ameliorating already evidenced drug effects. Drug rehabilitation programs are examples of tertiary prevention.

Modification of the Public Health Model terminology provided by Albee and Gullota (1991, cited in Bukoski 1991) may have particular meaning for health care professionals. The components of both models are essentially the same, but the terms in the latter model are more familiar and thus may be more meaningful. In the Albee and Gullota model, prevention is substituted for primary prevention, treatment replaces secondary prevention, and rehabilitation represents tertiary prevention.

Applying the Public Health Model to mother-infant dyads places the pregnant consumer of drugs in the tertiary or rehabilitation level of this model while simultaneously placing the infant in the secondary or treatment level of care (Figure 2). With the integration of the model for mother and infant, it becomes possible to enumerate a number of viable and necessarily integrated treatments.

A comprehensive rehabilitation program for mothers can assure that mother-infant dyads receive good prenatal care, both medical and nutritional. Prenatal visits can provide an opportunity for the health care practitioner to empower mothers to take care of their children. Simple confirmation of pregnancy has been noted to decrease the use of drugs for the duration of the pregnancy (Richardson, Day & Taylor 1989). The rehabilitation model as applied to mothers can also alert the obstetrician to the possibility of complications at birth and thus prevent perinatal complications for the infants. Nurses, physical therapists, and occupational therapists can anticipate the presence of neonates whose prenatal exposure to alcohol and other drugs may have compromised their autonomic and motor systems and may have caused the neonates to have poor control of sleep-awake behaviors as well as less than op-

Figure 2. The Public Health Model on Prevention as Applied to Infants Prenatally Drug Exposed and Their Mothers.

Focus of Concern	Primary Prevention (Prevention)	Secondary Prevention (Treatment)	Tertiary Prevention (Rehabilitation)
Parent using drugs.	Prevention programs for grade school children and high school youths.	Early identification and treatment for drug use.	Drug addiction programs for the pregnant teen-woman.

Focus of Concern	Primary Prevention (Prevention)	Secondary Prevention (Treatment)	Tertiary Prevention (Rehabilitation)
Child prenatally exposed to drugs whose mother **enters** a drug addiction program during the pregnancy.	None	Medical/nutritional programs for the pregnant teen/woman resulting in a healthier infant. Empowerment of mother in care of herself and her fetus. Anticipation of high-risk birth and, therefore, better care of the vulnerable infant. Empowerment of the family in the nursery and perhaps through follow-up home visits.	

Focus of Concern	Primary Prevention (Prevention)	Secondary Prevention (Treatment)	Tertiary Prevention (Rehabilitation)
Child prenatally exposed to drugs whose mother **does not enter** a drug addiction program	None		Medical treatment of an impaired child. Education for an impaired child. Assistance in parenting of the impaired child.

timal habituation and orientation responses. The health care team can work for bonding of parents and infants in the nursery and thus promote competency in caregiving on the part of the parent.

Failure to reach pregnant users of drugs may compromise the health and neurologic integrity of their infants and thus consign the infants in the rehabilitation level of this model. The growth and development of drug-exposed infants whose mothers do not enter rehabilitation programs is complicated by poor nutrition and absent health care. Unexpected perinatal complications as those noted earlier may further compromise the infants' health and neurologic integrity. If mothers are not entered into rehabilitation for their addictions, their prenatally exposed infants do not receive preventive care and may need special services within both the medical system (i.e., physical therapy, occupational therapy, and speech therapy) and the educational system (i.e., special education). In other words, the later the health system reaches out to these mothers, the higher the price paid by the infants.

A deceptively simple "treatment" of a woman early in her pregnancy, designed by Field and her associates, can result in detectable improvement in the health and welfare of high-risk infants (Field et al 1985, cited in Field 1992). This study involved introducing the individual mothers, through an ultrasound assessment, to the fetus while leaving a second group of mothers uninformed about the ongoing ultrasound assessment. The informed mothers had improved sleep throughout the pregnancy. There were fewer obstetrical complications at birth, and a significant increase in birth weight of the children within dyads receiving

the "treatment" compared to mother-child dyads not given early feedback. Infants whose mothers received information during the ultrasound procedure also demonstrated improved state control, habituation scores, and motor activity scores as measured by the NBAS. A decrease in maternal concern about the pregnancy and therefore a decrease in maternal stress is a plausible explanation for the rather powerful effect of such a simple treatment. The bonding of the mother with the infant at this early stage is a second working hypothesis. Certainly optimal health care of the pregnant woman deserves continued attention as does the care of her vulnerable newborn. Best practice for infants prenatally drug exposed necessitates commitment to the care of mother-fetus and mother-infant dyads.

The Synactive Model

Researchers in the intensive care unit have suggested theoretical models for the assessment and treatment of neonates whose health status is vulnerable. One of these models, the Synactive Model (Als 1986), provides a useful paradigm to guide health care practitioners and parents in the care of all neonates and infants. Care entails a process of observing behaviors (assessment), responding to the behaviors with the least intrusive interventions possible (treatment), and observing the response to the intervention. The interactive nature of the model allows the practitioner and parents to respond to the behaviors that they see at the moment. The wide range of behaviors which have been reported as associated with PDE and the variability of any one neonate/infant suggest that a parent or health care practitioner

Figure 3. The Synactive Model (which proposes that the neonate and infant must master five hierarchical levels of control, beginning with autonomic nervous system control and ending with the ability to self-regulate).

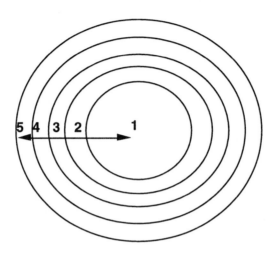

1. Autonomic Nervous System as seen in physiologic stability (heart rate, respiration, color, and visceral signs).
2. Motor System as seen in physical stability (posture and movement).
3. State Control as seen in ability to maintain appropriate level of alertness.
4. Attention and Habituation System as seen in the ability to attend to or ignore auditory and visual stimuli.
5. Self-Regulatory System as seen in the ability to maintain stability with appropriate input.

can make no assumptions about a neonate or infant and thus must be prepared to respond to the individual at the moment of interaction. An interactive model is particularly useful in the care of neonates who have been prenatally exposed to drugs.

Als (1986) assesses neonates' competence at five levels of observable behaviors. The cues are distinct for each of the levels (see Figure 3). The five levels comprise the autonomic nervous system, the motor system, the control of behavioral states, the ability to attend and interact, and the neonates' self-regulatory system. These levels are hierarchical in

that neonates must have the first level under control before they can master the next level.

Autonomic nervous system stability is the core or critical first layer of control. Neonates and infants must be able to maintain physiologic stability before they can control more complex behaviors. Thus, those who cannot seem to maintain core temperatures, stable heart rates, and respiration cannot be expected to control the more complex motor, state, and attention/interaction systems. Autonomic instability has been reported for neonates who have been prenatally exposed to drugs.

Physical stability (posture and movement) is the second layer of control needed. Neonates who startle easily, have frequent tremors, and have abnormal reflex behavior (reported for neonates who are PDE) cannot be expected to bring themselves into a quiet alert state. Likewise, infants who are tremulous, seem stiff in their movement, and have abnormal reflex behaviors (reported in polydrug-exposed infants) or who are so flaccid in tone that they cannot bring arms and legs forward (reported in neonates prenatally exposed to alcohol) cannot be expected to bring themselves into the next level of control.

Irritability as reported in neonates who are PDE demonstrates the lack of state control or third layer of control described by the synactive model. The neonates would need assistance in transitioning from one state to another (deeply asleep to drowsy to alert) so that they can attend to their environment.

Attending to or habituating to the many stimuli provided by persons or objects in the environment of the neonate represents the fourth layer of control. Habituation and orientation have been found to be less than optimal for neonates prenatally exposed to drugs.

Once neonates can, with assistance, control the autonomic, motor, state, and attention/interaction systems the goal becomes self-regulation by the neonates. The measure of competence becomes the amount (frequency and intensity) of facilitation necessary to assist neonates to self-regulate their behavior. There are frequent reports of the intense amount of care that some neonates and infants prenatally drug exposed demand.

Neurodevelopmental Model

Neurodevelopmental techniques have an intuitively simple but effective approach to assessment of a vulnerable child at any age. The assessment and treatment process is modeled on an understanding of normal development. Knowledge of the wide variations in normal development is essential. Four components of movement are assessed. They are muscle tone, primitive reflexes, automatic reactions, and volitional movement.

Normal tone allows for age-appropriate movement against gravity, that is, movement away from the supporting surface. For newborns lying on their backs this means flexing their arms to put fingers in their mouths, for five-month-old infants this means reaching for their mothers' face, and for toddlers this means rolling off their back, coming to sit, and getting into standing in seconds. Normal tone also allows for variation in movement patterns. For the neonates this means resting in a flexed pattern, but kicking legs alternately when awake. For five month olds this means lying on their backs and rolling to their stomachs. Toddlers demonstrate variation in movement patterns by changing sitting positions with ease. Neonates, infants, toddlers, and children with normal tone generally appear to move smoothly. Children with high tone (prenatal polydrug exposure) generally seem stiff. Children with low tone (FAS or FAE) generally seem floppy.

Primitive reflexes are specific movement response to stimuli which are normal in the neonate and should be outgrown (integrated) in the first year of life. The process of assessment of primitive reflexes entails establishing whether they are appropriately present or absent. Reflexes and norms for them are commonly known to healthcare professionals working with neonates and infants. As in normal tone, normal reflex integration is generally seen in variation of movement patterns. Stereotypic movement patterns are of concern. For example, if an infant moves the head to the left the left arms and legs always extend, the infant has a dominant or stereotypic asymmetrical tonic reflex, or ATNR. Though this reflex is normal in the neonate and infant, the stereotypic (obligatory) nature of the pattern is not normal. The key to assessing reflexes is to be aware and wary of obligatory movement patterns. Abnormal reflex behavior was reported for neonates and infants who were prenatally exposed to drugs.

Infants, toddlers, and children should also be assessed for righting and equilibrium responses. Righting (keeping head and trunk in alignment with each other) and equilibrium responses (responding to movement so as to maintain or regain the center of gravity) begin to develop in early infancy and are maintained throughout life. These reactions, once developed, are automatic. For example, as a child leads with the head or shoulders or hips to roll over, the rest of the body automatically follows or aligns itself. Once children develop head righting, they will keep their head upright as you move them around. A rule of thumb for assessment of righting and equilibrium response is to realize that the more developed the reactions the easier it is to pick up or carry a child. The normal child "feels" lighter in weight because his or her reactions are always monitoring alignment and constantly adjusting to maintain the center of gravity. An in-

fant or toddler is able to transition from one position to another because of righting and equilibrium responses. Thus rolling, coming to sit, getting to stand, and walking are possible because of these automatic responses. Head righting (control) and balance responses were noted as delayed in children who were prenatally drug exposed.

The fourth and final component to be evaluated is volitional movement. Volitional movement is the measure of development that is most often used by our society. Gross and fine motor milestones are assessed. Examples of gross motor skills include standing on one foot, climbing stairs, or throwing a ball. Fine motor skills include picking up a small object or stacking cubes. The normal child is the best model for age-appropriate volitional movement activities, and a wide variety of assessments are available to serve as a standard for normal volitional movement.

Equally important to treating infants is empowering parents with the knowledge that will allow them to take care of their infants. Neurodevelopmental models reinforce parent involvement in caregiving (Finnie 1975). Parents must be taught to position and move (handle) their children so that head and trunk righting occurs and equilibrium responses (early balance responses) are reinforced. Parents can be taught the techniques for helping their infants into midline and into flexion while feeding, dressing, holding, playing with, and positioning their infants for sleep. They can learn the importance of changing the infants' positions and thus varying the motor experience that the infants receive. This process, begun early at the birth of the infant, can enhance bonding and ease the transition to home.

Eclectic Model

The diverse findings of the studies on neonates, infants, toddlers, and children make it difficult to support one assessment or treatment model for all children born with prenatal drug exposure. The three models described have been of particular value because they support the philosophies of prevention, early assessment, and early treatment. However, as research on older children who are PDE is published it becomes obvious that other models offer viable methodologies for assessment and treatment. Motor learning as applied to the frequently documented low normal scores in gross motor and fine motor development should be given serious consideration. Behavioral techniques should be used for those children (reported most often for children with FAS and FAE) who have not learned the appropriate social skills of a preschooler or school-age child. Using play seems an appropriate methodology for achieving therapeutic goals for all neonates, infants, children, and toddlers, but would have specific application for children found to have decreased representational play. A combination of methodologies needs to be brought to the feeding problems reported for children diagnosed with FAS and FAE.

Intervention

It is apparent that use of one drug, and one drug alone, is rare in those women who are using drugs during the prenatal life of their children. Use of "toxic cocktails," a mix of legal and illegal drugs, is probably the norm rather than the exception. Poor nutrition, inadequate medical care, and other factors contribute to an unfavorable prenatal environment. Prenatal drug use is a concern across all economic, educational, and racial groups, although attention has been focused on inner city poor.

All of the unknowns make the task of selecting concise assessments and specific treatments and programs an art as well as a science. Thus recognition of strengths as well as needs for mother-infant dyads and their families must fall into the hands of an extended family of health care practitioners and other professionals. An Individualized Family Service Plan (IFSP) should be established. This process mandates the inclusion of family members in the planning of care and can be used to build a therapeutic relationship between the team of healthcare practitioners and the family. The ability of health care practitioners to establish exact diagnoses and to prescribe ideal treatments, given the complexity of the family unit of the prenatally drug-exposed infants, may remain an illusive goal. However, the process of involving the family in their care is a powerful way to empower families. It is critical, therefore, to apply "best practice" to all pregnant women and, subsequently all mother-infant dyads and their families. Physicians, nurses, physical therapists, occupational therapists, communication disorder specialists, psychologists, social workers, educators, and other health care practitioners who work in the arena of screening, assessment, and treatment of families must be committed to applying "best practice" to all families. In today's complex environment it may be that "best practice" is to anticipate problems, expect none, and respond to the concerns as they are presented. This requires a constant vigilance and a willingness to work with all families as well as our colleagues in health care.

An eclectic approach to intervention is recommended. The challenge for the health care practitioner and other professionals is to integrate the treatment approaches (prevention, synactive, neuro-developmental, motor learning, behavioral, and play) in a manner that is advantageous for infants and their families. Treatment techniques for each of the concerns posited by researchers are addressed. Treatment is a process of assisting neonates to achieve autonomic nervous system control, facilitating motor system stability, learning to respect the behavioral state of the neonates, enhancing the neonates' attention/interaction abilities, and, finally, withdrawing of support to allow for self-regulation by the neonate/infant. It is a process of reading cues (observation or assessment), responding to those cues by changing the neonates' environment (intervention or treatment), and reading the cues yet again to assess the response to the changed environment. Treatment is also a process of modulating the assistance that neonates receive so as to be able to interpret their ability to self-regulate.

For the full-term, mildly affected neonates/infants whose mothers were light to moderate users of drugs, swaddling to provide warmth may be sufficient treatment to assist neonates in gaining stability of their autonomic nervous systems. A slight mottling of the skin or bluing of the fingers may be one of several cues to swaddle and otherwise assist an infant to maintain normal body temperature.

If swaddling is the treatment selected, attention can be simultaneously turned to facilitating normal posture. Swaddling neonates/infants can facilitate the low-toned infant (prenatally exposed to alcohol) and the child with extended posture (PDE to polydrugs) into optimum midline and semi-flexion patterns. Bringing the head into a neutral position or into slight flexion, if tolerated, can be part of the swaddling. Assisting the head, trunk, and extremities into semi-flexion promotes active flexion. Bringing arms closer to the mouth in a way that neonates can reach their mouths with their fists should also reinforce flexion since the neonates, sensing the proximity of their own fists, may attempt to bring their fists to their mouths. Non-nutritive sucking reinforces flexion. Bringing the legs closer to the trunk assists the child to actively engage in movement away from the extension pattern. Changing the child to side-lying makes it easier for neonates, lightly swaddled, to move by themselves. Changes in positions, and therefore variety in movement experiences, are also provided. Working for semi-flexed and midline postures assists neonates to begin to control their own motor behaviors. The combination of warmth and motor stability created by the swaddling may decrease the tremors and startles frequently reported in neonates/infants withdrawing from drugs.

Neonates who have extension of neck and trunk present a substantial increase in the challenge to nurses, therapists, and parents who attempt to facilitate motor control. These neonates require gentle movement into the optimum midline and flexed postures, biomechanical containment to help the neonates stay in an appropriate position, and professional vigilance as to the neonates' responses to the movement and postures. Biomechanical containment of these neonates in the new postures requires the secure placement of rolls to assist them to stay in side-lying, to maintain their heads in a neutral position, and to bring their shoulders forward and extremities into semiflexion (Schneider, Griffith & Chasnoff 1989; Sweeney & Swanson 1990). Hydrotherapy as described by Sweeney (1983) may provide the key to assisting these more severely compromised neonates. (It is important to state that a child of this severity is rare in this population of neonates.) It is critical to help neonates avoid the behaviorally disorganizing hyperextension of the neck and trunk.

Once the autonomic and motor systems are relatively stable, neonates can succeed in maintaining an optimum control of their behavioral states. Habituating to nonthreatening sounds while maintaining a sleep state, or maintaining a quite alert state to attend to appropriate stimuli, are positive signs of state control. Treatment may involve simplifying the environment. Preparing a darkened silent room to decrease sensory stimuli, holding the swaddled infant without talking, or simply rocking with the child may be all that is needed to modulate the environment. Neonates and infants who have been successful at reaching and sucking on their own fists may begin to use that mechanism for self-quieting and thus begin to control their own behavioral states.

Neonates and infants who are able to maintain autonomic stability, who have controlled motor behaviors, and who can demonstrate state control can then be encouraged to attend to and interact with people and objects. The literature is replete with ideas on "stimulation." However, assisting neonates to attend to and interact with their environment should be carefully modulated. The health care practitioner must continuously attend to the autonomic, motor, and state cues that the neonates send. Stimulation should also be judiciously directed, with first priority given to parent-infant interaction over health care practitioner-infant interaction. Assisting the infant to a quiet alert state when a parent is present or recommending the best time for a parent to be present is critical at this time.

Self-regulation is the next step in treatment. It is the process of slowly removing support and observing that the neonate or infant functions successfully without that support. It is a weaning process that needs to be part of the health care professional's and the parent's repertoire.

The treatment, although hierarchical, is not unidirectional. By carefully controlling the environment at one level stability at a more basic level can be maintained. Field (1992), for example, reported that the use of pacifiers (motor system) appeared to be a simple intervention with a broad range of benefits. Used during heel sticks, pacifiers reduced manifestations of physiological stress for premature neonates receiving repeated blood draws.

As the children mature and other concerns take precedence, it is still important to assess the presence of autonomic control, physical stability, and state control, as well as to facilitate attention, interaction, and self-regulation. However, attention is directed to screening for those concerns that have been raised

(text continues on page 224)

Figure 4.   Goals and Intervention Strategies for Concerns Identified for Neonates Who Were PDE.

Concerns Identified by Researchers	Goals and Intervention Strategies (Using Synactive and Neurodevelopmental Techniques)
Autonomic instability	Assist neonate maintain autonomic stability by providing optimum environmental control. Attend to physiologic stability of the neonate by changing the environment (temperature, levels of sound and light). Position and handle the neonate only as needed.
Startles, tremors, abnormal reflex	Having established autonomic stability, provide physical stability by correctly positioning and handling the neonate. Position the neonate with head in neutral position or in slight flexion, shoulders slightly forward, arms and legs in flexion. Neonates may be placed side-lying or on their backs if this positioning can be maintained. Midline positioning and flexion help to prevent startles and prevent the neonate from eliciting the stimuli for most abnormal reflex behaviors. Once passive physical stability has been established encourage active movement into flexion and midline. Flexion provides the opportunity for the neonate to suck on fists. This sucking, in turn, reinforces flexion.
Irritability	Having established autonomic and physical stability, help the neonate maintain state control. This is achieved by noting the neonates' responses to stimuli. Sucking on fist is calming. Changes need to be made slowly when moving the neonate from one position to another, when providing a necessary medical procedure, or when waking the neonate to eat.
Less optimal habituation and orientation	Having established autonomic stability, physical stability, and state control, provide appropriate levels of stimuli. This is achieved by helping the neonate focus on or attend to a parent's face or voice. In response to signs of distress help the neonate quiet to a stimulus by modulating the stimulus.
Difficulty with self-regulation	Having established autonomic stability, physical stability, state control, and appropriate levels of stimuli, begin to withdraw support to allow the neonate to self-regulate. The entire process is interactive. Observe the neonates' responses (assessment), support the neonate when needed (intervention), assess the response to support (assessment), and modulate support (intervention).

Figure 5. Goals and Intervention Strategies for Concerns Identified for Infants and Toddlers Who Were PDE.

Concerns Identified by Researchers	Intervention (Using Synactive, Neurodevelopmental, and Behavioral Techniques)
High tone (cocaine/polydrug) Low tone (alcohol)	The posture in which the infant is positioned is the same for both high and low tone, though perhaps more difficult to maintain if the infant has very high tone. Positioning is the same as that noted for the neonate.
Retained reflexes	Positioning is the same as that noted for the neonate. Active and controlled movement into these positions should be encouraged by slowly withdrawing external support.
Tremulousness	Tremulousness is exacerbated by autonomic instability and inadequate postural stability. Therefore, provide control for the above, as for the neonate. Professionals and parents should interact with slow controlled movements, and quiet voices, and be prepared to provide an immediate response to signs of stress (loss of autonomic stability). Older infants and toddlers should be screened to rule out neurologic damage.
Delay in head righting (control)	A program should be established to reinforce head control through positioning and handling. For example, parents could be taught to gently facilitate their infant or toddler in rolling each time that a diaper is changed and each time the parent goes to pick up the infant or toddler. In this way the head is "righted" to accommodate to the movement. This activity needs to be modulated to the infant's or child's emerging abilities.
Delay in gross and fine motor development	In anticipation of possible delays, children should be periodically screened for gross motor and fine motor delays. Intervention would be provided specifically for the deficit. If balance delays and inaccurate slow fine motor movements have been identified as a possible problem in children it may be appropriate to anticipate these concerns and provide opportunities for toddlers to engage in developmentally appropriate activities which are fun.
Feeding problems (alcohol)	Positioning of the head in neutral and/or slight flexion enhances sucking for the infant and is best for the toddler as well. Infants can be placed in an infant seat where head and trunk are in alignment but upright at about 45 degrees. They can also be held in a slightly upright position. If sitting independently, toddlers need to be upright. Experience with different flavors, textures, and temperatures as developmentally appropriate should be provided. Severe feeding problems need to be referred to a therapist who is specifically trained in that area.
Behavior problems	A team approach, including parents, is needed to assess why the behavior was elicited. Measurement of the antecedents and consequences of the identified "problem" behavior needs to be taken. A program to modify this behavior should be initiated as soon as it is identified and followed by all.
Decreased representational play	Toddlers need to be screened for the possibility of this problem. The infant and toddler need to be given developmentally appropriate play experiences. This may necessitate assessing the environment where the child spends awake time.

Figure 6.   Goals and Intervention Strategies for Concerns Identified for Children Who Were PDE.

Concerns Identified by Researchers	Intervention (Using Neurodevelopmental and Behavioral Techniques).
Balance	Since this has been identified as a possible concern, children should be screened for balance problems. To try and avoid this problem, toddlers and children could be provided with developmentally appropriate experiences. Toddlers could be given the opportunity to manage uneven surfaces, walk between narrow lines, climb stairs, kick balls, and other activities which require early balance skills. Children could be given opportunities to run on uneven surfaces.
Fine motor: slower and less accurate	Since this has been identified as a possible concern, children should be screened for fine motor problems. To try and avoid this problem infants, toddlers, and children could be provided with developmentally appropriate experiences. Encourage an infant, who is developmentally ready, to finger-feed and then continues with more difficult fine motor tasks such as blocks and balls and release into smaller and smaller spaces is important toward possible prevention.
Visual motor planning and eye-hand coordination	Since this has been identified as a possible concern, children should be screened for fine motor problems. Research in this area appeared to indicate that the problem may well be motor. See above.

for infants, toddlers, and children who are PDE (Figures 4-6). If a delay exists for head righting and early balance responses, parents can be reinforced in their efforts to integrate exercise into their daily routine, such as picking up and carrying their infants and toddlers correctly and attending to sitting posture during meals. The potential for problems in balance may be anticipated by letting the toddler walk on uneven surfaces, climb up stairs under supervision, or kick a large ball. Delays in fine motor and visual motor skills and feeding problems can be addressed by having the parents provide finger feeding experiences so that the infant and tod-

dler can experience picking up small objects and at the same time gain experience with a variety of textures and food. The anticipation of behavior problems may be forestalled by the early attention to state and attention. It is wise to be available to assist parents with behavioral techniques. Play is always a positive way to get at most of the concerns we have discussed.

Using normal development as a guide, one can think of countless activities that could be used to reinforce an emerging (newly developing) motor skill in children with prenatal drug exposure. Screening for potential problems, using the many published standards of normal development, and enlisting the parents' commitment to address the problems facing their children are key to helping children who are mildly affected by PDE. However, at times, the combination of risk factors (i.e., parental self-medication with legal and illegal drugs, inadequate medical care, poor nutrition, unexpected birth complications) exceeds the biological resources of infants. These infants may be born with a neurologic disability and the focus for treatment is rehabilitation. The treatments suggested by the synactive model and neurodevelopmental techniques would still offer the most effective alternative. However, this level of impairment (problems with sucking and swallowing or limitations of movement due to abnormal tone) is considered beyond the scope of this chapter. Motor disabilities of this severity generally fall within the purview of health care practitioners who have a specialty practice in rehabilitation, that is, in clinical management of neurologically impaired infants. Rotert and Svien (1993) address treatment for children who have been impaired by prenatal exposure to alcohol. A conceptual framework for a developmental program for low birth weight, premature infants also offers applications that would be invaluable in the care of drug-exposed infants who have been severely compromised by their prenatal environment (Ramey et al 1992). Nurses facing the care of a child with this severity might wish to read these two articles as well as the work of Schneider, Griffith, and Chasnoff (1989) on neurodevelopmental techniques.

SUMMARY

Children prenatally exposed to drugs offer us challenges that must be met one child at a time and one family at a time. Although health care professionals must trust their judgment, based on their invaluable day-to-day contact with families who use drugs, it is equally important for us to assess input from researchers. The controlled focus of the researcher has given us a better understanding of the impact of some of the more commonly used legal and illegal drugs, while helping us to understand that we are in a position to change many of the variables which will ultimately impact the children in our care. The task of preventing the exposure of our children to legal and illegal drugs, which may cause them harm, demands the attention of our entire community.

REFERENCES

Als H. Assessing the neurobehavioral development of the premature infant and the environment of the neonatal intensive care unit: A synactive model of neonatal behavioral organization. *Physical and Occupational Therapy in Pediatrics 1986; 6*: 3-53.

Als H. Neurobehavioral organization of the newborn: Opportunity for assessment and intervention. In Kilbey MM, Asghar K eds. *Methodological Issues in Controlled Studies on Effects of Prenatal Exposure to Drug Abuse*. Rockville, MD: National Institute on Drug Abuse, 1991 (Research Monograph 114).

Arendt R, Singer L, Minnes S. Development of cocaine-exposed infants. Poster presented at the meeting of the Society for Research in Child Development, New Orleans, 1993 March.

Aronson M, Kyllerman M, Sabel KG, Sandin B, Olegård R. Children of alcoholic mothers: Developmental, perceptual and behavioral characteristics as compared to matched controls. *Acta Pædiatrica Scandinavica 1985*; 74: 27-35.

Bayley N. *Manual for the Bayley Scales of Infant Development*. New York: Psychological Corporation, 1969.

Barr HM, Streissguth AP, Darby BL, Sampson PD. Prenatal exposure to alcohol, caffeine, tobacco, and aspirin: Effects on fine and gross motor performance in 4-year-old children. *Developmental Psychology* 1990; 26: 339-48.

Beery KE, Buktenica NA. *The Beery Test of Visual Motor Integration*. Cleveland, OH: Modern Curriculum Press, 1967.

Bobath K, Bobath B. Cerebral palsy. In Pearson P, Williams C, eds. *Physical Therapy Services in the Developmental Disabilities*. Springfield, IL: Charles Thomas Publishers, 1975.

Brazelton TB. Neonatal Behavioral Assessment Scale. Rev. ed. *Clinics in Developmental Medicine* 1984; 88 (Philadelphia: JB Lippincott).

Bruinink RH. *Bruininks-Oseretsky Test of Motor Proficiency*. Circle Pines, MN: American Guidance Service, 1978.

Bukoski WJ. A definition of drug abuse prevention research. In Donohew L, Sypher HE, Bukoski WJ, eds. *Persuasive Communication and Drug Abuse Prevention*. Hillsdale, NJ: Lawrence Erlbaum Associates, 1991, pp 3-19.

Chandler LS, Andrews MS, Swanson MW. *Movement Assessment of Infants: A Manual*. Rolling Bay, WA: Infant Movement Research, 1980.

Chandler LS, Richardson GA, Day NL, Gallagher JD. Prenatal exposure to alcohol and marijuana: Effects on motor development of preschool children. Poster presented at the meeting of the Society for Research in Child Development, New Orleans, 1993 March.

Chasnoff IJ, Griffith DR, Freier C, Murray J. Cocaine/polydrug use in pregnancy: Two-year follow-up. *Pediatrics* 1992; 89 (2).

Coles CD, Brown RT, Smith I, Platzman KA, Erickson S, Falek A. Effects of prenatal alcohol exposure at school age. I. Physical and cognitive development.

Neurotoxicology and Teratology 1991; 13: 357-67.

Coles CD, Platzman KA, Smith I, James ME, Falek A. Effects of cocaine and alcohol use in pregnancy on neonatal growth and neurobehavioral status. *Neurotoxicology and Teratology* 1992; 14: 23-33.

Day NL. Effects of prenatal alcohol exposure. In Zagon IS, Slotkin TA, eds. *Maternal Substance Abuse and the Developing Nervous System*. Orlando, FL: Academic Press, 1992, pp 27-44.

Eisen LN, Field TM, Bandstra ES, Roberts JP, Morrow C, Larson SK, Steel BN. Perinatal cocaine effects on neonatal stress behavior and performance on the Brazelton Scale. *Pediatrics* 1991; 88: 477-80.

Field T. Interventions in early infancy. *Infant Mental Health Journal* 1992;13(4): 329-36.

Finnie NR. *Handling the Young Cerebral Palsy Child at Home*. New York: E. P. Dutton, 1975.

Frostig M, Lefver W, Whittlesey J. *The Marianne Frostig Developmental Test of Visual Perception*. Palo Alto, CA: Consulting Psychologist Press, 1966. (Swedish version: Stockholm: Psykologiförlaget, 1973).

Fried PA, Makin JE. Neonatal behavioral correlates of prenatal exposure to marihuana, cigarettes, and alcohol in a low-risk population. *Neurotoxicology and Teratology* 1987; 9: 1-7.

Fried PA, Watkinson B. 36- and 48-month neurobehavioral follow-up of children prenatally exposed to marijuana, cigarettes, and alcohol. *Developmental and Behavioral Pediatrics* 1990;11(2): 49-58.

Gesell A, Amatruda C. *Developmental Diagnosis: Normal and Abnormal Child Development: Clinical Methods and Practical Applications*. New York: P. B. Hoeber, 1941.

Griffiths R. *The Abilities of Babies*. London: University of London Press, 1954.

Griffiths R. *The Abilities of Young Children*. Chard, Sommerset: Young and Son, 1970.

Harris SR, Osborn JA, Weinberg J, Loock C, Junaid K. Effects of prenatal alcohol exposure on neuromotor and cognitive development during early childhood: a series of case reports. *Physical Therapy* 1993; 73: 608-17.

Janzen L, Nanson J. Neuropsychological evaluation of preschoolers with fetal alcohol syndrome. *Neurotoxicology and Teratology* (in press).

Kyllerman M, Aronson M, Sabel KG, Karlberg, Sandin B, Olegård R. Children of alcoholic mothers: Growth and motor performance compared to matched controls. *Acta Pædiatrica Scandinavica* 1985; 74: 20-6.

Mayes LC, Granger RH, Frank MA, Schottenfeld R, Bornstein MH. Neurobehavioral profiles of neonates exposed to cocaine prenatally. *Pediatrics* 1993; 91: 778-83.

Matthews CG, Kløve H. *Wisconsin Motor Steadiness Battery: Administration Manual for Child Neuropsychology Battery*. Madison, WI: University of Wisconsin Medical School, Neuropsychology Laboratory, 1978.

McCarthy D. *Manual for the McCarthy Scales of Children's Abilities*. New York: Psychological Corporation, 1972.

Ramey CT, Bryant DM, Wasik BH, Sparling JJ, Fendt KH, LaVange LM. Infant health and development program for low birth weight, premature infants: Program elements, family participation, and child intelligence. *Pediatrics* 1992; 3: 454-65.

Reitan RM, Davison LA. Clinical neuropsychology: Clinical status and applications. New York: Wiley, 1974.

Richardson GA, Day NL. Maternal and neonatal effects of moderate cocaine use during pregnancy. *Neurotoxicology and Teratology* 1991;13:455-60.

Richardson GA, Day NL, Taylor PM. The effect of prenatal alcohol, marijuana, and tobacco exposure on neonatal behavior. *Infant Behavior and Development* 1989; 12: 199-209.

Rodning C, Beckwith L, Howard J. Prenatal exposure to drugs: Behavioral distortions reflecting CNS impairment? *Neurotoxicology* 1989;10:629-34.

Rotert DA, Svien L. Fetal alcohol syndrome: implications for practice. *Occupational Therapy Practice* 1993 March.

Satz P, Fletcher J. *Florida Kindergarten Screening Battery.* Psychology Association Resources, 1982.

Schneider JW, Chasnoff IJ. Motor assessment of cocaine/polydrug-exposed infants at age 4 months. *Neurotoxicology and Teratology* 1992; 14: 97-101.

Schneider JW, Griffith DR, Chasnoff IJ. Infants exposed to cocaine in utero: Implications for developmental assessment and intervention. *Infants and Young Children* 1989; 2: 25-36.

Singer L. Personal communication, April 24, 1993.

Sparrow SS, Balla DA, Cicchetti DV. *Vineland Adaptive Behavior Scales: Interview form—Survey form manual.* Circle Pines, MN: American Guidance Service,1987.

Streissguth A. Fetal alcohol syndrome: an epidemiologic perspective. *American Journal of Epidemiology* 1978;107:467-78.

Streissguth A, Barr H, Martin D. Maternal alcohol use and neonatal habituation assessed with the Brazelton Scale. *Child Development* 1983; 545: 1109-18.

Streissguth A, Barr H, Martin D, Herman C. Effects of maternal alcohol, nicotine, and caffeine use during pregnancy on infant mental and motor development at eight months. *Alcoholism: Clinical and Experimental Research* 1980;4:152-64.

Sweeney J. Neonatal hydrotherapy: An adjunct to developmental intervention in an intensive care nursery setting. *Physical and Occupational Therapy in Pediatrics* 1983; 3: 39-52.

Sweeney JK, Swanson MW. At-risk neonates and infants; NICU management and follow-up. In Umphred D, ed. *Neurological Rehabilitation* St. Louis: CV Mosby, 1990.

Trites RA. *Grooved Peg Board.* Lafayette, IN: Lafayette Instrument Company, 1987.

Trites RL, Price MA. *Assessment of Readiness for Primary French Immersion.* Ottawa, Canada: University of Ottawa Press, 1978.

Tronic EZ, Beeghly M, Fetters L, Weinberg MK. New methodologies for evaluating residual brain damage in infants exposed to drugs of abuse: Objective methods for describing movements, facial expressions, and communicative behaviors. In Kilbey MM, Asghar K, eds. *Methodological Issues in Controlled Studies on Effects of Prenatal Exposure to Drug Abuse.* Rockville, MD: National Institute on Drug Abuse, 1991 (Research Monograph 114).

ANNOTATED BIBLIOGRAPHY

Day NL, Richardson GA. Prenatal alcohol exposure: A continuum of effects. *Seminars in Perinatology* **1991;15(4): 271-9.**
Day and Richardson have provided the reader with a comprehensive review of the literature on infants and children prenatally exposed to alcohol. This review addresses research on the adverse effects of alcohol on growth and morphology as well as neurobehavioral and cognitive development of infants prenatally exposed to drugs. The authors provide direction for future research.

Donohew L, Sypher HE, Bukoski WJ, eds. *Persuasive Communication and Drug Abuse Prevention.* **Hillsdale, NJ: Lawrence Erlbaum Associates, 1991.**
The National Institute on Drug Abuse (NIDA), researchers, and community practitioners interested in drug abuse prevention collaborated on the publication of this text which has as its focus the prevention of misuse of legal and illegal drugs. Professionals concerned with the care of infants and children prenatally drug exposed will find the text useful in reaching a better understanding of the subtle combination of events that have placed infants and children at risk. A variety of methods for preventing drug abuse surface from the pages of this text.

Kilbey MM, Asghar K, eds. *Methodological Issues in Controlled Studies on Effects of Prenatal Exposure to Drug Abuse.*
Rockville, MD: National Institute on Drug Abuse, 1991 (Research Monograph 114).
This monograph serves as a resource of current research and researchers on prenatal drug exposure and its consequences for infants and children. Efforts to quantify prenatal exposure and efforts to assess the outcomes of that exposure are presented.

Neuspiel DR, Hamel SC. Cocaine and infant behavior. *Developmental and Behavioral Pediatrics* **1991; 12 (1): 55-64.**
Neuspiel and Hamel have provided the reader with a comprehensive review of the literature in regards to the impact of cocaine on infant behavior. This thorough review addresses the published literature on human as well as animal research, using the combined wisdom of researchers in both arenas to suggest potential mechanisms for adverse effects of cocaine on neurobehavioral development of infants prenatally drug exposed. This article provides a balanced critique of published studies. The authors provide direction for future research.

Ramey CT, Bryant DM, Wasik BH, Sparling JJ, Fendt KH, LaVange LM. Infant health and development program for low birth weight, premature infants: Program elements, family participation, and child intelligence. *Pediatrics* **1992; 3: 454-65.**
This is a summary of an efficacy study on early intervention for low birth weight and premature infants. Eight sites throughout the United States participated in this study. Although the infants selected for this study to enhance health, behavioral, and cognitive status were not prenatally exposed to drugs there is much to learn from this extensive intervention protocol. The four-pronged intervention included pediatric follow-up, home visits, parent support groups, and a systematic educational program provided at developmental centers. IQ scores of the children at age three were highly correlated with a Family Participation Index.

11

Communication Development and Disorders of Children with Prenatal Alcohol and Drug Exposure and Pediatric AIDS

Marion D. Meyerson, CCC-SP/A, Ph.D.

Children prenatally exposed to licit and illicit drugs and those with the human immunodeficiency virus are reported to have speech, language, and hearing problems. A continuum of effects—from severely compromised to normal development—must be addressed in the context of the families and cultural communities. Thorough and individualized assessments followed by rational therapeutic approaches are needed.

For many years nurses have interacted professionally with speech-language pathologists and audiologists on team management of patients with communicative disorders (Shanks l983a,b). In rehabilitation units and extended care facilities these professionals have shared expertise and concerns working with head injury, stroke, and progressive neuromuscular disease patients. In community-based health centers and outreach programs, nurses have disseminated information about the need for intervention when delays are suspected. Preschool and school nurses have long cooperated in identifying children with a wide range of speech and hearing problems. Pediatric nurse practitioners are following children through their developmental milestones and are making referrals to communicative disorders specialists. They have overseen the continuity of care and services for at-risk children (Lewis l991). Nurses often assume the responsibility of prenatal, neonatal, and postnatal family counseling and convey information critical to the health, safety, and development of children.

There is a particular overlap of concerns shared by nurses and communicative disorders specialists in working with children who are prenatally exposed to drugs. Prior to addressing these common concerns, some general discussion of how language develops, why it goes wrong, and how it is assessed is appropriate.

Development of Speech and Language

The simple phrase or sentence uttered by a child represents an exquisite constellation of skills that are universal for humans. We are genetically programmed and environmentally reinforced to use respiration, phonation, and articulation in concert with linguistic and cognitive skills. Bees may give signals, chimps may make signs, and dolphins may communicate with each other. The human species, however, is unique, so far as we know, in the ability to generate spontaneously an infinite number of sentences. All over the world children develop language in a systematic and predictable way, following a biological timetable with both universality and range of normalcy (Lenneberg 1984).

Evidence of the development of receptive language is generally observed first as the child appears to understand comments by adults and recognize objects and persons in the environment. Expressive language emerges soon after. Even with vast cultural differences in child-rearing, the pattern is maintained. Some parents or caretakers talk very little; others talk to excess. Children exposed to any environment in this broad range usually begin to use language in the same way and at the same time (Lenneberg 1984). A serious handicap such as mental retardation, profound hearing loss, or severe neuromuscular disease can slow the biological timetable, but some development according to the universal pattern is still possible. Among humans, deprivation must be extreme for a child *not* to develop some language. Tales of feral children or virtually isolated children are few and interesting in their uniqueness. Many of the children reported to be raised in isolation do not live a normal life span and few develop appropriate language skills. It is not known whether they may have been retarded before abandonment or whether the absence of expected species contact precluded the development of cognitive and linguistic abilities (Lane & Molyneaux 1992).

Hearing is the primary modality for the acquisition of language. The particular language which is learned is the one the child hears, be it English, Spanish, Russian, or Xhosa. Which specific words are learned, which sounds or tones are included, what grammatical forms are used, are all incidental. The basis for learning by watching, listening, interacting, and then expressing concepts with a string of words is universal.

The Acquisition Timetable

Sounds of distress and contentment are the earliest recognizable signs of communication intent. Crying signifies distress or need or a desire to manipulate the environment. The random production of sounds and the repetition of those sounds are known as cooing and babbling. They are related to contentment and are an important form of vocal play. Babies with profound hearing loss begin babbling but the quantity and the quality of the babbling are different (Lane & Molyneaux 1992). Normal hearing children babble in imitation of their parents' prosody which combines the rhythm, stress, and inflection of spoken language (Moskowitz 1978). A baby raised in a Chinese language environment demonstrates inflectional patterns in babbling which indicate that he/she already can recognize different tones as different sounds, a feature of Chinese which is not part of English. Infants are often heard to utter a long stream of jargon with such accurate prosody and structure

that listeners wonder if they really uttered a sentence!

Close to the child's first birthday, a few true words usually emerge (Dale 1976). Each of these words represents a sentence concept, as if the entire sentence has been squeezed through a small channel. The simple word "out," or a close approximation of it, can reflect any one of a number of more complex ideas, from "Put on my jacket, momma, and take me outside with you," to "Look at that strange animal out in the yard tearing up my favorite toy." Accompanying gestures and contextual cues identify for the listener which of these concepts has been telegraphed as "out."

Receptive abilities significantly outdistance expressive skills during the second year of life. The caregiver can say "Don't spread out your fingers when I'm trying to get your arm in the sleeve; make a fist for me" and the child will react. She understands, although she is a long way from producing a sentence of equivalent length and complexity.

The child's vocabulary continues to increase after the first birthday. The particular number of expected words varies according to the source. One simple and reasonable measure is that we usually anticipate about 200 words at age two, 300 words at age three, and continued additions until at least 2,500 words are spoken at age six (Lane & Molyneaux 1992). Most children use many two-word sentences at age two. At ages three, four and five, sentences increase in length and complexity. Subtleties will be introduced. The four-year-old can give hints, pick up on cues, and modify conversation on the basis of listener reaction.

As the child matures, the motor

speech mechanism will function with increasing precision (Lane & Molyneaux 1992). Vowels have the fewest motor adjustments and are used first. Consonants develop logically with the simplest, such as /m/, /p/, and /b/, generally used early. The consonants which are the most complex (usually /s/, /r/, and /l/) are added later, often as late as seven or eight years of age. The spoken language of preschoolers, therefore, may not always be completely correct. However, if each of us could understand and speak several foreign languages as well as the average three or four-year-old speaks his own language, we'd be considered quite remarkable!

Children are raised in many cultural and linguistic environments, some of which may be different from the mainstream. The children may have large but different vocabularies, and alternate sentence structure and pronunciation. Their communicative behaviors are valid for their level of development whether or not they can be adequately assessed by tests adapted for the mainstream. Language and dialect differences should not be labeled as disorders, although the two can certainly coexist.

Children of all cultures participate in play. The process of play is important in exploring new items and concepts, in using language, in learning to interact, and in reducing anxiety (Lane & Molyneaux 1992). Unusual patterns of play, such as indiscriminate taking up and discarding of toys, may reflect problems in communication and social skills.

Communicative Disorders

Most children develop receptive and expressive language systems and motor speech abilities normally and naturally.

The major criterion in the acquisition of communication skills is an intact speaker with normal hearing, cognitive abilities, social interaction skills, neuromuscular functioning, and craniofacial morphology. Among the organic problems which can seriously compromise language and speech are hearing loss, mental retardation, autism, weakness or paralysis of the speech mechanism, and a variety of facial malformations. Many individuals demonstrating one or more of these problems have an identified syndrome of chromosomal, genetic, or unknown etiology (Meyerson 1985). The cause may also be teratogenic, the category which includes prenatal drug exposure.

Even with an otherwise normal profile, some children exhibit communicative disorders. Interestingly, among the most frequently seen types of problems at the average community or university speech clinic is the child with delayed language and/or speech for no readily apparent reason. Table 1 lists signs of communicative disorders and when referral to a speech-language pathologist is indicated.

With the significant strides in language acquisition during early childhood, any decrease in the reception of sound can impair speech development in some children. Recurrent otitis media is a common pediatric ailment. It often occurs during critical periods of perception and learning during the first year of life. Even after the infection is under control, there may be a temporary mild hearing loss that can interfere with language learning and precipitate auditory processing problems. Many of the children will eventually attain normal language and speech without intervention. Others

Table 1. Signs of Communicative Disorders.*

Refer to speech-language pathologist if the child:

Does not recognize own name, common objects by 18 months

Cannot respond to simple requests by 18 months

Has no words at age 2

Does not combine words into sentences at age 3

Has multiple articulation errors and is unintelligible to most people at age 3

Has frequent repetitions, prolongations, and hesitations of sounds at age 5

Is embarrassed by or fearful of dysfluency

Accompanies speech with nasal or facial grimacing

Has unexplained hoarseness of more than two weeks duration

Has breathy or strained voice quality

Has inappropriate high or low pitch or loudness

Has irregular breathing and a limited number of words on each breath

Is hypernasal or has excessive emission of air through the nose

Is hyponasal in the absence of transient rhinitis

Has an at-risk history and/or diagnosed birth defect

Refer to audiologist if the child:

Does not turn to source of sound by 6 months of age

Ignores spoken conversation and/or television unless it is loud

Requires visual cuing

Has a diagnosed birth defect

---

* The signs listed should alert the nurse or other professional to the need for consultation with a communicative disorders specialist. If the child has already been seen by a speech-language-pathologist and/or audiologist, an exchange of reports could benefit the total management of the child. If one or more of these signs is reported by the parent or noted by a teacher or nurse, and the child has not been seen for a speech and/or hearing evaluation, referral should be made.

experience frustration and early failure. Because it is difficult to determine which of the language-delayed children will develop appropriate skills eventually without therapy and which will fall behind, early intervention is generally recommended.

During the normal development of speech, many children exhibit dysfluencies such as word or phrase repetition or hesitation. Most of these dysfluencies are temporary and decrease as language skills improve. However, abnormal pitch and loudness variations, tremors while speaking, and signs of tension and fear indicate a need for intervention (Lane & Molyneaux 1992).

In order to prevent speech, language, and hearing problems, mass professional and family education in the prenatal and neonatal periods is critical. Good prenatal maternal health is primary. In neonates, prespeech feeding activities, critical to the development of articulation, should be assessed. The caregivers of at-risk infants who require tube feeding should be instructed to allow opportunities for sucking and chewing prior to using the tube for nutrition. Identification of lethargy in babies requires special attention so that adequate interaction and stimulation are not overlooked. At the other end of the spectrum, irritability requires other modes of intervention.

Assessment

If speech and language milestones are a concern, screening or formal assessment is appropriate. Ideally, all genetic, medical, audiological, developmental, social service, and psychometric reports are available so that the speech-language pathologist can view the child in the broadest possible context. In the actual speech assessment, body posture, respiration, and the structure and function of the speech mechanism are observed. Changes in prolonged and repeated utterances are noted. Spontaneous language samples are elicited with a broad view of real-life situations for the individual child. This requires a sensitivity to the cultural and linguistic background of the family and an appreciation of family and community values. A speech-language pathologist notes facial expression, fluency, pitch, loudness, articulation, hypernasality, oral muscle strength and movement, and stimulability. Gestures or inflectional variations that can augment a minimal vocabulary are assessed. Socialization skills, such as turn-taking, are evaluated as part of communicative interaction. If a child's expressive language is limited, receptive abilities can also be assessed through observation of response to simple commands and directions in everyday situations. Hyperverbalization sometimes masks language delays. Even if speech appears excessive, it must be analyzed for complexity and appropriateness.

A number of published screening and diagnostic tools are used in assessing language (Compton 1990; Villarreal, McKinney & Quackenbush 1992). Some of these are administered to the caregiver, who describes the child's development by drawing from observations in the home. Other tools are used directly with children. With the knowledge that a test score is *not* a diagnosis, and with every effort to incorporate published tests with observations so as to obtain a valid assessment, the information gleaned may help to direct the professional to areas requiring remediation. In an at-risk population, assessment should be ongoing in order to detect subtle problems that may not surface until the child enters school (MacDonald 1992).

Diagnostic reports should document all physical and communication features noted, not just the abnormal ones. Is the philtrum (the vertical midline groove above the upper lip) normal or flat? Is the voice quality normal or hoarse? Is the rhythm normal? Is hypernasality a factor or is it not? The report should be thorough. A copy of it should go to the family. If, in the judgment of the professional, the language of the report would not be easily understood by the family, another version of it should be composed and should include both the assessment findings and specific recommendations for intervention.

Recent literature concerning the development of children prenatally exposed to licit and illicit drugs generally mentions problems in speech, language, and hearing. The range of effects is from serious malformation and central nervous system compromise to completely normal development. Comprehensive speech and hearing profiles of children prenatally drug exposed are necessary in order to provide strategies for successful intervention, when needed.

Teratogens

Teratogens are agents that deform the fetus without altering the genetic makeup. They include legal and illegal drugs, chemicals, viruses, and other agents. Teratogens may affect the embryo early in pregnancy and cause specific malformations such as microcephaly. Behavioral teratology has uncovered a set of problems which incorporates many of the learning and language disabilities that are not always

evident until a child enters preschool or is school age. Among the known and suspected teratogens are alcohol, tobacco, cocaine, and other illicit drugs.

Fetal Alcohol Syndrome

Fetal alcohol syndrome (FAS) was delineated in the early 1970s, although it had been suspected since biblical times. Case studies and research protocols have helped to develop a profile of the child and adult with FAS (Shaywitz, Cohen & Shaywitz 1980; Hamilton 1981; Iosub et al 1981; Sparks 1984; Becker, Warr-Leeper & Leeper 1990; Greene et al 1990; Streissguth et al 1991; Brown et al 1991; Autti-Ramo, Gaily & Granstrom 1992; Majewski 1993). The physical characteristics include prenatal and postnatal growth deficiency, microcephaly, central nervous system involvement, and characteristic facies with short palpebral fissures because of poor eye and brain development, a perceived flat midface, enamel hypoplasia, and a flat philtrum.

The speech problems of children with FAS include delays in receptive and expressive language, which are reflective of the mental retardation in many children with the syndrome. Nanson (1992) described a number of children with both FAS and autism. Additionally, decreased processing and memory abilities, poor attending skills, impulsivity, perseveration, poor judgment, hyperactivity, and hypersensitivity to noise have been reported. Structural and functional deviations of the articulators, dysarthria, and voice and fluency problems have also been noted (Becker, Warr-Leeper & Leeper 1990; Coles et al 1991). Conductive and sensorineural hearing losses are frequent (Church & Gerkin 1988). In a comparative study with children with another syndrome matched for cognitive levels, those with FAS appeared to have better social speech and skills at simple word recognition than would have been expected (Hamilton 1981). The automatic social speech masked more serious linguistic problems. Abkarian (1992) noted similar qualitative language differences between children with FAS and peers matched for mental age. The issue of whether the language deficits of children with FAS are a direct result of cognitive impairment or an independent feature of the syndrome itself has not as yet been resolved (Carney & Chermak 1991).

The descriptions of communicative skills and problems in those with FAS have helped in the development of strategies for accurate assessment and effective remediation for the entire continuum: those with the full-blown syndrome, and those who have neither the characteristic dysmorphic features nor the mental retardation but still demonstrate speech, language, and behavior problems (Meyerson 1991). Similar data are needed for children exposed to illegal drugs.

Cocaine/Crack

The media abounds with articles about children who are prenatally exposed to cocaine. The challenge is for nurses, teachers, and other professionals to develop a database of the strengths and problems that we might expect in this population. The variables, such as polydrug exposure, are significant. Children exposed prenatally to cocaine may also have FAS or may demonstrate the influence of exposure to small or large amounts of alcohol, or to tobacco, marijuana, or other drugs. The quality of home life might be chaotic or tragic, further deterring success in speech and language development. On the other hand, many children prenatally exposed have normal motor and cognitive development and have speech and language strengths similar to nonexposed peers. Some have had communication disorders that might be totally unrelated to prenatal exposure. Therefore, each child must be evaluated without bias. Villarreal, McKinney and Quackenbush (1992) thought of labeling as acceptable when it is ultimately helpful in providing services and strategies for the child. A more valuable set of labels might describe how the child best learns (e.g., visually), what his or her level of energy may be (e.g., lethargic), and/or how he or she interacts socially (e.g., a loner). The risks of prenatal exposure must be understood but prejudgment and labeling may become self-fulfilling. Mayes and coworkers (1992) suggested that many of the children are victims of the broader social problems of poverty, unemployment, and inadequate education and should not be "written off" when they might indeed thrive. Neuspiel and Hamel (1992) suggested a model that assumed no basic deficits in children prenatally exposed to cocaine but recognized an increased *risk* of problems.

To reiterate, almost every published article and unpublished communication surveyed by this author underscores the confounding effects of polysubstance exposure, chaotic home life, and poor prenatal care. It is not likely that there has been a group of children who have a prenatal history of cocaine exposure, but not alcohol, tobacco, other drugs, poor prenatal care and nutrition, and a troubled environment. On the other hand, children who have not been prenatally exposed to drugs nor postnatally subjected to poor and chaotic care may also demonstrate delays and deficits. Nevertheless, a number of specific characteristics of children who have been prenatally exposed to cocaine have been reported. Anday and associates (1989) found that infants prenatally cocaine-exposed demonstrated increased reactivity to tactile and acoustic stimuli. The authors posited that cocaine-induced vasoconstriction reduced fetal blood flow and caused central nervous system dysfunction reflected in the abnormal startle response. At least one report linked a drug-induced vascular etiology with a diagnosis of the congenital facial paralysis known as Moebius' syndrome (Kankirawatana et al 1993).

The cry of the neonate may reveal his/her neurobiologic health and foretell the developmental consequences beyond infancy (Corwin et al 1992; Lester et al 1991). A number of birth defects (Down syndrome, 5p-(cri du chat) syndrome, and so on) have characteristic cries. Prenatal exposure to cocaine might present distinctive acoustic characteristics of the infant cry. Lester and colleagues (1991) found that the direct effects of cocaine on the fetal cry appeared to be an increased duration and higher pitch, characteristic of laryngeal tension and upper airway constriction. The indirect effects might be related to lower birth weight with less crying, lower amplitude, and more turbulence, as in other less responsive infants with poorer respiratory effort. Therefore, there is often a combination of excited and depressed cries. Corwin and associates (1992) found fewer cry utterances and shorter cries in

newborns prenatally exposed to cocaine and decreased arousal in neurobehavioral function. It was not known if this represented central nervous system injury or withdrawal symptoms. The authors posited that acoustical analysis of newborn cry might be used in the future to identify and evaluate outcome.

Other findings in children prenatally drug exposed are low birth weight, shorter gestation periods, microcephaly, respiratory complication, facial clefting, craniosynostosis, ocular problems, puffy eyelids, increased incidence of ankyloglossia (midline attachment of tongue to floor of mouth), tone and movement deficits and other neurologic impairment (Hubatch et al 1985; Ferriero, Partridge & Wong 1988; Fulroth, Phillips & Durand 1989; Chasnoff et al 1989; Kabori, Ferriero & Golabi 1989; Dominguez et al 1991; Good et al 1992; Harris, Friend & Tolley 1992; Chasnoff et al 1992; Beeram et al 1993; Chiriboga et al 1993). These problems place babies at risk for auditory, visual, cognitive, receptive, and expressive language and speech delays. Some children prenatally exposed to cocaine do not have serious structural or cognitive compromise, but may demonstrate uncoordinated sucking and swallowing, as well as other signs of mild neurologic compromise, lower developmental scores, attention deficit, poor interaction with peers, attachment problems, distractibility, abnormal play patterns and an absence of delight (Howard et al 1989; Lewis, Bennett & Schmeder 1989; Rodning, Beckwith & Howard 1989a, b; Dixon 1989; Giacoia 1990; Rist 1990; Sanders-Phillips 1990; Lewis 1991). Chasnoff (1992) reported a broad spectrum of language problems in children with prenatal cocaine exposure but felt that all responded well to speech therapy.

Davis and coworkers (1992), in a review of seventy cocaine-exposed children ranging in age from one month to five years, found significant developmental delays. These included speech and language deficits, gross and fine motor delays, deficient personal social skills, and paucity of symbolic play. The children pointed and cried to make their wants known at an older age than would nonexposed children, and examined and discarded items in a detached manner. Interestingly, 11% met the standard criteria for autism, using the *DSM III-R* criteria (American Psychiatric Association 1987). Many demonstrated perseverative acts, including running back and forth across the room and other seemingly nonpurposeful movements.

Abnormal auditory brain stem responses in cocaine-exposed infants suggest a risk for auditory system deficits (Shih, Cone-Wesson & Reddix 1988; Cone-Wesson & Wu 1992). Unpublished reports have suggested major speech delays, unusual tactile responses and tactile defensiveness, intermittent processing problems, decreased organizational skills, distractibility, indiscriminate attachment, and poor visual tracking. In addition, there have been reports of apraxia (the inability to perform purposeful motor acts such as forming speech sounds in the absence of motor or sensory impairment) and mild dysarthria (the weakness, paralysis, or incoordination of the speech musculature). Dysarthric and/or apraxic speech can be awkward and difficult to understand. The behavior of children prena-tally drug exposed has been compared to that of children with FAS.

Rivers and Hedrick (1992) polled eight speech-language pathologists in central Florida concerning the language of fifty children in their caseloads who had been prenatally exposed to cocaine. In general, there were marked delays in receptive and expressive language in this population. Additional problems included inappropriate use of gestures in the first two years of life. After age two, many children exhibited poor word retrieval, disorganized sentence structure, and difficulty with abstract concepts. Pragmatic deficits included excessive talking, poor turn-taking, reduced attention span, impulsivity, and problems staying on task.

Other Illegal Drugs

Speech and language effects of some additional illegal drugs to which fetuses have been exposed have been described (Wilson et al 1979; Wilson 1989; Sowder & Burt 1980; Hayford, Epps & Dahl-Regis 1988; Dixon 1989; Fried & Watkinson 1990; Milman 1990; van Baar 1990). Some children of heroin-addicted and methadone-maintained mothers demonstrated language defects such as limited vocabulary, articulation errors, poorer performance on perceptual and organizational tasks, distractibility, motor incoordination, behavior problems, and more difficulty adapting to new situations. Prenatal exposure to marijuana has been associated with reduced verbal, visual-motor, perceptual, and general cognitive skills. Studies of children whose mothers used angel dust, PCP, and/or amphetamines reported poor motor coordination, mildly retarded cognitive skills, and limited and atypical language. Astley and associates (1992), in an analysis of facial shapes of children prenatally exposed to a variety of substanes, confirmed distinctive patterns in those exposed to alcohol, subtle features of mild hypertelorism and midface flatness in the cocaine-exposed, and no anomalies associated with maternal marijuana use. Corkery (1992a) implicated amphetamines, PCP, and solvents like airplane glue in findings of decreased head growth, neurobehavioral delays, and long-term motor and language problems. Other authors (Kaltenbach & Finnegan 1989; Day & Richardson 1991; Hoegerman & Schnoll 1991; O'Connell & Fried 1991) found studies regarding prenatal marijuana and opioid exposure inconclusive, with some studies reporting long-term effects, some indicating behavioral differences, and others reporting no negative effects. A summary of published studies points to a wide range of findings, few longitudinal follow-ups, and the persistent variable of polysubstance use. There are no accepted profiles of children exposed primarily to heroin, to amphetamines, or to marijuana. As with prenatal cocaine exposure, there may well be a continuum of effects, with some children severely compromised and others delightfully normal.

Pediatric AIDS

Going along with problems of maternal drug addiction is the frightening increase in the number of children with human immunodeficiency virus (HIV). Most are born to infected mothers, many of whom were drug users themselves and/or had drug-using mates. Hammonds (1989) reported that 80% of the cases of pediatric AIDS were infected during the prenatal and perinatal period. The ratio of affected children is equal for males and females. The prognosis is grim; most, but not all, die in the first two years of life (Rogers 1988).

Not all offspring of infected mothers inherit the virus. Cohen and associates (1991) compared infected and noninfected children of infected mothers. The study bore out the cause of the symptoms—not poor nutrition, prenatal care, or drug use—but the infection itself. However, in any given child, the factors of prenatal drug exposure, long-term hospitalization, and chaotic home environment must be considered.

Ultman and colleagues (1985) divided cases of HIV-positive children into those with full-blown AIDS and those with AIDS-related complex (ARC) with no opportunistic infection in the latter. They found delayed milestones in both groups. Price and associates (1988) underscored the risk for children with AIDS and ARC for serious neurodevelopmental delays.

Ninety percent of children with AIDS have failure to thrive, low height and weight, enlarged liver and spleen, pneumonitis, central nervous system dysfunction, severe recurrent infections, recurrent diarrhea and other gastrointestinal problems, hepatitis, nephropathy, and malignancies. Stiff ankles and wrists, contracted digits, and dystrophic nails have also been reported. Retinopathy occurs in 50% of the patients (Brady & Van Dyke 1992). Candidiasis, a fungal infection of the moist mucosa, and parotid enlargement are common oral findings (Katz et al 1993). The candidiasis in the pediatric AIDS population is resistant to the usual antifungal therapies (Ketchem et al 1990). It can spread to the larynx, pharynx, and esophagus (Williams 1987) creating additional problems in breathing, eating, and speaking. Hass and colleagues (1987) noted episodes of hoarseness caused by fungal disease of many of their immunocompromised pediatric patients.

Hammonds (1989) summarized that 90% of children with AIDS have at least two of the following symptoms: failure to thrive, enlarged liver and spleen, pneumonitis, CNS dysfunction, and severe and recurring infections.

Neural symptoms are very common in children with pediatric AIDS and may be static or progressive. Among the common neurologic and/or developmental findings (Williams 1987; Diamond 1989; Schmitt et al 1991; Butler, Hittleman & Hauger 1991; Indacochea & Scott 1992) are mental and motor delays, loss of previously acquired milestones, acquired microcephaly, progressive bilateral pyramidal tract signs, ataxia, tremor, short-term memory probems, visual organization deficits similar to those exhibited by children with cerebral palsy, attention deficits, and behavioral changes. Mintz and Epstein (1992) reported depression, anxiety, and autistic behaviors in older school-age children with HIV. On the other hand, Cohen and associates (1991) reported that overall intellectual functioning can be stable for many years, even in children with other symptoms.

Progressive encephalopathy is marked by impaired brain growth, progressive motor problems, and loss of neurodevelopmental milestones (Mintz 1992). It can result in a severe loss of language skills and minimal social interaction.

AIDS dementia in children with accompanying loss of cognitive skills can be striking. The drug AZT can block propagation of the virus and appears, in combination with other drugs, to reverse this progressive dementia (Culliton 1989; Schmitt et al 1991). AZT is reported to improve neuropsychologic function in some children (Brouwers et al 1990). However, a safe and universally effective drug has not yet been found. Additionally, it is not known if AZT administered to a pregnant woman will harm the fetus or prevent fetal infection.

Facial dysmorphism in pediatric AIDS has been suggested but remains speculative (Nicholas 1988; Qazi et al 1988; Chanock & McIntosh 1989). It certainly needs to be explored with consideration of whether any distinctive facial features were due to alcohol or drug abuse rather than to the AIDS virus, and whether the facial abnormalities will affect development of speech.

Along with all the respiratory infections they contract because of the deteriorating immune system, children with AIDS have frequent bouts of tonsillitis and otitis media and a lower cure rate with standard drugs such as amoxicillin (Chow et al 1990; Principi et al 1991). In some cases, recurrent otitis may precede the manifestation of other opportunistic infections (Church 1987). Williams (1987) noted that 80% of children with AIDS have chronic or serous otitis media. In addition, many of the powerful drugs used for malignancies and infections are ototoxic. Certainly, if old and new drugs used in life-saving attempts truly work, we'll learn more about the long-term ototoxic sequelae in the survivors. In the meantime, both conductive and sensorineural hearing losses must be considered as potential deterrents to the normal development of speech and language skills and be assessed so appropriate intervention can begin early.

Pressman (1992) followed 150 children with prenatally or perinatally acquired AIDS. Almost 20% were developmentally delayed. Some demonstrated progressive encephalopathy with accompanying regression of language skills and increasing dysarthria. Many demonstrated receptive and expressive language delays, dysphagia, hypernasality, and dysarthria. The author recognized the multiple factors including prenatal exposure to alcohol and other drugs which may have been factors in the delays. Twelve percent had hoarse voices secondary to the spread of candidiasis. Twenty percent had dysphagia, the inability to swallow. Coughing and gagging accompanied attempts to eat or drink for some. Intervention with improved posture and the thickening of liquids for some proved helpful. Some children regressed in self-feeding abilities as their disease progressed. Nutritional management became a prime concern. For those with candidiasis, inclusion of purees and puddings in the diet and the elimination of juices with citric acid were recommended. In spite of the grim prognosis of those with progressive encephalopathy, many children in this study were reported to be stable and attending school regularly.

Abrams and Nicholas (1990) and Van Dyke (1991) noted that pediatric AIDS is a disease suffered by the entire family. Parents and siblings may demonstrate the relentless progression of fatal symptoms. A multidisciplinary professional commitment is essential. Lipson (1993), a psychologist, described the ethical and social dilemmas of disclosure of the AIDS diagnosis to the affected children.

Nebel-Gould (1991) reported a number of language and speech problems in children with HIV encephalopathy, including aphasia, depressed vocabulary, reading and writing deficits, decreased respiratory support for voice projection, and flaccidity or spasticity of the articulators. She recommended pragmatic language therapy and positioning for support of swallowing and feeding. Speech and language assessment of children with AIDS should take into account the progressive nature of the condition with respect to cognition and motor impairment, as well as hearing, speech, attention, and behavioral problems. For those with progressive encephalopathy, loss of motor skills may preclude the substitution of signing for verbal speech. In end stages, the arms are in a retracted position, thereby inhibiting pointing (Pressman 1992). Eye gaze communication and the use of augmentative devices can be attempted. Somehow, a mode of communication between patient and caregivers must be developed.

Issues of care and community response are critical in providing services to children with pediatric AIDS. Most have a poor prognosis but there are individuals who could benefit from school attendance (Chadwick 1992). Taylor-Brown (1991) stated that for children with AIDS, or those unaffected children whose parents died of AIDS, foster care which most resembles a family environment is preferable to a hospital or group home. The caregiver's fear of AIDS impacts upon care as well. A balance must be kept in reducing isolation and maintaining appropriate safety measures required for infectious diseases (Asha

Table 2.   General Suggestions for Prevention and Remediation of Communication Disorders.

Encourage development of pre-speech feeding skills by allowing for sucking and chewing time before supplemental tube feeding.

Stimulate placid children; calm agitated ones.

Find core vocabulary significant to family life; use these words often.

Consider culture and community in all aspects of planning and delivery of services.

Utilize peer teaching by older siblings, cousins, or school mates.

Balance need to have clear speech with efforts to expand language.

Keep learning areas clutter-free; minimize visual and auditory distractions; organize and label important items in the environment.

Treat tactile defensiveness by systematic desensitization with a variety of textures.

Treat hypersensitivity to noise by gradually increasing volume from low to high.

Set behavior limits in advance; develop clear signals for redirection.

Praise good behavior and efforts at attending.

1990). Meyers and Weitzman (1991) noted that the exacerbation of stigma and loss of family may result in post-traumatic responses similar to survivors of disasters. The families need physical, speech, occupational, and recreational therapy in a supportive environment.

Remediation of Communicative Disorders

Therapy strategies for all communicative disorders are determined through ongoing evaluation and with special regard for the culture, family, and community dynamics of the patients (Table 2). Effective treatment considers the needs of the children and the caregivers and includes guidance and feedback (Saylor, Lippa & Lee 1991). A familiarity with regional cultures and customs is critical but, at the same time, cultural generalizations must leave room for individual family variants. There is much in the literature concerning the influence of culture on the perception of etiology, treatment, and the pursuit of health and educational resources (Vincent et al 1990; Meyerson 1990; Toliver-Weddington 1990; Cheng 1990; Strauss 1990). Different ethnic groups (Latino, African-American, Asian, Native American, to name a few) demonstrate a variety of strengths in coping with a child who may need physical and speech therapy and/or special educational classes.

Early intervention with at-risk children of any cultural or linguistic background may reduce hazards to speech and language development. Beginning in the nursery, infants who demonstrate irritability should be handled in a slow and calm manner, with dim lighting and the possible use of quiet white noise (Lewis, Bennett & Schmeder 1989). Lesar (1992) suggested rocking and hydrotherapy to decrease irritability. Face-to-face quiet contacts and smiling as a response to irritability can foster trust. It is also recommended that caregivers of infants imitate pleasurable sounds and name items aloud in the daily environment so that linguistic stimuli are accessible.

In the event that tube feedings are indicated, encourage sucking and, later, chewing small quantities in an upright position with support for chin and back, so as to develop pre-speech feeding skills. After a few minutes of sucking, the tube can be introduced for supplemental nutrition. This will allow a balance of meeting nutritional needs and allowing sucking and swallowing activities. (See Gigliotti [1992] for review of infant interventions.)

Oral tactile hypersensitivity can be modified first by stimulation on other parts of the body and then gradually by slow, firm touching of the face and then the oral cavity (Alexander 1983). Posture, food texture, and utensils can be varied to determine the best strategy for appropriate swallowing.

In therapy with toddlers and young children, elimination of excess visual and auditory clutter will help to reduce distractions. Verbalization with normal gesture and prosody in a realistic situation should be encouraged with a core of significant words individualized to the child and family (Meyerson 1991). In fact, successful therapy takes into account the priorities as perceived by the patient and/or the family. If particular words are critical in the environment, those should be the ones targeted in therapy. It is important to balance the expansion of language with the improvement of verbal output. In other words, the goal is to allow the child to say clearly what it is that he/she knows.

Hypersensitivity to noise can be gradually deconditioned by presenting the offending sound (vacuum cleaner, television, etc.) on tape first at a low volume, and then in incremental increases in volume. A program of sensory integration and systematic desensitization using a variety of items and textures, perhaps in teamwork with an occupational therapist, may be effective in overcoming tactile defensiveness.

Clearly, any problems in social interaction should be identified and remediated. Role playing and behavioral reinforcements can be utilized to reduce problems with eye contact, turn-taking, fidgeting, and staying on the topic (Blondis et al 1991). Behavior limits should be clearly established and maintained. Poor judgment and lack of imagination in anticipating the consequences of actions must be addressed. This may include teaching important safety measures such as looking before crossing the street or not playing with fire. In other words, the children need to learn how to make good choices. Blondis and colleagues (1991) suggested catching the child being good, as well as when being disruptive, and continuing positive reinforcement of good behavior as he/she gets older. For children with attention deficits and/or hyperactivity, cognitive behavioral therapy has yielded improvement (Fehlings et al 1991). The method uses modeling and role playing to identify an aberrant behavior and to evaluate the alternative solutions. Cognitive behavioral therapy also shows mistakes and demonstrates how to cope with those mistakes. Corkery (1992b) recommends helping children develop visual imagery as well as verbal cues for self-soothing and focusing attention.

In the classroom, a minimum of interruptions in the daily routine is advised. Healey (1993) listed a number of behavioral problems and appropriate intervention strategies; for example, moving a disoriented child to an isolated area and minimizing visual and auditory stimuli. Teachers can set a fixed quiet organizational time between transitions; for example, after play/before snack or after storytime/before playground. Predictable daily routines should be planned (Sparks 1993). Seating a disruptive child next to a quiet one may be calming. Peer teaching in school or in the family often helps to enrich the lives and heighten accomplishment and self-esteem of both the children requiring remedial work and the children who are assigned to instruct them. Involving the whole family in an understanding of the processes and goals of therapy can be a valuable asset. Written instructions for helping and reinforcing the children for brief periods at home during the day usually result in improved compliance.

CONCLUSION

The nurse's coterie of colleagues should include speech-language pathologists and audiologists. The potential for meaningful cooperation in case management, for concerned family counseling, for increased learning, and for cross-referrals can grow from both formal and informal consultation among the professions. Speech-language pathologists (sometimes referred to as speech clinicians, speech therapists, or communicative disorders specialists) and audiologists are certified by the American Speech-Language-/Hearing Association and are also often licensed by individual states. Their names and qualifications, as well as information regarding services in any particular area, can be obtained from the American Speech-Language-Hearing Association at 10801 Rockville Pike, Rockville, Maryland 20852. Phone: 1-800-638-TALK.

REFERENCES

Abrams EJ, Nicholas SW. Pediatric HIV infection. *Pediatric Annals* 1990;19:482-7.

Alexander RP. Developing prespeech feeding abilities in children. In Shanks SJ, ed. Nursing and the Management of Pediatric Communication Disorders. San Diego: College-Hill Press, 1983.

Abkarian GG. Communication effects of prenatal alcohol exposure. *Journal of Communication Disorders* 1992; 25: 221-40.

American Psychiatric Association. *DSM-III-R.* 1987.

Anday EK, Cohen ME, Kelley NE, Leitner DS. Effect of in utero cocaine exposure on startle and its modification. *Developmental Pharmacology and Therapeutics* 1989; 12: 137-45.

Asha. AIDS/HIV: Implications for speech-language pathologists and audiologists. *Asha* 1990; 32: 46-8.

Astley SJ, Clarren SK, Little RE, Sampson PD, Daling JR. Analysis of facial shape in children gestationally exposed to marijuana, alcohol, and/or cocaine. *Pediatrics* 1992; 89: 67-77.

Autti-Ramo I, Gaily E, Granstrom M-L. Dysmorphic features in offspring of alcoholic mothers. *Archives of Diseases of Children* 1992; 67: 712-6.

Becker M, Warr-Leeper GA, Leeper HA. Fetal alcohol syndrome: A description of oral motor, articulatory, short-term memory, grammatical and semantic abilities. *Journal of Communication Disorders* 1990; 23: 97-124.

Beeram MR, Abedin M, Shoroye A, Jayam-Trouth A, Young M, Reid Y. Occurrence of craniosynostosis in neonates exposed to cocaine and tobacco in utero. *Journal of National Medical Association* 1993; 85: 865-8.

Blondis TA, Clippard DS, Scroggs DJ, Peterson L. Multidisciplinary habilitative prescriptions for the attention deficit hyperactivity disorder child. In: Accardo PJ, Blondis TA, Whitman BY, eds. *Attention Deficit Disorders and Hyperactivity in Children*. New York: Marcel Dekker, 1991.

Brady MT, Van Dyke RB. Involvement of the ear, sinuses, oropharynx, parotid, cervical lymph nodes, and eye. In: Yogev R, Conner E, eds. *Management of HIV Infection in Infants and Children*. St. Louis: Mosby Year Book, 1992.

Brouwers P, Moss H, Wolters P, Eddy J, Balis F, Poplack DG, Pizzo PA. Effect of continuous-infusion zidovudine therapy on neuropsychologic functioning in children with symptomatic human immunodeficiency virus infection. *Journal of Pediatrics* 1990; 117: 980-5.

Brown RT, Coles CD, Smith IE, Platzman KA, Silverstein J, Erickson S, Falek A. Effects of prenatal alcohol exposure at school age. II. Attention and behavior. *Neurotoxicology and Teratology* 1991; 13: 369-76.

Butler C, Hittelman J, Hauger SB. Approach to neurodevelopmental and neurologic complications in pediatric HIV infection. *Journal of Pediatrics* 1991; 119: S41-6.

Carney LJ, Chermak GD. Performance of American Indian children with fetal alcohol syndrome on the test of language development. *Journal of Communication Disorders* 1991; 24: 123-34.

Chadwick EG. Issues of daily life: Day care, foster care, and school attendance. In: Yogev R, Conner E, eds. *Management of HIV Infection in Infants and Children*. St. Louis: Mosby Year Book, 1992.

Chanock SJ, McIntosh K. Pediatric infection with the human immunodeficiency virus: Issues for the otorhinolaryngologist. *Otolaryngologic Clinics of North America* 1989; 22: 637-59.

Chasnoff IJ, Hunt CE, Kletter R, Kaplan D. Prenatal cocaine exposure is associated with respiratory pattern abnormalities. *American Journal of Diseases of Children* 1989; 143: 583-7.

Chasnoff IJ, Griffith DR, Freier C, Murray J. Cocaine/polydrug use in pregnancy: Two-year follow-up. *Pediatrics* 1992;89:284-9.

Chasnoff IJ. Cocaine, pregnancy, and the growing child. *Current Problems in Pediatrics* 1992; 22: 302-21.

Cheng L-RL. Asian-American cultural perspectives on birth defects: Focus on cleft palate. *Cleft Palate Journal* 1990; 27: 294-300.

Chiriboga CA, Bateman DA, Brust JCM, Hauser WA. Neurologic findings in neonates with intrauterine cocaine exposure. *Pediatric Neurology* 1993; 9:115-9.

Chow JH, Stern JC, Kaul A, Pincus RL, Gromisch. DS Head and neck manifestations of the acquired immunodeficiency syndrome in children. *Ear, Nose and Throat Journal* 1990; 69: 416-23.

Church JA. Human immunodeficiency virus (HIV) infection at Children's Hospital of Los Angeles: Recurrent otitis media or chronic sinusitis as the presenting process in pediatric AIDS. *Immunology & Allergy Practice* 1987; 9: 25-32.

Church MW, Gerkin KP. Hearing disorders in children with fetal alcohol syndrome: Findings from case reports. *Pediatrics* 1988; 82: 147-54.

Cohen SE, Mundy T, Karassik B, Lieb L, Ludwig DD, Ward J. Neuropsychological functioning in human immunodeficiency virus type 1 seropositive children infected through neonatal blood transfusion. *Pediatrics* 1991; 88: 58-68.

Coles CD, Brown RT, Smith IE, Platzman KA, Erickson S, Falek A. Effects of prenatal alcohol exposure at school age. I. Physical and cognitive development. *Neurotoxicology and Teratology* 1991; 13: 357-67.

Compton C. *A Guide to 85 Tests for Special Education.* Belmont, CA: Fearon Education, 1990.

Cone-Wesson B, Wu P. Audiologic findings in infants born to cocaine-abusing mothers. In: Rossetti LM, ed. *Developmental Problems of Drug-Exposed Children.* San Diego: Singular Publishing Group, 1992.

Corkery L. Fetal effects of exposure to amphetamines, phencyclidine (PCP), and solvents. *Clearinghouse for Drug Exposed Children Newsletter* 1992a; 3: 1-7.

Corkery L. *Guiding Our Children Beyond Risk: A Handbook for Caretakers of Prenatally Drug-Exposed Children.* UCSF: Clearinghouse for Drug-Exposed Children, 1992b.

Corwin MJ, Lester BM, Sepkoski C, McLaughlin S, Kayne H, Golub HL. Effects of in utero cocaine exposure on newborn acoustical cry characteristics. *Pediatrics* 1992; 89: 1199-1203.

Culliton BJ. AZT reverses AIDS dementia in children. *Science* 1989; 246: 21-2.

Dale PS. *Language Development: Structure and Function.* New York: Holt, Rinehart and Winston, 1976.

Davis E, Fennoy I, Laraque D, Kanem N, Brown G, Mitchell J. Autism and developmental abnormalities in children with perinatal cocaine exposure, *Journal of National Medical Association* 1992;84:315-9.

Day NL, Richardson GA. Prenatal marijuana use: Epidemiology, methodologic issues and infant outcome. *Clinics in Perinatology* 1991; 18: 77-92.

Diamond GW. Developmental problems in children with HIV infection. *Mental Retardation* 1989; 27: 213-7.

Dixon SD. Effects of transplacental exposure to cocaine and methamphetamine on the neonate. *Western Journal of Medicine* 1989; 150: 436-42.

Dominguez R, Vila-Coro AA, Slopis JM, Bohan TP. Brain and ocular abnormalities in infants with in utero exposure to cocaine and other street drugs. *American Journal of Diseases of Children* 1991; 145: 688-95.

Fehlings DL, Roberts W, Humphries T, Dawe G. Attention deficit hyperactivity disorder: Does cognitive behavioral therapy improve home behavior? *Journal of Developmental and Behavioral Pediatrics* 1991;12: 223-8.

Ferriero DM, Partridge JC, Wong DF. Congenital defects and stroke in cocaine-exposed neonates. *Annals of Neurology* 1988; 24: 348-9.

Fried PA, Watkinson B. 36- and 48-month neurobehavioral follow-up of children prenatally exposed to marijuana, cigarettes, and alcohol. *Developmental & Behavioral Pediatrics* 1990; 11: 49-58.

Fulroth R, Phillips B, Durand DJ. Perinatal outcome of infants exposed to cocaine and/or heroin in utero. *American Journal of Diseases of Children* 1989;143:905-10.

Giacoia GP. Cocaine babies in Oklahoma. *Journal of the Oklahoma State Medical Association* 1990; 83: 64-7.

Gigliotti E. Fetal effects of maternal alcohol and drug use. In: Naegle MA, ed. *Substance Abuse Education in Nursing.* Vol II. New York: National League for Nursing Press, 1992.

Good WV, Ferriero DM, Golabi M, Kobori JA. Abnormalities of the visual system in infants exposed to cocaine. *Ophthalmology* 1992; 99: 341-6.

Greene T, Ernhart CB, Martier S, Sokol R, Ager J. Prenatal alcohol exposure and language development. *Alcoholism: Clinical & Experimental Research* 1990; 14: 937-45.

Hamilton MA. Linguistic abilities of children with fetal alcohol syndrome. Doctoral Dissertation, University of Washington, 1981.

Hammonds KE. AIDS babies: a sociomedical dilemma. *Journal of the National Medical Association* 1989; 81: 629-30.

Harris EF, Friend GW, Tolley EA. Enhanced prevalence of ankyloglossia with maternal cocaine use. *Cleft Palate-Craniofacial Journal* 1992; 29: 72-6.

Hass A, Hyatt AC, Kattan M, Weiner MA, Hodes DS. Hoarseness in immunocompromised children: Association with invasive fungal infection. *Journal of Pediatrics* 1987; 111: 731-3.

Hayford SM, Epps RP, Dahl-Regis M. Behavior and development patterns in children born to heroin-addicted and methadone-addicted mothers. *Journal of the National Medical Association* 1988; 80: 1197-1200.

Healey T. Intervention strategies in children prenatally exposed to drugs; a continuum birth through school age. *Clearinghouse for Drug-Exposed Children Newsletter* 1993; 4: 1-6.

Hoegerman G, Schnoll S. Narcotic use in pregnancy. *Clinics in Perinatology* 1991; 18: 51-76.

Howard J, Beckwith L, Rodning C, Kropenske V. The development of young children of substance-abusing parents: Insights from seven years of intervention and research. *Zero to Three* 1989; 9: 8-12.

Hubatch LM, Johnson CJ, Kistler DJ, Burns WJ, Moneka W. Early language abilities of high-risk infants. *Journal of Speech and Hearing Disorders* 1985; 50: 195-207.

Indacochea FJ, Scott GB. HIV-1 infection and the acquired immunodeficiency syndrome in children. *Current Problems in Pediatrics* 1992; 22: 166-204.

Iosub S, Fuchs M, Bingol N, Gromisch DS. Fetal alcohol syndrome revisited. *Pediatrics* 1981; 68: 475-9.

Kabori JA, Ferriero DM, Golabi M. CNS and craniofacial anomalies in infants born to cocaine abusing mothers. *Clinical Research* 1989; 37:196A.

Kaltenbach KA, Finnegan LP. Prenatal narcotic exposure: Perinatal and developmental effects. *Neurotoxicology* 1989; 10: 597-604.

Kankirawatana P, Tennison MB, D'Cruz O, Greenwood RS. Mobius syndrome in infant exposed to cocaine in utero. *Pediatric Neurology* 1993; 9: 71-2.

Katz MH, Mastrucci MT, Leggott PJ, Westenhouse J, Greenspan JS, Scott GB. Prognostic significance of oral lesions in children with perinatally acquired human immunodeficiency virus infection. *American Journal of Diseases of Children* 1993; 147: 45-8.

Ketchem L, Berkowitz RJ, McIlveen L, Forrester D, Rakusan T. Oral findings in HIV-seropositive children. *Pediatric Dentistry* 1990;12:143-6.

Lane VW, Molyneaux D. *The Dynamics of Communicative Development.* Englewood Cliffs, NJ: Prentice Hall, 1992.

Lenneberg EH. *Biological Foundations of Language.* New York: Wiley, 1984.

Lesar S. Prenatal cocaine exposure: The challenge to education. In: Rossetti LM, ed. *Developmental Problems of Drug-Exposed Infants.* San Diego: Singular Publishing Group, 1992.

Lester BM, Corwin MJ, Sepkoski C, Seifer R, Peucker M, McLaughlin S, Golub HL. Neurobehavioral syndromes in cocaine-exposed newborn infants. *Child Development* 1991; 62: 694-705.

Lewis KD. Pathophysiology of prenatal drug-exposure: In utero, in the newborn, in childhood, and in agencies. *Journal of Pediatric Nursing* 1991; 6: 185-90.

Lewis KD, Bennett B, Schmeder NH. The care of infants menaced by cocaine abuse. *Maternal and Child Nursing* 1989; 14: 324-9.

Lipson M. What do you say to a child with AIDS? *Hastings Center Report* 1993; 23: 6-12.

MacDonald CC. Preinatal cocaine exposure: Predictor of an endangered generation. In: Rossetti LM, ed. *Developmental Problems of Drug-Exposed Infants.* San Diego: Singular Publishing Group, 1992.

Majewski F. Alcohol embryopathy: Experience in 200 patients. *Developmental Brain Dysfunction* 1993; 6: 248-65.

Mayes LC, Granger RH, Bornstein MH, Zuckerman B. The problem of prenatal cocaine exposure: A rush to judgment. *Journal of the American Medical Association* 1992; 267: 406-8.

Meyers A, Weitzman M. Pediatric HIV disease: The newest chronic illness of childhood. *Pediatric Clinics of North America* 1991; 38: 169-94.

Meyerson MD. The effect of syndrome diagnosis on speech remediation. *Birth De-*

fects (Original Article Series) 1985; 21: 47-68.

Meyerson MD. Cultural considerations in the treatment of Latinos with craniofacial malformations. *Cleft Palate Journal* 1990; 27: 279-88.

Meyerson MD. Speech, language, & hearing of children prenatally exposed to drugs: The need for data and direction. *Clearinghouse for Drug-Exposed Children Newsletter* 1991; 2: 6-8.

Milman DH. Letter to the editor. *Developmental & Behavioral Pediatrics* 1990; 11: 228.

Mintz M, Epstein LG. Neurologic manifestations of pediatric acquired immunodeficiency syndrome: Clinical features and therapeutic approaches. *Seminars in Neurology* 1992; 12: 51-6.

Mintz M. Neurologic abnormalities. In: Yogev R, Conner E, eds. *Management of HIV Infection in Infants and Children.* St. Louis: Mosby Year Book, 1992.

Moskowitz BA. The acquisition of language. *Scientific American* 1978; 239: 92-108.

Nanson JL. Autism in fetal alcohol syndrome: A report of six cases. *Alcoholism: Clinical and Experimental Research* 1992; 16: 558-65.

Nebel-Gould A. Pediatric AIDS: A speech-language pathology perspective. *American Speech-Language Hearing Association* (Special Interest Divisions) 1991; 1: 15-9.

Neuspiel DR, Hamel SC. Neurobehavioral sequelae of fetal cocaine exposure. *Journal of Pediatrics* 1992; 120: 661.

Nicholas SW. Controversy: Is there an HIV-associated facial dysmorphism? *Pediatric Annals* 1988; 17: 353-61.

O'Connell CM, Fried PA. Prenatal exposure to cannabis: A preliminary report of postnatal consequences on school-age children. *Neurotoxicology Teratology* 1991; 13: 631-9.

Pressman H. Communication disorders and dysphagia in pediatric AIDS. *Asha* 1992; 34: 45-7.

Price DB, Inglese CM, Jacobs J, Haller JO, Kramer J, Hotson GC, Loh JP, Schlusselberg D, Menez-Bautista R, Rose, AL, Fikrig S. Pediatric AIDS:

Neuroradiologic and neurodevelopmental findings. *Pediatric Radiology* 1988; 18: 445-8.

Principi N, Marchisio P, Tornaghi R, Onorato J, Massironi E, Picco P. Acute otitis media in human immunodeficiency virus-infected children. *Pediatrics* 1991; 88: 566-71.

Qazi QH, Sheikh TM, Fikrig S, Menikoff H. Lack of evidence for craniofacial dysmorphism in perinatal human immunodeficiency virus infection. *Journal of Pediatrics* 1988; 112: 7-11.

Rist MC. The shadow children. Research Bulletin, Phi Delta Kappa, 1990.

Rivers KO, Hedrick DL. Language and behavioral concerns for drug-exposed infants and toddlers. In: Rossetti LM, ed. *Developmental Problems of Drug-Exposed Infants.* San Diego: Singular Publishing Group, 1992.

Rodning C, Beckwith L, Howard J. Prenatal exposure to drugs: Behavioral distortions reflecting CNS impairment *Neurotoxicology* 1989a;10: 629-34.

Rodning C, Beckwith L, Howard J. Prenatal exposure to drugs and its influence on attachment. *Annals of the New York Academy of Science* 1989b; 562.

Rogers MF. Pediatric HIV infection: Epidemiology, etiopathogenesis, and transmission. *Pediatric Annals* 1988; 17: 324-31

Sanders-Phillips K. Developmental outcome of drug exposed infants. *Clinical Research* 1990; 38:165A.

Saylor C, Lippa B, Lee G. Drug-exposed infants at home: Strategies and supports. *Public Health Nursing* 1991; 8: 33-8.

Schmitt B, Seeger J, Kreuz W, Enenkel S, Jacobi G. Central nervous system involvement of children with HIV infection. *Developmental Medicine Child Neurology* 1991; 33: 535-40.

Shanks SJ. *Nursing and the Management of Pediatric Communication Disorders.* San Diego: College-Hill Press, 1983a.

Shanks SJ. *Nursing and the Management of Adult Communication Disorders.* San Diego: College-Hill Press, 1983b.

Shaywitz SE, Cohen DJ, Shaywitz BA. Behavior and learning difficulties in children of normal intelligence born to alcoholic mothers. *Journal of Pediatrics* 1980; 96: 978-82.

Shih L, Cone-Wesson B, Reddix B. Effects of maternal cocaine abuse on the neonatal auditory system. *International Journal of Pediatric Otorhinolaryngology* 1988; 15: 245-51.

Sowder BJ, Burt MR. *Children of Heroin Addicts.* Westport, CT: Praeger, 1980.

Sparks SN. Speech and language in fetal alcohol syndrome. *Asha* 1984; 26: 27-31.

Sparks SN. *When Children of Substance Abuse Go to School.* San Diego: Singular Publishing Group, 1993.

Strauss RP. Culture, health care, and birth defects in the United States: An introduction. *Cleft Palate Journal* 1990; 27: 275-8.

Streissguth AP, Aase JM, Clarren SK, Randels SP, LaDue RA, Smith DF. Fetal alcohol syndrome in adolescents and adults. *Journal of the American Medical Association* 1991; 265: 1961-7.

Taylor-Brown S. The impact of AIDS on foster care: a family-centered approach to services in the United States. *Child Welfare* 1991;70:193-209.

Toliver-Weddington G. Cultural considerations in the treatment of craniofacial malformations in African Americans. *Cleft Palate Journal* 1990; 27: 289-93.

Ultmann MH, Belman AL, Ruff HA, Novick BE, Cone-Wesson B, Cohen HJ, Rubinstein A. Developmental abnormalities in infants and children with acquired immune deficiency syndrome (AIDS) and AIDS-related complex. *Developmental Medicine Child Neurology* 1985; 27: 563-71.

van Baar A. Development of infants of drug dependent mothers. *Journal of Child Psychology and Psychiatry* 1990; 31: 911-20.

Van Dyke RB. Pediatric human immunodeficiency virus infection and the acquired immunodeficiency syndrome. *American Journal of Diseases of Children* 1991; 145: 529-32.

Villarreal SF, McKinney L-E, Quackenbush M. *Handle With Care: Helping Children Prenatally Exposed to Drugs and Alcohol.* Santa Cruz, CA: ETR Associates, 1992.

Vincent LJ, Salisbury CL, Strain P, McCormick C, Tessier A. A behavioral-ecological approach to early intervention: Focus on cultural diversity. In: Meisels SJ, Shonkoff JP, eds. *Handbook of Early Childhood Intervention.* Cambridge: Cambridge University Press, 1990.

Williams MA. Head and neck findings in pediatric acquired immune deficiency syndrome. *Laryngoscope* 1987; 97: 713-6.

Wilson GS, McCreary R, Kean J, Baxter JC. The development of preschool children of heroin-addicted mothers: A controlled study. *Pediatrics* 1979; 63: 135-41.

Wilson GS. Clinical studies of infants and children exposed prenatally to heroin. *Annals of the New York Academy of Science* 1989; 562.

ANNOTATED BIBLIOGRAPHY

Lane VW, Molyneaux D. *The Dynamics of Communicative Development.* Englewood Cliffs, NJ: Prentice Hall, 1992.
A thorough treatment of prerequisites for speech and language, theories of language acquisition, language assessment, bilingualism, and family concerns. The book is well referenced and is written with an interesting combination of reviews of the literature and clinical narratives. The book covers language behavior from birth to adulthood. It is addressed especially to advanced students preparing for careers in speech-language pathology, education, nursing, and pediatrics.

Pressman H. Communication disorders and dysphagia in pediatric AIDS. *Asha* 1992; 34: 45-7.
A report of the communicative disorders of ninety-six children with AIDS. Although addressed to speech-language pathologists, it reviews the broad range of problems which influence speech and language in this population. Receptive and expressive language skills were common. A number of children had articulation and voice problems and were dysphagic. The causes of the dysphagia determined those

intervention strategies that were especially useful.

Streissguth AP, Aase JM, Clarren SK, Randels SP, LaDue RA, Smith DF. Fetal alcohol syndrome in adolescents and adults. *JAMA* **1991; 265: 1961-7.**
A follow-up of sixty-one adolescents and adults with fetal alcohol syndrome. The article reviews early characteristics and the long-term progression of symptoms. The subjects tended to remained short, microcephalic, and mentally retarded. Poor judgment, attention deficits, and maladaptive behaviors were common. FAS is a disability of both childhood and adulthood.

Villarreal SF, McKinney L-E, Quackenbush M. *Handle With Care: Helping Children Prenatally Exposed to Drugs and Alcohol.* **Santa Cruz, CA: ETR Associates, 1992.**
A readable book of information and suggestions to teachers and caregivers of children prenatally drug exposed. It includes appendices of descriptions of abusable substances, tools for assessment, and helpful resources. The book covers developmental milestones, learning styles, and intevention techniques for infants, toddlers, and school-age children.

12

Establishing and Maintaining Connections: Strategies for Working with Children Prenatally Exposed to Alcohol and Drugs

Sue Bakley, B.F.A., M.A.
Mark F. Whitney, Ph.D.

This chapter examines characteristics of children prenatally exposed to drugs and defines the problems those behaviors create in both school and home settings. The authors support the argument that children at risk are best served not by special programs in segregated settings but by applying sound principles of child development and effective practice in early childhood programs. Strategies are included for managing difficult behaviors and learning problems, modifying the classroom environment, and collaborating with other community agencies. The authors also examine the potential effects of foster home placements, separation, and the chaotic home environments that are often typical of the substance-abusing home and offer suggestions for helping children cope with such life stresses. Strategies for home visits and interventions are included.

> *"T.J. just doesn't seem to settle in to play with toys like the other kids I've had. He forgets the things he learned last week and I have to teach him all over again. Why, just yesterday, he was so pleased because he had learned to lace up his shoes and today, it just baffled him! His teacher tells me it's the same in school."*
>
> *—T.J.'s Mother*

These and similar observations are being repeated by parents and teachers as they care for children who have been prenatally exposed to drugs. Are the behaviors they are seeing unique to these children or are they just the result of "kids being kids"? In this chapter, we will help to sort out the behaviors typically associated with prenatal drug exposure in the early childhood years, explore the impact of those behaviors on learning, and suggest strategies for the child both at school and at home.

The word connections was chosen to use in the title of this chapter because of its importance to helping preschool children at risk, whose ever-widening horizons include more than just the home. Establishing and maintaining connections with all of the adults and professionals involved with a child is critical. The connections include those between professional and child, professional and family, family and child, as well as those among professionals themselves. These connections can help not only to support what you do but to assure that the best and most efficient services are there for the children and their families.

A key to successfully meeting the needs of children prenatally drug exposed and their families is early intervention. Researchers at the National Association for Perinatal Addiction Research and Education found that intervention with families and children is most successful when parental drug abuse is identified and the treatment of the child is initiated as early as possible (Schneider, Griffith & Chasnoff 1989). The purpose of the early intervention is to prevent negative behavior patterns from being established that later lead to difficulties in school and social situations. At the suggestion of physicians, nurses, and social workers, many children who are at risk because of prenatal exposure to drugs are being enrolled in early childhood enrichment programs such as Head Start, preschools, and pre-kindergarten programs.

While the identification of children and subsequent connection with services are positive steps, they can lead to labeling and stereotyping that can work against families and children. Unfortunately, the children's problems have frequently been portrayed in a way that has led many people to believe that the children are hopeless throwaways of the drug culture. Though the physiological effects of cocaine on the developing fetus may create a degree of biological vulnerability (Schutter & Brinker 1992), to assume children prenatally exposed to cocaine are a biological underclass implies that the children are beyond hope and that it is useless to intervene on their behalf. It has been our experience that most teachers are eager to identify children at risk not in order to use that information to label and exclude such children from the classroom, but to address difficult classroom behaviors and help the children reach their maximum potential. Evaluations from a recent seminar on children prenatally exposed to drugs (UCSD Extension 1992) showed that the teachers were gratified to know which children were prenatally exposed for two distinct reasons. First, the identification helped them to understand the children's otherwise bewildering behaviors, and second, knowing this information helped the teachers sort out which strategies and techniques to use when working with the child.

To encourage a positive attitude, professionals might remember to use a "child first" rule when referring to this population. The rule is that the child comes first and the condition follows. When children are referred to as "drug babies" or "crack babies" they are dehumanized. The phrase "children prenatally exposed to drugs" is one that recognizes the child instead of the problem. Another term is children at risk, which will be used throughout this chapter. Children at risk are those who, because of their exposure to drugs in utero, are likely to show developmental delays and other deficits that interfere with learning.

Because drugs are often taken in combination with other drugs, there is no clear picture to help guide us through the bewildering array of resulting characteristics seen in the children (Los Angeles Unified School District 1989). A child born to a mother addicted to crack can display a variety of symptoms that reflect the use of that particular drug. The child of an alcoholic mother may display a different set of symptoms, and heroin use may result in still another possible array of symptoms (Grimm 1987). The most *common* use of a combination of drugs or drugs and alcohol makes the children's symptoms harder to define. However, several characteristics appear to be common to children at risk. Because of the impact of early experiences, interpersonal relationships, and the home environment on the developing child, it is necessary to consider such factors before examining these characteristics.

The Los Angeles Unified School District (1989) pioneered research on the effects of prenatal drug exposure on the young child's ability to learn through a program designed especially for this segment of the population. The staff emphasizes that the characteristics of children at risk are similar to those seen in children who are raised in dysfunctional, chaotic home environments where drug use is *not* a factor. Are the children's behaviors due to the prenatal exposure to drugs or to the postnatal environment? As is true for *all* children, they maintain that when an adult in the program provides strong, consistent emotional support and the day is structured in a predictable routine, the children do show marked improvement. When teachers make a concerted effort to connect with the children—with all that implies in time, patience, and effort—the results are often well worth the effort. To facilitate this adult-child connection, the Los Angeles program keeps the children with the same teacher until kindergarten. In doing so, they are able to assure that the children will have the maximum opportunity to bond with a caring adult.

The importance of bonding and attachment cannot be overstated. The result of a weak or absent bonding process impacts the very core of a child's internal environment and can affect physical, intellectual, emotional, and moral development (Magdid & McKelvey 1978). Through the process of bonding to the mother or other consistent caregiver, an infant develops the sense of trust and attachment that is essential to healthy psychological development. In healthy families, well-bonded children embark on the world with a strong sense of security. They are more likely to take risks, to cope with stress and frustration, to handle fear and worry, to become self-reliant, to develop subsequent relationships, and to cope with feelings of jealousy. Children freed from such distractions as fear, worry, frustration, and jealousy are better able to think logically and sort through perceptions as they learn about the world. The result is that well-bonded children are more likely to reach their fullest intellectual and social potential (Fahlberg 1979).

The picture changes considerably in substance-abusing families where the bonding process is often interrupted or absent altogether. Factors that can affect bonding include lengthy postnatal hospital stays, fretful infant behaviors that make it more difficult for mothers to give the care and attention necessary for successful bonding, and the infant's lack of response to the mother's attempts to interact. Many babies come from the hospital to chaotic home environments typical of substance-abusing families where the importance of using drugs takes priority over care of the baby. Nor is stability assured for those children who are placed in foster homes. Many experience three or more placements by the time they reach preschool. Sometimes children are moved in and out of foster homes as their families continue to abuse drugs or struggle to maintain stability. Other foster home placements are unsuccessful because of the challenges that at-risk children pose to their caregivers. The result is a cycle of placement followed by rejection followed by another placement, rejection, and so on. The child's already fragile emotional state can only be further damaged. Although many foster placements with relatives can and do provide nurturing and stable homes, still others perpetuate the dysfunctional patterns that precipitated the maternal drug use in the first place. So, while foster care can be used successfully to intervene on behalf of the child, it remains problematic.

Connections: A Case Study

To illustrate the combination of internal and external issues that can and often do impact a child's development and ability to learn successfully, let's revisit T.J. Three-year-old T.J. came to school for the first time, identified as being at risk for developmental delays due to his mother's prenatal drug use. Shortly after his birth, he went home from the hospital with his mother who had entered a recovery program rather than risk having her child placed in foster care. His father disappeared shortly after T.J. was born. A tumultuous first year began with his mother's relapse into a downward spiral that included trading sex for drugs, severe neglect of T.J., and her eventual incarceration for prostitution. T.J. was finally placed in a foster home with five other children ranging in age from infancy to age eight. Although initially withdrawn and distant, T.J. soon became impossible to handle. His foster mother recalls that he grabbed food off the other children's plates, couldn't wait his turn, and was so unpredictable in his reactions to everyday matters that she simply couldn't handle him. After a few months, she suggested that perhaps another foster mother could do a better job and he was moved to another home. This pattern was to repeat itself for two more homes until his latest, where his foster mother was more successful and looked forward to adopting T.J. However, his mother decided to try parenting again after her release from prison. When T.J. started preschool, he had been living with her for the past five months. Although she brought T.J. to school regularly, the teacher suspected that she had started using drugs again.

Many of the challenges that T.J. brought to his preschool were the inevitable result of living in five different homes. No amount of assurance could convince T.J. that food would be there if he was hungry. He couldn't be sure that the adults that he had come to trust would be there for him tomorrow. The bed that provided security for him one night might be a different one tomorrow night. Why would anyone be surprised when T.J. refused to share the toys he found at school or that he hoarded food? Would anyone wonder why he cried uncontrollably when his foster mother left him at the door each morning? Or, once he finally stopped crying, that he attached himself to the teacher? Or that he stubbornly refused to cooperate whenever there was a shift in activities? These were simply survival skills that T.J. had fine-tuned over his short lifetime. Until there was some stability in his life, T.J. could be expected to exhibit

these same behaviors. The suggestions that follow can be of help to teachers and group caregivers who have children like T.J. in their care.

Connecting with Children
I: Strategies for Children with Life Stresses

Arrange to have the same caregiver greet the children each day so the children can identify with the same friendly face. Show the children you care by being consistently responsive, friendly, and loving.

Make an extra effort to tune into the children's moods as they start the day. If a child is out of sorts, try to get more information by initiating conversation with the child. You might try labeling children's emotions as they are expressed through their actions or facial expressions. Ex: "You look like you're angry about something, T.J. Can you tell me about it so we can work it out together?"

Check to see if each child has had breakfast. Keep juice and crackers on hand to fill in if necessary. No child should be expected to learn until basic needs are met.

Help children express their emotions. Play can provide rich opportunities to work through the fears and worries in a child's life. Respect the child's need for nonverbal emotional expression such as crying or just time to be alone.

Art activities can provide a vehicle for nonverbal expression and can sometimes lead to insights that cannot be expressed through verbal communication. Materials such as markers, crayons, paints, and plenty of paper should be readily available.

Acknowledge the children's fears about abandonment and other related separation issues. Be as reassuring as you can while still being realistic. Help them to work through separation issues if you know in advance about an impending move.

Provide each child with a "very special cubbie." Make a big fuss over the fact that it belongs to no one but that child. Let the children choose their own labels or symbols with which to mark the cubbies. Encourage them to bring a special small comfort toy (a special stuffed animal or small pillow) from home to keep in the cubbie and use when reassurance is needed. Have some extras at school just in case a child doesn't have one.

Think of your room as a large swaddle—does it "wrap" the children in safety and security? One of the most successful techniques for infants who are in withdrawal is to swaddle the babies to calm and soothe them. If you apply that same concept to the older child, the results could yield the same soothing effect. Are there areas where a child can go to find comfort—large, soft pillows, a quiet corner for browsing through books or listening to music, a loft filled with soft teddy bears and a blanket or two? Is the room safe and secure? Does the environment say "yes" to children? Is it safe to explore? Is the block corner located away from the flow of traffic so structures won't be toppled unintentionally? Is the playground fenced and is the equipment in good repair? Are the adults willing and able to provide comfort and guidance when needed?

An adult rocking chair can be an important investment. Even better is the adult lap that is there when a child needs it. Children at risk can be expected to seek more opportunities than typical children to cuddle, to rock, to seek adults for comfort.

One of the most important things you can do is to **build security into the child's day by maintaining a consistent routine and schedule.** Sometimes it is impossible to avoid sudden changes in routine, and when that happens, it helps to explain to the children what will be different. This technique can help them to feel more in control and, consequently, more secure.

Strategies for Children with Life Stresses

- Try to have the same caregiver greet the children each day. Show the children you care by being consistently responsive, positive, and loving.

- Make an extra effort to tune into the children's moods.

- Help children to express their emotions.

- Use art activities to provide a vehicle for nonverbal expression.

- Acknowledge the children's fears about abandonment and other related separation issues.

- Provide each child with A Very Special Cubbie. Encourage children to bring a special small comfort toy from home.

- Think of your room as a large swaddle—is it safe and secure?

continued on next page

**Strategies for Children
with Life Stresses**

continued

- Are there places where a child can go to find comfort ?

- An adult rocking chair can be an important investment. Still better is the adult lap that is there when a child needs it.

- Build security into the child's day by maintaining a consistent routine and schedule.

The Philosophical Connection

In addition to the specific strategies just mentioned, the philosophical orientation of the school program is critically important. Before children can actively explore the world, they must feel secure in venturing forth. What goes on between the caregiver and child is at the very heart of effective intervention, for it is through interactions with people that children develop security. Emphasis must be placed on the development of quality, long-term human relationships and on the establishment of trust. Trust can be defined as a confident expectation that basic needs will be met. This necessarily involves a close tie with another individual.

Consistency in daily caregiving routines helps children develop their own basis for self-control and feelings of self-confidence. Through their interactions with the world around them, young children learn about trust, attachment-separation, adaptation, autonomy, initiative, sex-role identification, adequacy, self-control, and relatedness. Given such a range of developmental issues, even secure children from intact families and the best environments face numerous

challenges in growing up. Only when a foundation of trust is established and actively nurtured can children confidently move into the world. This is especially important for young children who have faced numerous life stresses and disrupted caregiving relationships.

Preschool children learn through active experimentation and exploration of their environment. Both home and school environments must be developmentally appropriate and emphasize safety, but must also provide challenging activities that allow children opportunities to do for themselves (National Association for the Education of Young Children 1991). Young children need opportunities to try and fail (without blame) and try again. Play provides an important vehicle for children to indirectly reveal the conflicts they are experiencing, to try out different roles, and to act out potentially aggressive or destructive feelings. Active learning and concrete experiences allow young children to construct their own knowledge from their own experiences. Thoughtful input by the adult at the "right" moment requires constant observation of individual child behaviors and the ability to adapt plans to individual circumstances and needs.

Parents and professionals must work together to create for the child consistent routines, age-appropriate expectations, and positive outcomes. The role of the adult in this process is often that of facilitator—one who supports, guides, and extends individual growth without determining learning. Interventions should be seen as opportunities for each child to explore and experiment with a world scaled to individual perceptions and capabilities. Because this approach toward development accommodates a wide range of individual differences, it naturally benefits the special needs of children at risk.

Young children at risk deserve the same respect as others. It is important to view them as unique individuals with their own perceptions, feelings, and capabilities. First and foremost, young children learn best when they have a positive self-concept and believe they are capable, worthwhile individuals. A positive self-concept allows a child to feel good about taking risks and challenges, to accept and learn from failures, and to work toward behavioral and developmental change. Young children are learning to value and respect other people's feelings and to experience life as interesting, significant, and worth living. Quality interactions with adults and peers provide the foundation for the development of significant lasting human relationships, respect for differences among people, and a sense of morality.

The Impact of Drugs on Children's Learning

It is important to know that not all the children born to substance-abusing mothers will be affected by exposure to the drugs in utero. Some children appear to be more resilient than others and so show fewer problems. Still others exhibit no developmental or behavioral problems whatsoever and yet some have severe physical and developmental effects.

Several characteristics are common to children at risk. They have difficulty initiating and maintaining positive relationships and sustaining productive interactions with people and objects in the environment. Attention deficit, hyperactivity, and emotional and behavioral disturbances clearly impact the ability of at-risk children to learn, yet may not be sufficient in themselves to qualify for special education services. It is interesting to note that children at risk often fall within the normal range of development on standardized tests through age two (Schneider, Griffith & Chasnoff 1989). In a typical assessment, the examiner has a one-on-one relationship with the child and the tasks are presented in a structured fashion with clearly stated expectations, thus contributing to a positive outcome. It is when the children are left to their own devices that the effect of the drug exposure often becomes apparent.

Free play requires children to organize themselves and the environment around them in a fashion that allows for learning. It requires that the children have some degree of organizational skills such as classification and sequencing. In order to put these skills to good use, the children must be able to screen out environmental distractors as they play. In a typical preschool or group setting, children at risk are more likely than typical children to have trouble focusing, and are more easily distracted once they begin a task. At-risk children lack the ability to self-organize, initiate, and follow through in their play. Once they do choose an activity, they frequently find it difficult to complete, experiencing excessive frustration when they are not immediately successful. While other children can be quite flexible and adapt to changes in routine, children at risk often find it impossible to tolerate disturbances in the routine of the day. Many cannot handle transitions from one activity to another. At-risk children often show extremes in behavior; some fly off the handle for no apparent reason, with the behavior then escalating beyond the point of retrieval of control. Others may become quietly withdrawn, unable to cope with the natural chaos of the group. Still others exhibit a holdover of the poor state regulation patterns seen in newborns. They vacillate between the two extremes: withdrawn and isolated one minute and out of control the next. Hyperactivity and impulsiveness are compounding problems that often accompany the unpredictable behavior patterns. In addition, short-term memory problems are common in children at risk; what they learn one day may be forgotten the next.

The impact of maternal drug abuse can be seen in children's fine and gross motor abilities as well. The tremors that are characteristic in the newborn can also be present in the older child. They may affect fine motor tasks that require reaching and stacking as well as the child's ability to manipulate materials such as pegs, beads, and puzzle pieces. Gross motor skills such as climbing, jumping, and acquiring ball skills are affected by poor balance and coordination. Many children show poor motor planning and tend to stumble and fall more frequently than typical children. Finally, at-risk children experience delays and disorders in communication. They may be difficult to understand and may not readily engage in verbal interactions with adults and other children. The following strategies are designed to address these challenges.

Connecting with the Child
II: Managing Difficult Behaviors

When working with young children, remember that what is *done* is often much more important than what is said. Your attitude is reflected in a variety of ways. In an attempt to provide a supportive and consistent environment, think about your choice of words and tone of voice, as well as posture, nonverbal signals, and touch. All of these messages communicate to children how you feel about them. Your honest, respectful approach to the children will make the difference.

Recognize that negative behavior may be the result of unmet needs. In some homes, the only way a child can get the attention of the adults is through negative behaviors. What may appear to be the immediate problem at hand may instead be a reflection of the child's insecurities and unresolved issues. Challenging behaviors often have at their core an unmet need. Understanding and sensitivity, consistent attention, and reinforcement of positive interactions can be effective in helping the children learn acceptable ways to get what they need.

Provide clear, consistent limits on behaviors. Because many children have not had consistent behavior management, they may not know what is expected or how to behave in a positive manner. When adults are consistent in their expectations, limits are clearly stated, and there are logical consequences for misbehaviors, the children have the guidelines to become masters of their own actions.

An effective technique to use when children act aggressively toward one another is to **help the children appreciate the cause and effect of their behaviors.** For example, if T.J. hits another child in order to get a toy he wants, it's time to step in. Point out to T.J. the child's unhappy expression, tears, and other signs of distress. Give T.J. some alternative solutions to use the next time. These include using words instead of hitting, waiting to take a turn with the toy, or asking the teacher for help. It does little good to ask the children involved to make up with a hug or handshake unless it's their idea. Be sure to acknowledge T.J.'s subsequent use of more appropriate strategies as you see him using them.

As you see that the children are using more acceptable ways of interacting, loosen your reigns by letting them do more social problem solving themselves. Step back and see if the children can practice what they've learned. Intervene only when you feel they need help.

Try concentrating on behaviors that are harmful to others. When a child has problems following class routines, is highly active, can't attend during group activities, and acts impulsively and aggressively, it can be overwhelming to the teacher. Instead of working on all of those behaviors at once, give the most disturbing one the highest priority. Let the others go until the basic safety of the other children is assured. Then start working on the others a few at a time.

Tell the children what *to* do, not just what not to do. Letting children know what to do gives them a direction to take the behavior and focuses on the positives while defusing the negatives. "T.J., put your feet on the floor, not on the table."

Avoid no-win confrontations. They only result in the child's diminished self-esteem and leave the teacher feeling frustrated and ineffective. Instead, try redirecting or offering a choice of activity or response. For instance, when a child refuses to come in from the playground, try saying, "We are going into the classroom now. You may carry the sand tools or the ball." Or, "When you get into the classroom, you may play with the puzzle or you may color with the new markers. Which do you want to do?" If the choices are enticing and within a developmental ability, the child is likely to comply.

Allow children to make choices. For children who come from homes where so many factors are beyond their control, the issue of choice is more important than many adults realize, for it allows children some measure of control over their life. If children are allowed to choose an activity of personal interest, they are more likely to enjoy it and sustain the activity. However, for some children who may be confused by the array of choices, it may be necessary to limit the number of activities offered.

When a child is clearly out of control, try holding the child securely until you sense that control has been regained. Consider prefacing your actions by saying, "T.J., I am going to help you to get control by holding you tightly in my arms." Using the term "control" rather than labeling the behavior as "bad" will let the child know that you understand that he is not being bad but that he needs help in controlling the behavior. However, some children who have experienced physical abuse may not welcome this kind of help and you will want to try something else.

Don't require children to stand in line when making the transition from one activity to another. It is difficult for most preschool children and is a sure trouble time for the at-risk child. Instead, make sure an adult is stationed near the next area to guide the children as they arrive or dismiss the children in small groups rather than en masse.

Managing Difficult Behaviors

- Recognize that negative behavior may be the result of unmet needs.

- Provide clear consistent limits on behaviors.

- Help the children to appreciate the cause and effect of their behaviors.

- Try concentrating on behaviors that are a threat to others. Give the most disturbing behavior the highest priority.

- Tell the children what *to* do, not just what not to do.

- Avoid no-win confrontations. Instead, redirect or offer a choice of response.

- Give children opportunities to make choices whenever possible.

- When a child is clearly out of control, try holding the child securely until you sense that control has been regained. Because some children may have experienced physical abuse, however, they may not welcome this help.

- Don't require the children to stand in line when making the transition from one activity to another.

Connecting with Children
III: Classroom Environments

The classroom environment can be one of the most important factors in determining the success of the children in a program. What is in a space and how it is arranged strongly affects how children relate to one another and to the activities provided by the teacher. What follows are guidelines for modifying the physical environment to be responsive to the needs of young children at risk.

Examine your room environment. Make sure that centers are clearly defined and toys are neatly stored on shelves, and that there are areas free of distractions where children can go for quiet times.

It has been suggested that reducing the amount of stimulus can help at-risk children. Perhaps the answer lies not in the amount but in *how* the stimulus is organized. Healthy clutter is necessary in any preschool classroom but disorganized, disheveled clutter can be confusing to children. Children who have organizational difficulties are more likely to be successful when toys are neatly stored on shelves, bins contain like objects, visual cues are provided for organizing blocks on shelves, and art materials are clean and ready for each new day.

Reduce the amount of noise in your environment. Soft music can have a calming effect but constant "clutter" in the background can be subconsciously distracting and reduce attention to tasks.

Provide cues in how the materials are to be used. For example, have four chairs, four brushes, and four smocks ready at the art table. The message is clear that four children at a time can be there and that smocks are to be worn.

Tape pictures of children using the materials near those activities. The children can check the pictures to remind themselves how the materials should be used. Look in educational or toy catalogs for pictures or take your own photographs.

Define where children are to sit or group by marking the floor with colored masking tape or by using individual carpet squares.

Cafeteria trays work well to help children define their spaces. They can be used for puzzles and other manipulatives, play dough, finger painting, art projects, and cooking activities. For children who grab food from others, trays can help to define which food belongs to them and which belongs to others.

Use hula hoops to confine individual floor activities such as small building units, bristle blocks, and tinker toys.

Make transition an activity itself with a beginning, middle, and end. The more consistently you use rituals such as songs or actions to accompany transitions, the easier it will be for the children to negotiate the transitions independently. It also helps to warn the children ahead of time about an impending change and to make the next activity an enticing one.

Keep your group times short and sweet. Two short circle times can be more effective than one long one. Actively engage the children and be sure to make your circle activities appropriate to

the developmental levels of the children. Avoid calendar activities and others that involve abstract thought. Young children need activities that relate directly to the here and now; the more concrete the better.

Children who clearly have difficulty attending during circle time could be allowed to leave the group to go to another quiet activity. The other children in the group can be helped to accept your modified expectations if you explain that while it is easy for them to sit for circle, it is too hard for others. When it becomes easier, they will join the group for the whole time.

Some children can focus more successfully during group times when they are allowed to hold a stuffed toy or bean-bag during the activity. It gives the children an outlet for their excess energy and allows them to concentrate better on the group activity. Some respond better when the toy is heavy or has an interesting texture.

If a child appears to be overwhelmed by free play options, **try reducing the number of choices to two instead of four or five.** Discussing what activities are planned for playtime can help children preplan what they want to do. For the child who has difficulty, you might suggest one or two activities to get started. Supervise the child until you see that he or she is fully engaged.

Children who suck their thumbs should be allowed to do so for a longer period than otherwise anticipated. Understand that some children may need to use thumb-sucking as an important source of comfort. It can help children organize internally and provide a valuable means of self-soothing.

Build in relaxation time and activities.
It can help children organize and focus.
Build into the day quiet times to rest and
relax in cozy corners and soft spaces.

**Beanbag chairs are wonderfully sup-
portive and secure** for quiet activities
such as magazine and book exploration.

**Provide lots of opportunities for large
motor activities.** Obstacle courses are
not only fun, they promote motor planning, balance, and coordination skills.
Plan the day to alternate quiet and active
times.

**Invest in a wide variety of
manipulatives so that you can accommodate developmental differences.**
When the materials range from simple to
complex and large to small, you can assure that all of the children will be successful, no matter what their developmental level.

**Make sure that the children are
seated in stable and secure fashion.**
Feet should touch the floor and tables
should be at a comfortable height.

**Understand that some children at risk
have difficulty retaining information.**
What they learn one day may not be
there the next. It's important to plan for
lots of practice and repetition, which
will eventually lead to mastery. Your
patient understanding is critical to the
children's feelings of self-worth.

Classroom Environments

- Examine your room environment.
  Make sure that centers are clearly
  defined and toys are neatly stored
  on shelves, and that there are
  areas where children can go for
  quiet times.

- Reduce the amount of noise in
  your environment.

- Provide cues in how the materials
  are to be used.

- Tape pictures of children using
  materials near activities.

- Define where children are to sit or
  group.

- Cafeteria trays work well to help
  children define their spaces.

- Use hula hoops for individual floor
  activities.

- Make transition an activity in itself.

- Keep your group times short and
  sweet. Actively engage the
  children.

- Children who clearly have
  difficulty attending during circle
  time should be allowed to leave
  the group.

- Allow child to hold a stuffed
  animal or toy during circle time.

- Try reducing the number of
  choices for children who are
  overwhelmed by too many
  options.

- Children who suck their thumbs
  should be allowed to do so for a
  longer period than otherwise
  anticipated.

- Build in relaxation time and
  activities.

- Beanbag chairs are wonderfully
  secure for quiet activities.

- Provide lots of opportunities for
  large motor activities.

- Plan the day to alternate quiet and
  active times.

- Invest in a wide variety of manipulatives so that you can accommodate developmental differences.

- Make sure the children are seated in stable and secure fashion.

- Allow many opportunities for repetition and practice.

Connecting with the Community: Working Together

Working with young children at risk and their families must mean connecting with other agencies. These agencies can include health and welfare agencies, mental health and drug rehabilitation programs, and a range of educational programs. These might include special education, Head Start and other publicly funded enrichment programs, day care, and community preschools. Parents may be involved in counseling and parenting classes. To be a successful early intervention professional, connecting with others must be a regular part of effective practice.

Educate yourself about all local agencies involved in early intervention services. It is important to know what agencies and programs are available to families in the local community. Be careful not to exclude programs not traditionally considered to be a part of early intervention efforts, such as preschool programs, child care centers, family day care homes, and respite programs.

Coordinate family case management services whenever possible. Search out all those involved with the families you serve and make an effort to communicate on a regular basis. Identify a lead person on the basis of parent desires and the need to streamline services.

Avoid duplicating your efforts and services by working together. Maximize your intervention efforts by sharing information and developing agreed upon strategies for service. Make sure the child's social worker updates you on the child's home placement if and when it changes.

Share nonconfidential child and family information to streamline the intake and assessment process. Use shared information and common assessment forms whenever possible to limit the extent to which families must duplicate information and efforts.

Identify barriers or gaps in existing services. Try to fill in what's missing. Listen to families to discover what problems they face in the intervention process. Share concerns with other professionals and problem-solve ways to reduce frustrations and expand services for all involved.

Rethink traditional disciplinary boundaries so that services can be more efficient. Move beyond the view of the family from a single disciplinary perspective. Make efforts to deliver *trans*disciplinary services that maximize efforts and minimize duplication. Provide guidance and support to other early intervention professionals through regularly scheduled forums and in-services.

Build your staff into a support team for each other. Take advantage of the expertise offered by the personnel on your staff. Emphasize the interpersonal nature of service delivery and the importance of empathy and concern for one another. Share your needs and listen to those of others.

Develop the vision and courage to examine familiar problems in new and innovative ways. Become an advocate for children and families. Look beyond the daily tasks and frustrations inherent in your job to see yourself as an important part of the larger picture. Ask "Why not?" instead of "Why?"

Connecting with the Community: Working Together

- Educate yourself about all local agencies involved in early intervention services.

- Coordinate family case management services whenever possible.

- Avoid duplicating your efforts and services by working together whenever possible.

- Share nonconfidential child and family information to streamline the intake and assessment process.

- Identify barriers or gaps in existing services. Try to fill in what's missing.

- Rethink traditional disciplinary boundaries so that services can be more efficient.

- Build your staff into a support team for each other.

- Develop the vision and courage to examine familiar problems in new and innovative ways.

Connecting with Families: Home Visits and Interventions

Communication is the key to successful relationships with the families and while it sounds simple, it is often easier said than done. Many factors affect communication among individuals, including cultural differences, body language, tone of voice, room arrangement, and who and how many people are participating in the process. When a professional goes into a home, the visit should be guided by the utmost respect for the family. Working with families of children at risk often means leaving your own values at the doorstep. The purpose of the home visit is to assist and empower families, not to discredit them. Your sensitivity toward the needs of the parents can serve to build a lasting relationship that will eventually make a difference for the child.

The importance of parent support cannot be overemphasized. Most parents will be effective advocates for their at-risk child given the adequacy of family resources. However, parents are less likely to see their child's need for education and therapy as immediately important when they are faced with financial and emotional stresses. Your knowledge of community resources can be used in helping families address their basic needs. Once they are stable, families will be able to focus on the child's needs more clearly.

In addition, the success of the programs often depends on helping parents to change the internal message of diminished self-worth to one of positive affirmation. Parents are simply not able to give what they don't have. Until the parents see themselves as worthy individuals, they will not be able to impart those same values to their own children. Some programs are designed to assist the mothers in restructuring their negative thought patterns to more positive ones. The next step is to develop the communication skills needed to convey those positive messages to their children. Russell and Free (1991) found that the mothers in their study had difficulty focusing on their children's needs until near the end of the ten-week sessions. They were more likely than other mothers to focus on their own social, health, and interpersonal needs than on those of their children. Rather than emphasize the problems and weaknesses of the families, the project recommends that case workers develop family goals based on family strengths. The project found that when given encouragement and assistance in pursuing the goals, the families responded more positively than when the focus was on weaknesses.

Where substance abuse is present or the parents are in recovery, the process of reaching stability is challenged. However strong the winds of instability blow, the message to keep the family together comes through clearly. Implicit in the recovery process is relapse along the way. Your support in helping a family pick up the pieces and start again can make the difference in their eventual long-term recovery.

Two additional factors need to be addressed in the effort to understand the dynamics of the substance-abusing family. First, childhood physical and sexual abuse by family members plays a prevalent role in the histories of women who abuse drugs. Although figures vary, it is estimated that from 75% to 90% of drug-addicted women started taking drugs to escape the pain of their own abuse as children. So, a mother's parenting style may reflect her own upbringing which, in a majority of cases, is far from ideal and may very well have included abusive measures.

Second, women in recovery often find parenting to be difficult for reasons beyond those of the usual child-rearing challenges. It has been established that the emotional and social development of the drug abuser comes to a standstill at the age of initial addiction. For example, a woman whose addiction began at age thirteen can be expected to have the emotional maturity of a young adolescent. Even if she is determined to stop using drugs, the combination of her interrupted emotional development and the demands of a drug-exposed child are a challenge that would overwhelm the most diligent mother. The need for recovery programs that include parenting classes, ongoing support, and counseling cannot be overstated.

Whatever the degree of your involvement with families, the ability to communicate is essential. Eleanor Lynch (1981) said it best when she wrote her list of "NEVER, EVERS" to guide professionals when communicating to parents.

- NEVER, EVER let your first contact be negative.
- NEVER, EVER talk down to parents. They're adults too.
- NEVER, EVER speak in jargon or "alphabet soup."
- NEVER, EVER assume that your training and experience have given you more knowledge about a particular child than his or her parents have.
- NEVER, EVER forget that each culture has its own traditions, values, and beliefs, and they may not be the same as yours.

- NEVER, EVER forget that both you and the family are working for the same person—the child.
- NEVER, EVER forget that parents do care about their children. Sometimes they just don't express it the way *we* think they should.
- NEVER, EVER forget that parents deserve respect, courtesy, and understanding—just like teachers.

Professionals must consider the needs and perspectives of parents and families when making suggestions and offering intervention strategies for the home. Many of the suggestions for teachers in the classroom are appropriate for home settings with some necessary revisions. Parents and foster parents can help their children at risk by using some of these strategies delineated in Table 1.

CONCLUSION

Good programs for young children are due primarily to the efforts of dedicated, committed, and often underpaid staff. Such is the nature of teaching and early intervention. While recognizing the challenge that children at risk may bring to the classroom, it is crucial to remember that effective interventions should focus on the exhibited behavior and not dwell upon the root "cause" of such behavior. To separate young children prenatally exposed to drugs from their peers in community programs only serves to reinforce negative stereotypes and contributes to the problem rather than addressing it constructively. It must be emphasized that despite the magni-

tude of the current problems facing the field, there is simply no justification for developing a separate and special "curriculum" solely for young children prenatally exposed to drugs. This chapter is intended to underscore the importance of sound principles in child development and effective practice in quality early childhood education programs. What is good for children born prenatally exposed to drugs is what is good for *all* children: positive and consistent human relationships, involved parents, understanding teachers, lower child/teacher ratios in all of our classrooms, less adult-directed "education" and more developmentally appropriate practice, and a view of the child based upon individual strengths instead of perceived deficits.

All children entering our classrooms will require a more individualized educational experience. Classroom teachers should insist that *all* children under their charge be provided the necessary resources to achieve their individual potentials. One ought not warn of the impending "invasion," but begin to develop the foresight and compassion necessary to help these children and their families. In the process, our society will have to attend to the needs of all those who care for and educate young children.

The "Connecting with Children" suggestions are based on the authors' work with at-risk children as well as the work of many other professionals in the field. Many teachers, social workers, nurses, psychologists, and doctors have developed successful strategies through their work with this population. The authors wish to ac-

Table 1.   Connecting with Children: Strategies for Parents

- Be extra patient and understanding when children have a difficult time separating.

- Make an extra effort to tune into the children's moods as they start the day.

- Help children express their emotions in acceptable ways.

- Find a special place where the children can keep their belongings.

- Invest in an adult-size rocking chair.

- Build security into the day by maintaining a consistent daily routine and schedule.

- Provide clear, consistent limits on behavior and model the behavior you want to teach.

- Help children appreciate the causes and effects of their behaviors.

- Try concentrating first on the behaviors that are harmful to others.

- Tell children what *to* do, not just what not to do.

- Avoid no-win confrontations.

- When a child is clearly out of control, try holding the child until you sense that control has been regained.

- Reduce the amount of stimulation and consider how the stimulation is organized.

- Reduce the amount of noise in your home.

- Help children make smooth transitions from one activity to another.

- Allow children self-soothing behaviors such as thumb-sucking for a longer period than otherwise.

- Build in relaxation times and activities.

- Provide lots of opportunities for outdoor play.

- Understand that some children may have difficulty retaining information from one day to the next.

knowledge specifically the contributions of the following pioneers in the field: the staff of the Los Angeles Unified School District Program for Children Prenatally Exposed to Drugs— Carol Cole, Vicky Ferrara, Deborah Johnson, Mary Jones, Marci Blankett Schoenbaum, Rachelle Tyler, and Valerie Wallace, as well as Marie Poulsen of Children's Hospital, Los Angeles. Also, Ira Chasnoff and Dan Griffith of the National Association of Perinatal Drug Addiction, Research, and Education; Kate Howze of the Juvenile Welfare Board of Pinellas County, Florida, and Clare Jones of Northlight Counseling Services, Scottsdale, Arizona. These people have also helped to define the characteristics typical of children at risk reviewed in this chapter.

REFERENCES

Fahlberg V. *Attachment and Separation: Putting the Pieces Together.* Michigan Department of Social Services, 1979 (DSS publication No. 429).

Grimm VE. Effects of teratogenic exposure on the developing brain: Research strategies and possible mechanisms. *Developmental Pharmacology and Therapeutics* 1987; 10:328-45.

Los Angeles Unified School District, Special Education Division. *Today's Challenge: Teaching Strategies for Working with Young Children Prenatally Exposed to Drugs/Alcohol.* Los Angeles: LAUSD (450 Grand, #120, Los Angeles, CA 90012), 1989.

Lynch E. *But I've Tried Everything! A Special Educator's Guide to Working with Parents.* State of California Department of Education, 1981.

Magdid K, McKelvey C. *Children Without a Conscience.* New York: Bantam Books, 1978.

National Association for the Education of Young Children. *Guidelines for Appropriate Curriculum Context and Assessment in Programs Serving Children Ages 3 through 8.* A position statement of NAEYC and the National Association of Early Childhood Specialists in State Departments of Education. Washington, D.C.: NAEYC (1834 Connecticut Avenue, N.W., Washington, D.C. 20009), 1991: 51-9

Russell F, Free T. Early intervention for infants and toddlers with prenatal drug exposure. *Infants and Young Children* 1991; 3(4):78-85.

Schneider J, Griffith D, Chasnoff I. Infants exposed to cocaine in utero: Implications for developmental assessment and intervention. *Infants and Young Children* 1989; 2(1):25-36.

Schutter L, Brinker R. Conjuring a new category of disability from prenatal cocaine exposure: Are the infants unique biological or caretaking casualties? *Topics in Early Childhood Special Education* 1992; 11(4):84-111.

University of California San Diego Extension. *What's a Teacher to Do? Practical Strategies for Succeeding with Preschool and Elementary School Children Who Have Been Prenatally Exposed to Drugs.* La Jolla, CA: UCSD, 1992.

ANNOTATED BIBLIOGRAPHY

Harpring J. *Cocaine Babies: Florida's Substance-Exposed Youth.* State of Florida Department of Education, Office of Policy Research and Improvement (OPRI) Prevention Center (no date). This publication is one of a series designed to keep educators and policy makers current on important issues and trends in education. The categories of effects of prenatal exposure, the impact of the child's environment, and the role of schools in meeting the challenges of this population are examined.

Los Angeles Unified School District, Special Education Division. *Today's Challenge: Teaching Strategies for Working with*

Young Children Prenatally Exposed to Drugs/Alcohol **1989. LAUSD, 450 Grand, #120, Los Angeles, CA 90012.**
This excellent resource provides a wide array of strategies for working effectively with the young child prenatally exposed to drugs. The booklet provides guidelines to assist teachers in adapting preschool programs to serve these at-risk children.

Villarreal S, McKinney L, Quackenbush M. *Handle with Care: Helping Children Prenatally Exposed to Drugs and Alcohol.* **Santa Cruz, CA: ETR Associates, 1991.**
This book provides an overview of the problems of drug use, substance abuse, and prenatal drug exposure as well as specific chapters devoted to the developmental outcomes, caregiving strategies, and the educational implications of working with chemically dependent parents and their children.

Zero to Three. Bulletin of the National Center for Clinical Infant Programs. **1989; 9(5) and 1992; 13(1).**
Both issues offer a number of excellent research articles examining the clinical and developmental issues as well as the myths and misunderstandings surrounding the cocaine-exposed infant. Included in each issue are articles addressing the nature of interventions with recovering mothers and the importance of a comprehensive community-based approach to the problem.

ADDITIONAL RESOURCES ON SUBSTANCE-EXPOSED CHILDREN

Austin G, Prendergast M. Young children of substance abusers. *Prevention Research Update* No. 8. Washington, D.C.: Western Center for Drug Free Schools and Communities, Department of Education, 1991.

Bauer A. *Parenting Children Who Have Been Prenatally Exposed to Drugs or Alcohol: A Handbook for Foster and Adoptive Parents*. Ohio: Cincinnati University Press, 1990.

Bredekamp S. *Early Childhood Education Drug Abuse Prevention Curricula/Materials Project*. Washington, D.C.: Office of Educational Research and Improvement, Programs for the Improvement of Practice, 1989.

Bredekamp S, Shepard, L. How best to protect children from inappropriate school expectations, practices, and policies. *Young Children* 1989; 44(3):14-24

Charlesworth P. Behind before they start? Deciding how to deal with the risk of kindergarten failure. *Young Children* 1989; 44(3):5-13.

Chasnoff I, Schnoll S, Burns W, Burns K. Maternal nonnarcotic substance abuse during pregnancy: Effects on infant development. *Neurobehavioral Toxicology and Teratology* 1984; 6:277-80.

Crittenden P. Teaching maltreated children in the preschool. *Topics in Early Childhood Special Education* 1989; 9(2):16-32.

Curry N, Johnson C. *Beyond Self-Esteem: Developing a Genuine Sense of Human Value*. Washington, D.C.: National Association for the Education of Young Children, 1990 (Research monograph, volume 4).

Feig L. *Drug Exposed Infants and Children: Service Needs and Policy Questions*. Washington, D.C.: Department of Health and Human Services, Office of the Assistant Secretary for Planning and Evaluation, 1990.

Frailberg S. Ghosts in the nursery: A psychoanalytic approach to the problems of impaired mother-child relationships. *Journal of the American Academy of Child Psychiatry* 1975; 14:387-421.

Greenberg P. Ideas that work with young children: Learning self-esteem and self-discipline through play. *Young Children* 1989; 44(2):28-31.

Greer JV. The drug babies. *Exceptional Children* 1990; 56(5):382-4.

Guralnick MJ. Social competence and early intervention. *Journal of Early Intervention* 1990; 14(1):3-14.

Harpring J. *Cocaine Babies: Florida's Substance-Exposed Youth.* State of Florida Department of Education, Office of Policy Research and Improvement (OPRI) Prevention Center (no date).

Hitz R, Driscoll A. Praise or encouragement? New insights into praise implications for early childhood teachers *Young Children* 1988; 43(5):6-13.

Honig A. Stress and coping in children *Young Children* 1986; 41(4):50-63.

Howard J. *A Prevention/Intervention Model for Chemically Dependent Parents and Their Offspring.* Washington, D. C.: American Psychiatric Press, 1991.

Howard J, Beckwith L, Rodning C, Kropenske V. The development of young children of substance-abusing parents: Insights from seven years of intervention and research. *Zero to Three* 1989; IX(5):8-12.

Howes C. Research in review: Infant child care. *Young Children* 1989; 44(6):24-8.

Howze K. *Taking Care of Crack's Kids.* St. Petersburg, FL: Juvenile Welfare Board of Pinellas County (no date).

Jones CB. *A Sourcebook for Attention Disorders.* Tucson, AZ: Communication Skill Builders, 1991.

McCracken J. *Reducing Stress in Young Children's Lives.* Washington, D.C.: National Association for the Education of Young Children, 1986.

Odom SL, McEvoy MA. Integration of young children with handicaps and normally developing children. In: Odom SL, Karnes MB, eds. *Early Intervention for Infants and Children with Handicaps.* Baltimore: Brooks, 1988: 214-67.

Revkin A. Crack in the cradle. *Discover* 1989; September:62-9.

Rist M. The shadow children. *The American School Board Journal* 1990; January:19-24.

Van Barr A, Fleury P, Ultee CA. Behavior in the first year after drug dependent pregnancy. *Archives of Disease in Childhood.* 1989; 64:241-5.

Vincent L, Poulson M, Cole C, Woodruff G, Griffith D. *Born Substance Exposed, Educationally Vulnerable.* Reston, VA: Council for Exceptional Children, 1991.

Weston D, Ivins B, Zukerman B, Jones C, Lopez R. Drug exposed babies: Research and clinical issues. *Zero to Three* 1989; IX(5):1-7.

Developmental Assessment of Infants and Children Who Are At-Risk Due to Prenatal Alcohol and Drug Exposure

Eleanor W. Lynch, Ph.D.

This chapter addresses issues in the developmental assessment of children who are at risk, especially those who are at risk due to prenatal drug exposure. It provides information about the assessment process, including planning, conducting, and interpreting data, and it describes commonly used strategies for gathering data. Throughout the chapter, the importance of interdisciplinary or transdisciplinary approaches and family-professional collaboration are emphasized with specific strategies provided for improving the latter.

At-risk conditions may be temporary or long term. They may be determined by characteristics that are inherent in the child, characteristics of family members, or characteristics of the environment in which the child and family live. The factors that cause a child to be described as "at-risk" may be single or multiple. They may be the results of problems in pregnancy, a difficult labor and delivery, a diagnosed disability, or environmental factors such as poverty or substance abuse in the home. Thus at-risk infants and children may have little in common. Even among those who are at risk because they were prenatally drug exposed (PDE), each child presents a very individual developmental and behavioral picture.

Determining whether or not these children need or are eligible for special programs or services requires a comprehensive assessment of their development, health status, and behavior. Many programs and services also assess the family's concerns, priorities, and resources to ensure that the needs of the entire family system are considered in planning interventions (Campbell 1991; Johnson, McGonigel & Kaufmann 1989; Trivette et al 1990). This chapter begins with a definition of developmental assessment and discussion of developmental assessment of infants and children from different professional perspectives. It continues by presenting the multiple purposes that developmental assessment serves, explaining approaches to assessment, and providing suggestions for supporting families throughout the process. The chapter concludes with a discussion of issues surrounding developmental assessment and a summary. Although assessment issues related to young chil-dren who have been prenatally exposed to drugs are highlighted in the chapter, the primary focus is on all children who are at risk for disability.

Defining Developmental Assessment

Developmental assessment of infants and children is included as part of the practice of many disciplines, but each of those disciplines conceptualizes it in a slightly different way. For nurses, developmental assessment includes the child's health status, physical measures such as length or height, weight, and head circumference, and screening of traditional developmental areas such as the child's performance on tasks in the cognitive, perceptual/fine motor, gross motor, speech and language, social-emotional, self-care, or adaptive behavior domains. Psychologists often rely on standardized tests to determine cognitive development such as the *Bayley Scales of Infant Development* (Bayley 1969), the *Stanford-Binet Intelligence Scale* (Thorndike, Hagen & Sattler 1986), or other psychometric tests (Drotar & Sturm 1989). Early childhood special educators have as their primary emphases the assessment of the child's functional skills in each of the developmental domains as well as the child's performance in the settings in which he or she spends the most time such as the home, preschool, or other community environments. They tend to rely on systematic observation of the child in natural settings, interviews with parents and primary caregivers, and developmental profiles and checklists (Hanson & Lynch 1989). Speech and language pathologists, physical therapists, and occupational therapists emphasize their own areas of specialty when conducting developmental assessments. Thus, a speech and language pathologist is especially concerned with how well the child is hearing, speaking, and understanding. The occupational therapist may focus on perceptual and fine motor skills, effective ways of positioning and handling the child, and the child's ability to suck and swallow. The physical therapist assessing the same child may concentrate on the child's muscle tone, strength, range of motion, and gait. Although each of the disciplines mentioned above conducts developmental assessments, the instruments and techniques they use to gather information, their philosophy of assessment, and the types of information they gather may differ considerably.

Developmental assessments are designed to gather both quantitative and qualitative information about the child. The number of words the child says or understands, the number of blocks counted or steps taken, and physical measures such as height and weight are considered quantitative. Although this kind of information is essential to have a complete picture of the child's functioning, qualitative information is often more important—particularly with children who are at risk. Qualitative data describe the "how" of the child's performance. Being aware of an infant's response to being talked to and rocked at the same time or recognizing the cues that indicate a need to pull back from interactions is critical information for both the family and the person intervening. Knowing how a child approaches and solves problems or how he or she initiates interactions may be far more important than knowing how many

problems he or she can solve or how many interactions he or she initiates. For example, when presented with a problem that is challenging but not beyond expectation for the child's age, does the child attend and persist to completion, immediately request help, quickly lose interest and move on to another activity, or become frustrated, cry, and have a tantrum? Or when initiating interactions does the child use words or gestures or is he or she more likely to use negative approaches such as hitting, crying, biting, or spoiling another child's work? These qualitative indicators are important in determining what interventions may or may not be needed and in prioritizing and developing those that are most appropriate.

Qualitative information is equally important when assessing the child's motor and language development. Knowing the quality of motor movement—whether it is smooth and effective, reflex-dominated, jerky, tremulous, or uncontrolled—is critical to designing appropriate motor interventions. The same is true for the qualitative aspects of prelinguistic, speech, and language behaviors. Does the infant maintain sustained eye contact, demonstrate differentiated crying, and imitate sounds? Is the young child's production of language repetitive and echolalic? Does it incorporate all of the elements of language appropriate to the age of the child? Is the voice quality typical for age and gender?

Although qualitative indicators are more subtle and sometimes more difficult to measure and describe, they are extremely important when conducting a developmental assessment. For infants, toddlers, or preschoolers who are at risk, especially those who have been prenatally drug exposed, attention to qualitative aspects of their development may make the difference in determining whether or not intervention is warranted.

The Team Approach to Developmental Assessment

From the preceding discussion of developmental assessment, it is easy to see that the process is multifaceted and complex. A variety of approaches and instruments are used, and professionals from different disciplines sometimes overlap and sometimes assess very different aspects of development. Because of these differences in types of assessment and professional approaches, parents have often reported that they found the process confusing. Some parents felt that assessors gave them mixed messages. Others thought that important aspects of their child's development were being overlooked while other aspects were assessed over and over again.

To eliminate the problems that parents were experiencing and to use resources more efficiently, team assessment emerged. In this model, professionals from a variety of professions work together to gather information about the infant or child (Hanson & Lynch 1989). The interdisciplinary or transdisciplinary team works with the family to determine what aspects of their child's health, development, or behavior they are concerned about and goes on to plan and conduct an assessment that addresses those issues. Such a model brings considerable expertise to the assessment process and enables professionals from different disciplines to combine their skills as they assess the child's strengths and needs. This assessment model reflects best practice according to many professionals who work with children who are at-risk or disabled and their families (Bailey & Wolery 1989; Foley 1990; Kjerland 1986; Kjerland & Kovach 1990). It is a model that respects the family's concerns, utilizes their knowledge, and supports a partnership between parents and professionals.

Family-Professional Partnerships in Assessment

The importance of an interdisciplinary or transdisciplinary assessment of infants and children who are at risk because of prenatal drug exposure is unquestioned. Because of the possible neurological, biological, developmental, and behavioral consequences of PDE, many professionals can contribute valuable information about the child's skills and performance. Nurses and physicians can provide information about the child's growth, health, and neurological and physical status. Psychologists may provide information about the child's attachment, temperament, and responses to the environment. Early childhood special educators can provide information about the child's performance in developmental domains; and the speech and language, physical, and occupational therapists can provide more refined assessments of specific motor and prelinguistic or language behaviors. The value of the interdisciplinary or transdisciplinary assessment is clear.

There have, however, been questions about the relevance—or even the possibility—of establishing a partnership with parents whose children have been prenatally drug exposed. Drug-using and drug-addicted mothers and family members are as heterogeneous a group as their infants (Weston et al 1989). Stereotyping them as disinterested, disaffiliated, and dysfunctional is as untrue as it is unfair. According to the Select Committee Hearing on Children, Youth, and Families (1989), pregnant women who seek help cannot get it. Two-thirds of the hospitals surveyed reported that they had no place to refer pregnant women who wanted to enter a treatment or recovery program, and one West Coast hospital reported a ten- to sixteen-week waiting period to enter drug treatment—even for pregnant women (Miller 1989). Thus, assuming that all parents who are or have been substance users or abusers do not want to become involved in caring and planning for their child is fallacious. As Myers, Olson, and Kaltenbach (1992) point out, "Resist believing the stereotypes and participating in the stigmatization of drug abusers. Truly accept that it could be you, it could be your sister." Although the partnership may be much more difficult to establish, be more tenuous, and require more support to maintain, reaching out to the family can be as important as reaching out to the child. The assessment process provides an important opportunity for professionals to reach out and support families and children alike.

Developmental Assessment: A Multipurpose Evaluation

Developmental assessments may be recommended for several different reasons, but each of the reasons relates to making decisions about the child's needs. Although different labels may sometimes be used, developmental assessments are typically conducted for one or more of the following purposes: (1) providing a baseline for ongoing monitoring of the child's performance and development; (2) screening for potential problems; (3) determining a diagnosis or eligibility for certain programs or services; (4) developing intervention strategies that match the child's/family's needs; and (5) gathering data for program evaluation (Hanson & Lynch 1989; McLoughlin & Lewis 1990).

Monitoring and Follow-Along

For children who are considered at risk, ongoing monitoring and follow-along are frequently provided through hospital or other community clinics. This monitoring enables those intervening to determine whether the child is developing typically or atypically. It also provides for contact with the family to determine their concerns, support their progress, provide requested information and linkages to other community resources, and observe the interactions between the parent(s) and child. The data that is collected through early monitoring and follow-along can be used as a baseline when assessing development in the toddler and preschool years.

Screening

Short forms of developmental assessments are used to screen for potential problems. Their purpose is to identify those children who may need additional assessments to determine whether the child's development is atypical or delayed. It is essential to decide on the specific intent of the screening before screening programs are implemented. In other words, a screening program with the purpose of checking children's hearing and vision would use different instruments and personnel from one designed to check for scoliosis or one checking for general developmental progress.

Screening programs and the instruments they use are characterized by simplicity, accuracy, comprehensiveness, cost-effectiveness, and involvement of parents (Hanson & Lynch 1989). Screening designed for infants typically includes measures of growth, vision, and hearing, sensory intactness, eating and sleeping patterns, and early cognitive, communicative, and motor behaviors. Screening for toddlers and preschoolers typically includes measures of hearing and vision as well as early skills in all of the developmental domains.

Most communities have established screening programs that are conducted through hospital health fairs, school districts, or public health departments. Although these community-based screening programs represent an important low-or no-cost resource for parents, children who have been prenatally exposed to drugs may need more systematic, individualized, and scheduled monitoring. In fact, all children who have been identified at birth as being at risk, those who have spent time in a neonatal intensive care unit, and those who are discharged from the hospital into homes where there is a history of drug use, violence, or limited ability to cope with daily demands should be followed routinely to help ensure more positive outcomes for both the child and family.

Determining a Diagnosis or Eligibility for Services

In medicine and allied health professions, determining the diagnosis is a critical step in deciding on treatment options. Therefore, health settings typically conduct developmental assessments that

are diagnostic in nature. These clinical evaluations are often critical in determining treatment options, ruling out certain conditions, or predicting the course of development. For example, knowing that a newborn is infected with the HIV virus may enable physicians to prescribe treatments that will slow the course of the disease. Or, recognizing that a newborn has fragile X syndrome enables genetic counselors to work with the family to determine the probability that they will have other children with the same condition. Thus, from the medical perspective, traditional, differential diagnosis is an important type of assessment.

In nonhealth settings, a different but parallel type of assessment is conducted. This assessment, known as an assessment for eligibility, is designed to determine whether or not the child meets the criteria for services established by the program or agency. For example, school districts are mandated to provide a free and appropriate education to all children from the age of three through twenty-one who meet the criteria for one of the handicapping conditions outlined in federal law. Before the school can serve the child, district personnel must determine whether or not the child meets the criteria. Often, a child may be behind his or her peers but not significantly behind to meet the criteria. Like schools, other agencies such as public health, mental health, social services, regional centers for people with developmental disabilities, Head Start, and others, all have established eligibility criteria. Their services can only be provided to those who qualify. Because of the complexities of differing eligibility criteria across systems, referrals that may seem logical may not always result in services.

Developing Intervention Strategies

One of the most important types of developmental assessment is one that is conducted to determine the child's strengths and needs in order to plan appropriate interventions. These are typically conducted by program staff with the assistance of family members. The findings are then used to establish specific goals, objectives, or outcomes for the child. The goals and objectives are typically written to increase skills in deficit areas and build upon existing strengths. For example, if a child has good social interactions with his or her peers but poor language skills, an objective that uses his or her social skills to develop language may be written.

Program Evaluation

Children's developmental progress is sometimes used as one measure of program effectiveness. In this instance, the children's rate of developmental progress, based upon periodic developmental assessments, is used to determine whether or not the program made a difference. When children accomplish their written objectives or reach a normal or near-normal rate of developmental progress, the program can use that information to claim success.

The Developmental Assessment Process

As described in the beginning of this chapter, not all developmental assessments are conducted in the same way; however, there are basic steps and best practices that can be used to guide practice regardless of professional discipline. This section focuses on the model described by Hanson and Lynch (1989).

Planning

Planning is a prerequisite for any developmental assessment. The strategies, techniques, and instruments to be used; the observations to be made; and the interview questions should all be preplanned. Careful planning does not mean that the assessor cannot deviate from the plan as needs arise or different concerns emerge, but preplanning ensures that the assessor and/or assessment team are well prepared. Involving parents and other appropriate family members in the preplanning is essential for two reasons. First, written parental permission must be obtained before an assessment can be conducted, and second, encouraging parents to talk about their concerns acknowledges their central importance in their child's life. Even if parents are unfamiliar with the assessment process or more concerned with other life crises and demands, consulting them demonstrates respect for the parental role and a belief that they, too, want the best for their child.

The preplanning process also enables the assessor in charge to make any special arrangements that may be necessary. A sign language or other language translator/interpreter may be needed for the assessment; or arrangements may need to be made to observe in a day care setting, at the grandmother's, or some other setting.

Conducting

Much of the what occurs during a developmental assessment looks like and is play. The child is asked to interact with the parent/caregiver or an assessor around a series of tasks that are similar to puzzles and games. Experienced assessors observe and score the child's re-

Table 1. Stages and Activities in the Assessment Process

Stages	Activities
PLANNING	Obtain parental permission for assessment.
	Clarify referral questions with an emphasis on parents'/caregivers' concerns and priorities.
	Review existing information.
	Determine roles and responsibilities of other team members in the assessment, including parents/caregivers.
	Arrange for sign language or other language interpreters/translators as needed.
	Develop assessment objectives.
	Develop assessment strategies.
	Schedule observation/interview/testing.
	Obtain assessment instruments/materials.
CONDUCTING	Organize materials and environment.
	Meet with child and parents/caregivers; establish rapport; explain assessment procedures, reemphasize parent/caregiver members' value and roles in the assessment process.
	Observe/interview/test.
	Alter plans as needed based on child's state, parental/caregiver concerns and priorities, new information.
	Encourage parental/caregiver input, suggestions, questions throughout.
	Close session with clear specifications of next steps in the process, timelines, and contact person.
INTERPRETING	Review notes, protocols, videotapes, language samples, work samples collected in relation to referral questions and assessment objectives.
	Review anything learned not related to specific referral questions and objectives for importance and relevance to program planning.
	Incorporate all information into a draft report to be shared with parents/caregivers.
	Review draft report for clarity, accuracy, and relevance to program development.
SHARING	Provide draft report to parents/family and team members.
	Discuss findings with team members and parents/caregivers in staffing in relation to child's strengths, weaknesses, and needs.
	Encourage and support parental/caregiver input and participation.
	Determine appropriate services and placement.
FOLLOWING-UP	Check on performance in setting, parental satisfaction, staff perceptions/concerns.

Adapted, with permission, from *Early Intervention: Implementing Child and Family Services for Infants and Toddlers Who Are At-Risk or Disabled,* by MJ Hanson and EW Lynch. Austin, TX: PRO-ED, 1989, p. 109.

sponses but do not limit their observations to the specific tasks. In this way, qualitative information can be gathered related to the child's approach to others, to the tasks, and to problem solving.

Unlike older children who have been socialized to respond to adult demands, young children may or may not want to "play the assessor's games." In fact, the presence of a stranger may be uncomfortable for some children at certain ages and stages. Therefore, assessors must be flexible, engaging, and willing to follow the child's lead in the interaction. Actively involving the parents or other family members present may help to elicit responses.

Many developmental assessments include structured and unstructured opportunities for observing the child. Presenting both structured tasks and allowing time for free play are especially important when working with children who have been prenatally drug exposed. Because testing that uses only structured tasks may result in spuriously high scores for these children, opportunities to observe them play on their own are critical (Howard et al 1989; Poulsen 1990). The difference between a child's performance in structured versus unstructured situations is another example of the importance of qualitative data. Qualitative, developmental differences exist between children who perform well only when operating with external controls and children who can perform well when relying solely on internal controls and organization.

Increasingly, play is becoming the cornerstone of developmental assessments for young children. Linder (1990) has proposed a model of play-based assessment and intervention for children

from six months to six years of age that incorporates families in the assessment process in nonthreatening, natural ways. This approach meets the guidelines of assessing relevant behaviors in the environments in which the child normally spends time.

Interpreting and Sharing

In the past, professionals typically planned, conducted, and interpreted assessment information without including families in the process. Today, best practice includes parents or other family members in all aspects of the assessment. Instead of professionals meeting together to discuss their assessment findings before they share that information with the parents/caregivers, parents and those whom they choose to participate are invited to share in all phases of the assessment process, including interpretation of the information. This does not mean that parents are asked to interpret technical information that is specific to knowledge in a professional discipline. However, it does mean that it is incumbent upon all professionals to describe the assessment findings and their interpretation of them in lay language, to solicit the parents'/caregivers' thoughts, and to use parental/caregiver input in developing recommendations for intervention.

In addition, reports of the assessment findings should not be considered final until parents/caregivers have had the opportunity to react to them and to discuss their interpretations of the data. For those working with parents who have limited abilities, who are addicted, and who are immobilized by the demands of daily life, this level of family participation may seem to be the imaginings of a writer in an ivory tower. However, failing to try to include parents and caregivers underscores their feelings of incompetence and low self-esteem—characteristics that lead to poor parent-infant interaction and inadequate parenting (Weston et al 1989). Asking a parent's opinion is a small gesture, but one that is too seldom made when the parents themselves do not meet our expectations.

Following Up

If the developmental assessment leads to actions such as referral to programs or services, it is the assessor's job to follow up on the outcome of the referral. Checking with the family and the program or agency to whom the child was referred completes the loop.

Components of a Developmental Assessment

Developmental assessments should be guided by the questions and concerns expressed by the child's parents/caregivers. Although assessors may want to gather additional information, parents' concerns take priority over all issues except those related to the child's safety or to a life-threatening health or medical need. The concept of assessing those things that are of critical importance to parents/caregivers is a relatively new concept in infant and early childhood intervention, but it is one that is supported in the best practice literature (Kjerland 1986; Lynch et al 1991; StevensDominguez, Beam & Thomas 1989; Winton & Bailey 1990).

New parents/caregivers may need help from professionals in articulating their concerns, because it is difficult to know what questions to ask until one knows the range of possibilities. Professionals can provide basic information about their concerns or about developmental expectations, which will help families identify and discuss their own concerns and frame the questions that they have about their child's progress. As parents/caregivers learn more about child development, are coached by professionals, and recognize that they are respected members of the intervention team, many will be able to contribute considerably more to positive outcomes for their child and their family.

The specific questions and techniques that assessors use to gather developmental information change with the child's chronological age, but developmental assessments typically include the following four components: (1) interviews with family members/caregivers, (2) observations of the child in his or her natural environments such as home, hospital, or childcare setting, (3) administration of structured test items or tasks, and (4) review or additional data gathering related to health and/or medical status. Each of the four components is briefly described in the paragraphs that follow.

Interviews

Interviewing has long been one of the most important techniques for gathering information about children's behavior, development, and health status. The purpose of an interview is to gather rich, qualitative information that would take far too long or be impossible to observe in a limited period of time. Interviews are conducted with parents/caregivers or others who know the child well in one or more settings. In the past, interviews were typically driven by a set of structured questions developed by the assessor.

Sometimes the questions were used no more creatively than a checklist. More recently, interviews to gather information about the child's development and behavior have become less structured, more open-ended, and more dependent on following the leads of parents/caregivers (Bailey & Simeonsson 1988; Winton & Bailey 1990). Specific and narrow questions such as: "When did Gavin roll over for the first time?" "What does he do when he is having a tantrum?" "When did you first notice that Gavin was having trouble understanding directions?" have given way to more global questions that allow parents/caregivers to focus on the concerns and issues that are most important to them. Questions or prompts like the following are typical in more family-focused interviews: "Tell me about your family." "Tell me more about Gavin." "What are your greatest concerns about Gavin?" "What do you feel good about when you think about Gavin?" These questions encourage the parents/caregivers to describe their child's strengths and needs in the larger family context, and understanding the child and the larger family context enables the professional to shape interventions that are more relevant and individualized. The family's/caregiver's responses in the interview also shape decisions about the next steps in assessment—what should be observed, where observations should take place, what structured assessments should be administered, and whether or not additional health or medical information needs to be gathered.

Observations

Observations of the child may occur in any setting where the child spends

time. For children who are hospitalized, the hospital would be the scene of the observation. Children who reside with their biological or foster families would probably be observed there, in a child-care setting, or other setting that is important to the parents/caregivers. For example, if an at-risk preschooler is impossible to take to the grocery store because of her behavior, the assessor may want to observe one of these outings to learn what seems to trigger the negative behavior.

Observing the child's interactions with parents/caregivers, peers, and toys or materials are all critical to developmental assessment. Increasing evidence in the literature suggests that the nature and quality of parent-infant or caregiver/infant interaction strongly influence developmental outcomes (Bromwich 1981). Nurses have long been familiar with formal strategies for measuring these interactions such as the Nursing Child Assessment Scales (Barnard & Bee 1981). More recently, less intrusive measures have been developed that are based on interviews and observations (Hanson & Krentz 1986). If parents/caregivers express concern about interactions or if the child's well-being appears to be significantly threatened because of the nature and quality of the interaction, an assessment of parent/caregiver-infant interaction is warranted.

As infants grow into toddlers, preschoolers, and young children, interactions and relationships with other children become increasingly important. Observations of the child with his or her peers is often included in developmental assessments. The primary purposes of this type of assessment are to determine the extent, quality, and types of interactions. The assessor may gather information about the range of interactions that take place. For example, some children initiate play with others; others allow themselves to be included in play, but do not initiate. Still others may choose to be alone and play or work in isolation. Knowing that a child only plays alone may suggest that the child has fewer opportunities to learn turn-taking, cooperation, and verbal strategies for managing behavior than those children who play in groups.

The ways in which a child handles and uses toys and other materials also contribute to our understanding of a child's development. Some children may play with the same materials repetitively with no attempt to use the toy or material for its designed purpose; others pick up one toy, put it down, and move on to something else without ever seeming to become involved in play. Other children use toys and materials to create simple or elaborate stories, games, or fantasies that incorporate reality and make-believe in highly imaginative ways. Thus, the quality of the child's play, compared to peers of the same age, gender, and culture, may reveal a great deal about the child's developmental progress and whether or not there is a need for intervention.

Structured Tasks or Test Items

Tests such as the *Neonatal Behavioral Assessment Scale* (Brazelton 1973), *Bayley Scales of Infant Development*, (Bayley 1969), *Kaufman Assessment Battery for Children* (Kaufman & Kaufman 1983) are frequently used by trained professionals to gather developmental information. These instruments provide norms or expectations to which an infant's or young child's performance can be compared. They highlight those areas in which there are delays or those areas in which the child's development is at or beyond age expectations. In the hands of an experienced assessor, they can also yield qualitative information about the child's development that can be used to determine whether or not intervention may be needed. Results are most often used to determine whether or not a child is eligible for a particular program or service or to determine the child's rate of development.

In addition to the instruments mentioned in the previous paragraph, a number of developmental and skill assessment batteries are used for program planning (Hanson & Lynch 1989). Tests such as *Developmental Programming for Infants and Young Children* (Schaefer & Moersch 1981) and the *Hawaii Early Learning Profile* (Furuno et al 1979) give parents/caregivers and assessors a comprehensive picture of the child's development in each of the traditionally measured areas including fine and gross motor, social/emotional, speech and language, cognition, and self-help skills. Because these measures were designed to assist in individualizing children's goals and objectives, they are especially useful for those who will be working with the child on an ongoing basis. Most are written in clear, understandable language that makes them easy for a trained professional to use and easy to explain to parents or other caregivers.

Reviewing Health and Medical Information

For all children who are at risk, reviewing health and medical information is an essential part of a complete developmental assessment. This review should be completed while at-risk children are still hospitalized after birth. Until the child is medically stable, no other interventions can begin. Even after the child has stabilized, his or her health and medical status continues to help shape intervention. Knowing that an infant is neurologically disorganized and incapable of managing multiple stimuli has direct implications for the assessment process and any proposed intervention. Knowing that a child is healthy, growing, and thriving with all of his or her sensory systems intact allows assessors and interventionists to develop a very different set of goals and objectives. Thus, information about physical health, growth, medical conditions, special precautions, hearing, vision, and medications contributed by physicians, nurses, and allied health professionals is essential to a good developmental assessment.

Supporting and Working With Families in the Assessment Process

Parents, family members, and other primary caregivers are the most significant people in the lives of young children. They are also the ones who spend the most time with the child. Parents and primary caregivers will always know the child better than professionals who interact briefly and are in and out of the child's and family's life. Even those parents for whom parenting is extremely challenging because of issues in their own lives know their children in ways that are impossible for others to know them. For this reason, involving parents or primary caregivers in planning and conducting the assessment is an impor-

tant step—important because it can be the first step in acknowledging their role, responsibility, and adequacy as parents.

Working with families in planning and conducting the assessment is important in another more pragmatic way. In almost all settings, the permission of the parents and/or legal guardian is required before any assessment may be conducted. Formal testing, observations, or other data-gathering related to the child's skills and abilities without appropriate permission is neither ethical nor legal. Therefore, before any developmental assessments are planned or conducted, professionals must seek written permission from the parent(s) and/or guardian.

Family-Professional Partnerships

The goal of developing a partnership with families is to enhance the child's development in the context of the family through a coordinated, complementary approach. Families and professionals working in concert create a powerful combination that is more effective than either working alone. To develop such a partnership takes time, mutual respect, training, and education for parents, and professional willingness to adapt to new roles and responsibilities. It requires listening, putting parents' or caregivers' priorities first, and helping families gain expertise in working with their child and with the system. Parent-professional partnerships do not come naturally. Like all other skills, they must be learned and relearned. Strong partnerships built over time result in informed, effective parents, systems that are more responsive to children's and families' needs, and work environments for professionals that are

Table 2. Tips for Improving LAB Skills: Language, Attitude, and Behavior

Language
- Address parents or caregivers as equals, using their appropriate titles such as "Ms.," "Mr.," or "Mrs." Don't assume that they want to be on a first-name basis.
- Remember that you are addressing other adults. Even those who do not understand your professional terminology appreciate professionals who are not condescending.
- Use "person first" language and avoid labels. If it is necessary to communicate that a child has been prenatally exposed to drugs, say it that way. Don't say "drug babies," or "the PDEs."
- Use words that are a part of daily conversation. When technical words must be used, explain what they mean. Don't expect parents (or professionals from other disciplines) to understand everything you have to say the first time.
- Write things down so families or other professionals can refer to something later, look something up, or ask others to explain.
- Arrange for translators or language interpreters for families who are deaf or who are non-English speaking prior to any meeting or interaction to ensure communication.

Attitude
- Show respect for the parents or caregivers as the individuals who know the child best.
- In every interaction expect to learn something from the parents or caregivers that will help you understand the child's and family's needs better.
- Approach all clients, patients, and families as people who care about their children and want to grow and learn. Some just need more assistance than others.
- Recognize that culture may play a significant role in parents' or caregivers' concerns and priorities. Respect their traditions and beliefs, but provide information about other alternatives and approaches from your own professional perspective.

Behavior
- Take time to listen, to teach, and to care. What may be routine to you is often a new and frightening experience for families.
- Demonstrate respect through making introductions, giving greetings, paying attention, answering questions, providing written information, and ensuring closures that are clear about "next steps" and follow-up.
- Advocate for children and their families. Evaluate the agency or system that you're in, as well as your own practice, to see how clients, patients, and consumers are treated. How would you feel on the other side of the examining table or desk?
- Be kind to yourself and your colleagues. It is a highly stressful time in health, social, and educational services. Strong, competent professionals are essential if we are to build family-professional partnerships. Take care of yourself; we need you.

more positive and more rewarding.

Building these partnerships is not always easy, especially when parents or caregivers are struggling with their own problems and have little physical or emotional energy to give to the needs of their child. Family-professional collaboration requires some LAB skills—language, **attitude**, and **b**ehavior on the part of the professional. Table 2 suggests some strategies that professionals can use as they work to develop colLABorative relationships with families.

Partnerships When Families Are At-Risk

Children who have been prenatally drug exposed come from families that are very challenging to professionals. Parents who use drugs, who lack parenting skills, and who live in poverty amidst violence and crime are not in a position to respond to typical approaches and interventions. These hard-to-reach families need help in learning to respect themselves, getting their own lives together, and developing social supports that can lead to self-sufficiency (Thurman & Berry 1992). Despite the difficulties and frustrations in working with families with such intensive needs, they, too, can benefit from the **LAB** skills discussed earlier. Although families with infants who have been prenatally drug exposed are often stereotyped as poor, dysfunctional, and disorganized, many parents who are drug users or abusers are affluent and influential. They may be successful in meeting their own and their children's material needs but unable to provide a stable, nurturing environment that promotes optimal development. However, whether the parent is rich or poor, addiction puts the child's

needs in the background and requires that professionals view the needs of the family as critical to meeting the needs of the child.

Special Considerations in Developmental Assessment

Research has begun to document some of the common clinical signs of children who have been prenatally exposed to drugs, and a cluster of physical, developmental, and behavioral effects has been identified (Fried & Watkinson 1990; Russell & Free 1991; Schneider, Griffith & Chasnoff 1989; Lewis 1991). Much of the recent research has been with infants who were exposed in utero to cocaine and/or polysubstances. The characteristics of some of these infants (detailed in previous chapters) such as hyperirritability, poor feeding patterns, irregular sleeping patterns, increased heart and respiratory rates, depressed interactional abilities, tremors, exaggerated startle behavior, and poor state control suggest that developmental assessments should include measures of these characteristics (Schneider, Griffith & Chasnoff 1989; Lewis, Bennett & Schmeder 1989; Lewis, Schmeder & Bennett 1992).

When these symptoms appear, additional assessment is warranted. However, caution must be observed. Searching for symptoms of drug exposure among young children and their families or conducting comprehensive evaluations of symptom-free children is a double-edged sword. On the positive side, knowing that a child has been prenatally drug exposed may cause the system to be more responsive and more alert to deviations in development. More support may be provided and more resources mobilized to ensure optimal development for the child and family. On the negative side, identifying the child as prenatally drug exposed may track him or her into a world of labels, lowered expectations, and an automatic "out" for service providers if the child fails to make expected progress. Professionals may draw faulty assumptions about the parents and curtail attempts to work with them. Thus, focusing on prenatal drug exposure as the primary criterion for assessment or intervention may result in negative outcomes. Instead, the physical status and behavior of the child and/or the family should determine whether or not assessment is necessary, not just the assumption of prenatal drug use.

What then is the role of nurses or other professionals when gathering developmental information or referring the child and family for developmental assessment? From an educational and behavioral perspective, the role is clear. Assessors need to gather information about the child and family that determines whether or not intervention is needed, and they need to gather information that suggests what those interventions should be. The diagnosis of prenatal drug exposure is often irrelevant and sometimes harmful. Children with similar characteristics, developmental patterns, and behaviors have been in the service system for many years, and effective interventions have been devised. The interventions for the parents/family/caregivers are less well documented and in need of refinement. Perhaps for both children and families the most important goal is not in labeling the problem but in developing an assessment process that pinpoints areas of need and creating interventions that make a positive difference.

Other Issues

Three additional issues related to developmental assessment are particularly important for professionals to consider. They include the anxiety caused by assessment, the timing of assessment, and the systems that are available to provide assessments of infants and children. The suggestion that a developmental assessment is needed often creates fear and concern in parents' or caregivers' minds. Suspicion of delayed development is a threatening picture that may cause some families to retreat from services. Therefore, it is especially important to build upon the expressed concerns of parents or caregivers. Suggesting assessment in response to a concern that they present about their child's development or behavior is ideal. When parents or caregivers do not express a concern, but professional experience and knowledge suggest that one is needed, it is important to be candid about the reasons for recommending an assessment, clear about what information it can and cannot provide, and clear about the parents' right to accept or refuse the assessment. Planning the assessment with families and including them in the conduct of the assessment can allay many fears. Remembering the threat that all of us experience under scrutiny may help professionals be more sensitive in their approach to parents and caregivers.

Because the predictive validity of infant assessments is low, the timing of assessments is a question that has been raised. One of parents' most common complaints is that they knew something was wrong with their child, but they could not get professionals to believe them. Many report that when they brought their concern to physicians or other professionals they were told that the child would probably grow out of it only to have their suspicions confirmed a year or two later. Based upon families' own experiences, it is probably never too early to conduct a developmental assessment. However, one should not assume that early test results accurately predict later performance. Using parental reports and checklists designed for parents/caregivers to complete has proven to be an effective strategy. Both family members and professionals learn more about the child, there is an ongoing source of data, and parents'/caregivers' concerns can be addressed more easily.

The final issue is related to referral for developmental assessment. Although all states and communities have service delivery systems that differ, all have programs, agencies, and systems that provide developmental screenings or assessments. School districts, regional centers for individuals with disabilities, public health nursing departments, and private nonprofit agencies are typically part of the assessment and service network. Learning the resources available in one's own community is an essential professional skill.

SUMMARY

Developmental assessment can provide families and professionals with a more complete understanding of the child's strengths and needs, but best practice dictates that any assessment be conducted with the permission and involvement of the parents or primary caregivers. Developmental assessments are multifaceted and typically include: interviews, observations, structured tasks, or test items. Although early developmental assessments should not be used as predictors of future performance, they can provide important information about the child's current growth, development, and behavior, and they can be used to shape effective interventions.

REFERENCES

Bailey DB, Simeonsson RJ. *Family Assessment in Early Intervention.* Columbus, OH: Merrill, 1988.

Bailey DB Jr, Wolery M. *Assessing Infants and Preschoolers with Handicaps.* Columbus, OH: Merrill, 1989.

Barnard K, Bee H. *The Assessment of Parent-Infant Interaction by Observation of Feeding and Teaching.* Unpublished manuscript, University of Washington School of Nursing and the Child Development and Mental Retardation Center, Seattle, 1981.

Bayley N. *Bayley Scales of Infant Development.* San Antonio, TX: Psychological Corporation, 1969.

Brazelton TB. *Neonatal Behavioral Assessment Scale.* Philadelphia: Lippincott, 1973.

Bromwich R. *Working with Infants and Parents.* Austin, TX: PRO-ED, 1981.

Campbell PH. Evaluation and assessment in early intervention for infants and toddlers. *Journal of Early Intervention* 1991; 15: 36-45.

Drotar D, Sturm L. Training psychologists as infant specialists. *Infants and Young Children* 1989; 2(2): 58-66.

Foley GM. Portrait of the arena assessment: Assessment in the transdisciplinary approach. In: Gibbs ED, Teti DM, eds. *Interdisciplinary Assessment of Infants: A Guide for Early Intervention Professionals.* Baltimore: Paul H. Brookes, 1990: 271-86.

Fried PA, Watkinson B. 36-and 48-month neurobehavioral follow-up of children prenatally exposed to marijuana, cigarettes, and alcohol. *Journal of Developmental and Behavioral Pediatrics* 1990; 11(2): 49-58.

Furuno S, O'Reilly K, Hosaka C, Inatsuka T, Allman P, Zeisloft B. *Hawaii Early Learning Profile.* Palo Alto, CA: VORT, 1979.

Hanson MJ, Krentz MS. *Supporting Parent-Child Interactions.* San Francisco: Project ISIS, Department of Special Education, San Francisco State University, 1986.

Hanson MJ, Lynch EW. *Early Intervention: Implementing Child and Family Services for Infants and Toddlers Who Are At-Risk or Disabled.* Austin, TX: PRO-ED, 1989.

Howard J, Beckwith L, Rodning C, Kropenske V. The development of young children of substance-abusing parents: Insights from seven years of intervention and research. *Zero to Three* 1989; IX (5): 8-12.

Johnson BH, McGonigel MJ, Kaufmann RK, eds. *Guidelines and Recommended Practices for the Individualized Family Service Plan.* Washington, DC: Association for the Care of Children's Health, 1989.

Kaufman AS, Kaufman NL. *Kaufman Assessment Battery for Children.* Circle Pines, MN: American Guidance Service, 1983.

Kjerland L. *Early Intervention Tailor Made.* Eagan, MN: Project Dakota, 1986.

Kjerland L, Kovach J. Family-staff collaboration for tailored infant assessment. In: Gibbs ED, Teti DM, eds. *Interdisciplinary Assessment of Infants: A Guide for Early Intervention Professionals.* Baltimore: Paul H. Brookes, 1990: 287-307

Lewis KD. *Behavioral Characteristics of PDE Infants Using the Lewis Protocol.* Unpublished Master's Thesis. San Francisco: University of San Francisco, 1991.

Lewis KD, Bennett B, Schmeder N. The care of infants menaced by cocaine abuse. *Maternal Child Nursing Journal* 1989; 14(5): 324-9.

Lewis KD, Schmeder N, Bennett B. Maternal drug abuse and its effects on young children. *Maternal Child Nursing Journal* 1992; 17(4): 188-203.

Linder TW. *Transdisciplinary Play-Based Assessment: A Functional Approach to Working with Young Children.* Baltimore: Paul H Brookes, 1990.

Lynch EW, Jackson JA, Mendoza J, English K. The merging of best practices and state policy in the IFSP process in California. *Topics in Early Childhood Special Education* 1991;11(3):32-53.

McLoughlin JA, Lewis RB. *Assessing Special Students.* 3rd ed. Columbus, OH: Merrill, 1990.

Miller G. Addicted infants and their mothers. *Zero to Three* 1989; IX: 20-3.

Myers BJ, Olson HC, Kaltenbach K. Cocaine-exposed infants: myths and misunderstandings. *Zero to Three* 1992; 13(1): 1-5.

Poulsen MK. Videotape: *Close Ups, A Conversation with Marie Poulsen: Cumulative Risk and Prenatal Drug Exposure.* San Diego, CA: Media Technology Services, San Diego State University, 1990.

Russell FR, Free TA. Early intervention for infants and toddlers with prenatal drug exposure. *Infants and Young Children* 1991;3(4):78-85.

Schaefer DS, Moersch MS, eds. *Developmental Programming for Infants and Young Children.* Ann Arbor, MI: University of Michigan Press, 1981.

Schneider JW, Griffith DR, Chasnoff IJ. Infants exposed to cocaine in utero: Implications for developmental assessment and intervention. *Infants and Young Children* 1989; 2(1): 25-36.

Select Committee Hearing on Children, Youth, and Families. *Addicted Infants and Their Mothers.* Washington, DC: Select Committee on Children, Youth, and Families, 1989.

StevensDominguez M, Beam G, Thomas P. *Guide for Family-Centered Services.* Albuquerque, NM: University of New Mexico, 1989.

Thorndike RL, Hagan E, Sattler J. *Stanford-Binet Intelligence Scale.* 4th ed. Chicago: Riverside, 1986.

Thurman SK, Berry BE. Cocaine use: Implications for intervention with childbearing women and their infants. *Children's Health Care* 1992; 21: 31-8.

Trivette CM, Dunst CJ, Deal AG, Hamer AW, Propst S. Assessing family strengths and family functioning style. *Topics in Early Childhood Special Education* 1990; 10(1): 16-35.

Turnbull AP, Turnbull HR. *Families, Profes-*

sionals, and Exceptionality: A Special Partnership. 2d ed. Columbus, OH: Merrill, 1990.

Weston DR, Ivin B, Zuckerman B, Jones C, Lopez R. Drug exposed babies: Research and clinical issues. *Zero to Three* 1989; IX: 1-7.

Winton PJ, Bailey DB. Early intervention training related to family interviewing. *Topics in Early Childhood Special Education* 1990; 10(1):50-62.

ANNOTATED BIBLIOGRAPHY

Bailey DG, Wolery M. *Assessing Infants and Preschoolers with Handicaps.* **Columbus, OH: Merrill, 1989.**
Written primarily for early childhood special educators, this text focuses on the philosophical and technical aspects of conducting assessments of infants and children. It describes the rationale for assessment, explains the psychometric properties of good tests, and suggests strategies for assessing children with sensory and motor impairments. A comprehensive chapter on observation provides guidelines for selecting observational strategies, example data collection sheets, and sample analyses. In addition to chapters devoted to assessment in each of the developmental domains, chapters on assessing environments, screening and assessing sensory functioning, assessing newborns including the assessment of behavioral states, and using assessment data to plan instructional programs are included.

Barnett DW, Macmann GM, Carey KT. Early intervention and the assessment of developmental skills: Challenges and directions. *Topics in Early Childhood Special Education* 1992;12(1): 21-43.
This article provides a critical review of the ways in which developmental skills are assessed, and it suggests alternative strategies for data gathering. Following a discussion of the technical inadequacies of commonly used assessment instruments and practices, the authors describe promising directions in assessment. Ecobehav-ioral interviews, observations, and curriculum-based measurements are defined and described; they are suggested as more appropriate strategies for data gathering. Because these measures are guided by problem analysis and interactive problem-solving in relevant contexts, they provide a more effective way of gathering information and making intervention decisions related to programs and services for young children who are at-risk or who have disabilities.

Gibbs ED, Teti DM, eds. *Interdisciplinary Assessment of Infants: A Guide for Early Intervention Professionals.* **Baltimore: Paul H. Brookes, 1990.**
This text is designed for early intervention professionals from a variety of disciplines. It is divided into sections that include chapters on: (I) Foundations, (II) Assessing Neuromotor Integrity, (III) Cognitive, Language and Developmental Assessment, (IV) Assessing Social Behavior and Characteristics of the Social Environment, (V)The Assessment Process, and (VI) Conclusions. The book highlights a variety of assessment instruments and procedures and provides a strong review of assessment from the perspective of many different disciplines. Of particular interest are chapters by Foley on arena assessment and Kjerland and Kovach on family-professional collaboration in infant assessment.

Hanson MJ, Lynch EW. *Early Intervention: Implementing Child and Family Services for Infants and Toddlers Who Are At-Risk or Disabled.* **Austin, TX: PRO-ED, 1989.**
Designed as a textbook for those working with children from birth to three who are at-risk or disabled, this book discusses the components of comprehensive early intervention programs. The book takes a family-centered, transdisciplinary approach to service delivery. Three chapters are particularly relevant to assessment. They are a chapter on screening, one on assessing children and identifying family strengths

and needs, and one on working with families. Each chapter includes a listing of best practices that can be used as a program self-evaluation.

Schneider JW, Griffith DR, Chasnoff IJ. Infants exposed to cocaine in utero: Implications for developmental assessment and intervention. *Infants and Young Children*, 1989; 2(1): 25-36.

This article presents information about the developmental characteristics of infants who were prenatally exposed to cocaine and draws implications for assessment and intervention. Suggestions for intervention relate to positioning, handling, feeding, playing, and carrying and are very practical and useful for parents and practitioners alike. The text is accompanied by photos that illustrate the suggestions being made.

14

The Impact of Family Diversity on Addiction, Treatment, and Recovery

Marci J. Hanson, Ph.D.
Marie Kanne Poulsen, Ph.D.
Lora-Ellen McKinney, Ph.D.

The population in the United States, particularly at this time in history, varies widely in terms of cultural and ethnic background, religious beliefs, languages spoken, age, socioeconomic status, and family structure. While differences add to the richness of the nation, this diversity presents special challenges for persons in the helping professions as they are called upon to consider many different perspectives in working with families. This chapter seeks to describe the diversity among families in the United States and the influence of this diversity on the provision of family services, including health, educational, and social service approaches related to chemical dependency and the effect on the child. The impact of cultural diversity is examined as it relates to addiction, treatment, and recovery. The importance, characteristics, and roles of extended family/kinship networks and foster family care in providing care for children of chemically dependent women are described. Finally, recommendations for the provision of services to families from a wide range of backgrounds and belief systems are presented.

Like the varied plants in a garden, we as individuals in this society share many needs in common, such as the needs for affection, shelter, and nurturance. However, just as the garden is made up of diverse plants, each with its own particular needs as to soil, water, and sunlight to help it achieve maximal growth and beauty, so too do the individuals who make up our society differ in terms of the environment and supports that will facilitate their growth and human potential (Hanson 1992). Also, like the garden, the makeup of our society is diverse. Particularly at this time in the United States, the population varies widely in terms of cultural and ethnic background, religious beliefs, languages spoken, age, socioeconomic status, and family structure. While differences add to the richness of the nation, this diversity presents special challenges for persons in the helping professions as they are called upon to consider many different perspectives in working with families.

This chapter seeks to describe the diversity among families in the United States and the influence of this diversity on the provision of family services, including health, educational, and social service approaches. Further, the impact of chemical dependency on family functioning and parenting is discussed. The importance, characteristics, and roles of extended family/kinship networks and foster family care in providing care for children of chemically dependent women are described. Finally, recommendations for the provision of services to families from a wide range of backgrounds and belief systems are presented.

Demographics of the United States

One can hardly open a newspaper or magazine without being reminded of the colossal changes that have transformed American families over the last several decades. Families today are defined from a much broader spectrum than the two-parent nuclear family. Families are characterized by variation in structure (e.g., two parent, single parent, extended, blended, adopted, foster), size, cultural identification, and age of parents, to name a few. Further, sociopolitical issues, such as poverty, have influenced the ways in which families operate.

Cultural Heritage and Ethnicity

For many years the United States was characterized as a "melting pot" made up of individuals from different cultures and backgrounds who had come together to forge a new society. Today, our nation is more typically and accurately described by its pluralistic nature. Recent information from the 1990 United States Census shows a resident population of 248,709,873 (US Census Bureau 1991). The percentage of the population described by race and Hispanic origin in the census is indicated in the following distribution: 80.3% White; 12.1% Black; 0.8% American Indian, Eskimo, or Aleut; 2.9% Asian or Pacific Islander; 3.9 % Other; and 9.0% Hispanic origin.

Though the largest percentage of the population of the United States traditionally has come from Anglo-European groups, the current population trend is toward a growing non-white, non-Anglo population. Estimates indicate that by the year 2000, 38% of the children under eighteen will be members of non-white, non-Anglo groups (Research and Policy Committee 1987). Population projections from the Children's Defense Fund (1989) indicate that by the year 2000, there will be "2.4 million more Hispanic children; 1.7 million more African-American children, 483,000 more children of other races; and 66,000 more white, non-Hispanic children. These population shifts can be accounted for by the increased immigration of non-Europeans and the greater number of women and higher fertility rates among women in non-white, non-Anglo groups (Hanson, Lynch & Wayman 1990).

Socioeconomic Status and Poverty

In 1989 more than 12.6 million children in the United States lived below the poverty line, as defined by family size and income (Children's Defense Fund 1991). In 1990, the following figures defined poverty: $8,420 or less for families of two, $10,500 or less for families of three; and $12,700 or less for families of four (Children's Defense Fund 1991). These figures are especially disturbing in that in 1989, 41% of children of poverty lived in families whose incomes were below *half* of the poverty line (Children's Defense Fund 1991).

"Every 35 seconds an infant is born into poverty" (Children's Defense Fund 1991). Over 20% of children were living in poverty by the end of the 1980s and the distribution of children who were impoverished differed by race and ethnicity with 15.4% of white children, 38.2% of Hispanic children, and 43.8% of African-American children classified as living in poverty (Center for the Study of Social Policy 1991). Further,

while poverty is widespread, the rate of increase differed across groups over the 1980s: 36% increase for white children, 31% increase for Hispanic children, and 16% increase for African-American children (Center for the Study of Social Policy 1991).

The impact of poverty on family life and individual outcomes alone can be devastating. The circumstance of poverty also may produce or interact with other risk factors and result in outcomes of concern such as poor health, high infant mortality, lack of child care, homelessness, poor educational outcomes, and crime (Hanson & Lynch 1992). Further, the impact of these circumstances may disproportionately influence particular cultural or ethnic groups. For instance, as reported by the Children's Defense Fund (Rosenbaum, Layton & Liu 1991):

"...in 1988 black infants were 3.88 times more likely to die from disorders relating to short gestation and low birthweight, 3.20 times more likely to die from homicide, 2.39 times more likely to die from septicemia, 2.09 times more likely to die from meningitis, and 2.64 times more likely to die from maternal complication of pregnancy."

Despite the fact that the United States is one of the richest nations in the world, the outcomes for many children in this country are diminished as a result of poverty and lack of adequate health care and support. Thus, the socioeconomic status of the family may play a great role in the family's ability to respond to a problem, seek treatment, and/or benefit from certain treatments and types of assistance.

Religion

Just as the population of the United States is diverse with respect to race, languages spoken, cultural background, and ethnicity, so too does the population differ widely with respect to religious beliefs. A recent newspaper article ("Religion Coats U.S." 1991) reported that 86.5% of people in the United States are Christians and they belong to a number of different Christian denominations (largest groups: 26% Roman Catholic, 19% Baptist, 8% Methodist, 5% Lutheran). Further, approximately 2% of the population is Jewish; Muslims represent 0.5% of the population. These data, from a study commissioned by the Graduate School of the City University of New York, indicated that more than nine out of every ten Americans in the United States identify with a religion and that a wide range of denominations are represented.

Religious and spiritual practices vary greatly across families. These beliefs and practices may strongly influence a family's approach to treatment, choice of treatment providers, and their receptivity to treatment and change. Service providers will benefit from becoming knowledgeable and respectful of practices that may be unfamiliar to them and learning to use families' spiritual beliefs as a support.

Age

Other population trends include changes in the age of childbearing. In recent years the age trends have extended in both directions (Hanson & Lynch 1992). Many women are deferring childbearing to later ages (Levitan, Belous & Gallo 1988). However, the most significant shift is in the number of teenage pregnancies. Figures indicated that 12.5% of births in the United States in 1988 were to women under age twenty (Rosenbaum, Layton & Liu 1991). Though the proportion of births in the United States to teenagers is falling as the number of young women in this age-group decreases, the number of births to teens (ages 15 to 19) increased between 1987 and 1988 with a birth rate of 43.7 per 1,000 for white women and 105.9 births per 1,000 for African-American women (Rosenbaum, Layton & Liu 1991). Further, childbearing in the teenage years is strongly associated with long-term poverty (Rosenbaum, Layton & Liu 1991).

Family Structure

The structure of American families is also undergoing change. Today families come in a variety of shapes and sizes, including two parent, single parent, teen parent, gay/lesbian, divorced, blended, extended, adoptive, and foster families. The proportion of nontraditional families is increasing (Masnick & Bane 1980). One of the greatest changes is the rise in the proportion of single parent households (Research and Policy Committee 1987) due primarily to divorce and nonmarital childbearing. Estimates indicate that 44 percent of children who were born between 1970 and 1984 will live in a single parent household before they are sixteen years old (Bumpass & Sweet 1989). In 1985, of these single women giving birth, over a third were teenagers (Levitan, Belous & Gallo 1988). According to the Children's Defense Fund (1991), "Every 31 seconds an infant is born to an unmarried mother. Every 64 seconds an infant is born to a teenage mother."

Summary

This discussion of demographics documents the diversity among families in the United States today. Families are no longer defined along the two-parent nuclear family structure that predominated for much of our history. These sociopolitical changes challenge the service delivery system to provide models and services which more closely match the needs of a wide variety of families. The need for adjustments in service delivery to meet the needs of families is underscored in services to families where drug use influences child rearing and family functioning.

Culture of Drug Use and Dependency

Many stereotypes exist with respect to the definition of the community or culture of drug use. The meaning of community, a description of drug use and dependency in this country, and the demographics of drug use in the United States are presented in this section.

Role and Definition of Community

Family, tribe, clan, culture, society, commune, community. These are just some of the terms used to explain or describe the ways in which human beings have traditionally banded together for a variety of purposes that may include shared bloodlines, ethnicity, experiences, protection from perceived enemies or environmental forces, political beliefs, or geographical proximity.

How a particular group defines their community is essential to their perception of their strengths and weaknesses as a group and as individuals and it is also important to their view of how they are perceived by the rest of the world. The story of Taya, a precocious preschooler of Japanese and French ancestry illustrates this point. Taya lived with her mother who was a visual artist. Taya's life was filled with artistic images, her personal art projects and the wide variety of painters, sculptors, poets, and actors who were her mother's friends. Discussions that occurred around her focused on the artistic process, on the financial difficulty of supporting oneself on money made through sales of art, and on the satisfaction or dissatisfaction that these artists felt when they viewed their finished projects. In the environment created by her mother, Taya's most salient culture was that of the artist; her community defined itself by its natural talent and its perceived creative vision. When outside her community, the perception of Taya focused more on her mixed racial and ethnic heritages. Once, when walking through a grocery store with a babysitter, Taya was asked, "What are you?" She looked perplexed for a moment, then replied, "I'm a little girl."

The woman who asked Taya this question was clearly uncomfortable with not being able to easily fit Taya into a designated racial category. But her question was not clear. "What race are you?" would have been a question that Taya could have answered, even though her community defined itself on artistry rather than race. Taya knew that she was of mixed racial heritage, she knew her gender, and she also knew that, in her world, what mattered most was finding the avenue of artistic self-expression that felt the most genuine. Taya was, in many senses, multicultural.

Many people, however, tend to view community as synonymous with culture, and culture as equivalent to race or ethnicity. In the United States, racial minority groups have frequently defined themselves by race because they had no choice. Native Americans, African-Americans, Asians, and Latinos are unable to hide their race in a predominantly white, Western culture, whereas those of European ancestry may choose whether and in what circumstances to embrace their broader ethnic origins. The proposed melting pot into which all races and ethnicities were once hoped to blend in harmony has never occurred and now is no longer universally viewed as desirable. So Americans are left to struggle with the varied definitions of who they are and why, how they are valued by others, and what forms of "difference" from the norm may be more or less acceptable than others. As in Taya's case, confusion over or negative connotations of race have often overlaid perceptions of the talents, abilities, beliefs, and values or unique characteristics that an individual or group might hold. In the case of those persons involved in the culture of drug use, this has often been the case.

The Culture of Drug Use and Dependency

In 1985 when the epidemic use of crack cocaine was first noted by public health authorities and law enforcement departments, television news programs frequently portrayed users of crack. Invariably the drug users shown in the media were African-American inner city dwellers. However, surveys conducted by the National Institute on Drug Abuse (1989) clearly indicated that crack was used by whites as well as blacks and by suburban as well as urban dwellers. In

fact, federal drug officials describe the prototypical cocaine user as a twenty-seven-year-old white male high school graduate living in a small city or suburb (NIDA 1989). Nonetheless, the war on drugs has focused most of its attention on poor, urban communities whose citizens are largely people of color.

The community of law enforcers, responding to racial and economically-based fears, focused their attention toward users and sellers of drugs who were easiest to incarcerate, often because of factors related to poverty. Inner city dwellers who are out of work spend more time on the street and may, therefore, be easier to arrest. Poor persons without resources for private attorneys or drug treatment programs may receive inadequate legal representation, be placed on long waiting lists for treatment services, and remain incarcerated for longer periods than suburban dwellers. What the legal system has often been slow to understand is that what users of drugs have in common, regardless of race, urban or suburban status, is the culture of drug use. These persons share an addiction to legal and illegal substances, a set of behaviors designed to hide the addiction during its initial stages, and patterns of behavior related to the manner in which drugs were acquired, shared, and used. For addicted persons, identification of community may take on a meaning that is separate from identification based on racial, ethnic, or economic factors. The community of addiction is most frequently defined by the common experience of drug-related patterns of behavior.

An important study that illustrates the degree to which racial attitudes in our culture affect perceptions of the chemically dependent, as well as racial differences in drugs of choice, was conducted by Chasnoff, Landress, and Barett (1990). Chasnoff and colleagues surveyed the rates of women who had toxicology screens positive for substance use upon delivery of their child in eleven hospitals in Pinellas County, Florida. He found that the rates at which black and white mothers had positive toxicology screens were not significantly different, though black women were ten times more likely than white women to be reported to social service agencies for child endangerment. Additionally, black women were reported to have toxicology screens that were positive for cocaine, whereas white women in this county preferred marijuana.

While the shared experience of using drugs may be the most salient description of community for addicted persons, the delineations of community and culture to which we more commonly refer nonetheless exist. There are often regional and sometimes even neighborhood differences in the terms used to describe drugs, in the drug of choice, in patterns of acquisition and use, and in knowledge about the possible consequences of abuse of a particular substance. For example, until 1991 Chicagoans addicted to cocaine preferred to use it in its powdered form, whereas New Yorkers for whom cocaine was the drug of choice preferred the alkaloid form, crack. Reports also indicate that ice (crystallized amphetamine) is more widely abused on the island of Hawaii than on the mainland. There may also be ethnic group trends in the belief structures about whether or not abusable substances are acceptable. For example, in some traditional Latino communities,

while addiction is generally regarded as negative, substance abuse by men may be tolerated if it does not interfere with their ability to provide financially for their families (Villarreal, McKinney & Quackenbush 1992).

The culture of drug use can provide an aura of social acceptability for the chemically dependent person. The addicted person surrounds himself or herself with other people who use drugs, who talk about them, who plan acquisition of them, and who discuss personal goals and obsessions related to drug use. In like company, addicted persons are less likely to view themselves as "different," or as having a problem. However, identification of oneself as a member of a community whose focus is addiction has considerable negative consequences, both for the addict and for persons outside of the drug culture. The drug culture, focused on supply and demand of illegal substances, places value on the economic structure of drug transactions but little on human life. Drug users and drug pushers frequently endanger family members, friends, strangers, and themselves in their pursuit of funds to purchase drugs, in their quest for drugs, and often, as a consequence of the ways in which drugs affect their judgment and behavior. Another significant consequence of the culture of drug use is the institutionalization of the exploitation of women. Women involved with drug-abusing men are frequently victims of domestic violence, but female addicts may exchange sex for drugs or become involved in prostitution or other illegal activity to support their drug habit.

Demographics of Drug Use in the United States

One need only walk through urban neighborhoods, listen behind suburban walls, or talk to hospital and social service staff to assess the range of human tragedies caused by the epidemic abuse of legal and illicit drugs. Since 1985 the media has bombarded us with stories about increasing drug use, most notably the use of crack cocaine. We have heard stories of women who abandon their children for drugs, Wall Street bankers who experienced personal ruin as a result of drug abuse, and children whose entry into the world of work was drug-related because drug sales were viewed as more financially rewarding than traditional, legal professions. We have also seen infants whose developmental status may be challenged by prenatal exposure to alcohol and other drugs. While the violent environment surrounding increased crack use has forced us to focus our national attention on substance abuse, a review of history in this country indicates that addiction to alcohol, tobacco, opiates, and other substances has been a long-standing problem.

Though prevalent in all communities, the significant impact of drug use and abuse is apparent within racial minority groups. For racial minority communities that may also be financially impoverished, substance abuse may serve as both a response to and a contributing factor for a variety of social stressors. Drugs of choice may also differ between ethnic and racial communities. African-American, Native American, and Latino communities have especially felt the brunt of the violence, financial devastation, and diminished resources contributed to by abuse of alcohol and other drugs. Estimates of rates of drug use by ethnicity indicate that, among teens enrolled in school, Native Americans have the highest prevalence rates for use of cigarettes, alcohol, and many illicit drugs. Asian-American students have the lowest rates of drug usage. With the exception of high prevalence rates for marijuana use, African-American students also had low rates of general drug use (National Institute on Drug Abuse 1991). (Because of the disproportionally high rates of African-American and Latino students who drop out of high school, these numbers may have been drawn from a skewed population of students.) Chasnoff's Florida study (1990) indicated a drug preference for marijuana among white women whose toxicology screens were positive whereas black women in this sampled population more often used cocaine.

Differences within drug-using communities of the drug of choice occur for many reasons. Persons in some communities may view drugs as recreational but nevertheless develop addictive patterns; others may use drugs for escape. Drug use may be considered acceptable in some communities if the substances are legal, whereas other communities prohibit use of any substances. And in yet other communities, substance use and abuse may be overlooked if the impact of the chemical dependency can be masked by the users or the evidence avoided by family and friends.

Presently, according to the expanded National Household Survey on Drug Abuse (National Institute on Drug Abuse 1991), estimates indicate an encouraging downward trend exists in drug use among adolescents and younger children. Older Americans who began drug use in the late 1970s and early 1980s present a more complex picture because they may decrease use of one drug and select another for continued use. The Drug Abuse Warning Network (DAWN) which provides estimates of drug-related hospital room visits, has reported increases of 10% and 13% in health emergencies related to abuse of heroin and cocaine, respectively. Many of these emergency room admissions involve women, some of whom deliver their infants having used cocaine to facilitate the birth. The recent increase in hospital visits was considered evidence of increasing medical complications and consequences among a stable population of chronic drug users (*Health and Human Services News* 1992).

Though legal and illegal drugs are noted to have potentially devastating effects on all users, recent concern has attended to the abuse of alcohol and other drugs by pregnant women and the effect of prenatal exposure to a number of abusable substances on the developing fetus. Data on the use of alcohol and illicit drugs by women are presented in Table 1.

The impetus for this book reflects the concern that, as economic and social conditions worsen, women are abusing drugs at alarming rates. While society has often overlooked or celebrated male abuse of drugs such as alcohol, the role of women as society's caretakers has created a much harsher, less understanding, and more punitive view of addictions among women.

When women of childbearing age abuse drugs, they run the risk of exposing their child prenatally to a range of medical, developmental, and social difficulties. Medical literature has yielded a significant amount of research on the possible effects of prenatal and perinatal

Table 1. Use of Alcohol and Illicit Drugs by Women in Different Age and Racial Groups.

Alcohol Use (Percent Used in the Past Month: Observed Estimate)			
Women By Age	**Whites**	**Blacks**	**Hispanics**
12-17	32.8	18.4	18.6
18-25	70.5	49.2	41.6
26-34	64.2	56.2	48.2

Illicit Drug Use (Percent Used in the Past Month: Observed Estimate)			
12-17	15.0	8.0	11.1
18-25	22.2	21.1	15.4
26-34	16.3	18.2	6.3

Taken from the National Institute on Drug Abuse (NIDA) *National Household Survey on Drug Abuse*, 1989.

Table 2. Recent Estimates of Drug-Exposed Children.

- 2,600,000 to Alcohol
- 1,300,000 to Cigarettes
- 611,200 to Marijuana
- 158,400 to Stimulants
- 92,400 to Hallucinogens
- 38,300 to Sedatives

Taken, with permission, from Gomby D, Shiono P. Drug-Exposed Infants. *Future of Children* 1991; 1 (Spring): 17-25 (Center for the Future of Children — The David and Lucille Packard Foundation, Palo Alto, CA).

drug use and abuse. Though the maternal abuse of many drugs does not necessarily lead to specific fetal disruption syndromes, the new field of addiction research indicates that prenatal exposure to a number of substances may place the developing child at a substantially increased risk for medical, behavioral, developmental, and social/emotional abnormalities. The Packard Foundation's Center for the Future of Children provides annual estimates of children who are exposed to legal and illegal drugs (see Table 2).

Characteristics of Substance-Using Women That May Influence Parenting

Drug use crosses all socioeconomic lines. However, women of poverty, particularly women of color, are more likely to be tested for drugs, reported to authorities, and have their children removed from their care than are middle-income mothers who use private health care. While it is important to see each recovering woman as an individual, it is equally important that service providers understand the unique hurdles recovering women may face.

A summary of research on substance-using mothers whose children are in the child protective service system reveals a picture of a single mother with minimal financial resources who has a history of physical abuse and/or sexual exploitation (Poulsen 1992). She may have a partner who is a drug user or who offers little financial or emotional support.

Many of these women experienced "out-of-home" placement as children or grew up in substance-abusing dysfunctional families, leaving a void of "good parenting" memories. Social isolation and loneliness result when a woman chooses to leave her "drug culture" community. Without intervention services, young recovering mothers don't have access to the "community of moms" that have helped young women learn how to parent for generations.

There are indications that women may abuse drugs for reasons that differ from those of men. The following list details a number of factors that may place women at particular risk for the abuse of alcohol and other drugs.

- Reports indicate that women of childbearing age and their children are more likely than men to be impoverished.

- Poor women are more likely to be undereducated and therefore to have fewer job options, resources, and opportunities.

- Women from all socioeconomic classes frequently have fewer, or less appropriate, job opportunities than men.

- Poor women often have limited access to health care, drug treatment programs, day care facilities, and other essential services.

- Women experience clinical levels of depression and low self-esteem more often than men.

- A significant number of women who abuse drugs were sexually, physically, or emotionally abused as children.

- As is the case with men, many women who later become chemically dependent had a parent who used drugs as a coping strategy. (Kronstadt 1989; Villarreal, McKinney & Quackenbush 1992).

Other data indicate that, once addicted, drug dependent/abusing women are more likely than men to:

- Have difficulty gaining access and entry to appropriate treatment services. Despite the increasing evidence that women are becoming addicted to drugs in record numbers, particularly since the introduction of crack, many programs do not provide treatment services for women. Some of the programs that treat women may not accept pregnant women, or women with children, for services.

- Be solitary, secretive drinkers or users. At home alone with their children or fearful of being out on the streets, these women often abuse substances in the privacy of their own home. Consequently, available statistics about drug use among women are thought to be vastly underreported.

- Be attracted to drugs that are swallowed (alcohol, pills) and smoked (marijuana, crack) rather than those that are injected. Though we have evidence that many women use drugs by injection, most women choose other methods of getting drugs into their bodies.

- Trade sex for drugs. Women who are chemically dependent and in need of funds for drugs may set up situations where they swap sex for drugs. In modern jargon, the sex for drug swap is called a toss-up. This behavior has become more common since the beginning of the crack epidemic. Engaging in toss-ups, which usually includes serial sexual partners, puts these women at increased risk for AIDS and disabling HIV disease.

- Metabolize alcohol differently than men because of the higher fat content in their bodies.

- Neglect or abuse their children. Those women who were themselves abused as children have not had appropriate models of parenting. Additionally, the nature of drug dependence often makes locating drugs temporarily more important than caring for their children. (Kronstadt 1989; Villarreal, McKinney & Quackenbush 1992).

The absence of healthy parent-child experiences has left many women naive about child development, behavior, intentions, and motivations. Interpretation of infant/child behavior often is filtered through the eyes of a mother who is dealing with issues of guilt, depression, fear, and the agitation of drug withdrawal. Many young mothers may need help in facilitating their children's development, as well as assistance in providing a protective environment that will enable the at-risk infant to organize his or her behavior and initiate interactions with persons and objects.

Anticipating child stress, diverting nonadaptive behavior, modeling language and play, encouraging the expression of emotion and decision making, and providing meaningful family rituals are critical dimensions of parenting programs designed for recovering mothers.

Central to parenting programs for women in recovery is the importance of building on the parental *strengths* of each woman. Videotapes that capture "good" parenting skills not only contribute to parental esteem, but provide an effective arena for the facilitation of positive parenting behavior for her peers.

Family Foster Care

Many children prenatally exposed to drugs are placed in the family foster care system because their mothers, fathers, and other relatives are not able to assume responsibility for their care. Over 360,000 children are currently in foster care placements, which represents a 33% increase since 1985 (Child Welfare League of America 1991). Over 42% of the children are under six years old. It has been reported that up to 80% of children referred to protective services are for drug-related reasons (Digre 1992). Although the exact number of children who have been prenatally exposed to drugs is unknown, the significant increase in foster placements is considered to be related to the increased use of substances during pregnancy (Klerman 1991). In addition, it has also been documented that a disproportionate number of children are from minority families in the foster care system (Child Welfare League of America 1991). Children from minority families and infants who have been prenatally exposed to drugs tend to be placed in foster care earlier, stay longer, and have more changes in placement.

Increased caseloads, increased numbers of high-need infants and young children, and the disproportionate number of minority children, combined with a significant decrease in the availability of foster families and lack of community support and services, has led to a foster care crisis.

Obstacles to Quality Foster Care

There is a scarcity of foster families available to meet (1) the social-emotional needs of the growing numbers of infants and young children requiring out-of-home placement; (2) the special needs of those infants who are medically fragile or at risk for behavioral, learning, or developmental problems; (3) the birth family relationship needs of children in out-of-home placement; and (4) the cultural and ethnic identity needs of children placed in their care. This is evidenced by several red-flag situations:

- **Infants remain in hospitals as boarder babies or in emergency shelters for extended periods of time**. Many communities are experiencing a "boarder baby" crisis. Infants are forced to live in hospitals beyond medical necessity because parents are not able to assume responsibility for their care, and kinship and foster family placements are unavailable. Boarder babies appear to be the victims of family poverty and homelessness. Most mothers are single parents from multiproblem families who lack permanent housing or extended family supports. A high percentage of boarder babies are born at-risk to substance-addicted women who received only minimal prenatal care (Huling & Stewart 1988).

  Because family preservation services and alternative out-of-home placements are lacking, babies are being hospital-raised in the regular nursery, neonatal intensive care units, or special care nurseries for extended periods of time. These babies have continuous contact with medical personnel, child development staff, and supervised community volunteers. However, the absence of the priceless family unit places these babies at enormous risk for emotional and so-

cial developmental vulnerabilities.

- **Infants are being raised in congregate care settings**. For the last thirty years, there has been a growing appreciation of the dangers that congregate care may present to the healthy development of the individual child. A child's unique sensitivities, strengths, and vulnerabilities may be overlooked in a group setting. Compliance to group norms may be deemed more important than the expression of individual needs (Provence 1989).

  In spite of the research, the need for out-of-home placement has led to a resurgence of small group homes and larger congregate care facilities serving six to fifty infants and children. Licensing requirements focus on the physical aspects of the environment, but currently there are no stated standards of quality developmental care to infants and young children.

  On paper, the assignment of a primary caregiver to each child and the clustering of small groups of children appears child-focused, but the reality of poor pay for care providers leads to high caregiver turnover, leaving the child with unstable, unfulfilling attachments to mothering figures and gaping holes in his or her emotional and social development.

- **Infants and young children are being placed with foster families in group homes whose licenses are restricted to given ages.** Licensing regulations and/or foster care placement practices have resulted in a proliferation of "baby-moms" and infant-toddler group homes that restrict care to children of designated age-groups. The rationale has been based on the notion that the care provider is specially trained to meet certain medical or developmental needs and that once stabilized the child will be transferred to a more appropriate placement. This allows needier infants and toddlers to be placed in these "highly prized" settings.

From a medical point of view, the situation may make sense. However, from a child development perspective, the damage of disrupted placement is a traumatic experience for a young child and should be avoided at all costs. The importance of stable primary attachments over time cannot be overstated. Infants, toddlers, and young children should have *one* out-of-home placement until reunification or relinquishment takes place. Children should never be re-placed in order to "free up a slot."

- **At-risk infants are being placed with foster families and extended family members who are overwhelmed by their special behavioral needs**. In most states, foster families receive extra training and financial support to care for medically fragile or disabled infants and children. However, these resources are not available for families caring for high-need infants and children with neurodevelopmental vulnerabilities caused by substance exposure, low birth weight, prematurity or other perinatal factors. Neither do parents or extended family members receive help in nurturing children at behavioral risk due to the traumatizing effects of separation and loss. As a consequence, the child's special

emotional and behavioral needs go unmet or they are returned to the system for re-placement. Re-placement is always traumatizing to the child, and yet estimates show that one-third to one-fourth of children in foster care have experienced re-placement (U.S. House of Representatives 1989).

- **Infants and young children are experiencing the added trauma of being separated from siblings**. Too often siblings are separated by the child protective service system. Siblings should be separated *only* when such separation is in the best interests of the child. The loss of parents is always a devastating event. When a child is also separated from siblings, the child is left with no anchors or connections to his or her past. Often, an older sibling has assumed the primary caregiver role for the younger children in a substance-abusing family and has developed a primary bond to the younger child. Every effort should be made to keep siblings together and to help the older sibling to recapture a life with continued attachment, but with less responsibility for the younger child(ren).

When maintaining sibling togetherness is not possible, every effort should be made to provide ongoing and frequent interaction among siblings. Formalized plans for sibling contact should be made for all children in the child welfare system.

- **Infants and young children are experiencing increased trauma of parental separation by out-of-home placement that is geographically distant and/or inaccessible to their birth families**. Parental visitations are extremely critical in maintaining parent-child relationships when they are separated. From a child development perspective, optimal visitation is a minimum of three times a week at two hours per visit. Daily visits are recommended unless medically contraindicated for the child (National Council of Juvenile and Family Court Judges 1991).

Fear, anger, and disgust may be experienced by the foster parents and advertently or inadvertently communicated to the child. Foster parents need support to resolve their own feelings and effective ways to discuss birth family issues with their foster children. Neutral locations need to be found when it is inappropriate for the foster family to have birth parents come to their home.

One of the most challenging tasks of the child welfare system is to help foster parents facilitate the relationship between a child and a substance-abusing family. Foster parents need information on ways to encourage the birth family-child relationship via the mail, tape recordings, phone calls, and photographs.

- **Children's self-esteem and ethnic/cultural identity are being compromised by placement in foster families with different cultural backgrounds**. The sense of belonging that comes with cultural, religious, and linguistic familiarity is essential to a child's feelings of worth. The social and emotional trauma of family loss when a child is in out-of-home placement is compounded when the child is placed in a home that is outside his or her racial, cultural, religious, or linguistic heritage.

Extra consideration needs to be given when children are placed in culturally different homes. Children need opportunities to know about their heritage and to value its heroes. Pictures, films, television programs, books, music, rituals, and rites need to be shared and discussed. Experiences with children and adults of similar heritage must be provided. Special training may be needed for caregivers whose cultural heritage may be different from the children in their care. Such training would be aimed at facilitating the caregivers' knowledge, understanding, and awareness of cultural beliefs and practices that may differ from their own.

The National Commission on Family Foster Care (1991) emphasizes that with adequate support from communities, and with state and federal support for foster home recruitment and retention, homes can be found to avoid placement across heritage lines. Communities need to set up a proactive recruitment plan for minority and non-English speaking foster families. Family foster care may be a foreign idea to recent immigrants who often have the expectation that godparents, community members, or relatives will be responsible for children whose parents cannot care for them. Non-English speaking foster parents need access to health, social service, mental health, and education professionals who speak their language and understand their culture.

Essentials for Quality Foster Care

To rectify these abuses within the welfare system, the *1991 National Commission on Family Foster Care* has identified the following child welfare practices as essential for the provision of quality foster care for infants and young children.

- Children should remain with their birth family whenever possible.

- Children should have *one* family foster care placement until reunification or relinquishment takes place.

- Children should be placed with their siblings.

- Children should be placed in geographical proximity to their birth family and in family foster care that is willing to promote birth family relationships.

- Children should be placed in family foster care that can provide for their special emotional, behavioral, developmental, and medical needs.

- Children should be placed in family foster care that is similar in ethnic and cultural identity.

- Children should be provided emotional support, counseling, and/or psychotherapy for unresolved separation, loss, attachment, abuse, and neglect.

Obviously the Commission's objectives for quality out-of-home care *cannot* be met by "an empty bed availability" criterion for child placement. Rather, thoughtful decision about the match between the child and the foster family must reflect careful assessment and planning for the child and foster family needs. Hasty decisions and lack of support lead to instability and the trauma of multiple placements which are *always* damaging to a child's emotional, social, and mental health.

Foster Family Support

All foster families must be provided with the training and support needed to meet the special developmental needs of infants and children placed in their care who have been affected by a negative birth and/or social history. Foster parents need to know how to provide an environment that will help a hypersensitive, hyperreactive child learn to master his or her vulnerabilities and to adapt to the challenges that confront every child in the process of growing up. In addition, foster parents need information and support to deal with a child's feelings and expression of anger, sadness, and fear that result from the separation from parents and siblings.

Foster parents may return children to the system for re-placement because they cannot deal with a child's acting-out behavior. Negative stereotypes about the potential of children prenatally exposed to drugs too often has resulted in the belief that these children cannot learn to deal adaptively with the world. Children born to drug-addicted women may be too quickly "written off" by care providers and professionals. Foster parents need resources to health, mental health, and developmental services and the instrumental supports of transportation, child care, and respite care that will enable them to provide a nurturing environment for their children and encourage them to keep children with challenging behaviors.

Case Management Issues

Health and allied health professionals

may play an important role in the case management of children in out-of-home placement. Careful health, developmental, behavior, and mental health assessments provide valuable information that will help child protective service professionals make appropriate placement decisions.

The child and foster family will benefit if the health and developmental follow-up can be continued by the same providers. This continuity of care gives a needed historical perspective in the development and modification of service delivery plans. Often a child loses his history in the mire of protective service bureaucracy. Countless children do not have records of their health, developmental, or childhood history. Significant health information that may influence future medical follow-up may be lost. Of equal importance is that a person without memory of significant childhood milestones or rituals loses a piece of self.

Many states have developed *medical, developmental, and/or educational passports* to ensure good record-keeping and the continuity of care for children in foster placements. *Passports* may include: names and addresses of the child's pediatrician, dentist, and school personnel; birth, health, and developmental history; records of immunizations, medications, medical, and mental health problems; developmental assessments; early intervention services; grade level performance; and special education services. Passports should be reviewed and updated regularly and are kept by the foster parent(s).

In addition to the *passports* that provide case management records, every child in foster care should have a *transi-*

tion plan that includes preparing the child for a new home, preplacement contact(s) between child and receiving parents whenever possible, opportunity for the child to say goodbyes, and the opportunity for the child to express feelings of separation and loss. For infants and young children, transition plans should include favorite foods and toys and a record of bathing, sleeping, eating, and dressing rituals that can provide some familiarity and security to the child even though the caregiver is new.

Recommendations for Service Provision

The Role of Extended Family and Kinship Networks in Intervention

While chemical dependency may begin as a result of an individual person's behavior, ultimately it is a family disease. Children born to addicted mothers may have significant developmental disabilities or challenges that require medical, developmental, or educational intervention (Coles et al 1991; Zuckerman et al 1989). Children and spouses/partners of addicted persons may experience abuse and neglect; they may become homeless as a result of drug-related behaviors (Farrow 1991). Family members may "enable" the chemically dependent person by supporting continued use of the substance in misguided attempts to keep their loved one happy or to protect themselves from the behaviors that might ensue if the drug is not available to their relative (Villarreal, McKinney & Quackenbush 1992).

Though the print and television media have, in the past, most often presented information about the challenge that chemical dependency presents for poor persons or people of color, we now know that addiction does not discriminate by race or socioeconomic status. However, racial and economic factors may influence access to resources or the manner in which the addicted person is perceived by the larger community. For example, families with more money may have increased access to treatment resources. This is particularly true as increased numbers of working-class Americans are employed in positions that do not provide health benefits. The middle- and upper-middle classes may have private insurance that can pay the cost of recovery programs whereas poor people may have to go to public treatment centers with longer waiting lists. State agencies tend to be less punitive and intrusive with middle-class families and with white families, reporting them less frequently to monitoring agencies. Finally, those with financial resources may be better able to hide indications of their drug abuse; if they can afford childcare services, for example, forays for drugs can occur without the physical abandonment of their children.

Though there may be differences in drug-related behaviors or community responses as a result of economic and racial status, there are nonetheless behaviors that are typical within the culture of drug-involved families. These families tend to become increasingly socially isolated as more and more emphasis is placed on relationships within the culture of drug users, addictive disease may lead to diminished impulse control and violence, and the drug abuser may develop serious physical or mental health problems. Relatives may develop the enabling behaviors mentioned earlier that facilitate drug use and children may

be abused or neglected.

It is not surprising, then, that drug-involved families are often quite suspicious of service providers. Their suspicions and fears are, of course, not unfounded. A chemically dependent pregnant woman may know that a positive toxicology screen at delivery may increase her risk of losing her child to a social service system. Children, even those who have been abused, may be very attached to their parent and fear placement in a foster home. For many within this family system, the known evil presented by substance abuse may at times appear preferable to unknown factors.

To increase the success of intervention strategies, information about the confluence of the definitions of community and culture surrounding drug use combined with the knowledge of racial, ethnic, regional, and familial beliefs about addiction is important for those who provide service to drug-involved or recovering families or persons. By attending to these factors the provider increases his or her ability to ask difficult questions in a sensitive manner, to ask questions appropriate to a particular group (of users of a specific substance or different racial or ethnic communities, for example), and to gain the trust of the clients they serve.

Increasingly, social service systems that work with drug-involved families have learned that family-centered services increase the likelihood for successful treatment outcome. Service providers must understand that the culture of drug use has created specific issues not only for the addicted person but for the children who fear that they will not be cared for, the parent who fears drug-related gang violence, the elderly persons concerned that their drug-involved child will approach them with violence, or the infant whose developmental outcome has been made uncertain by prenatal drug exposure. Understanding these factors increases the likelihood of creating a treatment environment where the goal is the empowerment of families rather than cessation of drug use alone. Depending upon the needs of a particular family, such empowerment may include not only emotional support and drug treatment, but employment training, remedial education, housing, family violence and abuse prevention, parenting skills, social/family support services, prenatal and postpartum care, child care, developmental support services for children, income assistance, legal aid, transportation services, and community, family, and media-based prevention strategies.

Of course, it is also vitally important for the service provider to maintain, as much as is possible, a flexible viewpoint. Each client (individual or family) regardless of their defined culture, is a unique entity rather than a stereotype of a particular group norm. In working with families affected by drug use, individual assessment guided by sensitivity to the varying definitions of community and culture is essential.

Family and Individual Assessment and Treatment Issues

Successful assessment of drug-involved families is a delicate task that requires attention to the needs of that particular family unit and may require coordination of a number of different service systems. Knowledge about the needs of various family members, fam-

ily specific culture, racial/ethnic factors, and economic status and available support can give the intervening clinician useful information for the provision of appropriate treatment.

Strategies used for family intervention may occur in a number of settings, both traditional and nontraditional. Assessment and treatment may occur in hospitals, health clinics, community centers, churches, family homes, or on street corners. The settings must be those in which the families are the most comfortable or those that are located in places that increase the likelihood that scheduled appointments will be kept. For persons who are still actively using drugs, keeping clinic appointments may be a difficult task. For them, a street-based intervention that targets the drug-using community of which they are a part or a community center within their neighborhood is more likely to be a successful site for service provision.

When working with drug-involved families several general strategies are important. These strategies are discussed below.

An interdisciplinary team approach. Because of the complex needs of drug-involved families, use of an interdisciplinary team is an essential strategy. No single provider can meet the myriad needs presented by chemically dependent families, though coordination of services through a central person, trusted by the family, can facilitate treatment success. Dependent on the needs of the family, the interdisciplinary team may consist of physicians, hospital, school, or community health nurses, drug and alcohol counselors, HIV counselors, psychologists/psychiatrists, nutritionists, developmental specialists, and religious leaders. The lack of trust that families may have in treatment systems is also lessened by the team approach; it may take several visits and several providers to gain a family's trust and to gather the information needed to assist the family.

A nonjudgmental approach. The service provider has the delicate position of being an ally for the chemically dependent person while setting limits that enhance chances for therapeutic success. Addicted persons frequently have poor self-esteem; being confronted by a service provider who reinforces that perception may cause the patient to avoid settings that could provide essential important services. For example, in states where women who expose their children to drugs prenatally can be arrested and incarcerated for child endangerment, rates of utilization of prenatal heath services are often low. While child health is compromised by exposure to drugs, lack of prenatal care can worsen the developmental outlook for that child and can also exacerbate poor maternal health factors.

A culturally sensitive approach to treatment. As discussed earlier, culture and community may be defined in many ways. However, a chemically dependent person has a connection with the culture of drug addiction as well as self-identification that may be based on gender, sexual orientation, race or ethnicity, or religion. For example, women whose experience of addiction has included being the victim of violence from men may require a treatment model focused on empowerment, rather than the more male-oriented, twelve step recovery model that stresses giving up personal power. Similarly, persons of a particular racial ancestry, religious affiliation, or sexual orientation may feel more emotionally prepared for recovery within a treatment model that stresses their most highly valued cultural beliefs and traditions. And finally, persons for whom extended family networks are an important source of support may require a familial model of assessment, feedback, or counseling that acknowledges and utilizes information from a wide variety of sources.

Additionally, when working with persons whose ethnic or racial identity differs from that of the treatment provider, the provider must recognize that the theoretical perspectives from which they work may be of limited use with other cultures. For example, Erickson's stage-related psychosocial theory of development is most appropriate when applied to children raised in nuclear families in industrialized countries. It may be less appropriate for children from extended family networks in Third World countries (Gibbs & Huang 1989).

Each individual and family has strengths as well as weaknesses. It is essential to use a model of assessment or treatment that focuses on strengths rather than on pathology alone. For someone who has used drugs daily for ten years, one day of sobriety is worthy of recognition and praise. For a parent whose drug abuse has caused them to neglect their children, arrival at a treatment site with clean or nicely dressed children is significant and noteworthy. Helping those in treatment recognize what is good about themselves in spite of the negative behaviors in which they may have engaged is an important step in helping them build feelings of self-worth that may have been forgotten. Praise and support for small steps towards health can provide the encouragement that a chemically dependent person or a drug-affected family needs for successful recovery.

Guidelines for Assessing Social and Cultural Factors Affecting Health

Cultural factors that affect health cover a number of areas important to assessment of individuals and families who seek or are referred to treatment. The professional working with families will want to be familiar with individual, familial, racial/ethnic, and other community standards and beliefs about health. This information can then be utilized to enhance the therapeutic relationship and in creation of the most appropriate treatment plan (Cross et al 1989; Randall-David 1989). Such factors may include:

How a Community Defines Health

- What are the general definitions that persons within a community have of the concepts of good health, illness, diagnosis and treatment of disease?
- What beliefs do individuals or communities have concerning the purpose and function of organ systems in the body?
- How does the concept of good health fit into the hierarchy of values espoused by a community?
- What attitudes do persons or communities have towards preventive health and mental health services?
- What are family-specific or community attitudes towards hygiene?

Beliefs About Death and Dying

- What are individual, family, and community beliefs and rituals about death and dying?

- Is grieving an overt or covert expression of loss?
- Is grieving part of the community ritual involving death?

Attitudes About Sexuality, Pregnancy, and Childbirth

- How is knowledge about sexuality shared within families and the community?
- What are the social and cultural beliefs about menstruation?
- What are the typical ages at which men and women first engage in sexual activity?
- What is the informational base about sexually transmitted diseases?
- How do children learn about sex?
- How does a woman determine if she is pregnant?
- Are there beliefs about the forces that influence pregnancy outcome?
- Does the community have special rituals or practices concerning pregnancy and childbirth?
- Who is present during childbirth? What are the roles of those present in the birthing process?

Understanding the Structure of a Community

- Who are the persons generally perceived as community leaders?
- How is information transmitted within a particular community?
- To whom should information or requests be addressed?

Understanding the Ways in Which Beliefs May Influence Service Delivery

- What views are held about health, illness, medical care, sexual behavior, and family responsibility?

- Are those beliefs transmitted to the families with whom the provider works?

- Are the beliefs of the provider similar or dissimilar to those of the individuals within communities in which they work?

- Do those differences create difficulties for the provider or the client in the assessment and treatment process?

Assessing Perinatal Substance Abuse in Women

In response to the increasing numbers of pregnant women with addictive disorders, medical and social service agencies have found it necessary to set policies about the ways in which perinatal substance abuse will be treated within the particular service system. In the past several years, large inner city hospitals and social service agencies have developed protocols designed to identify and treat pregnant substance-abusing women. The protocol guidelines summarized here are from Boston City Hospital, Martin Luther King/Drew Hospital in Los Angeles, Harlem Hospital in New York, and San Francisco General Hospital. All focus on appropriate identification and treatment within a system of support. Women are not automatically referred to child protective service departments if they have positive toxicology screens. Rather, they are assessed for the following factors:

- Length of substance abuse history

- Previous treatment experience

- Length of periods of sobriety

- Reasons for relapse

- Emotional support system

- Mental health history

- Physical health status

- Prenatal care history

- Economic status

- Access to community resources

Following assessment of these factors a treatment plan can be devised that determines what specific services are needed, who should provide them, what family or extended family members are essential to the treatment process, and whether children can remain with a parent. For example, a pregnant substance-abusing woman who is motivated for recovery, has previously experienced periods of sobriety, and has an intact support system may be considered an excellent candidate for drug treatment and for maintaining parental status. A woman who has a significant psychiatric history as well as an addiction, who has severely neglected other children, and for whom social supports are less available may require a referral to a facility that specializes in the treatment of dually diagnosed persons; her children may need to live with relatives or be temporarily placed in foster care until her recovery process has begun.

General Guidelines for Working with Families from Diverse Backgrounds

It is apparent that the population distribution in the United States is changing and that the population growth is greatest for non-white, non-Anglo European groups. At the same time the majority of service providers and graduates from professional schools in the helping sciences are still representative of Anglo-European and middle-class backgrounds. Thus, in order to avoid potential difficulties from cultural mismatches between families and service providers, programs engaged in personnel preparation must work to recruit and retain students from groups previously underrepresented in the helping professions. Further, all service providers must become increasingly aware of, sensitive to, and knowledgeable about working with families from cultures which may differ from their own (Lynch & Hanson 1992; Wayman, Lynch & Hanson 1990).

Working with families whose behavior patterns, traditions, and/or cultural backgrounds may differ radically from one's own may challenge interventionists to become more "culturally competent." Lynch (1992) suggests three areas that must be addressed in developing cultural competence: (1) self-awareness of one's own cultural heritage; (2) gathering specific knowledge and understanding related to understanding specific cultural practices; and (3) communication issues. Each is briefly described.

Everyone belongs to a culture. However, individuals vary widely with respect to their awareness of how these cultural values and beliefs may influence their day-to-day behavior, attitudes, and interactions. Thus, beginning with an awareness of one's own cultural heritage and its influence is the first step in becoming able to negotiate competently across cultures (Chan 1990; Lynch 1992). This can be accomplished through discovering one's own roots and becoming aware of the values, beliefs, and behaviors that are associated with one's particular background. For instance, privacy, individualism, and a futuristic perspective are typically associated with individuals in the United States who are of Anglo-European heritage.

A second strategy in developing cultural competence is learning more about specific cultures in one's community. Ways to gather this information include reading and studying the culture, talking to persons from that cultural group and participating with their families when possible in daily and special events, and learning the language of the culture. While this level of learning typically gives one a new perspective on the culture, it does not typically allow entrance or admission into that cultural community and expertise on the cultural practices. It is often recommended that an interventionist work with a mediator who is a member of the community and who can serve as a "cultural guide" to working closely with families from that community. Community members who function as guides or liaisons are invaluable in most treatment situations as they help both the helping professional and the family understand one another's perspective on the problem or the issue at hand, the potential treatments, the acceptability of different treatment protocols, and the outcomes of these treatment procedures.

A third and related issue in developing cultural competence involves issues of communication. Even though an interventionist may speak the language of the person within the other culture, unless the interventionist is a member of that community or has had a great deal of experience in that cultural community, the potential exists for communication difficulties. Cultures differ widely in their means of sending messages both verbally and nonverbally. What in one culture may be a positive word or sign may be highly offensive in another. Those who have traveled to other countries undoubtedly have experienced these communication difficulties. The same issues may apply as interventionists cross the cultures of the families with whom they work. A related communication issue is the use of interpreters or translators to communicate more effectively with families. This type of communication is much more complex than finding someone to translate word for word. A sense of the context, a knowledge of the culture, and nonverbal and verbal communication skills are all crucial to effective communication. Chan (presented in Lynch 1992) presents useful suggestions for working with interpreters and translators. These suggestions define the characteristics of effective interpreters, the cautions and concerns associated with using family members in this capacity, the cautions and concerns in using nonfamily members, the stress associated with being an interpreter, the preparation needed for being an interpreter, and guides for interventionists in working with interpreters.

Knowledge of one's own cultural heritage and the beliefs, values, and practices of other cultures with whom one works is essential. However, there is no substitute for a genuine appreciation of and sensitivity to individual differences, an understanding of and eagerness to learn new information and patterns, and respect and openness for working with individuals whose goals and perspectives may differ from yours.

SUMMARY

We all bring to our work the richness of our individual heritages. Who we are as people, as a result of racial, ethnic, religious, gender, and other important identifications, informs our world views and our ways of relating interpersonally to one another and to those we serve. In our professional roles, we are bound by our commitment to competent and compassionate treatment and our commitment to respect and understand the ways in which client culture, broadly defined, might have an impact on client health status, health beliefs and behaviors, and compliance with treatment protocols.

To address the comprehensive needs of individuals and families challenged by trying to avoid or overcome chemical dependency, a comprehensive approach is needed. Such an approach mandates, particularly in the fiscal climate of today, coordinated interdisciplinary community-based services. As we begin to tackle the difficulties in assisting mothers to overcome chemical dependency and support children who have been the victims of this abuse to overcome their own risks, the focus must be on the child and family as they are nested within their community. It brings to mind the African proverb, "It takes a whole village to raise a child." Indeed, the issues of chemical dependency are so pervasive and overwhelming that it will take the cooperation and support of the "whole village" to truly turn the tide of potential losses.

REFERENCES

Blackwell JE. *The Black Community: Diversity and Unity*. New York: Dodd, Mead, 1975.

Bumpass LL, Sweet JA. Children's experience in single-parent families: Implications of cohabitation and marital transitions. *Family Planning Perspectives* 1989; 21 (Nov/

Dec): 256-60.

Center for the Study of Social Policy. *Kids Count Data Book: State Profiles of Child Well-Being.* Washington, D.C.: Center for the Study of Social Policy, 1991.

Chan SQ. Early intervention with culturally diverse families of infants and toddlers with disabilities. *Infants and Young Children* 1990; 3(2): 78-87.

Chasnoff IJ, Landress H, Barett M. The prevalence of illicit-drug or alcohol use during pregnancy and discrepancies in mandatory reporting in Pinellas County, Florida. *New England Journal of Medicine* 1990; 332: 1202-6.

Child Welfare League of America (CWLA). *Initiative to promote culturally responsive child welfare practice: Recommendations from a colloquium.* Washington, D.C.: Child Welfare League of America, 1989.

Child Welfare League of America. *A Blueprint for Fostering Infants, Children and Youths in the 1990s.* Washington, D.C.: CWLA, 1991.

Children's Defense Fund. *A Vision for America's Future.* Washington, D.C.: Children's Defense Fund, 1989.

Children's Defense Fund. *The State of America's Children 1991.* Washington, D.C.: Children's Defense Fund, 1991.

Coles CD, Brown RT, Smith IE, Platman KA, Erickson S, Falek A. Effects of prenatal alcohol exposure at school age: Physical and cognitive development. *Neurotoxicology and Teratology* 1991; 13(4): 357-66.

Cross T, Bazron B, Dennis K, Issacs M. *Towards a Culturally Competent System of Care.* Rockville, MD: National Institute of Mental Health, Child and Adolescent Service System Program, 1989.

Digre P. Testimony before the U.S. Senate Finance Committee, 1992.

Farrow JA. Homeless pregnant and parenting adolescents. *Maternal and Child Health Technical Information Bulletin* 1991, pp 3-8.

Gibbs JT, Huang LN. A conceptual framework for assessing and treating minority youth. *Children of Color: Psychological Interventions with Minority Youth.* San Fran-

cisco: Jossey-Bass, 1989.

Gomby D, Shiono P. Estimating the number of substance-exposed infants. *Drug-Exposed Infants: The Future of Children* 1991; 1(10).

Hanson MJ. Families with Anglo-European roots. In Lynch EW, Hanson MJ, eds. *Developing Cross-Cultural Competence: A Guide for Working with Young Children and Their Families.* Baltimore: Paul H. Brookes, 1992: 65-87.

Hanson MJ, Lynch EW. Family diversity: Implications for policy and practice. *Topics in Early Childhood Special Education* 1992; 12(3): 283-306.

Hanson MJ, Lynch EW, Wayman KI. Honoring the cultural diversity of families when gathering data. *Topics in Early Childhood Special Education* 1990; 10(1): 112-31.

Health and Human Service News (US Department of Health and Human Services). 1992, Monday, January 27.

Henderson JL. *Cultural Attitudes in Psychological Perspective.* Toronto: Inner City Books, 1984.

Huling T, Stewart J. *Fragile Futures: Boarder Babies and Their Mothers.* (Policy Paper) New York: Federation of Protestant Welfare Agencies, 1988.

Klerman L. *Alive and Well? A Research and Policy Review of Health Programs for Poor Young Children.* New York: National Center for Children in Poverty, 1991.

Kronstadt D. *Pregnancy and Cocaine Addiction; an Overview of Impact and Treatment.* San Francisco: Far West Laboratory for Educational Research and Development, 1989.

Levitan SA, Belous RS, Gallo F. *What's Happening to the American Family? Tensions, Hopes, and Realities.* (Rev. ed.) Baltimore: Johns Hopkins University Press, 1988.

Lynch EW. Developing cross-cultural competence. In Lynch EW, Hanson MJ, eds. *Developing Cross-Cultural Competence: A Guide for Working with Young Children and Their Families.* Baltimore: Paul H. Brookes, 1992: 35-59.

Lynch EW, Hanson MJ, eds. *Developing

Cross-Cultural Competence: A Guide for Working with Young Children and Their Families. Baltimore: Paul H. Brookes, 1992.

Masnick G, Bane MJ. *The Nation's Families: 1960-1990*. Boston: Auburn House, 1980.

Matiella AC. *Positively Different: Creating a Bias-Free Environment for Young Children*. Santa Cruz, CA: ETR Associates, 1991.

National Commission on Family Foster Care. *A Blueprint for Fostering Infants, Children and Youths in the 1990s*. Washington, D.C.: Child Welfare League of America, 1991.

National Council of Juvenile and Family Court Judges. *Protocol for Making Reasonable Efforts in Drug-Related Dependency Cases*. Reno: National Council of Juvenile and Family Court Judges, 1991.

National Institute on Drug Abuse. *Drug Use Among American High School Seniors, College Students and Young Adults, 1975-1990*. Volumes I and II. Washington, D.C.: U.S. Department of Health and Human Services, National Institute on Drug Abuse, 1991a.

National Institute on Drug Abuse. *National Household Survey on Drug Abuse*. Washington, D.C.: U.S. Department of Health and Human Services, National Institute on Drug Abuse, 1991b.

National Institute on Drug Abuse. *National Household Survey on Drug Abuse*. Washington, D.C.: U.S. Department of Health and Human Services, National Institute on Drug Abuse, 1989.

Phinney JS, Rotheram MJ. *Children's Ethnic Socialization: Pluralism and Development*. Newberry Park, CA: SAGE Publications, 1987.

Poulsen MK. *Schools Meet the Challenge: Educational Needs of Children at Risk due to Prenatal Substance Exposure*. Sacramento: Resources in Special Education, 1992.

Provence S. Infants in institutions revisited. *Zero to Three* 1989; 9 (3): 1-4.

Pollack VE, Briere J, Schneider L, Knop J, Mednick S, Goodwin, D. Childhood antecedents of antisocial behavior: Parental alcoholism and physical abusiveness. *American Journal of Psychiatry* 1990; 147(10): 1200-3.

Randall-David E. *Strategies for Working with Culturally Diverse Communities and Clients*. Washington, D.C.: Association for the Care of Children's Health, 1989.

"Religion Coats U.S. with Many Colors." *San Jose Mercury News* 1991 April 10, pp. 1, 12.

Research and Policy Committee of the Committee for Economic Development. *Children in Need: Investment Strategies for the Educationally Disadvantaged*. New York: Committee for Economic Development, 1987.

Rosenbaum S, Layton C, Liu J. *The Health of America's Children*. Washington, D.C.: Children's Defense Fund, 1991.

Stabenau JR, Hesselbrock VM. Psychopathology in alcoholics and their families and vulnerability to alcoholism: A review and new findings. In Mirin SM, ed. *Substance Abuse and Psychopathology*. Washington, D.C.: American Psychiatric Press, 1984, 107-32.

Tyler R. Prenatal drug exposure: An overview of associated problems and intervention strategies. *Phi Delta Kappan* 1992; (May): 705-11.

United States Census Bureau. *Census Bureau Press Release CB91-100: Census and You*. Washington, D.C.: U.S. Census Bureau, 1991 April.

United States House of Representatives. *No Place to Call Home*. Washington, D.C.: Report to Select Committee on Children, Youth and Families, 1989.

Villarreal SF, McKinney L, Quackenbush M. *Handle with Care: Helping Children Prenatally Exposed to Drugs and Alcohol*. Santa Cruz, CA: ETR Associates, 1992.

Wayman KI, Lynch EW, Hanson MJ. Home-based early childhood services: Cultural sensitivity in a family systems approach. *Topics in Early Childhood Special Education* 1990; 10(4): 56-75.

Zuckerman B, Frank D, Hingson R, Amaro H, et al. Effects of maternal marijuana and cocaine use on fetal growth. *New England Journal of Medicine* 1989; 320(12): 762-8.

ANNOTATED BIBLIOGRAPHY

Blackwell JE. *The Black Community: Diversity and Unity*. New York: Dodd, Mead, 1975.
This book addresses the economic, social, and political issues that impact the health and well-being of African-Americans.

CWLA Initiative to promote culturally responsive child welfare practice: Recommendations from a colloquium, March 12-13, 1989. Washington, D.C.: *Child Welfare League of America*.
This document was designed to raise racial sensitivity about the significance of ethnic and cultural issues in child welfare policy and practice.

Cross T, Bazron B, Dennis K, Issacs M. *Towards a Culturally Competent System of Care*. Rockville, MD: National Institute of Mental Health, Child and Adolescent Service System Program, 1989 March.
This monograph on the provision of effective services for minority children who are severely emotionally disturbed was developed to assist communities in addressing issues of appropriateness of systems of care.

Henderson JL. *Cultural Attitudes in Psychological Perspective*. Toronto: Inner City Books, 1984.
This book discusses the ways in which psychological theories and perspectives are formed by accepted cultural norms.

Lynch EW, Hanson MJ. *Developing Cross-Cultural Competence: A Guide tor Working with Young Children and Their Families*. Baltimore: Paul H. Brookes, 1992.
Designed to help human service providers become more effective in cross-cultural interactions, this practical volume explores diversity issues and offers not just understanding, but helpful interaction strategies for working with children and families from diverse cultural backgrounds.

Matiella AC. *Positively Different: Creating a Bias-Free Environment for Young Children*. Santa Cruz, CA: ETR Associates, 1991.
This book for caregivers and teachers is designed to teach young children to recognize, respect, understand, and celebrate cultural diversity by constructing supportive, bias-free classroom and home environments.

Phinney JS, Rotheram MJ. *Children's Ethnic Socialization: Pluralism and Development*. Newberry Park, CA: SAGE Publications, 1987.
This book assesses the developmental process by which children come to understand the meaning of their own and other's ethnicity and culture.

Randall-David E. *Strategies for Working with Culturally Diverse Communities and Clients*. Washington, D.C.: U.S. Department of Health and Human Services, Office of Maternal and Child Health, Bureau of Maternal and Child Health and Resources Development, June 1989.
This manual, written in collaboration with the National Hemophilia Foundation, was designed to increase the awareness of the role of culture in shaping our health-related attitudes, values, and practices.

Villarreal SF, McKinney L, Quackenbush M. *Handle with Care: Helping Children Prenatally Exposed to Drugs and Alcohol*. Santa Cruz, CA: ETR Associates, 1992.
This guidebook—written for teachers, counselors, parents, medical providers, and volunteers—addresses the misleading statistics, labels, and stereotypes perpetuated about drug-affected children and families. It discusses the impact of substance abuse on families, the range of possible developmental outcomes that drug-exposed children may experience, and stresses a positive approach to intervention with children and families.

Legal Issues and the Rights of Infants and Children

Mary Anne Theiss, R.N., M.S., J.D.

The law is rapidly changing in the area of fetal and children's rights. States vary as to whether prenatal drug exposure is a form of child abuse or neglect so as to remove the child from the home.

Minnesota authorized involuntary commitment of pregnant drug abusers. Some states have even attempted to prosecute pregnant substance abusers for delivering drugs to the infant in the sixty to ninety seconds after birth before the umbilical cord is severed. These punitive approaches to addiction are counterproductive and drive the mother away from much needed treatment and rehabilitation.

Laws in each state are different. Nurses and other professionals can become aware of laws in their state by reading the current literature, attending conferences, and maintaining contact with the facility's attorney or legal advisor.

In the last several years, a number of important legal decisions have had an impact on the rights of the child and the unborn child. These cases will set the stage for future legislation and court decisions that may answer some of the medical communities' legal questions about the conflicting rights of parents and their unborn children.

This chapter discusses legal issues relating to the child, unborn child, and pregnant substance abuser. The mother's rights may conflict with what is in the best interest of the unborn child. The courts look strictly on any governmental intrusion or intervention that would restrict the pregnant mother's rights. The health care provider must be careful not to violate the mother's right to confidentiality, informed consent, and nonconsensual invasion of her bodily integrity. The health care provider must also stay within the guidelines of the state's reporting requirements and each state's Nurse Practice Act. Many times our perceived moral and ethical obligations to the unborn child interfere with our legal duty to the mother. The nurse must be informed of state laws and the requirements of these laws. Deviation from these laws places a nurse's license in jeopardy.

Rights of the Child

In the well-publicized case about a child switched at birth, Kimberly Mays petitioned the court to "divorce" her biological parents. Kimberly grew up with the Mays, who thought she was their biological child until genetic testing proved otherwise. Her biological parents (the Twiggs) received the Mays' biological child in the hospital where both children were born. The child the Twiggs received contracted a fatal illness. Prior to her death, genetic tests indicated she was not the biological child of the Twiggs. The Florida State court ruled that Kimberly's biological parents should have no contact with her but did not grant her request to "divorce" them. The court, however, did give Robert Mays the legal status of father and the right to proceed with adoption proceedings. Kimberly's biological parents appealed to the U.S. Supreme Court.[1] To complicate matters even more, Kimberly has recently chosen to move in with her biological parents. This case could continue until Kimberly reaches the age of majority, which is eighteen.

Florida had a similar case where the courts made a ruling about the conflicting rights of parents and children. A young boy named Gregory K. successfully filed a suit to "divorce" his mother who had abandoned him. Gregory sued in order to stay with the foster family he had lived with for a year. Gregory won and now lives with the foster family.[2]

More typically the courts have given credence to blood ties versus the best interest of the child. In 1991, a Connecticut teenager, Gina Pellegrino, gave birth to a girl at New Haven Hospital. Hours after giving birth she left the hospital where she had registered under a phony name. A search was made for both Gina and the child's father to no avail. Parental rights were terminated based on abandonment and the infant was placed for adoption. Several months later, Pellegrino sued to regain custody and subsequently won. The result for the child was taking her out of the adoptive parents' home and sending her to live with her biological mother in a homeless shelter.[3]

In another case with even more devastating effects on the child, the Illinois court returned a three-year-old boy, Joseph Wallace, to his biological mother who had been repeatedly admitted to mental institutions. Joseph spent most of his first three years in foster care. In the mother's petition to the court for custody of her son, she stated "I want to give him love, affection, something I didn't have." Two months after the child was returned, the mother was charged with her son's murder. The boy had been hung with an electrical cord.[4]

The highly publicized and heartrending case of Jessica DeBoer also brings to issue the balancing of the rights of children and their parents. In what is known as the "Baby Jessica case," the Michigan Supreme Court ruled that Jan and Roberta DeBoer, who had custody of Jessica while trying to adopt her for more than two years, had no parental rights. The DeBoers were the only parents Jessica knew. The court gave the DeBoers a month to turn the little girl over to her biological parents, Dan and Cara Schmidt.[5]

In the Baby Jessica case, the child was viewed more as a property right than as a person. The case raises the question about how judges consider the children's needs and best interests. Children have little or no say in the final decision that will affect their entire life. The Baby Jessica case and the others mentioned may spur legislators to enact new laws that consider the best interest of the child over the birth rights of the biological parents.

With the public outcry that accompanied these cases and new legislative concern, there is a growing trend to look at children's best interests versus birth rights of the parents.

Maternal-Fetal Conflict

Refusal of Treatment

Case law is more clearly defining the rights of the child, as well as balancing rights of mothers and unborn children. Recently, the Illinois court ruled that a pregnant woman did not have to undergo a cesarean section against her wishes.[6] The mother Tabita Bricci was informed that her unborn child was not receiving enough nutrients and oxygen from the placenta, and without immediate delivery by cesarean section, the child would be born dead or severely brain damaged. Mrs. Bricci, a twenty-year-old Christian Fundamentalist, refused the cesarean section and put her faith in God. Patrick T. Murphy, the legal guardian appointed for the unborn child, went to the court and sought an order for the cesarean. The order was denied by the lower court. This decision was upheld by the Illinois Appellate Court. The United States Supreme Court refused to hear the case.[7]

On December 29, 1993, the child was born by natural means and weighed four pounds, twelve ounces. Although the boy was underweight, he appeared otherwise healthy and in good medical condition. This case came to the attention of the court by the hospital reporting of the refusal of the mother to undergo cesarean delivery.[8]

In Re A.C., a similar case with a different outcome, the District of Columbia Court of Appeals issued an opinion leaving the decision as to whether or not to have a cesarean with the mother. The court held that "in virtually all cases, the question of what is to be done is to be decided by the patient—the pregnant woman—on behalf of herself and the fetus."[9] In June 1987, prior to the Court of Appeals hearing the case, the trial court issued an order to perform the cesarean on Angela Carder, who was dying. It is unfortunate that the Court of Appeals heard this case after the mother had been forced by the lower court to undergo the cesarean section. Both mother and the infant died shortly after the operation.

Angela Carder was a twenty-seven-year-old pregnant patient at George Washington University Hospital, Washington, D.C. She was considered high-risk because she had had cancer as a young woman. Her cancer had been in remission several years before she became pregnant. At approximately twenty-five weeks of pregnancy, a large tumor was detected in one of her lungs. She was admitted to the hospital and her condition deteriorated rapidly. It appeared that she would live no more than one to two days.[10]

She was highly sedated and could not communicate her wishes. At the hospital's initiation, a court hearing was held to determine if a cesarean section should be performed to save the twenty-six and a half-week-old-infant. The judge from the lower court ordered that a cesarean be performed. The court used a balancing-of-interests, and found that once the fetus became viable, "the State had an important and legitimate interest in protecting the potentiality of life" and that "with a viable fetus, a balancing of interests must replace the single interest of the mother, and as in this case, time can be a critical factor."[11]

Five months after Angela Carder's death, the District of Columbia Court of Appeals issued a written decision supporting the lower court's ordered cesarean. Upset about the decision, petitions

were filed by Angela Carder's parents and many others, including health care professionals, requesting that a rehearing be given. The rehearing was granted, and the November opinion was vacated. The Court of Appeals reheard the case in September of 1988, and issued an opinion in April of 1990.[12] The Court of Appeals reversed itself in the April 1990 opinion.

The Court of Appeals rejected the balancing of the maternal-fetal interests approach that the lower court used. The court stressed that once the patient's wishes are ascertained this must be followed in "virtually all cases," unless there are extraordinary or compelling reasons to override them.[13] The right to bodily integrity does not depend on the person's health or proximity to death. The court stated "[t]o protect that right against intrusion by other family members, doctors, hospitals, or anyone else, however well-intentioned we hold that a court must determine the patient's wishes..."[15]

The court went on to state that the right to bodily integrity belongs to both competent and incompetent persons. If the patient is not competent to make a decision, then the trial court must make a substituted judgment on behalf of the patient. Substituted judgment is what the patient's wishes would have been had the patient been competent to make a decision. Substituted judgment is determined by previously expressed wishes of the patient, either oral or written. The court will also consider previous decisions of the patient concerning medical treatment, especially when there is a consistent pattern of conduct or thought.[16] Angela Carder initially expressed the wish that the baby's life be saved at the expense of her own. When told of the court's initial decision to do the operative procedure, however, Carder verbally indicated that she was not in favor of the procedure. This was presented to the court but her change of heart was ignored. Angela Carder's objections would be important for the nurse to report and document in the medical record. This would give some evidence for the court to make a "substituted judgment." Any previous conversations that the nurse may have had that pertained to this issue are also important to document in the patient's record. Nonverbal communication should be documented if it tends to establish the patient's wishes. The court stated that since the lower court could not determine that Carder would have consented to or refused surgery, the court erred by placing this as a conflict between the interests of the mother and those of the fetus.[17]

The Court of Appeals, in this decision, recognized two other significant reasons for not overriding Carder's objections to surgery. Court-ordered intervention erodes the physician-patient relationship and may actually drive the patient away from the health care system. The second reason is that the nature of the judicial hearing convened in response to a medical emergency is not the proper forum for making such decisions.[18]

This case is important because of the judicial recognition of the autonomous decision-making authority of the pregnant woman. According to this legal opinion, a mother cannot be forced to undergo a surgical procedure or donate an organ for a living child nor can she be forced to undergo an invasion of her bodily integrity for the unborn child.

Maternal Rights versus the State's Interest in Protecting Life.

Angela Carder's and Tabita Bricci's cases set precedents and affirm pregnant women's autonomy in making their own health care decisions.

The welfare of the fetus is of the utmost importance to the majority of women, and only rarely is there a conflict between fetal and maternal interests.[19] Two areas where conflict may arise are: when the pregnant woman refuses the diagnostic or surgical procedure for the benefit of the unborn child, or the pregnant woman's behavior may jeopardize the health and well-being of the fetus.

There is a general societal expectation that the pregnant female has a duty to protect the unborn child. Most pregnant women will endure any procedure, and sacrifice many vices, for the safety and well-being of the unborn. The conflict arises when the mother's actions, such as taking illicit drugs, coincide with her pregnant state and she will not or cannot refrain from such behaviors during the pregnancy.

In the landmark abortion case, *Roe v. Wade*, the United States Supreme Court looked at the legal rights of the unborn child in relation to voluntary abortions.[20] The Supreme Court concluded that the unborn child is not a person entitled to protection of the Fourteenth Amendment of the Constitution. The court set up a timetable for balancing the woman's right to privacy and bodily integrity during pregnancy against the right of the state to protect the health of the unborn. The court stated that states may not interfere with a woman's decision whether or not to terminate her pregnancy during the first trimester. The decision was based in part on the rationale that through the first trimester the health risk to the pregnant woman is less for abortion than for natural childbirth. The court determined that the state's interest in the health of the expectant mother justified regulating abortions during the second trimester. A subsequent Supreme Court opinion held that during the second trimester the state "may not impose direct obstacles—such as criminal penalties—to further its interest in the potential life of the fetus."[21] The state's interest for life of the fetus in the third trimester is sufficient to justify restriction, or a complete ban, on elective abortion. The rationale for this standard is that in the third trimester the fetus is considered to be viable, or capable of sustaining life outside of the womb.

In the context of abortion and the Supreme Court decision of *Roe v. Wade*, the fetus is not a person entitled to constitutional protection.[22] In *Roe v. Wade*, the issue of state intervention to protect the interests of the unborn child from drug and alcohol abuse during pregnancy was not addressed. This issue was also not addressed in the Angela Carder case. The fact that the fetus is not a person under the Fourteenth Amendment does not mean that it is not entitled to legal protection.

The *Roe v. Wade* trimester framework for evaluating abortion regulation is not applicable outside the context of abortion. This case recognized the state's interest in protecting potential life, but did not decide that the fetus itself had any rights to life or health. *Roe v. Wade* is cited for balancing the individual rights of the mother versus the state's interest in protecting life. As a result of the balancing tests, we have the state's interest versus the rights of the mother. Nowhere in this landmark decision are fetal rights versus maternal rights addressed.

Compelled Hospitalization and Treatment During Pregnancy

If a woman refuses care, there is a trend toward intervening and forcing compliance to protect fetal life and well-being. Recent case law clearly indicates that we cannot force the mother to have invasive procedures on behalf of the fetus. However, the court, *In Re A.C.*, stated that the right to refuse treatment is not absolute; the court must have a truly compelling reason to override the mother's right to refuse medical treatment. The state has an interest in preserving life.[23]

Presently, few laws authorize involuntary treatment or commitment of pregnant substance abusers. Minnesota is the only state that authorizes involuntary commitment of pregnant drug abusers under their Child Abuse Laws.[24] The Minnesota law defines child neglect to include prenatal exposure to illegal drugs, as evidenced by withdrawal symptoms at birth, toxicology tests performed on mother or child at birth, or developmental delays during the first year of life.[25] This neglect must be reported to child welfare agencies. Health care providers must also report if they have reason to believe that a woman is using illegal drugs during pregnancy.[26] The Minnesota law does not apply to alcohol abuse during pregnancy.

In contrast, New York State, in February of 1993, proposed an amendment to its Civil Rights Law to state:

Preventive detention of pregnant women prohibited. Notwithstanding the provision of any general or special law to the contrary, no pregnant woman shall be subject to arrest, commitment, confinement, incarceration, or other detention or infringement upon her liberty of whatsoever nature solely for the protection, benefit, or welfare of her fetus. Neither shall any pregnant woman otherwise subject to arrest, commitment, confinement, incarceration, or other detention or infringement upon her liberty of whatsoever nature be subject to the same in any greater measure solely for the protection, benefit, or welfare of her fetus. Any person aggrieved by a violation of the provisions of this section may maintain an action in a court of competent jurisdiction for damages therefor.[27]

The legislative intent of lawmakers in New York was to recognize drug addiction as a disease and to treat it as such, that is, medically and not criminally. The imprisonment of women in New York State for alcohol and substance abuse problems has overburdened the prisons and the judicial and foster care systems; deprived women of their legal rights; and has been found to be counterproductive in that it adversely affects both maternal and fetal welfare.[28] Presently, the law has not passed but is before the legislature.

California provides criminal sanctions for failure to support an unborn child by not providing proper food and medical attention. The statute does not mention drug use as a form of abuse.[29] New Jersey allows for an application to be made to their Division of Youth and Family Services when a prospective mother is endangering the welfare of her unborn child. If, after investigation, the charges are founded, the division "may accept and provide such care or custody as the circumstances of such child may require."[30]

If the mother is in need of treatment but will not voluntarily seek it, what can the health care provider do legally? The Supreme Court of the United States in *Roe v. Wade* did not recognize the fetus as a person. The court did not address the issue of forced treatment to promote fetal health. In some states the medical community has looked to other areas of the law to compel hospitalization and treatment of addicted mothers.

Every individual has the right to personal autonomy and bodily integrity.[31] This right encompasses the freedom "from nonconsensual invasion of...bodily integrity" and preservation of the inviolability of the person.[32]

Governmental intrusions or interventions that would restrict the pregnant mother's rights are looked at closely. In order for governmental intrusions to pass constitutional scrutiny, the intervention must be justified under the circumstances and conducted in a proper manner, and be the least restrictive method of protecting the quality of potential life.[33] The health care provider's legal duties are to the mother. There may be an ethical or moral duty to the unborn child, but in many states there is no legal duty.

Given the pregnant mother's constitutional rights, it would be difficult for the state to be able to intervene and compel hospitalization and treatment. Many states have special statutes for the commitment of alcoholics and substance abusers.[34] These are involuntary commitment statutes. The argument has been made that these statutes could be used for the commitment of pregnant substance abusers. The statutory language in the Colorado law contains most of the standard elements necessary to commit under an involuntary commitment:

> A person who habitually lacks self-control as to the use of alcohol beverages or uses alcoholic beverages to the extent that his health is substantially impaired or endangered, or his social or economic function is substantially disrupted.[35]

Common to all of the statutes is the reference to habit or chronicity of abuse.[36] Some of the states include threat of an individual's condition to "others."[37] Arguably, the fetus could come under "other." States without specific statutory language for commitment of alcoholics or drug addicts allow commitment through broad interpretation of the general involuntary commitment statutory language.[38]

In most states that provide for involuntary commitment for substance abusers, provisions are made for notice to the abuser. Generally, the person to be committed is given a formal hearing at which medical evidence is to be presented to support the commitment. Several states confine a person on the basis of a medical certification without a hearing. The patient's due process rights are safeguarded in that the commitment usually requires two physicians to concur as to the necessity of treatment; the commitment is for a short period of time. For continued hospitalization there must be a court hearing. Arguably, if a pregnant woman meets the statutory definition of alcohol or drug addiction, there may be

a valid basis for court-ordered hospitalization to prevent damage to the fetus and the mother.[39]

Any intervention must be performed only when medically necessary to protect the fetus against substantial threat or to protect the mother from substantial harm to her health. The intervention must be the least restrictive means, and there must be medical benefits for the mother as well as for the fetus.

Opponents of fetal or maternal legislation that would allow forced intervention, such as drug testing and involuntary hospitalization, feel that the state can carry intrusive measures too far. Opponents are concerned about whether the state could also intervene if the mother was not eating a healthy diet or was smoking cigarettes. These intrusive interventions would infringe on a woman's right to bodily integrity and might drive her away from medical care and treatment.

At present drug treatment centers and programs are set up largely on the male model—used to treat men.[40] Many drug treatment centers refuse to treat pregnant women.[41] Many times prenatal health care providers lack the skill and expertise to diagnose substance abuse. In a study done by the House Select Committee on Children, Youth and Families (U.S. House of Representatives), it was found that women who seek help during pregnancy cannot get it.

Two-thirds of the hospitals surveyed did not have a place to refer substance-abusing pregnant women for treatment.[42] Actions of coercion—to force treatment—threaten the doctor-patient relationship and undermine the mother's autonomy.

It is hard for a person who is not or does not work with chemical abusers to understand how a mother can abuse drugs and carry a fetus. Even health care providers that work with these problems often have an initial response of anger and a feeling that the mother needs to be punished. The substance abuse must be seen as an illness that needs treatment, and not as a crime and grounds to send someone to jail. The well-being of the fetus is not necessarily protected in jail where drugs can be obtained from visitors, guards, and other prisoners.

Treatment centers are not always readily available for pregnant women who abuse drugs. The availability of public programs for uninsured women has diminished in the last ten years because of funding. The programs that remain experience a greater demand for services than they are able to meet.[43] Coupled with the risk of pregnancy is the added problem of the deleterious effects of the treatment drugs on the unborn child. There is a fear that treatment or withdrawal will cause miscarriage or harm to the fetus.[44] Many centers are not equipped, nor are they willing to deal with the added liability risks that these pregnant substance abusers pose. Most drug treatment centers would not be able to handle the high-risk pregnant mother and her special needs. Most pregnant addicts seeking treatment already have children and would be forced to place them in foster care. The length of waiting lists for treatment programs often means that the pregnant mother could not be admitted until after she delivers.[45]

Although many professionals believe that the unborn child should enjoy health and the right to be born chemically free, best efforts may result in merely an opportunity for the child to be born in a hospital and receive postnatal and hope-fully prenatal care. With proper counseling and treatment, future pregnancies may be chemical-free.

Consent of the Mother for Treatment

Any medical intervention to the mother or baby, for instance a urine test for screening of drugs and alcohol, must be done with the consent of the mother unless a specific statute mandates this type of intrusion. It may be medically necessary to do a drug or alcohol screen on the newborn to render proper care and treatment. If the mother will not give consent and it is an emergency the screen can be done without her permission with a doctor's order. Some hospitals do the screening of the newborn along with the mandated testing required of newborns. These hospitals do the screen under the general consent to treat the infant that the mother gives for the baby on admission. If the mother withdraws that permission and it is not an emergency, the hospital may have to petition the court for permission to do the screen unless there is a specific statute in the state allowing the screen.

The mother must be informed and must give her consent to do a blood or urine screen on herself unless it is a medical emergency involving the mother, or a specific statute mandates otherwise. The mother must also be informed of the testing of the infant. Depending on circumstances or institutional policy, the mother may be informed by either the physician or the nurse. Information given to the mother should be charted by the nurse. If the nurse is present when the mother is informed by the physician, she or he should also chart objectively what transpired between physician and client. Subjective charting that includes value judgments and opinions should be avoided. Objective documentation would include what the nurse saw, heard, and did. It must be specific. Generalizations are meaningless, especially in court when the medical record is the only recollection of what happened.

If consent to treat is not obtained and if there is no emergency or a specific state statute that mandates testing and treatment and the health care provider does a toxicology screen or procedure without permission, the institution and health care provider may be subject to a civil suit for battery or lack of informed consent. The institution should have very specific policy, procedures, and standards of care that outline what the professional can and cannot do.

Battery is the unauthorized touching of a person by another. If the health care provider treats a patient beyond what the patient consented to, this is battery.

An action for lack of informed consent may be brought when permission is not obtained from a patient to perform a specific test or procedure. The patient must be fully informed about the test or procedure. Generally, actions for lack of informed consent are brought against the physician. The institution or nurse may also be a target for such a suit if they have assumed that responsibility.

Postnatal Intervention— Child Abuse Statutes

A growing number of states explicitly make prenatal drug exposure a form of child abuse or neglect. Many states have made babies exposed to illegal substances subject to mandatory child abuse reporting resulting in removal of the child. Four states require fetal alcohol syndrome to be reported.

Other states fail to mention the unborn child or criminalization of a pregnant substance abuser in their laws. The Illinois abuse statute includes "any child born with fetal alcohol syndrome or an addiction to a controlled substance or is at substantial risk because the child's mother used alcohol or a controlled substance during pregnancy."[46] Similarly, Florida defines abuse or neglect as physical dependency of a newborn infant upon any controlled drug.[47] Oklahoma's law requires reporting of children born addicted to illegal drugs under their child abuse laws.[48]

The health care provider's duty to report under the child abuse statutes varies from state to state. Some states require reporting based on positive toxicology screens, whereas others require drug dependence or physical addiction of the mother or the baby.

Illinois' abuse statute includes, "any newborn whose blood or urine contains any amount of a controlled substance."[49] Similarly, Florida defines abuse or neglect as "physical dependency of a newborn infant upon any [controlled] drug."[50]

Some infants may be harmed by maternal drug abuse, whereas others may not. The severity of the symptoms depends on many factors, such as when the mother last abused the chemical, the regularity of abuse, the type of chemical abuse, timing of the abuse in relation to gestation and delivery, the mother's metabolism, and many other factors.

Some courts require that for charges of an abuse case to be indicated, the petitioner must prove how the infant had been harmed or endangered by the drug exposure.[51] Many times judges are reluctant to find abuse or neglect solely on the presence of drugs in the toxicology screen of the infant.

Courts have also considered the threat to the child as the basis of finding neglect with subsequent removal of the child from the biological parents. This is called prognostic deprivation—which is depriving a parent of custody based on the prediction of future actions.[52] Many states look to past treatment of older siblings by a substance abuser to remove an infant with a positive toxicology screen from a mother.

Indicators used in prognostic deprivation are the parents' history of mental illness, inability to manage their own affairs, threatening behavior, refusal to accept assistance from others, and heavy regular use of drugs and/or alcohol.[53] It is important for the nurse to document whether the parents follow advice, their ability to care for the child in the hospital, and if the child has special needs. If the parents are unable to care for the infant at the hospital, this may be indicative of the inability to care for the infant at home.

The school nurse and public health nurse may also have important input as to how the parent(s) have provided care to other siblings. Nurses may be required to testify in court proceedings that will determine whether or not the child is to be removed from the home.

Other courts predicate removal of the child on the basis that heavy chemical abuse can severely impair parents' judgment and ability to cope. If parents cannot care for themselves, they cannot care for a young infant or child.

There is evidence that drugs can make parents more violent toward their children. The Ramsey County (Minnesota) Department of Human Services, after reviewing 700 cases of households abusing cocaine, reported that these parents are "extremely volatile with episodes of normal behavior interspersed with episodes of unpredictable, dangerous and even violent behavior."[54] Many times the court system cannot remove the child if there is only a positive toxicology, but the threat of losing the child is often incentive for the mother to seek treatment.

Rights of the Father

What rights does the father of an unborn child have when a mother is jeopardizing the life, well-being, and health of an unborn child? The Supreme Court, in *Planned Parenthood v. Danforth,* recognized "the deep and proper concern and interest that a devoted and protective husband has in his wife's pregnancy and in the growth and development of the fetus she is carrying."[55] The father's interest in the unborn child is not the same as the mother's, the mother "...physically bears the child and who is more directly and immediately affected by the pregnancy."[56]

The rights of the mother when faced with governmental intrusion are greater than the father's. It is the female whose personal rights to privacy, liberty, and bodily integrity are directly affected.[57]

The constitutional rights of the mother may be greater than those of the father, but this does not negate the fact that he does have rights as far as the unborn child is concerned. He has the right as a parent to be protected from unwarranted governmental intrusion.[58] The rights of the father may be outweighed by the state's interest in protecting potential life. When the mother joins the state in opposition to the father, these combined interests will almost always prevail.[59] An example of this is when the mother wants to abort a previable fetus over the father's objections. Under the *Roe v. Wade* Supreme Court decision, she has a constitutional right to do so.[60]

If the mother engages in behaviors that will jeopardize the unborn child, such as abusing alcohol and drugs, the argument can be made that the father's parental rights should equal those of the mother. The paternal and state interests are now the same and the combination could potentially outweigh the mother's interests to intervene and protect the unborn child.[61]

Paternal rights are not weighed as heavily as maternal rights. However, when combined with a compelling state interest to protect the unborn child in limited circumstances, they may prevail over the rights of the mother.

Criminalization of Maternal Conduct

The most widely implemented "punishment" for the chemical abuser is the loss of custody of the infant. Recent efforts have focused on criminalizing maternal conduct through drug trafficking laws. The escalating numbers of children prenatally dug exposed have prompted states to take punitive action.

The theory behind the recent prosecutions is that the pregnant substance abuser is a drug trafficking felon. The mother is charged with delivering drugs to the infant in the sixty to ninety seconds after birth, but before the umbilical cord is severed. The drug is delivered through the umbilical cord by the mother.

In Massachusetts, Josephine Pelligrini was indicted for delivery of cocaine to a minor through the umbilical cord. The charges were dismissed based on Ms. Pelligrini's constitutional right to privacy.[62]

In Michigan, a state appeals court overturned a lower court decision allowing the prosecution of Kimberly Harding for umbilical cord delivery of a controlled substance. The court ruled that the drug trafficking statute did not apply to pregnant drug abusers.[63]

In July 1989, Florida successfully convicted Jennifer Johnson of delivering cocaine to a minor.[64] The case was subsequently reversed by the Supreme Court of Florida. The Supreme Court in reversing the lower court held that cocaine passing through the umbilical cord after birth, but before cutting the cord, did not violate statutory prohibition against adult delivery of controlled substance to a minor. The court reasoned that the legislative history of the statute did not show intent to use the word "delivery" in context of criminal prosecution of mothers for delivery of a controlled substance to infants by way of the umbilical cord.[65]

The prosecutor in the Johnson case argued that charging women such as Ms. Johnson provides a strong deterrent against unlawful use of drugs by pregnant women.

The medical community submitted many briefs on behalf of Ms. Johnson. The health care providers' position was that if women are subject to this type of criminal prosecution, they will be further driven away from seeking care during pregnancy. The end result would be even more devastating effects on the fetus and lack of care and treatment for the mother.

The Association of Women's Health,

Obstetrics, and Neonatal Nurses (AWHONN), formerly NAACOG (Nurses Association of American Colleges of Obstetrics and Gynecology), holds the opinion that drug and alcohol addiction are diseases, and that the punitive approaches to treatment and rehabilitation are not in the women's best interests and are counterproductive to the role of the health-care professional.[66]

The Committee on Ethics for the American College of Obstetricians and Gynecologists (ACOG) recommends encouraging responsible behavior through education and counseling. Actions of coercion to obtain consent or force a course of action limit maternal freedom of choice. The end result is that the doctor-client and nurse-client relationship is threatened. Such actions violate the mother's right to informed consent.[67] The use of the court system to protect the fetus violates the autonomy of the pregnant woman.[68]

Nursing Intervention and Recognition of the Chemically Dependent Mother

The health care provider must be able to recognize women who abuse drugs or alcohol in order to help them seek proper treatment. The mother who is chemically dependent, and therefore fearing reprise from the legal system, may seek prenatal care late in pregnancy or not until delivery is imminent. Late medical intervention may result in a fetus that is already harmed by the effects of drugs and alcohol.

Early intervention and treatment require a multiagency and multidisciplinary approach. Education and detection and establishing a trusting relationship are keys to early treatment.

The addicted mother may show signs of distrust, paranoia, hyperactivity, or hypoactivity. Many times she has severe mood swings—either low and depressed, or high and manic. She may also have difficulty making and keeping appointments for prenatal visits.[69] Her lack of weight gain may be a clue to her addiction.

This population of mothers has low self-esteem, guilt, and feelings of inadequacy.[70] The mother may already be in the legal system, and the nurse may receive a call from Child Protection or a Probation Officer informing of the mother's abuse of drugs.

Pregnant women from upper middle-class families who are chemically dependent may be more difficult to detect and assess. A detailed health care history that includes use of alcohol, cigarettes, prescription and nonprescription drugs needs to be obtained at the first prenatal visit of all mothers.[71] Ideally, legislation such as the one proposed in New York would encourage participation in prenatal care. The legislative proposal in New York is lacking in that it does not protect the addicted mother from actions for abuse or removal of the child by prohibiting the use of evidence obtained from the fetus in utero or within one week of birth to incriminate the mother.

The proposed statute in New York would allow an aggrieved mother to bring an action in court for damages if her civil rights were violated by incarceration or detention solely to protect the unborn child.

Nurses must educate women about the deleterious effects of drugs and alcohol abuse in a nonjudgmental manner. It is important to establish a trusting relationship. It is also important to have good interviewing and listening skills to elicit information needed to determine dependency.

If the expecting mother feels threatened, she will discontinue her prenatal visits and further jeopardize the health of the fetus and herself. It is important to be direct and truthful. Let the mother know that your goal is for her to be helped through treatment. Explain to her that you do not want her baby to be taken away or her to go to jail. Referral to a drug treatment center that accepts pregnant women would be an appropriate intervention.

The client may reveal that she abuses drugs and may request that the information be kept confidential. If the information is given to the nurse it must be documented in the client's health care record. Nurses must explain to the client that under the licensing laws of the state of their practice, they are obligated to document this information. Some states such as Minnesota require nurses to pass the information on to child welfare agencies. If nurses do not document the information, it may result in a potential license revocation or suspension. In addition to the licensure issues it may have malpractice implications if the information is not provided to other health care providers, such as the doctor, through means of the chart or direct communication. There may be resulting complications to the mother and the baby that could have been avoided if the substance abuse had been known. Inappropriate documentation may subject nurses to liability suits, in addition to defending their licenses against the state. A law such as the proposed law in New York State would eliminate nurses' fear of using appropriate documentation.

In states such as Florida and Illinois, which include a positive toxicology or physical dependency on a controlled substance in a newborn as abuse, this must be reported to the proper authorities. If the mother, such as the one mentioned above, discloses her drug abuse and asks for confidentiality, you must explain the reporting requirements of your state to her. It is imperative that nurses know the requirements of the state in which they practice.

If the nurse suspects that the client abuses drugs she or he should confront the mother and tell her of the suspicions. The nurse or health care professional that deals with prenatal chemical abuse should outline why she or he believes the mother is abusing drugs and ask the mother to be truthful about the matter. The nurse must be aware of and be truthful about the state's laws as to reporting and/or testing. The mother must be told of these requirements, if any. The goal of the health care provider is to be honest and truthful and to seek appropriate medical treatment for the mother.

If the mother denies her use of drugs or alcohol, the nurse should document objectively what she or he observes of the mother's conduct. The nurse should do a nursing assessment on the basis of objective observation.

An example would be:

S: "I don't seem to have any appetite."

O: Weight gain three pounds in five months; failed to keep the last five prenatal appointments; mother shaking and unsteady; eyes glassy and pupils dilated; mother brought in by probation officer. Refused to give urine sample.

A: Mother shows signs and symptoms of chemical abuse.

P: Confront mother about suspicions; ask for permission to do a chemical screen; inform mother of state mandates; communicate concerns to doctor: encourage mother's involvement in a drug treatment program.

Termination of parental rights or incarceration often results in long-term problems for the child and the whole welfare system. Placement of the child into foster care has its own set of problems. These children are often difficult to place because of poor memory, poor judgment, deficits in concentration, and behavioral and emotional problems.

If the state does not have mandatory testing and the mother will not consent, an application to the court may be necessary to obtain such testing. Prior to making such an application, the appropriate health care provider should discuss with the mother her or his concerns. Many times the mother will consent to treatment and/or screening if she understands that the goal is to protect her and the fetus, not to punish her or remove her child.

The Health Care Provider as a Witness

The health care provider may be called upon to testify in court. Being served with a subpoena may be the first notice the nurse gets. This simply notes the name of the action and the date, time, and place that the testimony is required. The subpoena may also require producing documents.

Generally, the attorney that is serving the subpoena will call and explain the purpose of the testimony and ask for information that the nurse may have. The nurse may call the attorney and ask for a conference prior to the hearing. The nurse has a right to know the purpose of the subpoena and what is to be expected. The attorney should also take time to prepare the nurse for the types of questions that will be asked. Nurses may be required to give testimony in a deposition, malpractice trial, licensure proceeding to revoke or suspend another health care professional license, child abuse hearing, criminal hearing, and/or probation hearing.

A deposition, sometimes called an examination before trial (EBT), is an informal hearing usually done in an attorney's office to gather facts before a trial. The testimony given at a deposition is sworn testimony and is taken down verbatim by a court stenographer. The purpose of the EBT is twofold: to gather information that will lead to further information that can be used at trial, and to keep witnesses in line so as not to change their testimony at the time of trial. If a witness changes testimony at the time of trial, the EBT can be used to impeach his or her credibility.

When giving testimony, nurses should remember that they are under oath and if they are untruthful they have committed perjury.

The nurse should take time with the attorney to review the medical record and what she or he and others have documented about the mother and/or baby. It would be inappropriate for the nurse to testify without such a review. The hearing may be months, or even years, after the nurse had an initial contact with the client. The documentation in the client's record is the best evidence of the care given or what the client related to the health care provider. If the medical record is deficient, the nurse may have a hard time convincing a judge or jury that she or he remembers a particular point. The nurse will also subject herself or himself to cross-examination by the opponent's attorney.

When testifying, the nurse must listen carefully to the questions asked. Many times the question calls for a yes and no answer. This is a double question. If the nurse simply answers affirmatively, she or he has answered yes to both parts of the question. If asked a double question or something that is confusing, the nurse should simply state that she or he does not understand the question and ask the attorney for clarification.

The purpose of legal proceedings is to discover the truth. The nurse should keep this in mind and try to be objective and not opinionated. The nurse should report the facts as they were observed and not be judgmental and take sides.

CONCLUSION

Health care providers should have as their goal the early intervention and treatment for the mother and exposed infant. The health care provider is the patient's advocate, and not informer or punisher. The nurse should clearly explain to the mother what her rights are and what medical care will be provided. The nurse should be very direct with the patient and share indications of a problem, and emphasize that the goal is to seek treatment and appropriate medical and psychological intervention not placement of the child in foster care.

Nurses and other health care providers should become involved in the legislative process and lobby for changes in the laws so that maternal abusers will re-ceive appropriate medical treatment in a facility that is capable of handling their unique problems and those of the infant or child and not punishment or removal of the child.

REFERENCES

1. Teen Wins Freedom From Birth Parents, But Judge Refuses to Grant "Divorce" *Syracuse Herald-Journal,* August 18, 1993, Al, Col 1.
2. Giggs N, "In Whose Best Interest?" *Time,* July 19, 1993, p. 48.
3. Idem, p. 48.
4. Idem p. 48.
5. Idem, p. 47.
6. Terry D. Illinois Is Seeking to Force Woman to Have Caesarean. *New York Times,* December 15, 1993, A. 22, Col 1.
7. Idem, p. A-22. The Court Refuses to Hear Appeal on Caesarean. *New York Times,* December 19, 1993, A. 35, Col 1.
8. Mom Who Said No to C-Section Gives Birth to Baby Boy. *Syracuse Herald Journal,* December 30, 1993, A. 1, Col 1.
9. *In Re A.C.,* 533 a.2d 611 (D.C. app. 1987), vacated 539 A.2d 203 (D.C. 1988); vacated and remanded 573 A.2d 1235 (D.C. 1990).
10. *In Re A.C.,* (1987) p. 612-3.
11. *In Re A.C.,* (1987) p. 614-5.
12. *In Re A.C.,* 533 A.2d 611 (D.C. App. 1987), vacated 539 A.2d 203 (D.C. 1988), vacated and remanded 573 A.2d 1235 (D.C. 1990).
13. *In Re A.C. (1990) p. 1252.*
15. *In Re A.C. (1990) p. 1247.*
16. *In Re A.C. (1990) p. 1249 & 1250.*
17. *In Re A.C. (1990) p. 1252.*
18. *In Re A.C. (1990) p. 1248.*
19. American College of Obstetricians and Gynecologists Ethics Committee Opinion No. 55; Patient Choice: Maternal-Fetal Conflict WHI Vol. 1, No. 1 (Fall 1990).
20. *Roe v. Wade,* 410 U.S. 113, 93 S.Ct. 705, 35 L. Ed. 2nd 147 (1973).
21. *Colautti v. Franklin,* 439 U.S. 379, 99 S.Ct. 675, 58 L. Ed. 2d 595 (1979).
22. *Roe v. Wade,* Idem p. 158.
23. *In Re A.C. (1990) p. 1252.*

24. Minn. Stat. Ann. 626.556 (2) (3) (West Supp. 1990).

25. Wilton M. Compelled hospitalization and treatment during pregnancy: Mental health statutes as models for legislation to protect children from prenatal drug and alcohol exposure. 25 *Family Law Quarterly* 149 (Summer 1991).

26. Minn. Stat. Ann. §5561(1) (West Supp. 1990).

27. New York State proposed bill #9286-C in the Assembly to amend 417 of New York State Social Services Law.

28. Legislative intent of New York State bill #9286-C in Assembly.

29. Cal. Penal Code 270 (West Supp. 1988).

30. N.J. Stat. Ann. 30:4C-22 (West Supp. 1991).

31. Meyers J. Abuse and neglect of the unborn: Can the state intervene? 23 *Dug. L. Rev.* 1, 58 (1984).

32. *Superintendent of Belchentown v. Saikewicz,* 373 Mass. 728, 739, 370 N.E.2d 417,424, (1977).

33. Townsend E. Maternal drug use during pregnancy as child neglect or abuse. 93 *West Va. L. Rev.* 1097 (citing *Roe v. Wade,* 410 U.S. at 155-6).

34. Brackel S, Parry J, Weiner B. *The Mentally Disabled and the Law* 22 (American Bar Found. Study, 3rd ed. 1985).

35. Idem, p. 41 citing, Colo. Rev. State, Section 25-1-302 (1) (Supp. 1980).

36. Idem, p. 41.

37. Idem, p. 41.

38. Wilton J. Compelled hospitalization and treatment during pregnancy: Mental health statutes as models for legislation to protect children from prenatal drug and alcohol exposure 25 *Family Law Quarterly* 149 at 165 (1991) (Citing 4 Co. 1236, 76 Eng. Rep. 1118 (K.B. 1603).

39. Idem, p. 165.

40. McNulty M. Pregnancy police: Implications of criminalizing fetal abuse, *Youth Law News* (1990), 33, 35.

41. Idem, p. 35.

42. Fink J. Reported effects of crack and cocaine on infants.*Youth Law News* 1990, 37, 39.

43. McNulty, Idem, p. 35.

44. McNulty, Idem, p. 35.

45. McNulty, Idem, p. 35.

46. Ill. Ann. Stat. Chs. 23 para. 2053(e) (Smith-Hurd Supp. 1990) & 37 para. 802-3(1) (c) (Smith-Hurd Supp. 1990).

47. Fla. Stat. Ann. 415.503 (9) (a) (2) (West Supp. 1993).

48. Okla. Stat. Ann. Tit. 21 846(a) (West Supp. 1989).

49. Ind. Code Ann., Section 31-6-4-3.1 (Burns 1987).

50. Fla. Stat. Ann., Section 415.503(7)(a) (Supp. 1988).

51. *Matter of Fletcher*, 141 Misc. 333, 533, N.Y.S.2d 241, 242-3, Fam. Ct., Bronx Co (1988).

52. Grimm B. Drug-exposed infants pose new problems for juvenile courts. *Youth Law News* 11 (1990).

53. Idem p. 11.

54. Clement D. "Babies in Trouble." *Minnesota Monthly*, March 1989.

55. *Planned Parenthood v. Danforth,* 428 U.S. 52 at 69 (1976).

56. Idem p. 71.

57. Meyers, p. 61.

58. Idem, p. 61.

59. Idem, p. 61.

60. *Roe v. Wade*, Supra.

61. Meyers, Supra at 62.

62. *Commonwealth v. Pelligrini*, No. 87970 slip op at 329 (Sup.Ct. Plymouth County, MA, Oct. 15, 1990).

63. "Fetal drug delivery case is overturned," *Wall Street Journal* April 3, 1991, B6, Col. 1.

64. *Johnson v. State*, 578 So.2d 419, 420, (Fla. 5th DCA 1991).

65. *Johnson v. State*, 578 So.2d 419 (Fla. 5th DCA 1991), rev. 602 So.2d 1288 (1992).

66. NAACOG - Substance Abuse in Women, Position Statement (May 1990).

67. American College of Obstetricians and Gynecologists — Ethics Comm. Op. No. 55; at 14.

68. Idem, p. 15.

69. Lewis KD. Pathophysiology of prenatal drug exposure: In utero, in the newborn, in childhood and in agencies. *Journal of Pediatric Nursing*, 1991; 6(3): 185.

70. Idem, p. 187.
71. Idem, p. 187.

ANNOTATED BIBLIOGRAPHY

Brakel S, Parry J, Weiner B. *The Mentally Disabled and the Law*. 22 (American Bar Found. Study 3rd Ed. 1985).
This reference work deals with the civil liberties of the mentally disabled. The book discusses the substantive and procedural rights of individuals in areas of involuntary institutionalization. It is projected that the fourth edition will be published in 1995 and should be an excellent source for individual state laws relating to commitment.

Grimm B. Drug-Exposed Infants Pose New Problems for Juvenile Courts. *Youth Law News* 11(1990).
The issues of whether evidence of prenatal drug exposure by itself, independent of any other harm to the child or the parent's ability to care for the child, is sufficient to assume jurisdiction are discussed. The questions of whether parental drug use justifies placement of the infant and/or siblings outside of the home and the impact that drug use should have on the welfare agency's obligation to keep the family together is explored.
The doctrine of "prognostic deprivation," which refers to depriving parents of custody based on a prediction of their future actions, is discussed.

McNulty M. Pregnancy Police: Implications of Criminalizing Fetal Abuse

Youth Law News **33 (1990).**
This article discusses the medical and legal communities' attempt to control women's behavior during pregnancy. With the concern over the effects of drug use during pregnancy "fetal rights" has emerged. The trend towards intervention, lack of services for substance-abusing pregnant women, criminalization of conduct during pregnancy, and constitutional issues are discussed.

Meyers J. Abuse and Neglect of the Unborn: Can the State Intervene? 23 *Duq L. Rev*. 1, 58, (1984).
The author contends that a framework should be developed to protect the rights of the unborn child. The legal status of the unborn child is examined through a historical examination of property, tort, and criminal law.

Wilton M. Compelled Hospitalization and Treatment During Pregnancy: Mental Health Statutes as Models for Legislation to Protect Children from Prenatal Drug and Alcohol Exposure. 25 *Family Law Quarterly* 149 (Summer 1991).
The legal analysis necessary to determine the limits of a woman's constitutional rights to privacy is discussed. The article discusses existing legal models for protecting maternal and fetal health, such as the mother's right to bodily integrity, child abuse statutes and mental health statutes. The author examines maternal and fetal health legislation and recommends specific legislation for protecting fetal health.

Resources

Dale Berry, R.N., B.S.N., P.H.N.
Keeta DeStefano Lewis, R.N., P.H.N., M.S.N.

Alcoholics Anonymous

P.O. Box 459
New York, NY 10163

See telephone directory for local listings. Information on alcohol addiction, including effects on the developing fetus. Group treatment and support for individuals with drinking problems.

Bay Area Addiction Research and Treatment (BAART)
The Family Addiction Center for Education and Treatment (FACET)

1040 Geary Street
San Francisco, CA 94109

Telephone: 415-928-7800
    Fax: 415-773-8747

Provides outpatient drug treatment to addicted pregnant women and their children. Services include pediatric and obstetric care, outpatient primary care, HIV antibody testing, acupuncture, nutrition counseling, psychotherapy/counseling, group therapy, 12-step groups, specialty groups for prenatal parenting, grief, LaMaze, cocaine, and cultural heritage. Other services include recreational outings, social service referrals, aftercare and relapse prevention, developmental testing, and on-site daycare.

Center for Comprehensive Health Practice

1900 Second Avenue, 12th Floor
New York, NY 10029

Telephone: 212-360-7792

Medical services for drug-abusing pregnant women and their families. Parenting groups, methadone treatment, counseling, and high school equivalency programs.

Center for Reproductive Law and Policy

120 Wall Street
New York, NY 10005

Telephone: 212-514-5534
    Fax: 212-514-5538

Legal advocacy for the purpose of protecting women's reproductive choices nationally and internationally. Clearinghouse on legal and public health issues relating to substance abuse and pregnancy.

Center for the Vulnerable Child

Children's Hospital Medical Center
747 52nd Street
Oakland, CA 94609

Telephone: 415-428-3783

Medical, psychosocial, and case management services to chemically dependent women, their babies, and their families. Medical, mental health, developmental, case management, and social support services for foster children and their families. Medical evaluations and psychosocial support services for sexually abused children. Related clinical research and health policy activities.

Child Welfare League of America

440 First Street, NW, Suite #310
Washington, DC 20001-2085

Telephone: 202-638-2952
  Toll-free: 800-8KIDS80
       Fax: 202-638-4004

A national membership organization which sets internationally recognized standards for child welfare practice, proposes national public policy initiatives, and provides technical assistance to member agencies. Membership fee of $5.00 or more.

Clearinghouse on Disability Information

Office of Special Education and Rehabilitative Services

US Dept. of Education
Room 3132, Switzer Building
Washington D.C. 20202-2425

Telephone: 202-205-8241 or 205-8723

Responds to inquiries, provides referrals, and disseminates information about national, state, and local services and resources for individuals with disabilities. Publications available free of charge include: a newsletter on issues of interest to individuals with disabilities (called "OSERS News in Print"), "A Summary of Existing Legislation Affecting People with Disabilities," and a "Pocket Guide to Federal Help for Individuals with Disabilities."

CSAP National Resource Center for the Prevention of Perinatal Abuse of Alcohol and Other Drugs

9302 Lee Highway, Suite #310
Fairfax, VA 22031

Telephone: 800-354-8824 or
              703-218-5700
       Fax: 703-218-5701

Information and referral services related to prevention and treatment of perinatal abuse of alcohol, tobacco, and other drugs. Provides access to reports, training guides, protocols, tools, contacts in the field, information of funding sources, state laws, and legislative activity. Includes modem-accessed computer system.

Easter Seal Society

70 E. Lake Street
Chicago, IL 60601

Telephone: 312-726-6200

Provides rehabilitation services to disabled persons. Conducts treatment, education, and research nationwide. Maintains over 2,000 programs and facilities.

The Family Center

Jefferson Medical College
Thomas Jefferson University
1201 Chestnut Street, 11th Floor
Philadelphia, PA 19107-4192

Telephone: 215-955-8577
              215-727-1640
       Fax: 215-568-4664

Comprehensive two-year residential drug treatment program for cocaine-addicted pregnant women and their children, ages birth to four. Women must be at least 18 years of age.

Juvenile Law Center

801 Arch Street, Sixth Floor
Philadelphia, PA 19107

Telephone: 215-625-0551
　　Fax: 215-625-9589
Toll-free (Pennsylvania only):
　　　　800-875-8887

A nonprofit, public interest law firm.
Represents individual children who are
involved in abuse and neglect cases in
Philadelphia County, and various classes
of children in Pennsylvania in lawsuits
involving juvenile justice and health issues. Works for reform and coordination
among child welfare, juvenile justice,
mental health, and public health care
systems. Provides legal advice to children and people working with children.

Legal Action Center

236 Massachusetts Avenue, NE
Suite #510
Washington, DC 20002

Telephone: 202-544-5478

153 Waverly Place
New York, NY 10014

Telephone: 212-243-1313

Information clearinghouse on women's
drug and alcohol problems. Concerned
mainly with confidentiality issues, effective treatment program models, liability
issues for treatment programs, and legislation.

Narcotics Anonymous

World Service Office, Inc.
P.O. Box 9999
Van Nuys, CA 91409

Telephone: 818-780-3951
　　Fax: 818-785-0923
　　TDD: 818-376-8600
A nonprofit, international, community-
based organization for recovering addicts. Members learn from one another
how to live drug-free and recover from
the effects of addiction in their lives.
Deals with any type of drug, including
alcohol. Meetings are anonymous, and
local telephone numbers can be found in
many directories.

National Abandoned Infants Assis-
tance Resource Center

University of California at Berkeley
1950 Addison, Suite #104
Berkeley, CA 94704

Telephone: 510-643-8390
　　Fax: 510-643-7019

Federally funded center to enhance the
quality of services for families who have
drug- and HIV-affected or medically involved children. Services include information, publications, training and technical assistance, telephone seminars, and
an annual national conference.

National Association for Perinatal Addiction Research and Education (NAPARE)

Telephone: 800-638-BABY or
                 312-329-2512

Provides assistance to professionals and lay people. Answers questions about exposure to specific drugs and gives tips on comforting prenatally drug exposed infants. Also provides local referrals, training, speakers, and an annual national conference. Sells informational materials related to perinatal drug use.

National Clearinghouse for Alcohol and Drug Information (NCADI)

P.O. Box 2345
Rockville, MD 20847-2345

Telephone: 800-729-6686

Individual referrals to alcohol and other drug abuse services. Consultation on available facts, figures, and statistics. Information on available prevention-based literature.

National Council on Alcoholism and Drug Dependence, Inc., (NCADD)

12 West 21st Street
New York, NY 10010

Telephone: 800-NCA-CALL

Telephone information and literature on addictive problems. Offers referral through locally affiliated offices to community-based programs across the nation.

The National Drug Abuse Treatment, Referral and Information Service

P.O. Box 100
332 Springfield Avenue
Summit, NJ 07901

Telephone: 800-COCAINE

Nationwide information and referral to the nearest inpatient or outpatient treatment center, self-help program, or private practitioner.

The National Federation Target Program

P.O. Box 20626
11724 N.W. Plaza Circle
Kansas City, MO 64195-0626

Telephone: 816-464-5400
 Toll-Free: 800-366-6667
       Fax: 816-464-5571

Assists state high school activity/athletic associations, school personnel, student participants, their parents, and community leaders to encourage healthy lifestyle choices among young people. Services include training programs, national resource hotline, substance abuse information, educational materials catalogs, conferences, and special events.

National Institute on Drug Abuse (NIDA)

5600 Fishers Lane
Rockville, MD 20857

Telephone: 301-443-6245
 Toll-Free: 800-662-HELP

The lead federal agency for research into

the incidence and prevalence of drug abuse, its causes and consequences, and improved approaches to prevention and treatment. Provides grants to support research. Conducts research at the Addiction Research Center in Baltimore, Maryland. Toll-free hot line refers callers to drug abuse treatment in their local area, provides drug abuse information and AIDS prevention information to intravenous drug abusers and their families.

National Training Center for Drug-Exposed or HIV-Infected Children and Their Families

1800 Columbus Avenue
Boston, MA 02119

Telephone: 617-442-7442
      Fax: 617-442-1705

Provides training, consultation, and technical assistance to professionals nationwide who are serving or planning to serve children who are drug-exposed and HIV-infected and their families.

Operation PAR (Parental Awareness and Responsibility)

10901-C Roosevelt Blvd, Suite #1000
St. Petersburg, FL 33716

Telephone: 813-570-5080
      Fax: 813-570-5083

Maternal substance abuse services, including inter-agency linkage and referrals; case management; outpatient, individual, and group counseling; day treatment; and child day care (including therapeutic and developmental services).

Shields for Families Project, Inc.

P.O. Box 59313
Los Angeles, CA 90059

Eight different therapeutic, nonresidential programs for drug- and alcohol-abusing women, their drug-exposed newborns, high-risk siblings, and affected family members.

Government Programs

Medicaid

This is the federal government's main program funding health care for the country's medically indigent population. Because some states have chosen to add benefits to the basic federal package, eligibility requirements and benefits vary by locale. Some states, such as California, have added benefits *and* changed the name of the final program (Medi-Cal, in this instance). Your local department of health or social services (also known as human services or welfare) should be able to provide information and application forms.

Eligibility is determined by application, whereby income and assets are reviewed. Special categories of eligibles might include foster children, pregnant women, and others, varying by state.

Benefits include some coverage for most health problems, but there are limits and exclusions.

An individual or family not eligible for full benefits may still be able to find some relief through "Share of Cost." This is essentially a monthly "deductible" which must be paid prior to becoming eligible for the remainder of the month's medical expenses.

Crippled Children's Service (CCS)

This is a federal program designed to assist and provide specialty care for children with severe health problems. As with Medicaid, CCS benefits and eligibility (as well as the name of the program) may vary among states.

CCS covers some children who do not qualify for Medicaid because family income exceeds the Medicaid limit. CCS, however, covers only certain types of medical conditions which are *listed*. Physicians or other health workers may refer to CCS for a condition believed to be eligible. For a child with a serious health condition, you should inquire at the local health or social services agency. Families may go without medical care or without other necessities in order to pay medical bills because they do not know of this program and no one has thought to refer them.

Services include specialty care, physical therapy, and case management.
Note : Families may be required to apply for Medicaid prior to applying for CCS.

Early and Periodic Screening, Diagnosis and Treatment (EPSDT)

Another federal child health program, EPSDT was established to detect health problems at the earliest possible age, refer for treatment of any problems found, and encourage low-income families to keep their children current on routine immunizations, thus protecting the individual child from preventable illness and also the general population from epidemics. Ask the local health or social services department about this program.

Eligibility again varies among states. Generally, everyone under the age of twenty-one who qualifies for Medicaid also automatically qualifies for EPSDT. Some states provide similar services for many children who do not qualify for Medicaid.

Services include regularly scheduled, thorough health examinations, including routine immunizations, hearing and vision tests, referrals for needed specialty care, and available local assistance in finding and using resources.

A telephone call to the local county or regional health department, social services department, or school district office will assist persons in finding other resources which may exist in their locale.

Index

A

ABR: *see* Auditory Brainstem Responses
Abortions, spontaneous
    cocaine use, 70
    heroin use, 40
    smoking, 46
Abruptio placentae: *see* Cocaine
Abuse and neglect
    fetal alcohol syndrome & fetal alcohol
        effects, 125
    legal issues, 326, 331, 335-336
    maternal chemical dependency relation-
        ships, 142, 157, 269
    neurobehavioral characteristics, 157
    risk factors, 158(t.)
    See also Opiates, fetal neonatal effects
ACOG: *see* American College of Obstetri-
    cians and Gynecologists
Acetaldehyde, 113
Addiction
    access to treatment, 7-8
    disease concept, 5, 6
    emotional/social development of the
        mother, 269
    females, 7
    history, 5-6
    risk factors, 6
    women & men, relationship to, 3-4
    See also Chemical dependency
Aggressive behavior in children
    effect on cognitive development, 173
    teachers' response, 173
Alcohol
    attention deficit disorder and prenatal
        exposure, 178
    care of infant exposed, 97-101
    history of use, 9, 10
    in pregnancy, 113
    motor development, 208-209(t.)
    neonatal neurobehavioral organization
        and prenatal exposure, 175-6
    physical symptoms, 64(t.)
    withdrawal symptoms, 64(t.)
Alcohol Related Birth Deficits (ARBD): *see*
    Fetal Alcohol Effects and Fetal
    Alcohol Syndrome
Alcoholics Anonymous, 347
Alertness in infants and children: *see*
    Arousal

American College of Obstetricians and
    Gynecologists (ACOG): *see* Legal
    issues, American College of Obstetri-
    cians and Gynecologists
American Speech and Hearing Association
    (ASHA), 152, 245
Apraxia, 239
ARBD: *see* Fetal Alcohol Effects and Fetal
    Alcohol Syndrome
Arousal, alertness
    levels, 180
    mother-infant attachment, 194(t.)
    motor state control, 216(t.), 217
ASHA: *see* American Speech and Hearing
    Association
Assessment: *see* Developmental assess-
    ment, Growth assessment, Hearing
    assessment, Vision assessment, Women
Association of Women's Health,
    Obstetrics & Neonatal Nurses: *see*
    Legal issues
Attachment, 169, 171
    bonding process, 256-257
    effects of foster home placement, 174,
        257
    infant neurobehavioral status, 191, 194(t.)
    teacher, 256
Attentional problems
    behavioral diaries, 181
    children at risk model, 261
    children with fetal alcohol effects and
        fetal alcohol syndrome, 178, 180
    communication disorders, 244-245
    interventions, 180-182
    self-regulation, 180
    See also Cocaine, long-term effects
Audiologist, referral, 234(t.)
Auditory Brainstem Responses (ABR), 33,
    152
Auditory System: *see* Hearing
Autism, 36-37, 239
AWHONN: *see* Association of Women's
    Health, Obstetrics & Neonatal Nurses

B

BAART: *see* Bay Area Addiction Research
    and Treatment
"Baby Jessica case": *see* Legal issues

BAER: *see* Brainstem Auditory Evoked Response

Bay Area Addiction Research and Treatment (BAART), 347

Bayley Scales of Infant Development (BSID)
developmental assessment, 277, 287
effects, 36
use, motor assessment, 207, 208(t.)

Behavioral interventions, 262-264
motor development, 222-224

BER, BSER: *see* Brainstem Evoked Response

Berry Test of Visual Motor Integration (VMI), 208(t.), 211

Blood brain barrier, 3

Boarder babies, 310

Boggs Act, 14

Bonding: *see* Attachment

BPD: *see* Bronchopulmonary dysplasia

Brainstem Auditory Evoked Response (BAER), 152, 239

Brainstem Evoked Response (BER-BSER), 152, 239

Brazelton Neonatal Behavior Assessment Scale (NBAS), 33, 205-206, 208(t.), 287

Breast-feeding, 29(t.)
alcohol, 99-100
cocaine, 30(t.)
HIV infections, 138
marijuana, 30(t.), 104
methadone, 30(t.)
narcotics, 30(t.), 96
PCP, 30(t.), 44
tobacco, 30(t.), 104

Bronchopulmonary dysplasia (BPD), 132

Bruininks-Oseretsky Test of Motor Proficiency, 211

BSER: *see* Brainstem Evoked Response

BSID: *see* Bayley Scales of Infant Development

C

California state law, 332

Cancer, childhood
effects of maternal tobacco use, 48
See also Marijuana, cancer

Cannabinoids: *see* Marijuana

Carboxhemoglobin, 46

Case management, 200-201, 267. *See also* Foster care, case management

Catecholamines, 45

Center for Comprehensive Health Practice, 347

Center for Reproductive Law and Policy, 347

Center for the Vulnerable Child, 347

Cerebrovascular accidents, prenatal, cocaine-related, 32

Chemical dependency
defense mechanism, 62
disease model, 5-6, 61, 332
emotional and social development, 269
evaluation, 65-67
postpartum relapses, 73-74
pregnancy, historical perspective, 59
treatment programs, 7-8, 61-62, 331-335
view of males and females, 7
women, historical patterns, 8-17
See also Addiction

Chicago Center for Perinatal Addiction: *see* Long-term studies

Child Welfare League of America, 347-348

Childbearing age, 301

Children at risk model, 256, 261-262

Children, drug exposed, demographics, 307(t.)

Chlamydia
maternal infection, untreated, 140
neonate infection, 140

Classroom environments, 245, 264-267

Clearinghouse on Disability Information, 348

Clinical measurements, 154-155

CMV: *see* Cytomegalovirus

Cocaine, maternal use, 28(t.)
abruptio placentae, 27, 33
alcohol and opiate combination, 23, 237
appetite suppressant, 27
auditory effects on neonate/infant, 33
breast-feeding, 30(t.)
congenital anomalies, 32-33
effects on newborn and growing child during pregnancy, 28(t.)
epidemiological estimates, 15-16, 25
growth effects on fetus/neonate, 31-32, 156

history, 3, 4, 15-16, 25-29
long-term effects, 35-37
meconium aspirations, 71
motor development of neonate/infant, 206, 207, 209(t.) 210
neurobehavioral/developmental effects on fetus/neonate, 33-35, 100(t.),176
nursing care of newborn prenatally exposed, 101-102
ophthalmic effects on neonate/infant, 33
pharmacologic effects, 25
physiologic effects and symptoms, 25-26, 28(t.), 64(t.)
premature rupture of membranes (PROM), 27, 30
sensory effects on newborn exposures, 33, 151, 152
speech/language development in children prenatally exposed, 237-239
sudden infant death syndrome (SIDS), 35-36
vasoconstrictive action, 26, 32
withdrawal symptoms, 64(t.)
Codependency, nurses with, 60
Cognitive development, infant and child, 169
attachment, 169, 174
behavioral problems, 173
contributing factors, 170-175
foster home placement, 174-175
head circumference, 175
homelessness, 173-174
parenting styles, 172
physical growth, 169
play activities, 169
relation to intrauterine growth retardation, 175
relation to motor development, 170
relation to poverty, 172
research issues, 175
sense of self, 170
Colorado state law, 333
Communicative disorders, 233-235
behavioral reinforcements, 244-245
dysfluencies, 235
remediations and interventions, 243-245
See also Speech and language development

Community
addicted persons in their, 304
definition, 302
drug use, 304
schools/agencies/family cooperation, 267-271
See also Culture
Conditioned Orientation Reflex (COR), 154
Connecticut court case: see Legal issues
Consent, informed: see Legal issues
COR: see Conditioned Orientation Reflex
Crib-O Gram, 152
Criminalization of mothers: see Legal issues
Crippled Children's Service (CCS), 352
CSAP National Resource Center for the Prevention of Perinatal Abuse of Alcohol and Other Drugs, 348
Culture
communication disorders, 243
community context, 192(t.), 195
cultural competencies, 320-321
drug use, 303
family health, 160(t.)
foster home identity and placement, 309, 312
health belief factors/standards, 318-319
heritage and ethnicity, 299
interventions, 314-321
poverty, 300
Cytomegalovirus (CMV), maternal and congenital infection, 136-137

D
Delta-9 tetrahydrocannabinol (THC), 37
Demographics
drug use of adults, 305-307
drug use of children prenatally drug exposed, 307(t.)
Deposition, legal definition, 340
Developmental assessment
components, 285-288
definition, 277-279
educational eligibility, 281
fear, 291
health and medical status, relation to, 287-288
interviews, 285

language, attitudes, behavior and skills (LABS), 289(t.), 290
maternal expectation, 192(t.)
medical diagnosis, 281
nursing, 277
observations, 286
parental inclusion, 284-285, 290
process, 283(t.)
program evaluation, 282
purpose, 280-282
qualitative and quantitative, 278-279
referral, 292
screening, 280-281
team approach, 279
tests, 387
timing, 291-292
value, 291, 292
See also Nursing assessment; Motor assessment; Psychological assessment
Developmental Test of Visual Perception (DTVP), 212
Diphtheria, pertussis and tetanus (DPT) immunization, 156
District of Columbia: *see* Legal issues
Dopamine: *see* Neurotransmitters
DPT: *see* Diphtheria, pertussis, tetanus (DPT) immunization
Drug use
categories, 66
prevalence, male/female, 12-13(t.)
See also Culture; Community; Demographics; Women
DTVP: *see* Developmental Test of Visual Perception
Dysarthria, definition, 239

E
Early and Periodic Screening, Diagnosis and Treatment(EPSDT), 352
Easter Seal Society, 348
EBT, Examination Before Trial, **see** Deposition
Eclectic model, 219-220
Educational assessment,
fetal alcohol syndrome, fetal alcohol effects, 125
See also Developmental assessment; Mental retardation

Epinephrine: see Neurotransmitters
Examination Before Trial (EBT): *see* Deposition
Expressive language: *see* Speech and language development

F
FAE: *see* fetal alcohol effects
Failure to thrive (FTT)
definition, 141
etiology, 141
fetal alcohol syndrome, 116
Families
assessment with, 284, 288, 316-318
connections, 268-271
environmental stress, 192(t.), 195
extended family/kinship networks, 314-316
health questions, 160(t.)
interventions, 314-321
professional partnership, 279-280, 288, 290
structural change, 301
See also Individual Family Service Plan (IFSP); Poverty; Religion
Family Center, The 348
FAS: *see* fetal alcohol syndrome
Fetal alcohol effects (FAE)
characteristics, 115, 122
cognitive development, 177-180
motor development, 205
Fetal alcohol syndrome (FAS)
acetaldehyde, relationship to, 113-114
behavioral and social skill problems, 120, 121
central nervous system abnormalities
adolescent/adult, 121
child, 120
infant, 116, 119
characteristics, 117(Fig.), 98(t.)
adolescent/adult, 121
child, 120-121
infant, 115-120
diagnosis,115
effects, 117(Fig.), 118(Fig.)
epidemiology, 113
facial anomalies
adolescent/adult, 121

child, 120
    infant 115-116
growth deficiencies,
    adolescent/adult, 121
    child, 120
    infant, 116
hearing loss, 152
heart defects, 119
history, 9, 10
identification and interventions, 122-125
infant care, 97, 99-101
legal issues, 335
marijuana use studies, 38
mental development, 119, 120, 121
motor development, 119, 205, 207, 208-
    209(Fig.), 211-212
pregnancy outcome continuum, 114(Fig.)
related mediating factors, 113
skeletal anomalies, 119
speech and language problems, 236-237
twin studies, fraternal, 24
visual motor planning, 211
Fine motor assessments, 211, 262
Florida state law, 335
    court cases, 3, 337
    legislation, 335, 339
Foster care
    case management issues, 313-314
    effects on children, 174-175
    emotional-social factors, 197, 199-200
    demographics, 309
    family support, 313
    PASSPORTS (medical, developmental,
        educational), 314
    philosophical framework, 260-261
    quality care concerns, 309-313
    strategies for children, 199(t.)
    transition plans, 314
    See also Attachment
FTT: see Failure to Thrive

G
Gastrointestinal feeding, 235, 244
Griffith Mental Development Scale, 208(t.)
Grooved pegboard, 211
Gross motor assessment, 211, 262
Growth
    assessment, 154

head circumference, 154
    risk factors, 155(t.), 157(t.)

H
Habituation
    effects, 34
    motor, 206, 217
Hair analysis
    nursing care and responsibilities, 88
    toxicologies research studies, 24, 59
Hallucinogens, history 16,
    See also Lysergic acid diethylamide
        (LSD); Phencyclidine (PCP)
Harrison Narcotic Act, 3, 8, 16
HB: see Hepatitis B
Health assessment
    school, 150-157
    social and cultural factors, 318-319
    See also Families
Health education, in assessment, 67
HEAR Kit, 154
Hearing
    assessment, 151-154
    cranial malformation, relationship to, 152
    drug-related effects, 152
    risk factors for loss in newborn 153(t.)
    See also Audiologist; Auditory
        Brainstem Response; Cocaine, auditory
        effects on neonate/infant
Hepatitis B
    cocaine use, increased risk, 27, 63
    definition, 139
    heroin use, increased risk, 40
    neonatal infection, 139-140
    HBV, Hepatitis B Vaccine, newborns,
        85, 139, 155
Heroin: see Opiates
Herpes simplex virus (HSV)
    acquired neonatal infection, 137
    maternal infection, 137
    treatment, 138
HIV: see Human immunodeficiency virus
    (HIV)
HOME: see Home Observation for Mea-
    surement of the Environment
Home Observation for Measurement of the
    Environment (HOME), 47
Home visits, 158-159

connecting with families, 268-271
personal safety issues for professionals, 160-161
Homelessness
cognitive development, relation to, 173
family stress, 195
HSV: *see* Herpes simplex virus (HSV)
Human immunodeficiency virus (HIV)
cocaine use, increased risk, 27
encephalopathy in infants/children, 141, 241
immunizations for children, 140, 155
infants/children, definition, 138, 140-141, 240-243
neurologic symptoms, 241
otitis media, 152, 241
revealed in medical history, 63
therapy for children, 140
upper respiratory tract infections, 241
See also Speech and language development
Hypersensitivity
maternal-infant attachment, 194(t.)
noise, 244
See also Oral tactile hypersensitivity

I
IFSP: *see* Individual Family Service Plan
IHP/IHCP: *see* Individual Healthcare Plans
Illicit drug use, high schoolers, 11(t.)
Illinois case law: *see* Legal issues
Illinois state law, 65, 74, 335, 339
Impedence audiometry, 154
Immunizations, 85, 139, 155-156
    See also Diphtheria, pertussis and tetanus (DPT) immunization; Human immunodeficiency virus,
Individual Family Service Plan (IFSP), 150, 161
health assessment and objectives, 162
Individual Healthcare Plans (IHP/IHCP), 162
Informed consent: *see* Legal issues
Interventions
behavioral, 262-264
classroom, 264-267
community collaborations, 267-268
comprehensive approaches, 319-321
early preventative need, 196, 243(t.)

interdiscipline/transdiscipline with families, 268-271, 316-317
neurodevelopmental model, 217-219, 222-224(t.)
nonjudgmental approach, 317
strategies, 258-260, 282
    foster home, 199(t.)
strengths, basis for, 317-318
See also Communicative disorders; Eclectic model; Families; Motor development/skills; Public health model; Speech and language development; Stimulation; Synactive model; Teachers
Intoxication, physical symptoms of mother, 64(t.)
Intrauterine growth retardation (IUGR), definition, 133
effects, 24, 31
head circumference, 31, 175
long-term problems, 133
marijuana, 37, 38
microcephaly, 31
opiates, 40, 42
postnatal nutrition, 32, 42, 156
tobacco, 103, 175
Intraventricular Hemorrhage (IVH), cocaine-related, 33
IQ, smoking use and effects on children, 47
Irritability, 217
IUGR: *see* Intrauterine growth retardation (IUGR)
IVH: *see* Intraventricular hemorrhage

J
Juvenile Law Center, 349

K
Kaufman Assessment Battery for Children Development, 287

L
Language development: *see* Speech and language development
Lead exposure, 154-155
Learning, 261-262

Learning environments: *see* Teachers, response

Legal Action Center, 349

Legal issues

    American College of Obstreticians and Gynecologists (ACOG), 338

    Association of Women's Health, Obstetrics, & Neonatal Nurses (AWHONN), 338

    "Baby Jessica," 328

    battery, definition, 335

    chemical dependency treatment, 331-335

    Connecticut case law, 327

    criminalization of maternal conduct, 337-338

    District of Columbia Court of Appeals, 328

    drug trafficking laws, 337

    Illinois case law, 328

    informed consent, 334-335

    involuntary commitments, 333

    Kimberly Mays, 327

    legal witness by a healthcare worker, 340-341

    maternal-fetal conflict, 328-330

    Michigan state Law

        Appeals court, 337

        Supreme court, 328

    Nurses Association of American Colleges of Obstetrics & Gynecology, 338

    nursing

        interventions, 338-340

        liabilities, 339

    refusal of treatment, 328-330

    rights of the child, 327-328

    rights of the father, 336-337

    Roe v. Wade, 330-331, 332, 337

    See also Deposition; Legislation; Prognostic deprivation; Urine toxicology, legal issues

Legislation

    Federal PL 94-142, 149

    Federal PL 99-457, 149, 161

    Federal PL 102, 119, 149

    See also California state law; Colorado state law; Florida state law; Illinois state law; Legal issues; Massachusettes state law; Michigan state law; Minnesota state law; New Jersey state law; New York state law; Oklahoma state law

Lewis Protocol, 34

Long-term studies

    abuse and neglect, 158

    auditory abnormalities, 152

    Chicago Center for Perinatal Addiction, 36

    cognitive development, 175, 178

    current study problems, 178-180

    growth abnormalities, 154-155

    motor development, 205, 208-209(t.)

    nutritional concerns, 156-157, 175

    prenatal care, 175

    tobacco use, 175

    visual abnormalities, 150

    See also Cocaine; Marijuana; Opiates; Research

Low birth weight (LBW)

    cocaine effects, 31

    definition, 31

    DPT vaccine, 156

Low threshold, infants and children

    behavioral and cognitive development, 176

    environmental effects, 181

    non-prenatally exposed, 177

    response by caretakers, 176

    risk behaviors, 198(t.)

    stimulation, 180-181

    teacher response, 176, 181-182

    vulnerability and resiliency, 190, 195

LSD: *see* Lysergic acid diethylamide

Lysergic acid diethylamide (LSD), 16

M

MAI: *see* Movement Assessment of Infants

Marijuana

    animal studies, 37-38

    breast-feeding, 30(t.)

    cancer, 39

    effects during pregnancy on newborn and growing child, 28(t.)

    effects on heart and lungs, 37

    fetal neonatal effects, 38

    history of use, 3, 14-15

    immune system effects, 37

long-term effects, 39, 205
maternal effects, 38
motor development, 208-209(t.)
neonate, conflicting studies regarding, 15
neurobehavioral and developmental
	effects, 38-39, 103, 104
PCP and misrepresentation, 43
pharmacologic effects, 37
physical symptoms, 64(t.)
reproductive system, effects on, 37
speech and language delays, 240
visual effects and strabismus, 150
urine testing, 37
withdrawal symptoms, 64(t.)
Massachusetts state law, 337
Maternal rights vs. fetal rights: *see* Legal
	issues, maternal-fetal conflict
Mays, Kimberly: *see* Legal issues
McCarthy Scales of Children's Abilities
	motor and perceptual subscales, 211
	motor development studies, 208(t.)
	narcotics, 43
	See also Opiates, long term effects
McMunn's elixir: *see* Opiates
Measles, mumps, rubella (MMR), 156
Meconium analysis
	nursing responsibility, 87-88
	research use, 24, 59
Media coverage
	reasons for erroneous perceptions, 189-
		190
	stereotypical images/views created, 170,
		189
Medicaid, 351
Mental health services, 200
Mental retardation
	head circumference, 175
	FAS leading cause, 113, 119, 120, 121,
		177
Methadone
	breast-feeding, 30(t.)
	effects, 40-41
	labor and delivery, 71
	language delays, 239
	neonatal abstinence syndrome, 42, 89-
		90
	pregnancy, 67, 40-41
	preterm infants, 41-42
	relation to birth weight, 42

strabismus, 43, 151
Michigan case law, 337
Middle-class mothers and substance abuse,
	338
Minnesota state law, 326, 331, 336, 339
MMR: *see* Measle, mumps, rubella (MMR)
Motor development/skills
	assessment of infant and child, 24-25
	automatic motor reactions, 218
	children, 210-212
	cognitive development, 170
	cocaine use, 35
	eclectic approach, 216
	infant/toddler, 207, 210
	interventions, 222-224(t.)
	neonates, 205-206
	neurodevelopmental approach, 217-219
	polydrug exposed, 209(t.)
	public health approach, 213-215
	qualitative assessment, 278
	studies, 208-209(Fig.)
	synactive approach, 215-217
	See also Automatic reactions; Interven-
		tions; Primitive reflexes; Research;
		Tonicity; Volitional movement
Movement Assessment of Infants (MAI),
	207, 208(t.)

N
NAACOG: *see* Nurses Association of
	American Colleges of Obstetrics and
	Gynecology
NAPARE: *see* National Association for
	Perinatal Addiction Research and
	Education
NAS: *see* Neonatal abstinence syndrome
Narcotics
	breast-feeding, 29(t.)
	definition, 39
	effects, 28-29(t.)
	illegal semisynthetics - heroin, 40
	medicinal semisynthetics, Methadone,
		Percodan, Dilaudid, Talwin, 39-40
	See also Neonatal abstinence syn-
		drome, Opiates
Narcotics Anonymous, 349
National Abandoned Infants Assistance
	Resource Center, 349

National Association for Perinatal Addiction Research and Education (NAPARE), 255, 350
National Clearinghouse for Alcohol and Drug Information (NCADI), 350
National Council on Alcoholism and Drug Dependence (NCADD), 350
National Drug Abuse Treatment, Referral and Information Service, 350
National Federation Target Program, 350
National Institute on Drug Abuse (NIDA), 350-351
National Training Center for Drug-Exposed or HIV-Infected Children and Their Families, 351
NBAS: *see* Brazelton Neonatal Behavior Assessment Scale
NCAST: *see* Nursing Child Assessment Satellite Training
NCADD: *see* National Council on Alcoholism and Drug Dependence
NCADI: *see* National Clearinghouse for Alcohol and Drug Information
Necrotizing enterocolitis (NEC), 132
Neonatal abstinence syndrome
    alcohol intoxication, 99
    central nervous system
        care/concerns, 94
        relation to, 34
    gastrointestinal system concerns, 96
    integumentary system concerns, 96-97
    IQ relation to, 42
    methadone, 40-42
    nursing care, 89, 94, 96-97
    opiates, 40-42
    premature infants, 41-42
    respiratory system concerns, 96
    scale, 33-34, 41-42, 134
    subacute withdrawal syndrome, 42
    symptoms/signs, 3, 72(t.), 91(t.), 134
    treatment with drugs, 95(t.)
    tobacco exposure, 103
    withdrawal scoring tool, 92-93(Fig.)
    See also Methadone, paregoric
Neonatal Behavior Assessment Scale (NBAS): *see* Brazelton Neonatal Behavior Assessment Scale
Neonate
    alcohol exposed, 97-101

assessment area, 85-87
    cocaine, 100(t.), 101-102
    complications, 84(t.)
    high-risk, essential support and equipment, 86(t.)
    nursing responsibility, 81-105
    opiate withdrawal, 90, 94
    postnatal nursing care goals, immediate, 83, 85-87
Neurobehavioral development
    alcohol exposure, 175-180
    central nervous system, 34
    mother/infant attachment, 194(t.)
    motor development, goals & interventions, 222-224
    social environment effects, 25
    vulnerability & resilience, 190-195
    See also Cocaine; Brazelton Neonatal Behavioral Assessment Scale; Marijuana; Opiates; Phencyclidine (PCP); Tobacco
Neurotransmitters
    dopamine, 26
    epinephrine, 26, 45
    norepinephrine, 26
    See also Phencyclidine (PCP), pharmacology
New Jersey state law, 332
New York state law, 338, 339
    amendment to Civil Rights Law, 331-332
Nicotine: *see* Tobacco
NIDA: *see* National Institute on Drug Abuse
Nurses Association of American Colleges of Obstetrics and Gynecology, *see* Legal issues
Nursing
    assessment, 63-67, 277
    diagnoses of infant PDE, 88-89
    discharge planning, 73-74
    documentation and charting, 334-335
    education regarding maternal drug/alcohol use, 61-62
    infant exposed to alcohol, 97-101
    infant exposed to cocaine and amphetamines, 101-102
    infant exposed to opiates, 89-97
    infant exposed to tobacco, 103-104
    legal interventions, 338

liabilities, 335
  witness responsibility, 340-341
maternal interventions and referral, 67-69
perinatal/postnatal interventions, 70-74, 81-104
public health model, 213-215, 336
response to maternal chemical dependency, 60-61, 338-340
school assessment, 125, 148, 162, 336
speech and language coworkers, 231
See also Codependency; Neonate, nursing responsibility
Nursing Child Assessment Satellite Training (NCAST), 157
Norepinephrine: **see** Neurotransmitters
Nutrition
  counseling during pregnancy, 69
  feeding patterns and mother/infant attachment, 194(t.)
  inadequate, risk factors, 157(t.)
  infants prenatally exposed, 156
  measurement, 157
  NCAST feeding scale, 157

O
OAE: *see* Otoacoustic Emission Testing
Oklahoma state law, 335
Operation PAR (Parental Awareness and Responsibility), 351
Ophthalmology: *see* Vision
Opiates
  effects, 28(t.)
  fetal neonatal effects, 41-43
  heroin, 16, 39-43
  history of use, 3, 16
  infant care, 89-97
  long-term effects, 43
  maternal effects, 40-41
  McMunn's elixir of opium, 4
  meconium aspirations, 71
  neurobehavioral and developmental effects, 42
  pharmacology, 39-40
  physical maternal symptoms, 64(t.)
  speech & language, 239-240
  strabismus, 43
  sudden infant death syndrome (SIDS),
    43
  Talwin, Stadol, use with, 71
  withdrawal symptoms, maternal, 64(t.)
Oral tactile hypersensitivity, 244
Organogenesis/teratogenic effects, 24, 236
  hallucinogens, 16
  PCP, 44, 62
Otoacoustic Emission Testing (OAE), 152

P
Pain management for mothers, 71
Paregoric (tincture of opium)
  as treatment, 4, 16, 42, 95(t.)
  in preventing miscarriage, 4
Parents/caregivers
  child cognitive development, 172
  mothers using drugs, 195
  strategies, 270(t.)
Passive smoke
  infant/childhood cancers, 48-49
  infant/childhood illnesses, 47-48
Patent ductus arteriosus (PDA), 132
PCP: *see* Phencyclidine (PCP)
PDA: *see* Patent ductus arteriosus
PDI: *see* Psychomotor Developmental Index
Phencyclidine (PCP)
  breast-feeding, 29(t.)
  fetal/neonatal effects, 28 (t.)
  hallucinogen,16, 43-44
  maternal effects, 44
  misrepresentation with marijuana, 43
  neurobehavioral and developmental effects on child, 44-45
  neurotransmitter effects, 44
  pharmacology, 43-44
  urine testing, 44
Phenobarbital, in treatment of neonatal abstinence syndrome, 42, 95(t.)
Physical growth, relation to cognitive development, 169
Play activities
  childhood assessment, 284
  children at risk and free play, 261-262
  cognitive development, exploratory, 174
  emotional security, 174
  self-awareness, 169
Polycythemia, smoking and elevation, 46

Polydrug use
    effects, 23, 256
    historical perspective, 17
    home environments, 36
    PCP use and problems, 43-44
    visual abnormalities in children ex-
        posed, 150-151
    speech and language development, 237
Poverty, 300
    effects on cognitive development, 172
    family-stress-related, 195
    social and economic status, 300
    teenage childbearing, 301
    See also Cultural issues
Premature rupture of membranes (PROM)
    effects of cocaine use, 27, 30, 70
    effects of heroin use, 40, 70
Prematurity, 132-133
    bronchopulmonary dysplasia, 132
    cocaine and methamphetamines, 30, 132
    heroin, 40
    PCP, 45
    respiratory distress syndrome (RDS), 132
Prevention: *see* Public health model
Primitive reflexes, 217-218
Prognostic deprivation, 336
PROM: *see* Premature rupture of mem-
    branes (PROM)
Psychologist
    assessment by, 277
    See also Bayley Scales of Infant
    Development
Psychomotor Developmental Index (PDI),
    207
Public health model
    infants with prenatal drug exposure,
        214(t.)
    primary, secondary, tertiary, 213

R
RDS: *see* Respiratory distress syndrome
Receptive language: *see* Speech and
    language development
Refusal of treatment: *see* Legal issues
Rehabilitative programs, 213, 215
Religions, 301
Research
    biological variables, 24

cofounding factors affecting, 25, 26(t.)
    methodological challenges & questions
        to ask, 25
    review, 23-25
    self-reporter's reliability, 23
    See also Long-term studies
Resiliency, childhood
    contributing factors, 192(t.)
    counterbalance with children prenatally
        drug exposed, 190
    developmental and neurodevelopmental
        factors, 191
    emotional and social competencies, 190
    temperament, 193
Respiratory distress syndrome (RDS), 132
Rights of the child: *see* Legal issues

S
Screening programs for developmental
    levels, 280-281,
Sedatives, hypnotics
    intoxication and withdrawal symptoms
        of, 64(t.)
Self-reporting, 59
    alcohol, 33
    marijuana, 33
    See also Research
Sense of self
    behaviors, 198(t.)
    cognitive development, 169
Sensory effects: *see* Hearing; Hypersensi-
    tivity; Vision
Sensory integration
    communication disorders, 244
    deficits related to FAS, 120
Separation, family issues and strategies,
    199(t.)
Sexually transmitted diseases
    cocaine use, increased risk, 27
    historical perspective with opiate use, 16
    See also Chlamydia; Hepatitis; Human
        immunodeficiency virus (HIV); Syphilis
SGA: *see* Small-for-gestational age
Shields for Families Project, 351
SIDS: *see* Sudden infant death syndrome
    (SIDS)
Sleeping patterns, mother infant attachment,
    194(t.)

Small-for-gestational age (SGA)
  cocaine and frequency, 31
  definition, 31
  PCP and frequency, 45
Social services
  case management during pregnancy, 69
  postpartum needs, 73
Speech and language development
  acquisition timetable, 232-233
  assessment, 235, 245
    qualitative, 278-279
  expressive language, 0-2 years, 232
  HIV, infants and children, 242
  marijuana and related delays, 239
  play and its effect on, 233
  receptive language, 0-2 years, 232-233
  therapy referral, 234(t.)
  See also Cocaine; Communicative
  disorders; Tobacco
Spermatozoa
  effects of cocaine use, 24
  effects of marijuana use, 37
  paternal substance use and abuse, 24,
    131
Stadol use with opiates, 71
Stanford-Binet Intelligence Scale, 277
Stimulation, internal and external
  cognitive development, 169
  intervention, 180-182
  low-threshold infants, 176
Strabismus, infant/child with cocaine,
  marijuana and opiate use, 150
Sudden infant death syndrome (SIDS)
  effects of secondhand smoke, 48
  postnatal drug exposure, 35-36
  prenatal drug exposure, 35
  See also Opiates, Tobacco
Support services, community, 200-201
Swaddling, 220
Synactive model
  children, goals and interventions, 224(t.)
  five hierarchical level, 216(T)
  goals and interventions, 222(t.). 223(t.)
  infants and toddlers, goals & interven-
    tions, 223(t.)
  interactive model, 215-217
  neonates, goals & interventions, 222(t.)
Syphyilis
  congenital infection, 134-136

rates, 90

T
T-ACE screening tool, 66, 66(t.), 124
Talwin, use with opiates, 77
Teachers
  assessment by early childhood special
    education, 277
  behavior problem management, 73, 262-
    264
  behavioral diaries of target behaviors, 181
  children's learning, 261-267
  classroom communication disorder
    therapy, 245
    learning environment, 182, 264-267
    strategies, 258-260
  community agencies, connection with,
    267-268
  curriculum programs used by, 270
  early childhood interventions, 255
  family connections, 268-271
  identification labels for children with
    PDE, 256
  low-threshold infant, 176-177, 181-182
  parent communication "never, evers,"
    269, 270
  philosophical framework, 260-261
  self-regulation responses by children,
    181
  withdrawn child, 173
  See also Attachment, Cognitive
  development
Temperament
  caregivers response, 192(t.), 193, 195
  definition, 193
Ten Question Drinking History (TQDH), 66,
  123-124(t.)
Teratogens, definition, 236
Thalidomide, 5
THC: *see* Delta-9 Tetrahydrocannabinol
Tobacco
  appetite suppressant qualities, 46
  breast-feeding, 30(t.)
  deaths related to, 46
  effects of use, 29(t.)
  fetal/neonatal effects, 46-47
  historical perspective on addiction, 4, 7,
    10, 14

intrauterine growth retardation, 103
long-term effects, 47-48
maternal effects, 46
middle ear infections in children, 152
neurobehavioral and developmental
    effects, 47, 104, 176
passive smoking effects, 48-49
pharmacology and origin, 45-46
poor health in infants/children, 48
sudden infant death syndrome (SIDS),
    48
use rate in pregnancy, 45-46
Tonicity, infant/child
    fetal alcohol syndrome, 211
    maternal/infant attachment, relation to,
        193, 194(t.)
    muscle development, 217
    physical stability, 217
TQDH: *see* Ten Question Drinking History
    (TQDH)
Transdiscipline: *see* Interventions,
    interdiscipline/transdiscipline
Tube feeding: *see* Gastrointestinal tube
    feeding

U
Ultrasound assessment, 215
Urine toxicology screening
    detection timetable, 70(t.)
    general procedure, 23-24, 59, 69, 70
    in infants, 82, 87, 88
    legal issues, 334-335
    marijuana, 37, 103
    PCP, 44
Uteroplacental blood flow
    effects of tobacco use, 46

V
Valium, intreatment of neonatal abstinence
    syndrome, 95(t.)
Vasoconstriction, smoking-related, 46
VER: *see* Visual Evoked Response
Verbal reasoning, 171
Vineland Adaptive Behavior Scale, 121,
    212, 208(t.)
Violence, cognitive development, 173-173
Vision

abnormalities, risk factors for, 151(t.)
assessment, 150, 151
effects of drug use, 33, 450-451
prophylactic care in newborns, 83
See also Cocaine; Marijuana; Opiates
Visual Evoked Response (VER), 151
Visual motor planning
    children with FAE/FAS, 211
Visual Reinforcement Audiometry (VRA),
    154
Vitamin K, parenteral use in infants, 83
VMI: *see* Berry Test of Visual Motor
    Integration
Volitional movement, 218
Volstead Act, 8
VRA: *see* Visual Reinforcement Audiom-
    etry
Vulnerability, childhood
    behavioral characteristics, 196-197
    contributing factors, 192
    early interventions, 196
    family separation, 199(t.)
    foster care, 197, 199-200
    neurobehavioral status and mother/
        infant attachment, 194(t.)
    temperament, 193

W
Withdrawal symptoms, maternal, 64(t.)
Women
    addicted/abusing, special concerns, 308
    assessment of perinatal substance abuse,
        319
    characteristics of substance use, 307
    drug use, 306(t.)
    risk factors, 308
Women's Christian Temperance Union, 8